Lhundrup

CENTRAL

30

LHASA

To Chamdo
& Chengdu

TIBET

Tsetang

GATSE

29

Gyantse

28

Bhutan

N

90 91 92 27

THE TIBET
GUIDE

FRONTISPIECE *Spires on the roof of the Jokhang.*

THE TIBET GUIDE

Stephen Batchelor

Foreword by
the Dalai Lama

WISDOM PUBLICATIONS
LONDON

First published in 1987

Wisdom Publications
23 Dering Street
London W1, England

© Wisdom Publications 1987

British Library Cataloguing in Publication Data
Batchelor, Stephen
The Tibet Guide.
1. Tibet (China) — Description and travel
— Guide-books
I. Title
915.1′50458   DS786

ISBN 0 86171 046 0

Designed by Humphrey Stone

Set in 9½ on 12pt Linotron Palatino
by Character Graphics of Taunton, Somerset
and printed and bound in Melbourne, Australia
by Valentine Sands

CONTENTS

MAPS DIAGRAMS AND TABLES

THE DALAI LAMA

THEKCHEN CHOELING
McLEOD GANJ 176219
KANGRA DISTRICT
HIMACHAL PRADESH

FOREWORD

I am happy to know that Wisdom Publications is bringing out a guidebook on Tibet. This is welcome.

With the slight opening of Tibet to the outside world, many foreign tourists have gone to Tibet. I am told that the number will continue to increase in the future. Though I welcome the fact that many tourists are visiting Tibet, I regret the lack of general and correct information on Tibet available to the visitors. This lack of information covers not only basic facts but also the general political, cultural and religious conditions in Tibet. The fact that these days Tibetans are being permitted to worship openly may mislead visitors into assuming that there is religious freedom in Tibet. True religious freedom means the freedom to propagate one's religious beliefs. Not only is this prohibited but what is also happening in Tibet is that the present trend towards liberalisation, mainly in the economic field, is accompanied by stringent and tightening control on the political life of the Tibetan people.

I hope that the present guidebook will fill this gap and contribute towards the outside world's understanding of Tibet and its people.

August 27, 1986

PREFACE

A question that I have frequently been asked since returning from Tibet to research this book is, 'Well, what's it like there?' My usual response has been to say that it is simultaneously inspiring and tragic. The landscape, with its vast open plains and soaring mountains and its crystalline, rarified atmosphere is inspiring. So too are the noble, resilient people. The religious sites, which evoke the memory of the saints and yogins who lived and practised there in the past, are also inspiring.

At the same time Tibet is a land of tragedy. The scenes of wanton destruction that greeted us at the sites of many monasteries, the tales of imprisonment and torture we heard from the mouths of men and women who had been subjected to these things since the Chinese takeover, and the constant reminders of the systematic attempt by a foreign power to impose its will upon another people are all immensely tragic.

I do not intend either to condone uncritically the former regime or to acquiesce in the Chinese occupation of Tibet as though it were an irreversible fact. Pre-1959 Tibet was neither the mystical paradise of some Western writers nor the medieval hell of Chinese propaganda. It was a land where a high degree of spiritual freedom co-existed with what for most of us would be an unacceptably backward and rigid feudal society. Yet the 'Tibetan Question' has nothing to do with a comparison of the relative merits and demerits of the past and present state of affairs. It is a question of the rights of a people to political self-determination and religious freedom. The current Chinese policy of respect for 'ethnic minorities' and the cultural achievements of the past should not mislead us into thinking that the rulers in Peking have budged an inch on the issue of Tibetan independence.

A few days after arriving in Lhasa we were visiting the Potala. Many Tibetans were there and I was glad to be able to speak freely with them. However, that same evening a Tibetan man called on us in our hotel. He explained that he had been at the Potala that morning and had overhead some of the remarks I had made, in particular my use of the term 'Bö gi rang-tsen' (Tibetan independence). He warned me never to use that phrase in public again. 'Were someone in authority to hear those words,' he told me, 'you would be taken away and shot.' Although I could not recall having used that phrase, from then on I was not only more careful of what I said, but more aware of the reality of the Tibetan situation, which is usually well-concealed behind the jovial faces of the people.

In compiling the information in this book I am especially grateful to all the Tibetans who guided us around the sites and explained the history and significance of the places we were visiting. Much of what is written here is based on their oral explanations. Another invaluable source was the *Bod.rgya.tshig.mdzod.chen.mo*, a recently published three volume Tibetan-Chinese dictionary, which I managed to obtain in Lhasa. Far more than being a mere dictionary between the two languages, it is a comprehensive encyclopedia of Tibetan religion and culture, meticulously researched and compiled by Tibetan scholars.

If it hadn't been for the constant encouragement of Nick Ribush of Wisdom Publications, this book would probably never have been written. I am very thankful to him and Wisdom for having commissioned me to undertake this task.

I am also grateful to a number of people who have helped bring this book to completion: Robert Beer for the *Iconographical Guide*; Brian Beresford and Sean Jones for the section on *Western Tibet*; Chris Shaw for doing the maps and diagrams; Bradley 'Stone Routes' Rowe for many details about temples and places that I was unable to visit; Ven. Geshe Wangchen of Manjushri London for clarifying several details about religious customs and practices; Humphrey Stone for the design and layout; Beth Solomon and John Newman; Nick Dawson; Michael, Scott and Rajan; Althea and Richard; Rosemary and Katerina, and many others.

Finally I must thank my wife, Martine, who accompanied me to Tibet and provided invaluable support throughout the entire project.

Things are changing rapidly in Tibet, and in order to keep reprints of *The Tibet Guide* accurate and up-to-date we ask travellers to write to Wisdom with information on where this book may now be incorrect. Also, if you have suggestions as to how subsequent editions could be improved they would be glad to hear them. If they use your corrections or suggestions in a new edition, they will acknowledge your help and send you a free, updated copy of the book.

STEPHEN BATCHELOR
Sharpham North
September, 1986

xiii

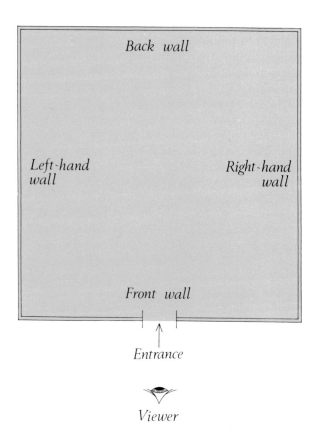

Entrance

Viewer

In descriptive passages, 'left' and 'right' always refer to the viewer's left and right. To say, for example, that a particular chapel is to the left of a certain building means that it is to the left of the viewer when the viewer is facing the entrance of that building. In describing a room, 'front wall' means the wall through which you enter the room; 'back wall', the wall you face from the entrance; 'left-hand wall', the wall to your left as you stand at the entrance; and 'right-hand wall', the wall to your right as you stand at the entrance. This should be clear from the accompanying diagram.

HOW TO USE THIS BOOK

The Tibet Guide has been written primarily to provide visitors to Tibet with a comprehensive description and explanation of what they will see when they are there. All the major places in the history of Tibetan culture and religion are covered, with special emphasis on those in the provinces of Central Tibet and Tsang.

The book is divided into several sections, and those on **Lhasa, Central Tibet, Tsang** and **Western Tibet** are further divided into forty-seven consecutive chapters, each of which covers a particular site. Each chapter is divided into three parts: travel details, history, and a description of the site. The numbers on the *plans* refer to *buildings* included in the description of the site.

Technical Buddhist terms and names of important historical figures are listed in the **Glossary.** The **Iconographical Guide** enables you to identify the most common deities and lamas depicted in Tibetan Buddhist paintings and statues.

A simplified and non-scholastic method of transcribing Tibetan words is used; it does not differ greatly from the systems used in other books on Tibet. If a Tibetan word ends in *e,* that *e* is *always* accented. *Gyantse,* for example, is pronounced *Gyantsé (Gyantsay); Sera Me, Sera Mé (Sera May),* and so forth. The section **Useful Words and Phrases** transcribes the words in a way purely designed to convey the approximate English sound equivalents.

Unless stated otherwise, the shrines, chapels, statues, paintings and other objects mentioned at religious sites are always described in the order they are passed by a pilgrim circumambulating the site in a clockwise direction.

Throughout the book prices are sometimes given in 'RMB' and sometimes in 'FEC'. This confusing system arises from the Chinese introduction of a special currency for foreign visitors. These special notes are called Foreign Exchange Certificates (FEC), while the local money is called Renminbi, 'People's Money' (RMB). Theoretically, the two currencies have exactly the same value, but in practice their respective values vary according to black market rates. FEC have to be used for most day to day business, shopping etc. Please beware that prices are constantly changing. For further details about currency in Tibet, see pp.382-3 and p.413.

THE LAND AND ITS PEOPLE

Three hundred million years ago what is now Tibet was covered by the Tethys sea, a vast ocean that covered much of India and Asia. The Mediterranean is but Tethys's last remaining puddle. Forty million years ago immense pressure from the southern Indian land-mass started very slowly to force the area to the north upwards, resulting in the soaring Himalayan range and, swelling beyond it, the vast Central Asian plateau. The high open land of Tibet rests on this plateau and stretches for two thousand kilometres from India in the west to China in the east, and for a thousand kilometres from Nepal in the south to the Chinese province of Xinjiang (Turkestan) in the north. Its average elevation is four thousand metres above sea level. On three sides it is bordered by some of the loftiest mountains in the world: to the south by the mighty Himalayas, to the west by the peaks of the Karakoram and to the north by the Kunlun and Tangla ranges. The land gradually descends eastwards, its vast barren spaces interrupted by subsidiary mountain ranges and deep gorges, until it meets the lowlands of China's westernmost provinces of Sichuan and Yunnan.

Some of Asia's greatest rivers have their sources on the Tibetan plateau. In the far west, near the sacred Mount Kailas, the Indus and Sutlej begin their long courses westward and join each other in the plains of Pakistan. Close by springs the Brahmaputra, which then flows eastward through southern Tibet like a massive life-giving artery, finally breaking through the Himalayas in a series of dramatic gorges and emptying into the gulf of Bengal. And in the far east of the country the Salween and Mekong rivers begin their long journeys into South-East Asia, while the Yangtse flows due east as far as Shanghai and the Yellow River pours into the East China Sea south of Tianjin.

The northern half of Tibet is a virtually uninhabited desert called the Jangtang, or 'Northern Plain'. Only occasional hunters and collectors of salt and borax roam this barren wasteland. To the south of this plain is an extensive area of mountainous grazing-land inhabited mainly by nomads and their herds of sheep, goats and yaks. These people, wild and unkempt in appearance, live in black animal-hair tents, surviving on meat and dairy products. Even today they maintain traditional life-styles that may well date back over two thousand years. Periodically

OPPOSITE *Nomad pilgrim outside the Jokhang.*

OVERLEAF *The Himalayas from the Tong-la pass.*

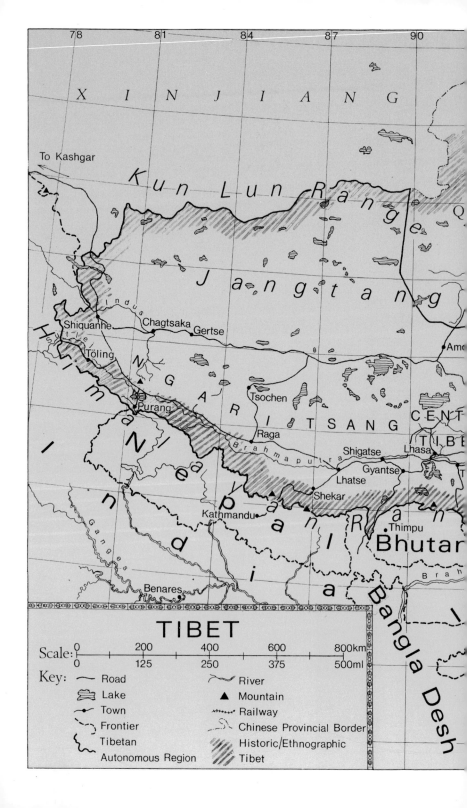

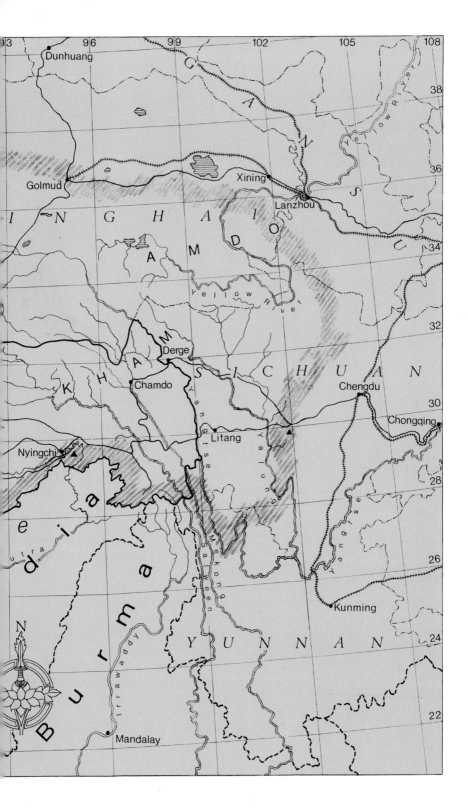

Farm buildings in Shekar. Fuel is stacked around the edges of the flat rooves.

they bring supplies of dried meat, wool, butter and cheese down from the highlands into the towns and trade them for *tsampa*, cloth and simple manufactured goods.

The majority of Tibetans, however, live in the southern part of the country in the area irrigated by the Brahmaputra and its tributaries, and in the eastern province of Kham. These more hospitable regions of gentle, protected valleys produce the crops upon which the Tibetans depend: barley, wheat and a small variety of vegetables. Animal husbandry is also practised and on the farms you will find cows, goats, pigs and horses. There are numerous scattered villages, many of which consist only of a couple of farming compounds. A typical compound is a single storeyed, whitewashed, quadrangular complex with an entrance leading into an open courtyard. Around the courtyard is the living area for the farmer and his family and storage rooms and barns for his livestock. Flags, often shredded and faded by the harsh winds, stream from masts erected from the flat rooftops. These are replaced every new year as an auspicious sign to usher in the spring. Fuel, such as wood, brush and dried yak-dung, is often stored on the roofs.

These southern valleys are the places where Tibetan culture and civilisation developed. Until the Chinese started on their campaign of

Nomad tent life: the younger woman churns butter while the elder woman cuts cheese.

systematic destruction, monasteries, nunneries and hermitages dotted the landscape. These varied in size from small establishments containing a single shrineroom and living quarters for a handful of monks or nuns to vast institutes of learning with populations of up to several thousand monks. There are few towns of any size, Lhasa, Shigatse, Gyantse, Tsetang and Chamdo being the largest. Traditionally these were centres of trade and the seat of a regional governor. Until 1952 Lhasa, the capital, had a population of only about 25,000, although this has nearly quadrupled in recent years due to the presence of the occupying Chinese army and administration.

The influence of Tibetan culture has spread beyond the borders of 'political Tibet', i.e. the area actually or nominally under the control of the Lhasa government. The Himalayan kingdoms of Bhutan, Nepal, Sikkim, Ladakh and a few other areas in north India such as Spiti and Lahoul are still repositories of ancient Tibetan learning. Ethnically, too, it seems that many of the people living in these areas are descended from Tibetan stock.

It is believed that the Tibetans originated from certain non-Chinese nomadic tribes who wandered into the country from the north-east around two and a half to three thousand years ago. They are a hardy,

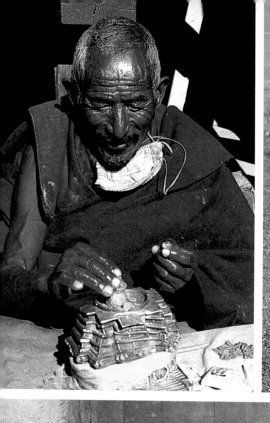

OPPOSITE BELOW *Two young novices at Drigung Monastery.* OPPOSITE ABOVE RIGHT
Nomad girl. OPPOSITE ABOVE LEFT *Old monk at Ganden making clay impressions of
Tsongkhapa's tooth.* ABOVE *Gyantse woman with coral and turquoise jewellery.*

independent people, whose natural warmth and good humour have
been noted by most Western travellers who have ventured into Tibet
since the seventeenth century. It is difficult to know the exact population of the country. The Dalai Lama's office claims that there are six million Tibetans, whereas a recent Chinese census puts the figure much
lower at 1,650,000. Undoubtedly a great many lost their lives during the
decade of the cultural revolution. Hugh Richardson, the head of the
British Mission in Lhasa in the forties, considered two to three million
to be an accurate estimate of the population. At present there are
100,000 Tibetans living as refugees abroad in India, Nepal, Bhutan,
Europe and America.

Until the Chinese takeover in 1959, this nation of nomads, farmers
and traders lived a simple but, according to most accounts, contented
life. Most people readily accepted their place within a society consisting
of aristocratic landowners, peasants, clergy and merchants. The population was kept stable by approximately one third of men and a great
many women living as monks and nuns and thus the agricultural

Yaks carrying their burdens down a hillside.

resources of the land were sufficient to provide all with plenty to eat. Despite the number of monks a system of polyandry – where one woman had more than one husband – existed. Compared with other Asian countries, there was a relatively high degree of literacy and the majority were at least able to read and recite the commonest prayers. A simple code of law was devised in the seventh century and elaborated by subsequent rulers, but in practice local custom often determined the sometimes brutal punishments inflicted for crimes. Taxes were levied from all levels of society: landowners had to give a certain percentage of their income; peasants had to provide labour, army service and travel assistance; and monks repaid their endowments with prayers and rituals. People journeyed either by foot, on horseback or, where possible, in leather coracles. Except for a couple of cars owned by the Thirteenth Dalai Lama, there was no wheeled transport in the entire country until the 1950's.

Few of these traditional ways of life continue today. Nomads and farmers are still the mainstay of the economy but many of the latter have been forced to become part of communes and work units. Apart from a few craft-centres, there is still virtually no manufacturing industry in Tibet. Landowners have been replaced by the state, which in effect means the alien Chinese government. The clergy have been disbanded

Lush farming valley in summer.

and stripped of all their privileges, although under the present climate of liberalisation are tentatively beginning to re-emerge. Still, most of the country's 6,500 monasteries have been totally destroyed.

The balance between population and agricultural resources was catastrophically upset by the massive influx of Han Chinese, resulting in famines from 1959-63 and 1968-73. Instead of paying taxes to the Lhasa government, Tibetans had to hand over their produce to feed the Chinese army and even the masses in the 'motherland'. Young Tibetan men are now conscripted into the People's Liberation Army. The laws of Communist China have been imposed making it a crime for any Tibetan to suggest publicly that the present system is unjust. Schools have been built but the majority of classes are taught in Chinese, and Tibetan students are at a constant disadvantage. A network of roads and bridges has been constructed which now connects all the major towns, but a plan to extend the Chinese railway system to Lhasa from Golmud has been abandoned. Hydro-electric plants have been installed providing electricity for most townships. The Chinese have now recognised that many of their policies in Tibet have not worked and in the last few years have lifted certain restrictions. Current relaxations might be leading to greater economic freedom and regional autonomy for Tibet but this is far from certain.

THE HISTORY OF TIBET

The Yarlung Kings (629–842)
The two great civilisations bordering Tibet – India and China – were at first barely aware of the movements of the people scattered over the high, inhospitable regions beyond their frontiers. They considered them as unkempt, illiterate, barbarian tribes who occasionally had to be pushed back across the border where they belonged but for the most part could be ignored. This situation began to change in the seventh century AD when a mighty king called Songtsen Gampo suddenly made his presence felt in both countries with the threat of invasion by a powerful, swift and well-organised army.

Tibetan historians regard Songtsen Gampo as the thirty-third king in a line that began with the magical descent from the skies of a man called Nyatri Tsenpo. This man appeared on a mountain called Yarlha Zhampo at the head of the Yarlung valley in central/southern Tibet. The people of the region declared him their chieftan and he built a palace from where to rule called the Yumbulagang. While allowing for the mythological aspects of this story, Nyatri Tsenpo can be dated at about 500 BC. It is also possible that he was Indian in origin, since theTibetans consider him to be related to one of the Indian dynasties contemporary with the historical Buddha. Although the significance of Nyatri Tsenpo and the early Yarlung Kings has no doubt been embellished by later historians, his appearance probably coincides with the first stirrings among the Tibetans of the notion of a social and political identity.

The first twenty-seven kings of the Yarlung dynasty adhered to the native Bön religion, an animistic cult governed by exorcists, shamans and priests, the early nature of which remains veiled behind centuries of Buddhist antagonism and Bön's own self-imposed transformation as a means of keeping up with the Buddhists. During the reign of the twenty-eighth king, Lhatotori (4th century AD), the first Buddhist scriptures appeared in Tibet. They also fell from the sky and had the good fortune to land on the Yumbulagang, where the king lived with his court. This event can be understood as the first suggestion of Buddhism being acknowledged in the ruling circles. Bön, however, was not to be easily swept aside, and conflicts between it and the imported Buddhist faith were eventually responsible for the collapse of the dynasty.

OPPOSITE *Yumbulagang*, 1950.

The birthplace of King Songtsen Gampo in the Gyama valley east of Lhasa.

Songtsen Gampo

Songtsen Gampo was born in 617 and ascended to the throne at the age of thirteen. He ruled for twenty years, during which time he established the borders of a powerful empire that extended far beyond the immediate area of the Yarlung valley. Tibetan forces were active from the plains of Northern India to the Chinese frontiers in the east and the borders of the Turkish empire in the west. Songtsen Gampo moved the capital from Yarlung to Lhasa and built a palace on the Red Hill (the site of the Potala). As a gesture of friendship towards their threatening neighbour, Nepal and China each offered the king a bride from their own royal families.

In broadening his horizons the king became aware of the Buddhist civilisation prevailing not only in its country of origin, India, but also as an inspiring force in the newly formed T'ang dynasty of China. The prestige and significance of Buddhism was further impressed upon him by his Nepalese and Chinese wives and the dowries they brought with them containing magnificent statues of the Buddha. Whether this warring man actually became the devout Buddhist king that popular tradition makes him out to be is open to question. But it is certain that he encouraged the building of temples to house the images brought by his wives and was probably responsible for the construction of several other religious shrines throughout the land. He also sent his minister Tönmi Sambhota to India to create a written script suitable for the transcription of Tibetan. This enabled the Tibetans to start translating the Buddhist scriptures into their own language.

Trisong Detsen

The second great ruler of the Yarlung dynasty, Trisong Detsen, did not begin his reign until 755, more than a hundred years after the death of Songtsen Gampo. He inherited a strong empire, consolidated by the four kings who had ruled since Songtsen Gampo, and launched further military expeditions into the heartlands of China and India. But despite these political advances it seems that Buddhism had not progressed much and the country was still very much in the grip of the Bön tradition. In the face of considerable resistance from Bön factions in the court, Trisong Detsen started on a widescale restoration of the Buddhist temples erected by Songtsen Gampo and invited a number of notable

Woman making ritual offerings at Drakmar, King Trisong Detsen's birthplace, near Samye. Mt. Hepori is visible in the distance.

Padmasambhava (Knowledge Holders' Chapel, Potala Palace, Lhasa)

Indian Buddhist masters to Tibet. Principal among these were Shantarakshita and Padmasambhava.

The monk-philosopher Shantarakshita, even today known to the Tibetans as the 'Great Abbot Bodhisattva', established the monastic order in Tibet and inspired the construction of the first major monastic institute of Samye. On his advice, the king invited Padmasambhava, an Indian tantric adept and sorcerer, to Tibet to help pacify the local demons who were still hindering the propagation of the new religion. Padmasambhava was able to beat the Bön priests at their own game and more than anyone else was responsible for turning the tide in favour of Buddhism. His charismatic personality lodged itself firmly in the Tibetan imagination and became a lasting symbol for the victory of the wisdom, compassion and power of Buddhism over the more primitive and less universal beliefs of Bön. The king was also deeply impressed by Padmasambhava and even offered him his wife of two years, Yeshe Tsogyel, as a consort; an act that scandalised the Bön faction and forced Padmasambhava to flee into hiding.

Ralpachen
After the death of Trisong Detsen in 797, his sons, Mune Tsenpo and Tride Songtsen, continued the policy of disseminating Buddhism. Wars with China also continued. The third and last great king of the Yarlung period, Tri Ralpachen, came to power in 815. He made a treaty with the Chinese and established peaceful relations with them. He was also responsible for undertaking a new and more reliable set of translations of Buddhist writings from the Sanskrit. However, scandal, jealousy and infighting between the different factions in his court resulted in his assassination in 838. His death sadly augured the break-up of the dynasty.

Ralpachen's elder brother Langdarma took the throne. This king was a supporter of the Bön faith and immediately set out on a violent persecution of Buddhism. Temples and monasteries were desecrated and monks forced to disrobe or flee. Within a few short years Buddhism was almost entirely suppressed in Central Tibet. The Buddhists, however, were to have the last word. In 842, during the performance of a play, a monk called Lhalungpa Pelgyi Dorje shot the king dead with a well-aimed arrow. Pelgyi Dorje escaped to the eastern district of Kham and joined the handful of monks and translators who had managed to find refuge there beyond the reach of Langdarma's fury.

The Middle Ages (842–1642)
After Langdarma's assassination the unified Tibetan kingdom broke up into a number of small principalities and fiefs ruled over by diverse members of the previous aristocracy. One branch of the royal family settled in Western Tibet and established the prosperous kingdoms of Guge and Purang and continued to support Buddhism. In the others, though, support for Buddhism declined and Central Tibet entered a kind of spiritual dark age that lasted for nearly two hundred years. Var-

ious Tibetan clans still harrassed the Chinese and Khotanese border areas, occasionally establishing small centres of power. But with the collapse of the T'ang dynasty in 905, China and Tibet drifted apart and had no formal relations with each other for another three hundred years.

The Buddhist Revival

A renewed interest in Buddhism started during the beginning of the eleventh century. Much of this was inspired by the arrival of the Indian master Atisha in the western kingdom of Gu-ge in 1042. Atisha was invited by King Yeshe Ö and his grand-nephew Jangchub Ö. Yeshe Ö was a devout ruler who was a supporter of another influential Buddhist figure of the time, the monk and translator Rinchen Zangpo. A famous story recounts how Yeshe Ö was captured by a Turkic army and held for ransom, the sum for his release being the weight of his body in gold. Although most of this sum was raised, the king forbade it to be used for his release and insisted instead that it be spent on inviting Atisha to Tibet. As a result of this act of self-sacrifice, Atisha spent the remaining twelve years of his life in Tibet, travelling from Gu-ge to Central Tibet and spent his last years in Netang, near Lhasa. Atisha's disciples founded the Kadampa order of Tibetan Buddhism.

A well-known Tibetan contemporary of Atisha was the translator Marpa. He came from a wealthy family in the Lhodrak region of Southern Tibet and travelled on several occasions to India to gather texts and study with a number of Indian masters. His main teacher was the former abbot of Nalanda Monastery turned tantric yogin, Naropa. Marpa became the teacher of the poet-saint Milarepa, who in turn taught Gampopa, through whom the main lineages of the Kagyu order of Tibetan Buddhism were founded.

At the same time Könchok Gyelpo, a monk from the powerful Khön family in Southern Tibet, received the lineages that the translator Drokmi had been initiated into by his Indian masters. In 1073 he founded a monastery in his homeland of Sakya. He and his son Kunga Nyingpo then established the Sakya order of Tibetan Buddhism.

This period of Buddhist revival is often called the 'Second Dissemination of the Doctrine in Tibet'. It was a time of great learning and spiritual creativity during which the foundations of much of what we now call 'Tibetan Buddhism' were laid. Translation work was started again producing a complete reworking of the translations done at the time of the early kings. Monasteries (such as Reting, Tsurpu, Densatil, Drigung, Talung, Tsel Gungtang, and Sakya) were built on a grand scale and the life of the country became more and more absorbed in religious matters.

Although politically ununited, the various chieftans, princes and head lamas of Tibet lived in relative harmony and none of them made a serious effort to bring the country under his own control. This period of peaceful, innocent independence came to an end at the beginning of the thirteenth century when the rising power of the Mongols began to make itself felt throughout China and Central Asia. Under the brutal leadership of Genghis Khan, the Mongolians were in the process of forcing the entire area to submit to their rule. Envoys were sent to Tibet demanding submission and the Tibetans yielded without any resistance. For the time being this saved them from further interference, but in 1239 Genghis's grandson Godan Khan sent raiding parties into Tibet that penetrated as far south as the monasteries of Reting and Drigung.

The Sakya Dynasty

Five years later, sensing the influence wielded by the great lamas of the land, Godan invited the head abbot of the Sakya order, Sakya Pandita, to his court. In return for a guarantee of no more Mongolian incursions into Tibet, Sakya Pandita offered Tibet into the hands of the Khan, an act that did not endear him to his rivals in Tibet. As a reward he was made regent of Tibet with a post in the Mongolian court. This relationship took on further dimensions under the respective successors of Godan Khan and Sakya Pandita. Godan's son Kublai Khan was so impressed by the spiritual qualities and teachings of Sakya Pandita's nephew Pakpa that in return for initiation into the secret teachings of Buddhism, he bestowed upon him the title of 'Imperial Preceptor', i.e. de facto ruler of Tibet.

This arrangement was to have repercussions all the way into the twentieth century. Basically a deal was struck between a certain religious order and a prevailing political power. The religious order provided spiritual guidance and was rewarded with political control over the inner affairs of Tibet, while the political power became the overlord of the country and guaranteed peace in return for submission. A major consequence of this was the increased politicisation of the Tibetan Buddhist orders. They began competing with each other for the favours of the most powerful rulers of the day, thus intensifying the sense of division between them. Being based upon compromise and sectarian self-interest, this attitude of trading spiritual for political authority weakened the political integrity and independence of Tibet.

Independence

With the support of the Mongolian Yuan dynasty, Sakya hierarchs ruled Tibet for almost exactly a century. But as the power of the Mongolians in China declined, a nationalist movement arose in Tibet under the leadership of Jangchub Gyeltsen of the Pamotrupa family based in the Yarlung valley. In 1354 he overthrew the Sakya leadership and was acknowledged by the Mongolians as ruler of Tibet. When the power of the Yuan rulers in China finally collapsed and they were replaced by the indigenous Chinese Ming dynasty, the Tibetans ignored the former 'patron-priest' arrangement they had had with Mongolian-ruled China and embarked on a three hundred year period of genuine independence.

Jangchub Gyeltsen regarded his rule as a return to the golden days of the Yarlung Kings. There was a renewed appreciation of the deeds of Songtsen Gampo and Trisong Detsen that amounted almost to a form of worship. This was also the period of the discovery of texts concealed by Padmasambhava, which further inspired a sense of the greatness of the spiritual traditions of the past. This new dynasty was also governed mainly by lamas, this time from the Pamotrupa line of the Kagyu order. Meanwhile, the other Buddhist orders continued to vie with each other for regional political influence and formed alliances with different local chieftans and families in the country. High lamas were also received at the Mongolian and Ming courts, but now as spiritual teachers rather than potential political allies.

Silver statue of one of the Karmapas.

Rock carving of Tsongkhapa, with Atisha and Drom Tönpa above his shoulders, in Tsongkhapa's hermitage at Ganden Monastery.

The Pamotrupa dynasty ended around 1435 and was replaced by the secular rule of the princes of Rinpung, an area south-west of Lhasa, which lasted for a hundred and thirty years until 1565. They were succeeded by four kings of Tsang, who ruled from Shigatse. Both of these dynasties were governed by lay rulers who were allied with the powerful lama, Karmapa, the head of another Kagyu sub-order at Tsurpu monastery near Lhasa.

But this epoch of independence came to a violent end in 1642, when the Mongolians appeared on the scene again and forcibly replaced the last Tsang king with the towering figure of the Fifth Dalai Lama.

The Rule of the Dalai Lamas (1642 – 1959)

The Rise of the Gelukpa Order
During the period of Pamotrupa rule in Tibet there lived and taught a monk called Tsongkhapa, named after the region of Eastern Tibet where he was born in 1357. Tsongkhapa was a brilliant and noble figure who studied widely with lamas of the various Buddhist orders of his time, without getting involved in the sectarian and political manoeuvring that absorbed some of their more worldly members. He produced a lucid and synthetic vision of Buddhist thought and practice and lived a

monastic life that paid strict attention to the ethical values embodied in the ordained community. He attracted a wide following during his lifetime among whom were many devoted disciples who sought to preserve his influence after his death.

These disciples established a number of monasteries in Central Tibet that swiftly grew in size, and a distinctive new order of Tibetan Buddhism began to emerge. Initially it was known as the Ganden Order, named after Tsongkhapa's monastery near Lhasa, but later acquired the title 'Geluk' (the 'Virtuous Order') by which it is known today. The Gelukpa were concerned with the teachings of Tsongkhapa, which emphasised a return to the spirit of the purity of doctrine and ethics introduced in the eleventh century by Atisha. At this stage they must have appeared as a fresh, dynamic and somewhat idealistic order untarnished by the stains of political ambition that now clung to most of the Sakya and Kagyu schools in Central Tibet.

The leadership of this order passed from the older to the younger disciples of the master, finally being granted to Tsongkhapa's nephew, Gendun Drup, the founder of Tashilhunpo Monastery in Shigatse. Following the example of the Karmapas, Gendun Drup announced that he would deliberately take rebirth in Tibet and gave indications to his followers to enable them to find him. His successor was called Gendun Gyatso, a learned and powerful man who, as head abbot of Drepung Monastery near Lhasa, further consolidated the prestige of Tsongkhapa's tradition. During his time Drepung grew into the largest monastery in Tibet, with more than a thousand monks.

The next successor to the leadership of the Gelukpa order was Sonam Gyatso, born in 1543. The prominence of the Gelukpas now began to attract the attention of the Mongolians, who since their eviction from China had returned to their northern homelands. Altan Khan, a descendent of Genghis, invited Sonam Gyatso to meet him. Upon meeting the Khan in North-Eastern Tibet, Sonam Gyatso was given the title 'Ta-le', the Mongolian word for 'ocean' (in Tibetan, 'gyatso'), which is now written as 'Dalai'. This title was retrospectively bestowed upon Sonam Gyatso's two predecessors, and thus Sonam Gyatso became the Third Dalai Lama. No formal political alliances were entered into by the two men. It seems that Altan Khan was sincerely impressed by the spiritual teachings of the Dalai Lama and encouraged the conversion of the Mongols to Buddhism. But when Sonam Gyatso's reincarnation turned out to be a great-grandson cf Altan Khan, the danger of further Mongolian political involvement in Tibet became apparent.

OPPOSITE *The Fifth Dalai Lama (Nechung Monastery, near Lhasa).*

The Fifth Dalai Lama

The rulers of Tibet at that time, the Tsang king and his ally the Karmapa, were understandably alarmed by the prospect of a Mongol/Gelukpa alliance. Tension between the two groups rose, leading to the king attacking Drepung and Sera monasteries. The Fourth Dalai Lama, Yönten Gyatso, fled from Central Tibet and later died under suspicious circumstances in 1616 at the age of twenty-five. The following year a successor was found in the figure of Ngawang Losang Gyatso, born to a Nyingmapa family in the Chonggye valley. The Mongolians continued to support the Gelukpa and make threatening gestures in the direction of Tibet. Finally Gushri Khan, the leader of the newly powerful Qosot Mongols, proposed to the Gelukpas that he invade Tibet and put an end to the conflict with the Tsang king. This he did, emerging victorious in 1642. The king of Tsang was murdered, the Karmapa order stripped of its authority, and Losang Gyatso, the Fifth Dalai Lama, was enthroned as regent over Tibet.

With the support of his Mongolian backers the newly empowered Fifth Dalai Lama set out to unite the country under Gelukpa rule. He travelled widely, inspecting the state of the monasteries and administration of the different provinces, making changes where he saw fit. By 1656, the year of Gushri Khan's death, most of Tibet from Kailas to Kham was under his control. Since Gushri's successors showed little interest in Tibet, Mongolian influence waned and the Dalai Lama became virtually an absolute ruler. This was the first time in the history of Tibet that a single, indigenous regime, uniting spiritual with secular authority, truly dominated the land. The Dalai Lama was generally recognised as a wise and tolerant ruler who brought back a sense of national unity and strength to Tibet. The lasting symbol of his rule is still visible in the grandeur of his Potala Palace.

Manchu Overlordship

Despite the Fifth Dalai Lama's achievements, his death (in 1682) exposed the weaknesses inherent in the machinery of succession by reincarnation. There being an inevitable gap of around twenty years before the next Dalai Lama could assume control, an unstable political vacuum was liable to emerge in this interim between one ruler and the next. And since the successor was chosen not on his merits but by the auspiciousness of his birth, it was always uncertain whether or not he would be a suitable leader. Such were the dangers when the Fifth Dalai Lama died. Initially his regent, Desi Sanggye Gyatso, concealed his death, maintaining that the Dalai Lama had entered a long period of meditation. Later, the choice of successor turned out to be an unfortunate one, for Tsangyang Gyatso, the Sixth Dalai Lama, showed little interest in either religious observances or political responsibility and preferred the life of a poet and libertine. Tibetans generously explain this behaviour as the enlightened, unfettered activity of an advanced tantric yogin, but it nonetheless contributed to events which were to have detrimental and lasting consequences.

In China at this time the Manchus had just established the Ching dynasty, which was to last until 1911. The powerful emperor K'ang Hsi, the second ruler of this dynasty, was determined to keep the danger of the Tibetans and Mongols on his borders in check. He recognised the instability and tension in Lhasa arising from the death of the Fifth Dalai Lama and chose to intervene. Thus in 1706 he encouraged the ambitious Mongolian prince Lhabzang Khan to invade Tibet and mount a coup. This was successful and Desi Sanggye Gyatso, the regent of the Fifth Dalai Lama, was killed. Lhabzang offered the country as tribute to the emperor and was rewarded with the post of govenor. To dispose of the inconvenient Sixth Dalai Lama, Lhabzang and the emperor decided to bring him to China, but he died in Eastern Tibet before reaching the border.

Lhabzang Khan's position was soon under threat from another group of Mongols, the Dzungars, who were former allies of Desi Sanggye Gyatso. In 1717 they invaded Tibet, murdered Lhabzang and set out on a vicious rampage of burning and looting. K'ang Hsi immediately intervened with an army of 7,000 men, who forced the Dzungars to retreat. To further impress themselves as saviours on the Tibetans, they brought with them the young Seventh Dalai Lama, Kelsang Gyatso, who, until then, had been in Kumbum Monastery in North-Eastern Tibet. In 1720 the Seventh Dalai Lama was enthroned and in the following year the emperor decreed Tibet to be a protectorate of China. Two Chinese representatives, called 'Ambans', were left in Lhasa to oversee relationships between the two countries.

The Seventh Dalai Lama was a religious man who played a minor role in the governing of the country. This was left to lay administrations, the most effective being that of Polha Sonam Topgye, who ruled until 1747. The Eighth Dalai Lama, Jampel Gyatso, was also largely uninvolved in matters of state, but from the time of his rule, the administration was put in the hands of a council of four ministers, one of whom would be a monk. Towards the end of his reign, in 1792, the Chinese army had to be called in to drive out the Nepalese Gurkhas, who invaded from the south and reached as far as Shigatse. This was the final intervention of Chinese forces on behalf of the Tibetans and for more than a century their role in Tibet became a mere formality, with all power shifting to the Dalai Lama's regime and the Gelukpa order.

None of the next four Dalai Lamas, from the Ninth to the Twelfth, had

any influence over Tibetan affairs, since they all died before reaching the age of majority. Whether they were murdered or died of natural causes is still an open question. A series of regents governed in their stead and the quality of their rule varied considerably with their personality and ability. During the nineteenth century Tibet adopted a xenophobic policy and closed its borders to all foreigners. With China occupied by its own internal decline and the suspect British and Russians refused entry, the Tibetans settled into a period of conservative, church-dominated stability.

The Thirteenth Dalai Lama
The next great national leader of Tibet to emerge was Tubten Gyatso, the Thirteenth Dalai Lama. He presided over Tibet's entry into the twentieth century and its initial response to the tumultuous events that were to transform the political situation in Asia. He was a perceptive ruler who recognised the precarious position of Tibet and the need to reach agreement with its neighbours (China and British India) over the exact political status of Tibet. He was forced into exile twice during his reign; firstly to Mongolia when the British, suspicious that the Tibetans were dealing with the Russians and eager to establish their own trade agreement with Tibet, sent an expedition under Colonel Younghusband into Tibet in 1904; and secondly to India when the Manchus invaded in 1910 in an attempt to convert Tibet into a province of China. Although the British won their trade agreement, the revolution in China in 1911 obviated all authority that the Manchus in Lhasa might have had and the Tibetans drove them out. The Dalai Lama returned in triumph to his capital in 1913, declaring an independent Tibet free from even the formality of Chinese overlordship.

Later the same year the British arranged a conference in Simla between themselves, the Tibetans and the Chinese in order to establish the exact nature of the relationship between them. The Chinese insisted that Tibet was an 'integral part of China', the first time such a claim had ever been made. The Tibetans fiercely repudiated this suggestion and it was up to the British to work out some kind of compromise. The convention carried on for six months, at the end of which a series of points were drafted for official approval by the three parties concerned. The rather complex agreement hinged on the notion that Tibet was an autonomous state under the suzerainty of China. The British and Tibetans were willing to sign the agreement but the Chinese government refused. A separate Anglo-Tibetan declaration was made instead in . which the British recognised Tibetan autonomy but would not recognise Chinese suzerainty over Tibet unless the Chinese signed the Simla accord (which they never did).

Tubten Gyatso, the Thirteenth Dalai Lama, shortly before his death, 1933.

The Thirteenth Dalai Lama returning to Tibet from exile in 1913.

For the remainder of his rule the Thirteenth Dalai Lama had to contend with continual tension and fighting on the Chinese border as well as internal resistance to change and modernisation from the powerful, conservative elements within the Gelukpa hierarchy. It would not be long before the British, Tibet's tenuous connection to the outside world and only security against Chinese invasion, would leave India, and China taken over by a Communist regime with decidedly imperial intentions.

Shortly before his death in 1933, the Dalai Lama issued a stern warning to his people of the dangers they faced in the years ahead. But no sooner had he died than chaos and factionalism beset the government, producing just the instability that Tibet could least afford at this critical time. In 1935 Tenzin Gyatso, the Fourteenth Dalai Lama, was found in a humble family in the north-east of Tibet near the Chinese border. The young boy was taken to Lhasa and grew up in the seclusion of the Potala and Norbulingka palaces, slowly and painfully becoming aware of the crisis towards which his country was heading.

The Chinese Occupation (1959 –)

India gained independence from Britain in 1947 and two years later Mao Tsetung announced the formation of the People's Republic of China. In the excitement of their new beginnings the two countries asserted the renewal of a long, but fictitious, history of mutual friendship (an assertion the Indians were soon to regret). Having successfully liberated the

Chinese trucks arriving in Lhasa on the newly constructed highway, January 1955.

Chinese people, the following year the communist government decided
'to liberate the oppressed and exploited Tibetans and reunite them with
the great motherland'. The PLA invaded Eastern Tibet in October 1950
and swiftly captured Chamdo. A few months later they had convinced
the Tibetan governor there, Ngapo Ngawang Jigme, to sign (with no
authority from the Lhasa government) a seventeen-point agreement for
the 'peaceful liberation of Tibet'. The Tibetans were ill-prepared to cope
with this invasion and with a minimum of resistance the Chinese army
made its way into Lhasa in September 1951.

The Chinese arrived on a wave of optimistic promises and good-will
with which they tried to win the Tibetans over to the idea of a just and
equal socialist society. The Dalai Lama's government tentatively agreed
to cooperate with a number of measures aimed at improving the Tibetans' lot by introducing certain features of modern life, such as roads
and electricity. This uneasy alliance did not last long. Suspicious of the
communists' motives, the Khampas in Eastern Tibet staged a revolt in
1956 that soon became a full-scale insurrection. Tensions mounted in
Lhasa and an armed resistance movement was soon active in Central
Tibet. In March 1959 the general of the Chinese forces in Lhasa made an
unusual request for the Dalai Lama to attend a theatrical show inside the
Chinese military base. This was immediately interpreted by the Tibe-

The Fourteenth Dalai Lama with his younger brother, Ngari Rinpoche, and Khampa guerillas en route to India, 1959.

tans as a ploy to kidnap their leader, and they reacted with a series of popular demonstrations in Lhasa and outside the Norbulingka, the grounds of the Dalai Lama's summer palace. This explosive confrontation finally erupted on March 17th. The Chinese started shelling the city and that evening the Dalai Lama and his entourage fled south in the direction of India. The demonstrations turned into an outright rebellion against the unwanted Chinese presence in Tibet that was met with the full fury of the Chinese military. Fierce fighting broke out in Lhasa but the superior Chinese forces quickly overwhelmed the Tibetans, inflicting heavy casualties and damaging many buildings.

From now on the Chinese dropped any pretence of 'peaceful liberation' and set out to incorporate Tibet into the People's Republic. They were assisted in this task by a number of Tibetan collaborators, such as Ngapo Ngawang Jigme. The former institutions of Tibet were dismantled, monasteries were stripped of all authority, and a Chinese dominated bureaucracy supported by a massive military presence was established to govern the region. The wishes of the Tibetan people were ignored and any hint of resistance was immediately suppressed by force. In September 1965, it was proudly announced that Tibet was now the Xizang (=Tibetan) Autonomous Region of the People's Republic of China.

Desecrated Buddha statue outside Palhalupuk, Lhasa.

During the next decade China became embroiled in one of the greatest disasters any country has ever imposed upon itself: the cultural revolution. Although much of Tibet's cultural heritage had already been destroyed as part of the process of peaceful liberation, what remained was now systematically reduced to ruins. Red guards, some of them young Tibetans, tried to uproot every last trace of the former system. Monasteries in the most isolated places were taken down stone by stone. Religious paintings and inscriptions were effaced. 'Reactionaries' were jailed by the thousand for merely refusing to denounce their faith in the Dalai Lama. And in Tibet the cultural revolution served the additional purpose of seeking to obliterate the very idea of a people's separate identity as a nation.

Since the death of Mao in 1976, the policy of the Chinese government has mollified somewhat and become more 'realistic'. The destruction wrought by the cultural revolution is now officially mourned and a programme is underway throughout China to repair some of its damage. The Tibetans too have benefited from this liberalisation and in recent years the Chinese have admitted to errors in their handling of the Tibetan situation. Taxes and other restrictions have been lifted and certain economic and religious freedoms have been granted. But none of this alters the fact that Tibet remains firmly under the domination of an alien and unwanted power.

Tibetans in Exile

Two weeks after he left Lhasa, the Dalai Lama reached India. In the months that followed he was joined by about a hundred thousand fellow refugees. Prime Minister Nehru readily granted political asylum to the Tibetan leader and his followers but refused to take any further steps against the Chinese. Despite the guarantee by the British that their support for Tibet (as embodied in the Anglo-Tibetan declaration of 1914) would be continued by their Indian successors, Nehru offered no recognition of the Dalai Lama's government and instead affirmed his support for the recent Indo-Sino treaty, which promised that neither country would involve itself in the internal affairs of the other, thereby tacitly acknowledging Chinese sovereignty over Tibet.

The Dalai Lama then appealed to the world community for support. The Internal Commission of Jurists investigated his case and concluded that Tibet was indeed a sovereign state and that the Chinese were guilty of what amounted to genocide. But when the issue was brought up before the United Nations later in 1959, a resolution was passed in Tibet's favour merely demanding 'respect for the fundamental human rights of the Tibetan people'. Led by the Russians, the communist bloc countries simply repeated the Chinese view of the affair and accused the West of fabricating the issue as another weapon in the cold war. The Indians and the British, the only two countries with a good knowledge of the situation, both emphasised the ambiguities of the Tibetan case and refused to take a firm stand for the rights of the Tibetans to independence.

Although the outside world continued to express sympathy for the plight of the Tibetans, it did nothing to support their cause and simply turned a blind eye to what the Chinese were doing. Discouraged by this ineffective response of the world community, the Dalai Lama recognised that he had no real allies. He turned his attention instead to the building up of the Tibetan community in exile and concentrated on the immediate problems of sheer physical survival and the preservation of Tibet's unique but threatened culture.

The Tibetans in exile have proven to be a remarkably resilient and resourceful people, establishing in less than twenty years a thriving refugee community in India and abroad. The Dalai Lama has created a government in exile at his home in Dharamsala and critically restructured the political apparatus. Many of the major monasteries have been reestablished in the Tibetan settlements in South India and Buddhist teachers have founded centres and monasteries throughout Europe and America, thus making the Tibetan religious heritage accessible to a wider audience than ever before.

In June 1978 the Chinese surprised everyone by allowing Tibetans in exile to return freely to Tibet (the only condition being that on their visa applications they give their nationality as Chinese). Postal communication was also reestablished. In these ways the refugees suddenly were able to gain first-hand knowledge of their families and friends left behind nearly twenty years before. Even more surprising was the Chinese acceptance of a series of fact-finding missions from Dharamsala to travel extensively through the country to evaluate for themselves the present situation. The first of these delegations left in August 1979, composed of senior members of the Dalai Lama's government as well as his immediately elder brother, Lobsang Samten. This was followed in 1980 by two further delegations. Everywhere the missions went they were beseiged by crowds of tearful Tibetans imploring the Dalai Lama to return. Feeling rose to such a pitch during the second delegation's visit to Lhasa that a crowd gathered outside the hotel where the delegates were staying and began shouting for Tibetan independence. The delegation was duly dispatched back to Hong Kong the next day accused of 'inciting the Tibetan people to break with the motherland'. Although the third delegation completed its tour, a planned fourth team was never sent. The Chinese, aware of the deep national feelings of the Tibetans, realised that they could not possibly contain the presence of the Dalai Lama on Tibetan soil without risking an uprising. The conditions for a possible visit by him in 1985 were made unacceptable to the Tibetans and the situation returned to stalemate.

Members of the Dalai Lama's second delegation with the Panchen Lama (fourth from left), Peking, May 1980.

Conclusions

The Tibetans are a race with a language, culture, religion, history and customs entirely distinct from the Chinese. They have functioned as a de facto independent state for thirteen hundred years, for the most part as a peaceful, deeply religious neighbour of India and China. Even during the periods of overlordship by Chinese dynasties, it was *non-Chinese* rulers (Mongolians and Manchurians) who exercised that overlordship. For the communists to maintain that Tibet has always been an integral part of China has no basis at all in history or fact.

Not only have the Chinese incorporated Tibet into China but they have partitioned it as well. Although the wider area to which Tibetan culture spread was often only nominally controlled by the government in Lhasa, the people of those regions have always considered themselves Tibetans rather than Chinese and regard the Dalai Lama as their spiritual and temporal leader. Now Amdo, the north-eastern region of Tibet, has become part of Qinghai and Gansu provinces, and much of Kham, the eastern region, has been included into Sichuan and Yunnan. The so-called Tibetan Autonomous Region refers mainly to Central Tibet, Tsang and Western Tibet.

China's avowed aim of liberating the oppressed masses of Tibet was merely an ideological justification for pursuing the imperialist ambitions of the Han Chinese, first voiced at the outset of Sun Yat Sen's Republic, to incorporate all the bordering territories of Mongolia, Manchuria, Xinjiang and Tibet into China. Its main purpose was strategic: to secure its western border and to dominate the highland of Central Asia, giving it access to India, the Middle East, and the crucial areas of European Russia. So far it has achieved considerable success with military force, but in so doing has entirely compromised its standing as a socialist society, reverting instead to the role of a colonialist power insensitive to the demands of the people it has conquered. 'A people that enslaves others,' wrote Karl Marx, 'forges its own chains'.

The cost of this conquest in terms of human suffering has been enormous. Millions of people have lost their lives or been forced to spend the greater part of them in prisons and labour camps for such 'crimes' as 'harbouring bourgeois tendencies'. Families have been separated, cultures and religions persecuted, and traditional ways of life abandoned. People have been subjected to racist discrimination in education and employment, the privileged positions almost always being given to the occupying Han Chinese.

In foreign affairs the Tibetans have at times acted naively, preferring a short term, expedient solution without considering the longer term implications of their actions. Had they been less willing to acquiesce to the nominal overlordship of the Yuan and Manchu dynasties, been

xenophobic during the nineteenth century, and formed more solid contacts with the outside world during the early decades of the twentieth century, they may have been able to prevent the tragedy which has overcome them. The notion of 'patron-priest' was a conveniently ambiguous one that in traditional Asian political relations could work to the advantage of both parties without either of them feeling to be the underdog. To the politically-minded Mongols and Manchus, the patron naturally held a superior position to that of the priest. But to the religiously-minded Tibetans, the priest held the real and higher power, since he was in touch with eternal truths, while his patron was mired in the inherently unsatisfactory and transient half-truths of the world.

By Western standards Tibet was a backward and feudal society with its fair share of injustices and shortcomings, but by all accounts it was a country where people were content with their lot, adequately fed and clothed, of a cheerful and friendly disposition, and nourished by deeply rewarding spiritual values. It may well turn out that they were preserving something that we in our arrogance have discarded.

THE DALAI LAMAS

1.	Gendun Drup	1391-1474
2.	Gendun Gyatso	1476-1542
3.	Sonam Gyatso	1543-1588
4.	Yonten Gyatso	1589-1616
5.	Ngawang Losang Gyatso	1617-1682
6.	Tsangyang Gyatso	1683-1706
7.	Kelsang Gyatso	1708-1757
8.	Jampel Gyatso	1758-1804
9.	Lungtog Gyatso	1805-1815
10.	Tsultrim Gyatso	1816-1837
11.	Khedrup Gyatso	1838-1855
12.	Trinle Gyatso	1856-1875
13.	Tubten Gyatso	1876-1933
14.	Tenzin Gyatso	1935-

PREVIOUS PAGE *Lhamo'i Lhatso: the 'Oracle Lake' in which visions are sought by those searching for the reincarnations of the Dalai Lama.*

TIBETAN BUDDHISM

A common misconception still prevails about Tibetan Buddhism that it is a shamanistic form of Buddhism heavily influenced by the indigenous Bön religion of Tibet. This misconception can be easily reinforced by visiting Tibetan monasteries at first hand and seeing all manner of ferocious, seemingly demonic deities peering at you from the murals and *tangkas*. But in every culture where Buddhism has spread, from Sri Lanka to Japan, the same phenomenon can be observed: instead of denouncing and stamping out the local gods, the Buddhists have simply converted them to their own cause. People are thus able to continue making use of their traditional religious symbols but within the context of a more highly evolved system of value and meaning. Tibet is no exception to this. The traditional religion of the country, in this case Bön, has conditioned the form Buddhism has assumed, but has had little influence on its meaning. In fact the opposite is true; since the arrival of Buddhism in Tibet both the form *and* the meaning of Bön have been completely transformed by its presence.

Buddhism entered Tibet from India in two principal phases (about ninety percent of the wrathful, Bön-type deities one sees are actually Indian in origin). The first phase was during the reign of the Yarlung kings, in particular Trisong Detsen, the Indian figure most associated with this period being Padmasambhava. The second phase was during the eleventh century, Atisha and Milarepa being the best known figures of this time. Although both Tibetan and Western scholars like to see the introduction of Buddhism as a systematic and almost deliberate effort, it is more likely that it was the gradual product of centuries of cultural and religious influence filtering from India and China into the Tibetan highlands. Only much later was this process simplified and categorised by the minds of historians.

For the Tibetans, Buddhism was their introduction to higher culture as such. Until the communist takeover in 1959 it informed their entire view of life: the origin and nature of the world, the role of the individual in society, the relation between mind and matter, the principles of ethics, the arts, medical science, and of course religion. Their lives were permeated by Buddhist values. It is impossible to understand Tibetans without knowing the basic tenets of Buddhism and how they interpreted them. And only in this way can we perhaps peel away some of the layers of exotic fantasy that have built up around these people.

One of the most distinctive features of Tibetan Buddhism is the way it has integrated the three principal trends of Indian Buddhism into a coherent, systematic whole. These three trends are the Hinayana, Mahayana and Vajrayana, which mean the 'lesser', the 'great' and the 'diamond' vehicles to enlightenment. The Hinayana presents the basic teachings of the historical Buddha Shakyamuni, still preserved in their original form by the Theravada tradition of Sri Lanka and South-East Asia; the Mahayana introduces the further evolution of ethical and philosophical understanding that started to emerge in India about five hundred years after Shakyamuni; and the Vajrayana is seen as the culmination of the two other traditions, a powerful, direct path that utilises symbolic imagination, mantric sound and subtle physical energy to effect a complete psycho-physical transformation.

Hinayana

Buddhism starts by recognising the frustrating and essentially unsatisfactory nature of normal human existence. It then goes on to point out that the source of this frustration and unfulfilment lies not in the nature of the world itself or in the intention of God or the Devil, but in the intellectual bewilderment and emotional confusion within ourselves. It maintains that the suffering we experience in life can be brought to an end by ridding ourselves of this confusion. And it offers a way to realise this goal by following a path of personal development that includes the examination and changing of one's attitudes, behaviour, livelihood and psychological habits.

The basic teachings of Buddhism emphasise the need for strict moral discipline combined with a rigorous training in meditation and insight as the means to liberate oneself from the negative, inner bondage to suffering. These elements are likewise stressed in Tibetan Buddhism and find their classical expression in its monastic institutes. The monk or nun consciously adopts a way of life that has been found to be the most conducive to the cultivation of these qualities. Although many of the minor rules of Indian Buddhist monasticism were put aside in Tibet, usually for practical reasons of climate, local customs etc., the main vows, such as not taking life, celibacy, not stealing and not lying about one's spiritual attainment, were upheld. Ideally a monk would devote the remainder of his life to study and spiritual discipline, aspiring to set an example to society by his own embodiment of the values of Buddhism. In practice, though, many Tibetan monks were also employed in the administration of their monasteries and would spend all but the last years of their lives engaged in official work that often had political impli-

OPPOSITE *Statues of lamas from the lineage of the Stages on the Path to Enlightenment* (lam-rim) *in the Potala.*

Decorative wood-carving above the entrance to Pelkor Chöde, Gyantse.

cations. Other monks would be specially trained in the performance of the complex rituals found in Tibetan Buddhism and much of their time would be taken up by long sessions of chanting and praying either in the homes of the laity or in the monastery itself.

The monks and nuns are also the living symbols of the Buddhist spiritual community or 'Sangha'. As in all Buddhist societies, the Tibetans believe that a continued monastic presence is vital to the preservation of Buddhism. Thus one of the responsibilities of the lay community is to support the monasteries either by donating food or money directly to it or by sponsoring one or more monks. It was also a custom to donate a son to the monastery both for his education and as a contribution to the manpower of the order. Although this practice was denounced and forbidden by the Chinese after they assumed power, in the last couple of years it has resumed and many of the young monks you see in the monasteries today are there because their parents have sent them to help revive the monastic tradition.

Another important feature of basic Buddhism is the commitment of

A finely carved pillar capital (Drepung).

'Taking Refuge in the Three Jewels'. The Three Jewels, or the Triple Gem, are the Buddha, the Dharma and the Sangha. It is by committing one's life to these three principles that one is considered to be a Buddhist. This commitment is the fundamental spiritual focus of Buddhism. It means directing one's inner life towards the enlightenment and compassion personified by the Buddha; practising the Dharma (the 'law' or path revealed by the Buddha) as the means of realising enlightenment; and devoting oneself to the community (Sangha) of men and women who are likewise engaged on this path to enlightenment. In Tibetan Buddhism this triad is often supplemented by a fourth refuge, the lama, or spiritual teacher, and even by a fifth, the *yidam*, or personal tantric deity (about which more will be said below). Quite early in their lives most Tibetans will attend a formal ceremony of 'taking refuge' in the presence of a lama. During their daily practice this commitment is repeatedly renewed and as a preparation for the more advanced tantric practices it has to be recited, together with visualisation and contemplation, one hundred thousand times.

The mantra OM MANI PADME HUM *carved on a boulder on Hepori. It concludes with the seed syllable* HRI.

Mahayana

The 'Great Vehicle' of the Mahayana is based upon and includes the Hinayana doctrines and practices but emphasises a different ethical standpoint. The Mahayana grew up in India as a critique of certain tendencies in the Hinayana to renounce any further involvement in the plight of the world and strive instead for one's own release in the unconditioned, deathless realm of Nirvana. The Mahayanists believed that by severing every last trace of attachment to the world one failed to acknowledge the essential connectedness one has with life and to discover the meaning of one's fundamental participation in existence. For them true spiritual nobility was found primarily not in detachment and release but in compassion and love. The Mahayana ideal is the *bodhisattva*, the person who selflessly aspires to realise enlightenment for the sake of everything that lives.

From the very beginning of the introduction of Buddhism into Tibet, the Tibetans were exposed to the ideas of the Mahayana. They accepted them readily and there was never any actual conflict between followers of the Hinayana and Mahayana traditions. The Tibetans understood the Mahayana critique as a critique of the tendency within oneself to centre spiritual practice around one's own personal needs and desires alone. Compassion became a central theme in Tibetan Buddhism and explains the tremendous devotion the Tibetans have for the archetypal bodhisattva of compassion, Avalokiteshvara, or, in Tibetan, Chenrezi. Avalokiteshvara is the personification of enlightened compassion and is represented in a number of symbolic forms. Songtsen Gampo, the Tibetan king who first accepted Buddhism, and the Dalai Lamas are revered as human emanations of Avalokiteshvara.

When that enlightened compassion is symbolised in sound it becomes the mantra OM MANI PADME HUM. This is the melody of Tibet, murmured constantly by the devout as they count their beads. As a mantra it is used as a means of concentrating the mind upon the meaning of compassion while its associations and vibratory resonance evoke corresponding feelings in the heart. Its syllables are those most commonly carved on the rocks and stones around holy shrines. In some places you can see them outlined in white rock on distant hillsides. Before the Chinese occupation roads were lined with 'mani walls', long piles of stones carved with the mantra slowly built up by pilgrims and local people. Sadly most of these have been demolished.

The bodhisattva realises that to overcome the world's frustration and despair, ultimately it is necessary to uproot the spiritual origins of suffering. Since from a Buddhist point of view this is achieved through enlightenment, he sets out to gain this goal in order that he will be in a position to lead others to a similar state. Thus he recognises that the optimal benefit he can bring to the world is his own inner illumination, compassion and freedom. The path he treads is outlined in the Mahayana teachings as consisting of six central qualities: generosity, ethics, tolerance, energy, meditation and wisdom. Of these six, wisdom is the key to enlightenment which, to be effective, must be supported by the moral and psychological strength of the other five.

Slate carving of Manjushri and Avalokiteshvara embedded in the wall surrounding the Potala.

The wisdom of enlightenment consists of direct, non-conceptual insight into the ultimate meaning of existence. In Mahayana Buddhism, the term used to refer to this truth is *shunyata,* which literally means 'emptiness'. This notion of emptiness is frequently misinterpreted to mean that Buddhism is life-denying and nihilistic. But nothing could be further from the truth. A well-known Tibetan lama was once asked by a Western student how, if everything were empty, one could still appreciate the beauty of nature. He replied that it is only when you have realised emptiness that you can fully appreciate the beauty of nature.

Emptiness does not deny the presence and beauty of people, animals, trees, mountains, and flowers. It simply negates the fictions we project upon these things that prevent us from experiencing them as they really are. Chief among these fictions is the sense that things are self-contained and essentially separate from everything else. This is most evident in the case of our sense of ego-identity. Of course, intellectually we may know that this is not so, but the doctrine of emptiness does not merely challenge our intellectual views: it puts into question our pre-intellectual sense of how things are. For it is not false concepts alone that prevent enlightenment, but a much more deeply rooted clinging based upon patterns, tendencies and habits inherited from our past conditioning. Thus the philosophy of emptiness, profound and far reaching as it may be, has to be driven home by the power of a concentrated, meditative awareness capable of counteracting the very force of conditioning itself.

Tibetan monks may spend many years studying, reflecting and meditating upon the meaning and implications of emptiness. They read texts, receive explanations, debate among themselves, and go into solitary retreat to deepen their understanding. Volumes of commentaries to the key Indian works on emptiness as well as original writings have been composed over the last thousand years by lamas from all the different orders of Tibetan Buddhism.

The aim of Mahayana practice is to harmonise wisdom and compassion. The wisdom of emptiness in no way diminishes the love the bodhisattva has for the world. By stripping his mind of fictitious notions, he breaks down the barriers that create the sense of separation between self and others. In this way emptiness reveals the rich and dynamic interrelatedness of all things. True wisdom and compassion mutually deepen each other and culminate in the liberated yet engaged enlightenment of the Buddha.

OPPOSITE *An itinerant lama chanting his prayers outside the Potala. The large drum indicates that he is doing* Chö *(ego-slaying) practice.*

Monks from the upper and lower tantric colleges of Lhasa during the yearly consecration (rab-ne) *ceremony at the Jokhang. The monks are consecrating newly made religious images. They are wearing the special robes and headdress of tantric initiates.*

Vajrayana

The diamond vehicle of the Vajrayana has the same objective as the Mahayana, the realisation of enlightenment for the sake of others, but employs its own particular means to achieve that goal. The Vajrayana is based upon the teachings of the Buddhist tantras. As opposed to the sutras, which were discourses given by the historical Buddha to a general audience, the tantras are esoteric instructions given to selected groups of disciples. Vajrayanists believe that these teachings were also taught by Shakyamuni, albeit often through his magically assuming a special form. The tantras reveal a path to enlightenment that is swifter than the ordinary Hinayana or Mahayana paths but no less arduous. They often speak in a language enriched with evocative symbols. States of spiritual attainment are illustrated not by psychological descriptions but by vibrant, personalised gods. By invoking these symbolic figures, the practitioner of the Vajrayana enters into a living relationship and identification with enlightenment as personified by the 'deity' with whom he or she has the greatest affinity.

The Vajrayana is a path of transformation. Instead of seeing the spiritual quest as the simple rejection of evil and achievement of good, it recognises how every psychological condition of humankind – whether beneficial or harmful – is essentially a process of energy. Raw energy is in itself neither good nor bad. Only when it is channelled by people towards constructive or destructive ends does it get praised or blamed for the moral consequences. The Vajrayana uses yogic techniques to channel our energy towards enlightenment instead of allowing it just to perpetuate the cycle of confusion. Contrary to a lot of popular misinformation, the Vajrayana does not abandon ethical constraints; in common with every Buddhist path, it is bound to the ethos of enlightenment. Because of the dangers involved in the utilisation rather than the suppression of emotional energies, it demands if anything an even higher degree of ethical integrity.

The often bewildering array of deities you see in Tibetan temples and monasteries illustrate the 'deities' of the Vajrayana who personify the multifaced phenomenon of enlightenment. Some depict the peaceful aspects of Buddhahood, smiling with encouragement and love. Others show its wrathful side, urging the practitioner to overcome his hesitation and engage in the awesome, compassionate dance of liberated consciousness. The numerous, waving hands clutch symbols that denote the spiritual tools needed for the task of transforming an ordinary person into an enlightened one. The stamping feet trample on the obstacles that hold you back from the fulfilment of your existential responsibilities.

The circular, symmetrical mandalas you sometimes see are symbolic descriptions of the deity in the context of his or her world. When visualised during Vajrayana practice, mandalas are not flat circles but three-dimensional, luminous spheres. The deity resides in the centre of this sphere, often in the company of the minor deities of his entourage. The mandala itself symbolises the complete transformation of experience wrought by enlightenment, only for such transformation affects not only the quality of one's own consciousness but also the way in which the world itself appears.

There are two stages involved in this process of transformation. First it is necessary to rid oneself of conventional ideas and perceptions of who one is and what reality is. On the tantric path this is achieved by imaging oneself as a deity and the world as the mandala of that deity. One's speech likewise becomes the mantra of the deity. (The particular deity one chooses for this purpose is called one's *yidam*, or tutelary deity.) The initial practice of the Vajrayana entails systematically familiarising oneself with this transformed view until it can be sustained in meditation without any distraction for several hours. In the second

The mandala of Kalachakra, the 'Wheel of Time', one of the most complex practices of the Vajrayana.

stage the practitioner uses his powers of imagination and concentration to free and rechannel the subtle energies that are the physical basis of psychic life. This gives him or her access to the 'founding stratum' of existence, which is known by a number of descriptive terms: 'clear light', 'primordial Buddha', 'Dharmic presence' and others.

In the course of normal human existence, this fundamental clear light only becomes apparent to us shortly after clinical death. But without spiritual preparation during life, we usually pass over it in a haze of inattention. The yogic techniques of the Vajrayana enable one to experience this luminous ground of life and death in meditation and on that basis recreate the quality of one's existence. Through constant practice one learns to arise from this meditation imbued with the dynamics of the deity instead of the habits and conditioning of one's former self.

The Tibetans also possess other methods of meditation that lead to an experience of the clear light but do not necessarily involve the stages of tantric practice described above. These are the practices of the 'Great Gesture' (*chak-chen*, or *mahamudra*) and the 'Great Completion' (*dzog-chen*). Such methods propose a direct breakthrough to the ultimate nature of consciousness and being, as do in a similar way the Zen traditions of China and Japan. In most cases, though, they are taught in conjunction with and often as the culmination of the traditional tantric path of deity yoga.

The Wheel of Life

These spiritual practices and disciplines are interpreted as a meaningful response to the kind of world the Tibetans believe themselves to inhabit. This world is the one they inherited from India over a thousand years ago and it is only within the last thirty years that it has been seriously challenged by the modern scientific outlook introduced by the Chinese. The traditional Buddhist world view conceives of the universe as temporally and spatially infinite. It has no beginning and only theoretically an end (should all sentient beings realise Nirvana). It is composed of countless world-systems, all of which are inhabited by six basic forms of life: humans, animals, celestials, titans, ghosts and denizens of hell. These life-forms dwell in the sky, on the earth, in the water and beneath the ground of a world that is dominated by a majestic mountain called 'Sumeru', protruding into the heavens from the centre of a vast ocean. We humans live on a continent called Jambudvipa, situated in the ocean to the south of Sumeru.

The mind, or stream of consciousness, of each individual being is considered as beginningless and endless. Until we recognise our dilemma and adopt a spiritual path to liberation, we are condemned to pass through an infinite succession of births within the six forms of life. The driving force of consciousness is the accumulated impetus of our actions, which propels us from one realm to the next according to the ethical quality of our deeds.

This process is vividly depicted by an illustration called the 'Wheel of Life', a painting of which is sometimes found at the entrance of Tibetan temples. At the hub of this wheel are three animals: a pig, a snake and a cock, respectively symbolising the ignorance, hatred and desire that motivate the actions that keep us bound to a meaningless cycle of birth and death. In the circle around the hub are shown various beings rising to divine heights only to fall again into hellish agony. Around this circle are six (sometimes only five) sections that show the realms of existence into which beings are propelled and then ejected. The outer rim contains a circle of twelve pictures that symbolise the twelvefold sequence of conditioning that leads from ignorance to ageing and death. The entire wheel is held by the demonic figure of Yama, the personification of death, who contains it in his mouth, ready to bite at any moment. Outside the wheel stands a Buddha pointing to a moon, which symbolises the completeness of spiritual liberation.

Although the Tibetans often interpret this diagram quite literally, it can also be seen simply as a powerful symbol of the human condition. It illustrates how our habitual psychological forces propel us into a cycle of frustrating life-situations from which we seem incapable of disentangling ourselves. Yet by recognising the mechanism of this process we have the potential to counteract the power of conditioning and reach an inner psychological freedom and completeness.

Religious Practice

When in Tibet you may be struck by the apparently superstitious aspects of religious practice that conflict with what you have read elsewhere about the profounder insights of Buddhist philosophy. From a superficial observation it is easy to conclude that Tibetan Buddhism is just a corrupt form of the original teachings of the Buddha. But as with all religions, a wide spectrum of different spiritual needs and abilities has produced an equally wide range of spiritual understandings and practices. The way in which a well-trained monk understands Buddhism will be a far cry from the way it is perceived by an old woman in the market. But nowadays, since most of the monks were driven into exile or imprisoned or killed by the Chinese, it is rare to meet a learned monk or lama to counteract the impression of Tibetan Buddhism as a simple folk religion.

In the large Gelukpa monastic universities around Lhasa the monks who chose to follow the full course of philosophical training would be required to study a number of demanding subjects that would often take fifteen to twenty years to master. They would begin with a two to three year course in basic philosophy, epistemology and formal logic before proceeding to the main subjects of Buddhist Doctrine, Madhyamika Philosophy, Buddhist Phenomenology, and Monastic Discipline. Upon successful completion of these studies they would be awarded the degree of Geshe, which is more less equivalent to our Doctor of Divinity. After this they would often go on to do tantric studies and practices. In the Kagyu and Nyingma orders a similar but usually less extensive course of study was followed, it being more common for monks to enter tantric practice at a younger age to master the meditative and yogic techniques required for completion of the Vajrayana path. In all the orders, a basic tantric retreat was a three year undertaking, either alone or with a small group of fellow practitioners. Some monks, as well

The Wheel of Life. In addition to the usual features, this representation of the wheel shows a lama leading beings out of hell along a ray of light up to Sukhavati, the 'Western Paradise' of the Buddha Amitabha. This picture may have been commissioned by a Chinese sponsor since the figures at the bottom left are dressed in Chinese fashion, playing mahjong. The skeletons remind the players of the transitoriness of their pleasurable lives.

as unordained yogins, would spend several years in the remote mountainous areas as hermits devoted to intensive spiritual practice.

These traditions were severely interrupted by the Chinese occupation and they have been preserved mainly among the exile communities in India. In recent years several Westerners have begun to train as Geshes, with so far one Swiss monk being awarded the degree. A number of others have completed three year tantric retreats under the guidance of Tibetan lamas in Europe and North America. In Tibet today, cautious moves are being made to restore these systems of training but considerable obstacles, a principal one being the lack of qualified instructors, still stand in the way.

On the level of popular, devotional practice, Buddhism is still a strong force throughout Tibet. Although public displays of faith were forbidden during the cultural revolution, as soon as the restrictions were lifted in the early 1980's, the country witnessed a huge resurgence of religious expression. The recitation of mantras and prayers, prostration, circumambulation, and the making of offerings to the temples constitute the core of popular practice. Whether these acts are accompanied by merely blind faith in their efficacy or whether they are supported by a deeper religious understanding cannot easily be judged from the outside.

Upon visiting temples and monasteries in Tibet, one will often meet pilgrims and devotees offering various things to the deities on the altars. Tibetans offer white greeting scarves (*katag*) and drape them on the statues as a formal gesture of 'meeting' the deity symbolised by the image; they pour butter into the lamps to keep them burning and thus symbolically dispel the darkness of ignorance; they offer incense and flowers and ring bells as acts of dedicating the experience of sense pleasure to enlightenment. The simplest offering is that of seven bowls of fresh water lined along the altar, which, among other things, stands as a gift of one's essential, unpolluted pure nature to the realisation of Buddhahood. Prostrations too are a form of offering. In performing them one gives up one's pride and arrogance, often combining this with a confession of the things one has done that have caused harm to oneself and others.

The turning of prayer wheels is another ubiquitous practice that for many people has come to typify popular Tibetan Buddhism. The cylindrical wheels – both the hand-held variety and the larger ones lined along the walls of shrines and temples – are filled with rolls of paper printed with mantras and prayers. As one turns the wheel and recites a

OPPOSITE *An altar and throne at Palhalupuk, Lhasa. The breads are* kabtse, *a traditional new year offering. An image of Ling Rinpoche, the late senior tutor to the present Dalai Lama, is placed on the throne.*

A young girl holding a butter lamp begins a circumambulation of Drepung Monastery. As she passes through each chapel she will pour some of the melted butter from her lamp into the larger lamps (BELOW) before the altars as an offering.

mantra, usually OM MANI PADME HUM, it is believed that additional merit is gathered because of the spinning around of the mantras packed inside. Perhaps this constant turning of sacred words also represents the continuous turning of the wheel of Dharma. In practice, though, the turning of a prayer wheel helps to concentrate one's attention and keep one's mind focused on the recitation of the mantra.

Among the stranger aspects of popular practice are the rubbing of hands or other parts of the body on stones, rocks, pillars, walls or other objects with religious associations. This is probably done with the hope that merit will be accrued or bodily ailments healed. Pins and needles are stuck into the brocade clothing of statues and around *tangkas* in the belief that this will sharpen one's intelligence. Clumps of wool are tied to trees and shrubs around monasteries in the hope that the about-to-be slaughtered animal to whom they belonged will somehow benefit. Similarly sheep and cows may be led clockwise around a monastery as their final act on this earth. The people performing many of these popular practices may not be able to give a reasoned explanation as to what they are doing. No more than I was able to explain to a Tibetan lama in Europe what Christmas trees were and why everyone was busy putting them up.

The Lama

'Lama' is the Tibetan term used to translate the Sanskrit 'guru', which simply means 'spiritual teacher'. Thus a lama is someone who is qualified to guide others along the path to enlightenment. A lama need *not* be a monk and most monks are not lamas. Some of the greatest lamas in the Tibetan tradition, Padmasambhava, Marpa, Milarepa, Kunga Nyingpo and Drom Tönpa, for example, took no monastic vows and lived as laymen and yogins. The term for a monk in Tibetan is 'trapa' not 'lama'. Moreover, to call Tibetan Buddhism 'Lamaism' is also a misuse of words. The Tibetans call their Buddhism *nang-pa'i-chö*, which means 'the Dharma of the insiders'. 'Lamaism' was a term coined by Western scholars and gives the impression that Tibetan Buddhism is something quite different from mainstream Buddhism.

In Tibetan Buddhism, the spiritual teacher plays a very important role, especially in the Vajrayana. Before embarking upon a tantric practice it is necessary to find a qualified guide who is willing to initiate you into the mandala of an appropriate deity and instruct you in the subsequent stages of meditation. Such a teacher will henceforth be considered your lama and you will be expected to devote yourself wholeheartedly to his instructions. This special role of the lama in the Vajrayana has been applied throughout the whole of Tibetan Buddhism, giving a strong devotional quality to the religion.

The term 'lama' also has some specialised usages. If you go to a monastery and ask how many lamas are there, you will be told, perhaps, that there are two. This would mean that the monastery honours within its ranks two lines of reincarnating teachers. This system of recognising the reincarnations of particularly great teachers dates from the end of the twelfth century when a great master called Karmapa declared that he would deliberately take rebirth in Tibet, and a few years later a young boy was subsequently recognised as his successor. Most monasteries of any standing would have at least one lama, the larger monasteries up to three or four. These men would serve not as abbot, which is more a post within the monastic administration, but as the spiritual head of the monastery. They are also referred to by the titles of 'tulku' and 'rinpoche'.

The two best known lamas must be the Dalai Lama and the Panchen Lama. The First Dalai Lama and the First Panchen Lama were both disciples of the founder of the Geluk school, Tsongkhapa. The present Dalai Lama is the fourteenth in his line and the present Panchen the tenth in his. Although the Dalai Lama escaped to India in 1959, the Panchen Lama was in China at the time and was unable to leave. Since then he has been constantly under the wing of the Chinese authorities. In the early 60's he disappeared from public life after making some pro-Tibetan statements and did not resurface until the end of the cultural revolution. It is fairly certain that he was imprisoned and probably tortured during this time. He now lives mainly in Peking, occupying a high-sounding post, and only rarely visits Tibet. Recently he visited the West for the first time as part of a Chinese delegation to Australia. The Tibetans revere him as a religious symbol but many of the people I spoke to expressed doubts about his current role under the Chinese. As for the Dalai Lama, he leads an active life both in the Tibetan community abroad and as an internationally recognised religious leader. The rumour that he will be the last Dalai Lama has never been confirmed or denied by him; he has simply said that the Dalai Lama will reappear only if the need for him continues to exist.

The Yellow Hats and the Red Hats
In many books written about Tibetan Buddhism you will come across the two orders of the Red Hats and the Yellow Hats. One gets the impression that the history of Buddhism in Tibet is dominated by the conflicts between these two groups, with the Yellow Hats finally emerging victorious. Unfortunately, this view is a vast oversimplification and only adds to the confusion surrounding the four principal Buddhist orders: the Nyingma, Sakya, Kagyu and Geluk. Although the Yellow Hats can be identified with the Geluk order, it makes no sense to group the other three together as the Red Hats. The historical conflict upon which the Yellow/Red distinction is based is that betweeen the Mongolian backers of the Geluk and the Tsang kings who supported the Karma Kagyu sub-order, during the seventeenth century. This becomes all the more confusing when the Karmapa, head lama of the Karma Kagyu, is commonly known as the Black Hat Lama, in distinction from another leader of the same order, the Sharmapa, the Red Hat Lama. The problem gets even more knotty when you try to include the Sakya and Nyingma orders. Unfortunately, to understand the different orders we have to look beyond what they wear on their heads.

The Tibetans sometimes distinguish between what they call the Old Ones and the New Ones, the former being the Nyingma order, who base their teachings on the first translations that were done from the seventh century onwards, the latter being the Sakya, Kagyu and Geluk orders, who base their traditions upon the later translations begun in the eleventh century. This is a much more helpful distinction than that of the Red and Yellow Hats. Another way of dividing the orders is by historical division: the Nyingma are the earliest order; the Sakya and Kagyu are the middle orders; and the Geluk the later order. About three hundred years separate the emergence of one group from the next.

Another problem is that around the four main orders there exist several minor orders and sub-orders. Some of these smaller orders are confined to a handful of monasteries that follow the teachings of a particularly great lama of that area. Examples of these would be the Bu order of Zhalu Monastery and the Bodong order of Samding Monastery. Although no longer a separate tradition, the Kadam order based at Reting Monastery was and still is very influential. It is often considered as the forerunner to the Geluk order.

It is much more difficult to try and distinguish the orders on doctrinal grounds. Such differences as do exist between them here have often been emphasised more for political than theological reasons. Although representatives of these orders continue to stress the uniqueness of their tradition as opposed to the others, the similarities that unite them are far greater than the differences that separate them.

Religious Art

Sadly, a great deal of the religious art of Tibet was destroyed during the Chinese occupation. Also, many statues and paintings were taken to China, where they were either channeled to the art market in Hong Kong, reduced to their raw materials or simply stored away. A small amount is now trickling back to Tibet and it will be interesting to see how much eventually returns. It also seems that the Tibetans concealed a considerable number of statues and *tangkas* and if the political situation proves to be stable, these too may start reappearing. The handful of artists and craftsmen who survived the persecutions of the sixties are now able to work again at their traditional skills and train young apprentices as well. Much of the work you see on display in renovated temples and monasteries today is theirs.

The most common forms of religious art in Tibet are statues, *tangkas* (painted scrolls) and murals. The vast majority of statues depict lamas, Buddhas, bodhisattvas, tantric deities, and protectors. These vary in height from a few centimetres to several metres and are made from substances ranging from clay to gold. The *tangkas* and murals likewise show lamas and deities but often surround their subject with details from the life of the main figure. Mandalas and 'lineage trees' (i.e. the entire lineage of teachers belonging to a certain tradition) are also common subjects. Around the walls of many temples are murals depicting scenes from the former lives of the Buddha.

Apart from a certain number of folk themes, Tibetan art has a purely religious function. The statues that line the altars in the monasteries are a focus of faith and a source of inspiration for the devout. The *tangkas* serve as aids to meditation, their exact details reminding the practitioner of the deity or mandala he is visualising. The richly painted

An aspect of Samvara and consort. A mural at Tsaparang, Western Tibet.

murals that fill the walls from floor to ceiling flood impress with an over-view of the Buddhist path and goal. Until recent interest from the West, paintings were never evaluated in terms of their antiquity, artistic merit or monetary value. If a beautiful, old *tangka* were too faded to be of further use as a meditation aid, it would often be ceremoniously destroyed and replaced with a new one, perhaps of inferior artistic worth. Art for the Tibetans is not an end in itself but merely a means to help realise a higher spiritual meaning.

The motifs found in Tibetan art may strike one as highly stylised and repetitive, allowing no room for the individual creativity of the artist. Such creativity is also a value not highly regarded in Tibet; more impor-tant is a humble submission of the ego to reproduce exactly the sacred forms of the past. But as you study the wide range of sculptures and paintings preserved in the monasteries, you will soon begin to distinguish the works of a master artist from those of an uninspired apprentice. Artistic genius finds its expression nonetheless.

The symbolism of Tibetan religious art is too intricate to discuss here. The symbols operate on a number of levels, possessing different meanings according to the depth of the viewer's spiritual insight. However, it is worth mentioning the sexual symbolism that is often found in the representation of tantric figures. Certain deities are often shown in sexual embrace with a consort. Sexual union is used as a vivid symbol for the integration of the male and female components of the spiritual path. The male aspect of the path is compassion and active engagement whereas the female aspect is wisdom and depth of understanding. Final enlightenment is present only when these two aspects are fully united with each other. The deities in sexual embrace do not hint at some secret erotic practice, but confront us with the challenge of integrating the male and female dimensions within ourselves, which are often tragically split apart.

Sacred Literature

Like art, literature in Tibet is almost exclusively used for religious purposes. A script for writing the Tibetan language was primarily created by Songtsen Gampo's minister Tönmi Sambhota in order that the Buddhist scriptures could be translated from Sanskrit. It took the Tibetans about six hundred years to complete that monumental task of translation, the result of which was 108 volumes of discourses attributed to the historial Buddha and a further 227 volumes of Indian commentaries to those discourses. The collection of discourses is called the 'Kangyur' in Tibetan, which means, 'translation of the word', while the

Illuminated title-page from a text on monastic discipline.

set of commentaries is call the 'Tengyur', the 'translation of the commentaries'. These scriptures, which consist of four to five hundred pages each, are printed on long, unbound leaves of tough, fibrous paper (about 75 cm long), placed between wooden covers and wrapped in cloth. They are often stacked on shelves in chapels and worshipped as reverently as the statues and other holy objects.

In addition to the Kangyur and Tengyur there is a vast quantity of indigenous writings by Tibetan lamas that for the most part are further commentaries to the Indian texts. Every lama of note has his 'Sung-bum' (Collected Works), which frequently runs into ten or twenty volumes. These writings explore in detail the meaning of Buddhist doctrine, philosophy and logic as well as more secular subjects such as medicine and astrology. Numerous works exist deciphering the esoteric meaning of the tantras and a great number of original liturgical texts have been composed. In addition the Tibetans have evolved their own styles of composition and textual structure. Only a fraction of this literary heritage has been translated into Western languages and most of it still remains unknown to the outside world.

Stupas

When the historical Buddha was cremated, his body was placed in a traditional Indian funeral cask to be burned. This cask is called a stupa (in Tibetan, a chöten) and has subsequently become for the Buddhists what the cross is for the Christians. It is the preeminent symbol for the Buddha and his enlightenment, the parts of the stupa representing the different stages on the way to the goal. There are eight principal forms of stupa, each of which stands for a particular aspect of the Buddha's enlightenment. The Enlightenment Stupa symbolises his illumination, the Victory Stupa, his conquest of 'Mara', the devil, the Nirvana Stupa, his passing away, and so forth. The reason for there being eight stupas is that after Shakyamuni's body had been cremated, the relics were divided into eight parts, placed in eight smaller funeral casks and taken to the eight major areas of India where the Buddha had been active. In Tibet when a great lama died, his body would likewise be cremated in such a funeral cask and the relics then enshrined in a more ornate stupa.

'Sky Burial'

Although lamas and monk would be cremated, the most common way to dispose of the dead in Tibet was to take the corpse to a specially designated area outside the town or village, often at the top of a mountain, chop it into pieces and wait for the vultures and other birds of prey to come and eat it. The final religious rites would be performed by monks and relatives before taking the body away. According to Mahayana

The 'Sky Burial' outside Lhasa.

Buddhist beliefs, consciousness leaves the body about three days after clinical death. From this moment on the corpse is considered as truly lifeless, its purpose fulfilled. The manner of disposal is considered as a final act of generosity, enabling other animals to be nourished by one's remains.

This practice has greatly aroused the ghoulish curiosity of many foreign visitors and it has become almost *de rigueur* while in Tibet to see if you can stomach the sight of this gruesome procedure. Initially the Tibetans tolerated the presence of foreigners but recently they have become more and more offended by the blatant, morbid voyeurism of some observers, especially when these people have insisted on photographing the occasion. Some unpleasant incidents have occurred in the last year resulting in Tibetans throwing stones at those who still try to take a candid photograph. The Chinese are also none too happy about foreigners attending this 'barbarian' ritual and it is quite possible that visitors may soon be banned from going altogether. If you do go to witness the 'sky burial', do so with a respect both for the dead and their families, and Tibetan customs. Keep a good distance and do not even show a camera. Try to follow the example of the Buddhist monks and yogins who deliberately lived in such places in order to deepen their insight into the transitoriness of life and the imminence of death.

Religious Festivals

Prior to 1959 the most jubilant and colourful events in Tibetan life were the different festivals that occured throughout the year. These were soon banned by the Chinese and denounced as wasteful and indulgent. Only since 1985 have moves been made to reinstate them. In the early spring of 1986, the greatest festival of all, the 'Mönlam' or 'Prayer' festival, took place again for the first time in nearly thirty years. This festival follows the Tibetan New Year ('Losar') celebrations and begins on the fourth day of the first lunar month. Huge butter sculptures are erected outside the Jokhang cathedral in Lhasa, monks and pilgrims pour into the city, and there is a long procession around the Barkor carrying a famous statue of Maitreya, the future Buddha. The Mönlam festival was started by Tsongkhapa in the early years of the fifteenth century and continued unbroken until the Chinese occupation. What takes place now is apparently only a poor imitation of what it was like before.

Another important festival is the 'Sakadawa' festival on the fifteenth day (full moon) of the fourth lunar month, which celebrates the birth, enlightenment and death of Buddha Shakyamuni. On this day Tibetans

OPPOSITE *The festival celebrating the Buddha's birth, enlightenment and death (Sakadawa), which occurs on the full moon of the fourth lunar month. A large appliqué* tangka *depicting the historical Buddha Shakyamuni is often displayed on this occasion (Ganden Monastery).*

RIGHT *Monk dressed in tantric costume in preparation for a religious ceremony involving ritualised dance, circa 1940.*

The A-che Lhamo Opera being performed at the Norbulingka, circa 1946. This was traditionally performed during the seventh month of the lunar year by companies from all over Tibet as a form of tax.

often devote themselves to religious practices and abstain from eating meat. The monasteries perform elaborate ceremonies and devotees make offerings to the monks.

The other major religious festivals are the 'Chökor Duchen', which celebrates the Buddha's first teaching in Sarnath near Varanasi, on the fourth day of the sixth lunar month; the 'Lhabab Duchen' on the twenty-second day of the ninth lunar month, which commemorates the Buddha's return to earth after his ascent to the heavens to teach his mother; and the 'Festival of Lamps' on the twenty-fifth day of the tenth lunar month, which commemorates the death of Tsongkhapa, the founder of the Geluk order.

In addition to these festivals there were numerous other national and regional celebrations. At some of these, monasteries would display beautiful embroidered *tangkas* from high walls often built solely for that purpose. Others would be less religious occasions when the people would enjoy the performance of open air opera and sports. At present it is difficult to say to what extent these events will be permitted to start again.

The Tibetan lunar month is usually about a month behind the Western calendar, with new year taking place sometime in February. However, each year fluctuates and sometimes a whole month has to be added. Thus in any given year it is difficult to know exactly when these festivals will occur without referring to a Tibetan calendar.

LHASA

1. THE CITY OF LHASA

Lhasa, the capital of Tibet, is situated on the north bank of the Kyichu River in the province of U (Central Tibet). The present population is about 150,000, seventy percent of whom are the Han Chinese who make up the administrative and military occupying force. The Chinese consider it to be the regional capital of the Tibetan Autonomous Region.

Hotels

If you are with a tour group you will probably stay at the **Lhasa Hotel**, *which is a large, very modern building to the west of the city by the Norbulingka. It is shortly to be taken over by the Holiday Inn group. At present, its impressive exterior belies its rather shabby and poorly equipped interior. Although the hotel does its best to provide Western comforts, it only barely succeeds. The atmosphere is deadening and the sense of being in Tibet zero. For the privilege of staying here you must pay 120 FEC for a double room per night. Tour groups may also be billeted at the* **Tibet Guesthouse**. *It is a little further out past the Lhasa Hotel and costs about 80 FEC per night.*

Most individual travellers, however, stay at either the **Banak Shöl Hotel** *(Banak Shöl Drönkhang) or the* **Snowlands Hotel** *(Gangjong Drönkhang). Both of these places are located in the old Tibetan part of the city and enable you to experience the atmosphere of Lhasa around you. Neither is particularly clean or well-equipped but they are both friendly and cheap. A bed costs 10 FEC per night (but this might well change!). The Banak Shöl has the advantage of having more small rooms (with very thin walls), a more sociable atmosphere, a high percentage of Tibetan guests and staff, and better room service (hot water in vacuum flasks three times a day!). Its biggest drawback is its location at the very eastern edge of the old city. The main advantage of the Snowlands is its central location, just around the corner from the Jokhang. Its rooms are bigger and marginally cleaner. Both hotels have their own restaurants attached and rent out bicycles for the day. At present neither have shower facilities but the Banak Shöl is opening one soon.*

Two new cheap hotels have just opened in the area of the Banak Shöl. The **Kirey Hotel** *is just down the road from the Banak Shöl, closer to the centre of town. It charged 10 FEC per night and has showers. The* **Plateau Hotel** *is the large building on the crossroads opposite the telecommunications office and also*

OPPOSITE *Dhritarashta, the guardian king of the eastern direction. Detail from a mural at the entrance of the Potala Palace.*

charges about 10 FEC. It is likely that more hotels will spring up in the coming years.

Another possibility is the **No. 1 Guesthouse** at the western end of the Mi Mang Lam across the road from the bookshop. This is entirely Chinese run, cleaner and slightly more expensive than the Tibetan hotels. It has solar heated showers and a laundry service. The main drawback is its lack of character and absence of Tibetans.

Restaurants

I find it difficult to recommend any restaurant in Lhasa for consistently good or even tolerable food. So much depends upon a wide variety of factors that are always in flux: the person who happens to be cooking that day, how fresh the meat and vegetables are, the number of customers (the more there are the less time there is to cook each wok-ful), and how clearly you have managed to communicate what you want. Restaurants in Lhasa have yet to find their own character, let alone to maintain it with any consistency. Consequently, the quality of food fluctuates wildly and the only remotely reliable barometer is the consensus of opinion prevailing among the community of visitors at the time you are there.

Only a few places have priced menus. In most restaurants the prices vary as much as the quality of the food. My suspicion is that it is often cheaper the first time you are seen in the restaurant only to increase slightly with each subsequent visit. It is always wise to establish the price before you eat.

We personally preferred to eat in the kitchen of the Banak Shöl, downstairs from the hotel (which is where we stayed). The staff are very friendly and after they got accustomed to our tastes were able to produce reasonable meals with fair regularity. This is an advantage of patronising the same place. The best place for Chinese food was the **Welcome Restaurant**, *on the main road just past the turning to the Snowland Hotel on the way to the Potala. The* **Electric Restaurant** *(so called because it is next door to the electricity generating office around the corner from the Banak Shöl Hotel) serves good wontan soup (meat dumplings in thin broth) but nothing else other than tea and tukpa. In any of these places, though, bad experiences were always possible. Many people have found that the several Muslim, or halal, restaurants scattered throughout Lhasa serve good meals at reasonable prices.*

The restaurant of the Lhasa Hotel was disappointing. When we were there only Chinese food was available. It was equivalent to mediocre fare in any city in China but far more expensive.

OPPOSITE *View of the medical college on Chakpori from the village at the foot of the Potala before 1959. A religious ceremony is in progress. The western gate of Lhasa is visible on the right at the base of Chakpori and Palhalupuk Temple can be seen clinging to the hillside to the left of the gate.*

Panorama of Lhasa, 1904.

Transport
There are no city buses in Lhasa. It is barely big enough to justify them anyway. Thus you are left with two alternatives: foot or bike. Everything within the old city is best visited on foot, but it takes about half an hour to walk from the Banak Shöl to the Potala and for this and any further distance it is worth hiring a bicycle (the standard rate is 5 RMB per day or 70 Fen per hour). There are, however, buses from the city to both Drepung and Sera Monasteries.

HISTORY
Originally Lhasa was called Rasa. It was a town built by the Otang Lake and was so-called because when the water in the lake was stirred by the wind its waves would make the sound 'ralasa'. In the seventh century, at the time of Songtsen Gampo, this lake – perhaps it was more of a marsh – was filled in and the Jokhang Cathedral built on the site. It first became the capital of Tibet during his reign. Although the king moved here from the traditional capital in the Yarlung Valley, the rulers continued to be buried in the Chonggye Valley near Yarlung for the remainder of the dynasty he inaugurated. There are still nine sites in or around Lhasa that are associated with Songtsen Gampo. The most important of these are the chapels of the Potala that he built, and the Jokhang and the Ramoche Cathedrals.

Songtsen Gampo gave the town the name 'Lhasa', which means 'Ground of the Gods'. The Tibetan etymology of the name runs thus: The city is called Ground (*sa*) of the Gods (*lha*) because it is as though a lofty realm of the gods had fallen to the ground through the richness of the Dharma.

When the Yarlung dynasty collapsed in the ninth century the unity of the country was destroyed and power reverted to local feudal lords and princes. Throughout this period Lhasa remained an important city but only nominally could be considered as the 'capital' of Tibet. When the country was next united under the Mongols, Sakya became the de facto capital on account of the power given to the Sakya lama Pakpa by Kublai Khan. After the end of the Sakya dynasty, the centre of political authority shifted to other powerful regions in Tsang. It was only when Gushri Khan, another Mongolian emperor, defeated the local Tibetan king in

The former western gate of Lhasa before its destruction.

1642 and installed the Fifth Dalai Lama as leader of Tibet, that Lhasa again became the centre of government.

Hence the city underwent two principal periods of development, which correspond to the two major periods of its political importance. The earliest period is that of Songtsen Gampo (7th Century) and the later period that of the Gelukpa Church and the Dalai Lamas (15th to 20th Centuries). Little remains from the time of the early kings and most of what one sees in terms of old buildings and monasteries dates back only to the later period.

A third, modern period could also be included; for present-day Lhasa now carries the strong mark of Chinese utilitarian architecture. A sprawling 'new town' of single- and double-storey government buildings spreads out around the old Tibetan city extending far beyond the Potala, continuing half way to Sera. Wide tarmaced avenues divide this new town into neat rectangles and squares. Compared with most towns in China, it is featureless rather than ugly.

THE BARKOR

The old city of Lhasa is the section of town east of the Potala, most of which is contained between the main avenue (Dekyi Shar Lam) and the river. It has changed little in layout and external appearance since pre-Chinese times. Two-storey, whitewashed town houses line narrow,

Young woman and child in the Barkor.

A view of the western districts of Lhasa from the roof of the Jokhang, overlooking the recently built plaza. Chakpori and the Potala are visible in the background. For a description of the steles in the foreground, see pp.81-2. The two white conical structures behind the steles are incense burners.

winding cobbled streets on which dogs, cattle, sheep, goats and people are all equally at home. All these alleys are connected in one way or another to the Barkor, the quadrangle of streets surrounding the Jokhang Cathedral. 'Barkor' literally means the 'Intermediate Circuit' and refers to the circumambulation route immediately around the complex of buildings surrounding the Jokhang Cathedral. (A longer circumambulation circuit called the 'Lingkor' used to run around the outside of the old city, along the river and round the Potala. Most of this has now been erased through incorporation into modern roads). The Barkor is at once the religious and mercantile focus of old Lhasa; pilgrims endlessly walk clockwise around it, pausing in their devotions every now and again to inspect some merchandise and haggle over its price. Both sides of the road are lined with shops and stalls selling all manner of goods from trinkets to tantric ritual objects. The Barkor is unsurpassed for having absorbed whatever traces of ancient Tibet are still present in the souls of the rich diversity of people who religiously pace its well-trodden streets.

Only one major change has been made to the centre of the old city. In 1985 a large area of old town houses facing the entrance to the Jokhang was cleared to make way for a spacious plaza giving easy and direct access to the building. The plaza itself is poorly conceived. The planners seem to have had in mind a European city square dominated by a large cathedral. But the Jokhang impresses one not by any lofty Gothic grandeur but by its solemn, weighty presence. Such presence is far more powerful and moving when suddenly encountered from a narrow enclosed street. It is only diminished when set off by a large open square. The plaza is further marred by phoney, vertical-walled Tibetan-style houses and grotesque street lamps. However, it is appreciated by the Tibetans as a meeting place and recreation area in the middle of the city.

To the north of the Barkor, before you reach the Dekyi Shar Lam, is an open air food market selling meat, butter, vegetables, grains and other goods. Huddled in the middle of this area are usually a crowd of Khampas, noticeable by the red braid in their hair and their dashing looks, engaged in buying and selling the wares that furtively pass between them.

To the south-east of the Barkor is the mosque and the Muslim district of town. Muslims from Kashmir have lived in Tibet for generations as traders and butchers. Recently they have been joined by fellow Muslims from other parts of China, who have come to Tibet because of the greater freedom to trade. It is possible to visit the mosque, which is easily spotted by the minaret sporting the characteristic Islamic crescent. It is surprising to see a mosque built in a Tibetan style, with pillars and decoration similar to those you would find in a Buddhist monastery. It was destroyed during the cultural revolution and has recently been reconstructed.

CRAFT CENTRES

There are a number of places in the city of Lhasa where you can see traditional crafts being practised. Just north of the mosque, up a narrow alley, is a newly erected, Tibetan-style building that houses a cooperative specialising in *tangka* painting. On the top floor you can see the master artists at work with their twenty or so young apprentices. Close by, eastwards along the Tsang Gyu Shar Lam, is the Carpet Factory, where you can study how colourful Tibetan rugs are made by hand on traditional looms. Another interesting workshop is the Tent Factory situated just off the Dekyi Shar Lam near the Taxi Company. Here it is possible to order strong cotton tents decorated with motifs designed according to one's own specifications. At all these places it is possible to purchase the goods. Although the prices are no cheaper than on the open market, the choice is generally wider.

2. THE JOKHANG

The old city of Lhasa is literally built around the Jokhang. It is the easiest place in town to find. You can approach it either by following the Barkor (the quadrangle of roads lined with stalls in the centre of the old city) until you reach its main entrance, or by going straight to the plaza (just down the road from the Snowlands) that faces it. It is open from 9 am to midday every day except Sunday. When special ceremonies are being performed it may stay open in the afternoon. There is a notice saying that foreigners must pay 3 RMB to visit but this is only half-heartedly enforced.

HISTORY

The Jokhang is without doubt the most sacred temple in Tibet. It was established in the seventh century by King Songtsen Gampo in order to house the image of Akshobhya (Mikyöba) Buddha offered to him by his Nepalese wife, Trisun (Bhrkuti). At this time it was called the 'Trulnang' temple. Only later, when the Jowo Shakyamuni statue given to the king by Wen Cheng, his Chinese wife, was moved here from the Ramoche Temple, was it given its present name 'Jokhang', the 'Shrine of the Jowo'. (The Akshobhya statue changed places with the Jowo and was installed in Ramoche). The Jowo statue was part of the Chinese princess's dowry. It was originally given to her father, T'ai-tsung, the second emperor of the T'ang dynasty, by a king from Bengal. The Tibetans believe it was originally crafted by the celestial artist Vishvakarman at the time of the Buddha. When Wen Cheng came to Tibet, she was accompanied by many Chinese artisans, who built the Ramoche Temple to house it. The Jokhang, however, was originally designed by Nepalese craftsmen on behalf of Queen Trisun. She had perceived the form of a demoness in the landscape of Tibet, and to subdue her conceived the idea of building temples on the most prominent parts of her body. The Jokhang was built on the site of a lake that had previously been filled in with earth by a sacred goat and which the queen thought to be the heart of the demoness. There are four other temples in Tibet called the 'Extremity Subduing Temples', built on her hips and shoulders (see Chapter 29, **Trandruk Temple**).

It is unclear exactly why the change-over of the two statues took place. The records state only that when Songtsen Gampo died, Wen Cheng moved the Jowo statue from Ramoche to the Jokhang for protection against an invading Chinese army and concealed it in one of the

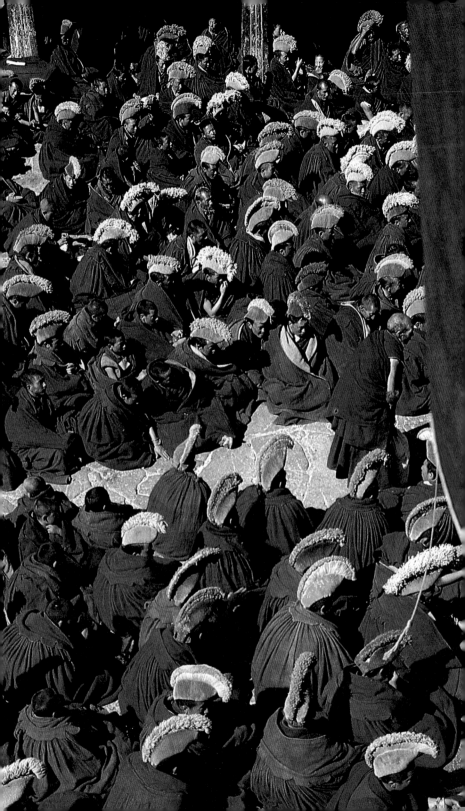

chapels. There is still a chapel called 'The Shrine where the Jowo was Hidden'. On our plan this is Chapel 17, which presently houses Amitabha and the Eight Medicine Buddhas.

Since its founding, the Jokhang has been considerably enlarged and embellished, in particular during the reign of the Fifth Dalai Lama. Some of the worn wooden carving around the doorways to the chapels, on the capitals of several pillars and on the ends of some beams may date back to the seventh century, but apart from the Jowo itself, very few statues are that old. Most of the images are modern, remade to replace those destroyed during the cultural revolution. There are currently sixty-eight monks residing here.

THE SITE
Directly in front of the entrance to the cathedral are three stone steles in two separate enclosures. The taller of these carries a bilingual inscription of the Tibetan-Chinese agreement of 821 between the Tibetan king, Tri Ralpchen, and the Chinese emperor, Wen Wu Hsiao-te Wang-ti. This agreement, clearly between equals, makes interesting, though in

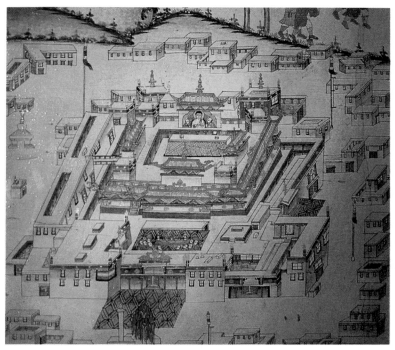

ABOVE *Stylised representation of the Jokhang (Norbulingka Palace).*
OPPOSITE *Monks assembled in the inner courtyard during the Great Prayer Festival (Mönlam Chenmo).*

A queue of pilgrims bearing traditional offering scarves (katag) waiting for their turn to enter the Jokhang.

retrospect ironic, reading. It states, for example, that *'Tibet and China shall abide by the frontiers of which they are now in occupation. All to the east is the country of Great China; and all to the west is, without question, the country of Great Tibet. Henceforth on neither side shall there be waging of war nor seizing of territory. If any person incurs suspicion he shall be arrested; his business shall be inquired into and he shall be escorted back'.* The other two steles are inscribed in Chinese and tell of the dangers of smallpox and means to cure it. They have been worn away in many places, presumably by Tibetans who supposed that the stone itself must be able to cure the disease. Immediately behind these two steles there used to grow a large willow tree planted by Queen Wen Cheng, of which now only the dead stump is still visible.

The forecourt leading to the main entrance of the Jokhang is invariably filled with pilgrims and devotees prostrating themselves full-length in the direction of the Jowo. To the left are two massive prayer wheels, which people turn as they enter and leave the cathedral.

As one walks through the main portals, the first images one sees, two to the right and two to the left, are large seated statues of the Four Guardian Kings. From here one enters an inner courtyard (2), the centre of which opens to the sky. Traditionally, this was the main assembly area for the monks. If you look up to the left you will see an ornate covered balcony adorned with beautiful golden figurines and pinnacles. This balcony leads to the private quarters of the Dalai Lama, where he would stay during the Mönlam festival and observe the monks engaged in philosophical debate in the courtyard below.

On your left as you enter the courtyard is a wall painting of the Mongolian emperor Gushri Khan in conversation with Desi Sanggye Gyatso, the regent who ruled after the death of the Fifth Dalai Lama. The detailed murals that cover the remaining wall space depict the thousand Buddhas who will appear during this current aeon. These are all recent paintings commissioned by the Thirteenth Dalai Lama. At the far end of the courtyard is a long altar usually ablaze with butter lamps. Behind this altar is another doorway, which leads to the interior of the Jokhang itself.

To enter the main hall of the Jokhang you proceed down another dark corridor, which runs past two small chapels. On the left (4) is a room containing five figures, both male and female, with wrathful expressions. On the opposite side of the hallway (3) is another chapel with three, more benign-looking beings. The wrathful beings are Raksas, malefic, cannibalistic spirits, and the benign ones Nagas, an intelligent subterranean species. According to tradition, these beings appeared to Songtsen Gampo as he was building the temple and, after having been subdued, vowed to protect it against harmful influence until the end of time.

Pilgrims standing outside the main entrance to the Jokhang. The Dharma-wheel and two deer are a traditional symbol of the Buddha's teaching.

Facing you as you enter the large inner chamber of the Jokhang are several large statues. To the left sits Padmasambhava (a), to the right Maitreya (c). Between them and slightly behind stands a thousand-armed Avalokiteshvara (b). To the right of the main Maitreya figure are two other images of Maitreya, both facing inwards. The smaller of these two, Barzhi Jampa (d), is named on account of the Barzhi family who commissioned its construction. The larger is called the Miwang Jampa (e) on account of its being commissioned by the nobleman Miwang Polha. Behind the image of Avalokiteshvara is another small encased statue of Padmasambhava (f).

Normally a queue of Tibetans murmuring mantras and carrying prayer wheels and butter offerings moves clockwise around these central figures. This line of people hugs the walls and weaves slowly in and out of the numerous small chapels, which are entered by regularly placed low doorways. The best (and only) way to visit these chapels is to join the queue.

The Chapel of Tsongkhapa and his Eight Pure Disciples (5)
The first chapel, immediately to the left of the entrance, is dedicated to the founder of the Geluk order, Je Tsongkhapa. He is the main figure facing you as you enter, and is accompanied by a group of monks known as the Eight Pure Disciples. The most famous of these are his two chief disciples, Khedrup Je and Gyeltsab Je, who are seated to Tsongkhapa's right and left. When Tsongkhapa had completed most of his teaching activities in Tibet, he withdrew from the world and spent several years in remote hermitages. These eight disciples are the ones he chose to accompany him during his retreats.

The Stupa of Examination [or Permanence?] (6)
The original of this white and gold stupa was made by Sakya Pandita. In the centre of the stupa one can see a small golden image of the female deity Vijaya.

The Chapel of the Eight Medicine Buddhas (7)
Eight rather undistinguished images adorn this small room.

The Chapel of the Fivefold Self-Originated Avalokiteshvara (8)
The main figure in this chapel is a thousand-armed, eleven-headed Avalokiteshvara, the original of which is said to have miraculously appeared at the time of King Songtsen Gampo. Its name indicates perhaps that it assumed its form out of five separate substances. One tradition maintains that Songtsen Gampo and his two wives were absorbed into the statue at death. Two wrathful protectors stand on

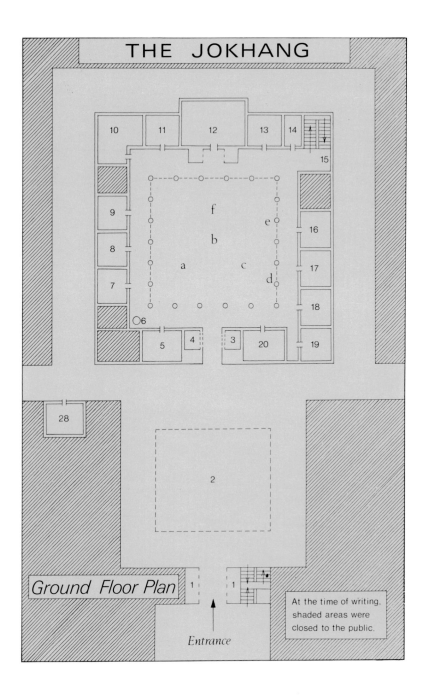

THE JOKHANG

10 · 11 · 12 · 13 · 14

15

9

8 · f · e · 16

b

7 · a · c · 17

d · 18

○6

5 · 4 · 3 · 20 · 19

28

2

Ground Floor Plan

1 · 1

Entrance

At the time of writing, shaded areas were closed to the public.

guard to either side of the entrance. On the left are three seated figures: Jigten Wangchuk (a form of Avalokiteshvara), and Tronyer Chenma and Özer Chenma (two forms of Tara who sprang from the tears falling from the two eyes of Avalokiteshvara). The three figures seated along the opposite wall are Sarasvati, Tara and Avalokiteshvara Karsapani.

The Chapel of the Maitreya of Purification [Jampa Trudze] (9)

To the right of the main image of Maitreya, seated along the wall, are small, fine statues of four principal bodhisattvas: Manjushri, Avalokiteshvara, Vajrapani and Tara. On the opposite wall is an image of Tsongkhapa with a stupa to either side.

Before reaching the final chapel along this wall you pass another image of a thousand-armed Avalokiteshvara enshrined in a golden glass and wood case.

The Chapel of the Statue that Resembles Tsongkhapa (10)

During Tsongkhapa's own lifetime several statues of the master were commissioned by his followers. Upon seeing this one, Tsongkhapa is said to have remarked on how closely it resembled him. Another tradition maintains that this image was created miraculously by the protector Dharma-raja. Yet another tradition claims it was commissioned by a later Mongolian emperor. Behind Tsongkhapa to his left is a series of his teachers from the Sakya tradition. This raised corner section is sometimes called the Chapel of the Lake.

The Amitabha Chapel (11)

Guarding the entrance to this chapel are two wrathful protectors. To the left stands the blue figure of Vajrapani and to the right the red form of Trolme-wa Tsekpa, an aspect of Hayagriva. Inside, Amitabha, the Buddha of Infinite Light, is flanked by two small ferocious guardians. Along each wall are four seated bodhisattvas. This room is sometimes called the 'room where obstacles are dispelled'. Since this is the shrine immediately before that of the Jowo, here the pilgrim prays that his or her karmic hindrances to seeing the Jowo are fully cleared away.

Between the Amitabha chapel and the Jowo are four raised, seated figures. The central image is King Songtsen Gampo. To the left is his Nepalese queen, Trisun, and to the right his Chinese queen, Wen Cheng. The fourth smaller statue in the corner is an old and much revered image of Padmasambhava. This image is markedly realistic and makes an interesting contrast to the traditional stylised representations of the Guru.

OPPOSITE *Jowo Shakyamuni, the most highly revered image in Tibet.*

The Chapel of the Jowo Shakyamuni (12)

This central and most important shrine in the Jokhang is also the most elaborate and impressive. As you stand at its wide entrance, make sure to look up at the beautifully carved and painted woodwork on the ceiling above. Upon entering the shrine, you pass standing, life-size images of the Four Guardian Kings before climbing a number of steps leading to the interior of the chapel. The Jowo is heavily bedecked with brocade clothing and jewelry. Before him burn massive silver butter lamps. A small doorway on the left and another on the right allow the pilgrims to touch their heads to his leg and make whatever prayers and wishes they may have. Immediately behind the Jowo is an old Buddha image of which only the head and shoulders are visible. It is said that this was the main image prior to the arrival of the Jowo. When the Jowo was to be installed in its place, it apparently proclaimed that it would never move but would remain to care for the new image. Around the high walls of this chapel are twelve standing bodhisattvas known as the Six Holy Sons and the Six Holy Daughters. At the back of the room are also found images of the Seventh Dalai Lama, Kelsang Gyatso; the Thirteenth Dalai Lama, Tubten Gyatso; Je Tsongkhapa, and a large seated Buddha.

As you leave the Jowo shrine and proceed to the next chapel, you encounter three seated images. The central figure is that of Atisha. To the left is the translator Ngog Legpa'i Sherab and to the right the layman Drom Tönpa, Atisha's main disciple. On the wall behind them is a painted image of Tara, 'the Saviouress'.

The Chapel of the Protector Maitreya [Tri-Tri Jampa] (13)

This chapel is guarded by two worldly deities from Indian mythology, Brahma (to the left) and Indra. The central image is a form of Maitreya historically (or mythologically) connected with the king Tri-Tri (Krkin), a benefactor of the former Buddha Kashyapa. It is said to have been brought to Tibet by Trisun, the Nepalese Queen of Songtsen Gampo. The eight seated bodhisattvas around him are all aspects of Tara. Formerly the stove of Wen Cheng was kept in this chapel in the front left-hand corner.

On your way to the next chapel you will also pass three seated figures. The central figure is that of the Tibetan lama, Jonang Taranata. Although strongly criticised by Tsongkhapa and his followers for some of his philosophical statements, he is still highly revered for his erudition and spiritual attainment. To the left is Avalokiteshvara and to the right Amitayus.

The Chapel of Avalokiteshvara who Roars like a Lion (14)

The main figure worshipped in this shrine is not the large Buddha Amitabha placed at the end of the chapel, but the smaller image of Avalokiteshvara seated on a lion, which is the first statue on the left as you enter. The other five bodhisattvas are also aspects of Avalokiteshvara.

Against the wall between this chapel and staircase leading to the upper storey is a short pillar with a hole at the top. Many pilgrims place an ear to this hole in the hope of hearing the sound of the 'Angba' bird beating its wings. According to legend, the Angba bird lives at the bottom of the lake upon which the Jokhang was built.

At this point one may either follow the majority of pilgrims upstairs or continue to visit the remaining chapels on the ground floor. Here we shall describe these remaining chapels first before covering the upper storey.

Shrine to Padmasambhava (15)

Tucked away in a corner beneath the stairs are two images of Padmasambhava together with, on the right, a statue of King Trisong Detsen.

As you leave this shrine you may notice a Buddha image on the wall to the left protected by a metal grille. This marks the place where nine Buddhas are said to have spontaneously manifested from the Clear Light, the ultimate nature of reality.

The Chapel of Maitreya [Jampa Che Zhi] (16)

The small, delicately wrought image of Maitreya that stands as the central figure of this chapel is the one traditionally carried around the Barkor in the procession during the Mönlam festival. To the left of Maitreya stands Manjushri and to the right Avalokiteshvara. An image of Tara sits to either side of these bodhisattvas. Four wrathful protectors against the walls guard the shrine. To the right of the entrance stands Vaishravana and to the left Jambhala. Seated by the altar is a statue of Lama Gyelwa Bum, renowned for having constructed a barrage against the river in Lhasa, thus saving the city from being flooded. If you look carefully in the lower left hand corner of the chapel as you enter, you will see a small stone carving of a goat. This is the sacred goat (Dungtse Rama Gyelmo) which, according to legend, filled with earth the lake upon which the Jokhang was to be constructed.

The Chapel where the Jowo was Hidden (17)

This is the chapel where the Jowo statue was concealed by Wen Cheng when she moved it here after the death of her husband Songtsen

The statue of Jampa Che Zhi (Maitreya) being ceremoniously carried around the Barkhor during the Great Prayer Festival. See chapel 16.

Gampo. Now the central figure is that of Amitabha. Along both side walls are the Eight Medicine Buddhas.

The Chapel of the Seven Mighty Buddhas (18)
These seven Buddhas, which include Shakyamuni as the main figure and six others, are shown here in the *sambhogakaya* or 'archetypal' form. When depicted in the *nirmanakaya* or 'emanated' aspect they are known as the Seven Heroic Buddhas. Going clockwise they are called All Protecting, Golden Power, All Seeing, Shakyamuni, World Destroyer, Head Protrusion, and Kashyapa.

The Chapel of the Nine Forms of Amitayus (19)
Amitayus is one of the bodhisattva aspects of Buddha Amitabha and is often worshipped to achieve longevity.

The Chapel of the Dharma Kings (20)
The images in this chapel are some of the very few that miraculously escaped destruction during the cultural revolution. The central figure is

Songtsen Gampo. To the left is King Trisong Detsen and to the right King Ralpachen. These three rulers reigned at the height of Tibet's glory as a Central Asian empire and were responsible for the introduction and consolidation of Buddhism in Tibet. To the left of the door as you enter is Songtsen Gampo's minister Gawa. Next to him is the Nepalese queen of Songtsen Gampo and next to her the first (quasi-mythological) king of Tibet, Nyatri Tsenpo. To the right of the door is Tönmi Sambhota, the minister of Songtsen Gampo who created the Tibetan alphabet, and next to him the king's Chinese wife.

The mural on your left as you leave this chapel and return to the entrance of the cathedral describes King Songtsen Gampo's founding of the Jokhang. In the centre of this painting is a lake with a white stupa in the middle. Songtsen Gampo had thrown his ring in the air and proclaimed that he would start building wherever it fell. When the ring fell into the lake a stupa was miraculously produced. A sacred goat then appeared, to fill the lake with earth. On this foundation the Jokhang was constructed. To the left of the lake you can see the image of the Jowo being carried in a palanquin from China. Further to the left is a painting of the Potala palace in the original form constructed by Songtsen Gampo. To the far left is the medical college founded on the neighbouring Chakpori hill.

We continue our visit to the Jokhang by climbing the two flights of stairs leading to the upper storey. The stone that protrudes from the wall on the landing between the two staircases has no particular significance even though it is plastered with butter, coins and other offerings. It merely indicates how anything slightly unusual in a place of pilgrimage such as the Jokhang can readily be endowed with supernatural significance.

The Chapel of Shakyamuni and his Disciples (21)
After passing three locked chapels, the images of which have yet to be restored, one enters a bare chamber containing a single statue of Buddha Shakyamuni. The accompanying images of his disciples have yet to be replaced.

The Chapel of the Five Protectors (22)
This is one of the several tantric shrines found on this upper level of the Jokhang. The central deity here is the wrathful protector Hayagriva, the 'Horse-Headed One'. To the left is Pelden Lhamo, the female protectoress much revered in Tibet. Guarding the doorway are (to the left) Dutsen, a spirit being, and (to the right) Lutsen, a Naga. The five remaining wrathful deities are the protectors to whom the shrine is dedicated. They are the guardians of the centre and the four directions.

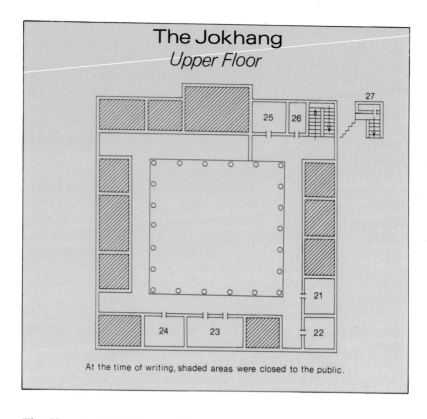

The Jokhang
Upper Floor

At the time of writing, shaded areas were closed to the public.

The Chapel of the Dharma King Songtsen Gampo (23)

This spacious shrine located directly above the main entrance to the Jokhang is dedicated to the founder of the temple, King Songtsen Gampo. A large statue of the king dominates the shrine. As usual he is flanked by his Nepalese queen, Trisun (to the left), and his Chinese queen, Wen Cheng (to the right). Behind the three main figures are the Seven Heroic Buddhas (see Chapel 18). Against the left wall of the chapel are three smaller images of the king and his two wives. To the right are Tsongkhapa and his two chief disciples. In front of the king is a large, ornate silver pitcher. This was the receptacle in which the king kept his supply of *chang* (barley beer). The silver casing probably houses an earthenware vessel and is of a later date. Before the Chinese occupation, once a year this pitcher would ceremoniously be carried around the houses of the nobility and a serving of *chang* offered to each family.

The Chapel of Avalokiteshvara (24)

The central image here is a simple representation of Avalokiteshvara, the bodhisattva of compassion. Along the walls are the six Buddhas who are the special protectors of each of the six realms of existence: the hells, the hungry ghost realm, the animal realm, the human realm, the titan realm and the celestial realm. Each Buddha is responsible for the welfare of the beings in each realm. The guiding principle of their activity is compassion, hence Avalokiteshvara stands as the main image in this chapel. Numerous small identical images of Amitayus are painted in red on the cream-coloured walls.

All the chapels to your left as you leave the Avalokiteshvara shrine are closed. One of these was the meditation cell of Songtsen Gampo. You must now retrace your steps in order to find the stairs by which you reach the remaining tantric chapels at the rear of the upper storey.

The Padmasambhava Chapel (25)
Traditionally, Padmasambhava is said to have manifested in eight different forms during his stay in Tibet. As an accomplished tantric master he was capable of assuming different appearances, each one appropriate to the particular situation he was dealing with. These eight transformations of the Guru are depicted along the two side walls of this chapel. The central figure is the most common form of Padmasambhava, 'Guru Nam Si'. On the altar in the centre of this shrine you can see skull-cups filled with *chang* offered to the Guru. Such offerings are made only to tantric figures.

The Samvara Chapel (26)
This chapel houses a single statue of the tantric deity Samvara with consort. Samvara belongs to the highest class of tantric practice and is worshipped by all orders of Tibetan Buddhism. He is often considered to be the Buddhist transformation of the Hindu deity Shiva, as well as the tantric manifestation of Avalokiteshvara.

The Chapel of Pelden Lhamo (27)
Pelden Lhamo is often regarded as the principal protectress of Tibet, especially among the Gelukpa. There are two statues of her in this shrine: the one to the right is the peaceful form; the one to the left, wielding a sword, her face covered by a cloth, is the wrathful aspect.

The monk in the Pelden Lhamo shrine may allow you to enter another chamber that is reached by a small flight of stairs at the rear of the chapel. This chamber, the Pelchok Dukhang, has no statues but has been richly decorated with tantric murals. The walls are black and the paintings beautifully outlined in white, gold and red. The figures depicted are the main protective deities of the Gelukpa: Yamantaka, Mahakala, and Pelden Lhamo. This chamber is the place where the

A gilded rooftop of the Jokhang. The figures are called ja-shang-shang, *a mythical bird, and the spires* gen-ji-ra.

monks who live in the Jokhang gather to perform their rituals, in particular the tantric rite of *gangso*.

This chamber leads directly onto the roof of the Jokhang. Although the monks may be reluctant to let you go up here, it is well worth visiting, so try to get permission. (Another entrance to the roof is found by the staircase leading out to the main forecourt [behind (1)].) There are presently no chapels at this level, which is where the monks have their rooms. The golden rooftops are exquisitely embellished with dragonheads and figurines. Beaten golden plaques placed at regular intervals around the tops of the walls portray all manner of Indian and Tibetan Buddhist symbols. Of particular note are the delightful murals of Tara painted around the entire length of the outer walls of the rooms below the main roof.

Before leaving the Jokhang it is worth circumambulating the main building. As you leave the main entrance, turn right. This will lead you to a long corridor lined with prayer wheels. Just as you approach this corridor, however, you will pass another chapel to your left.

Detail of the lower Jokhang roof.

The Tara Chapel (28)
Immediately in front of the door to this shrine you will notice a roundish piece of carved masonry on the ground. This marks a stone that is said to resemble the pointed hat of Tsongkhapa. The chapel itself is devoted to the female deity Tara. A large image of Tara sits in the centre of the room. Behind her in glass cases are the 'Twenty-One Taras', the principal manifestations of this female aspect of enlightenment. On the right of the chapel are six other statues. The first three depict the Indian masters Shantarakshita and Padmasambhava and, to the right, their patron, King Trisong Detsen. The remaining three images are those of Tsongkhapa and his two chief disciples.

The circumambulation path takes you around the Jokhang and ends back at the main inner courtyard (2). The walls to both sides are covered with detailed murals depicting one hundred and eight stories from the Buddha's previous and final lives. They are based on the *Paksam Trishing (Avadanakalpalata)*, a work by the Kashmiri poet Ksemendra, and were commissioned in the early part of this century by the Thirteenth Dalai Lama.

ABOVE *View of the Potala from an island in the Kyichu River.*

PREVIOUS PAGE *The Potala as seen from Chakpori.*

3. THE POTALA

The Potala is a landmark impossible to miss. It is located at the west of the city and is reached simply by following the Dekyi Shar Lam westwards from the old city. Although guided tour groups will enter the Potala by the back from a gate at the western end, individual visitors and Tibetan pilgrims must walk through the old, crumbling houses of the village beneath the palace and climb up the wide, stone staircases that lead into the spacious inner courtyard, before which rises the massive front wall of the Red Palace. It is open from 9 am to midday every day except Sunday. On Wednesdays and Saturdays it is open all day. These are the two days of the week when traditionally the palace is visited by Tibetans and you must expect long queues. There is an entrance charge of 3 RMB and you must buy a ticket at a small booth as you enter the inner courtyard. An additonal 20 Fen is charged to view the Dalai Lama's private audience room and chambers. With a valid student card you may get a 2 RMB reduction.

HISTORY

Songtsen Gampo was the first Tibetan ruler to establish a palace on this outcrop, the 'Red Hill', which dominates the city of Lhasa. Although his palace which was called the Kukhar Potrang, was burned down by an invading Chinese army during the reign of his successor, Mangsong Mangtsen, there are still two rooms inside the Potala that supposedly date from his time. But it is impossible to tell how extensive this first palace was and what it was like.

Old pictures of the Potala often show a tall stone stele rising up from the ground in front of the palace. It now stands on the opposite side of the main road by the Potala. This is the ancient 'Zhöl' pillar, erected about 764 by the loyal minister and general of Trisong Detsen, Ngenlam Tagdra Lugong. It modestly records how the Tibetan armies successfully overran most of Central Asia and finally occupied the Chinese capital of Chang-an (Xian). The rewards bestowed upon Tagdra Lugong by the king are also recorded on the pillar.

Construction of the present palace began in earnest in 1645 during the reign of the great Fifth Dalai Lama. By 1648 the White Palace was completed. To finish the rest of the building, known as the Red Palace, his chief advisor, Desi Sanggye Gyatso, had to conceal the Dalai Lama's death and pretend that he was in a prolonged retreat. The Red Palace was completed in 1694, twelve years after the Dalai Lama's death.

The building is named after Mt. Potala in South India, one of the holy mountains of the Hindu god Shiva. The Buddhists, however, dedicated this mountain to Avalokiteshvara, the bodhisattva of compassion, and gave the name 'Potala' to the Pure Land where Avalokiteshvara resides. Since both Songtsen Gampo and the Dalai Lamas were considered to be incarnations of Avalokiteshvara, 'Potala' was the right name for their dwelling.

The Potala has served as the home of successive Dalai Lamas and their monastic staff from the time of the Fifth until that of the present Dalai Lama, the Fourteenth. From the latter half of the eighteenth century it has been used as the Winter Palace, the Norbulingka being the place where the rulers would retreat during the summer months. With the exception of a section added on to house the tomb of the Thirteenth Dalai Lama, the palace is much the same as when it was first built.

The Potala was slightly damaged during the popular Tibetan uprising against the Chinese in 1959 and was fortunately spared from further destruction during the cultural revolution, apparently through the personal intervention of Chou En Lai, the red guards being kept at bay by the Chinese military.

THE SITE
The first impression you may have of the Potala is that it is not located at the great height that most photographs suggest. Compared to the surrounding mountains, the rocky outcrop on which it stands is tiny. Nonetheless, as you slowly acquaint yourself with the dimensions and proportions of this incredible building, the awesome grandeur of its architecture becomes so much more tangible and real that even the most rapturous description seems hopelessly inadequate. It is well worth circumambulating the Potala with Tibetan pilgrims, riding around it on road by bicycle, and observing it under different light conditions, in order to appreciate fully its external perfection.

The Dalai Lamas lived and worked in the Red Palace, the central, squarish structure that rises out of the mass of the surrounding White Palace. From the inner courtyard you enter the Red Palace by a steep wooden stairway to find yourself in the main foyer. On the left of this opening are two handprints of the Thirteenth Dalai Lama placed beneath an edict written in the cursive Tibetan script. Around the other walls are murals depicting the construction of the Jokhang, the Potala and the medical college on Chakpori. The Four Guardian Kings are also portrayed.

Several more flights of stairs bring you out onto the roof of the palace and it is from here that you actually enter the building itself, slowly working your way down. This is where the Dalai Lama's personal monastic staff, the Namgyal Tratsang, also lived. They were responsi-

The Inner Courtyard of the Potala Palace. The door at the far end leads into the Red Palace.

ble for performing all the complex rituals required by the Tibetan head of state, and for the upkeep of the numerous chapels and shrines situated in the maze of rooms that make up the four storeys of this multi-storeyed labyrinth. The roof affords a superb view over Lhasa and the Kyichu valley basin.

The Dalai Lama's Quarters

The only room on the roof level that is permanently open at present is the **Official Reception Hall**, which is just around the corner as you come up the stairs. This opulent room is dominated by a large throne, to the right of which hangs a realistic portrait of the Thirteenth Dalai Lama and to the left of which the Fourteenth. A small ante-chamber to each side of the raised platform leads to their respective private quarters.

CITS groups and individual tourists who manage to tag along behind them are also allowed to visit a set of the Dalai Lama's private quarters behind the official reception hall. The first room you enter is a smaller audience chamber where individuals and private groups would be received. Set in the right-hand wall are three large cabinets containing a number of exquisite bronzes. The three animal-headed deities and the statue of Vijaya are of particular note. From here you will enter a small, square protector chapel. The principal deities are a six-armed Mahakala, Pelden Lhamo and Dorje Drakden. The final room in third section is the small but very ornate bedroom of the Dalai Lama. The large altar houses statues of the longevity triad of Amitayus, Tara and Vijaya. A beautifully painted mural of Tsongkhapa is visible above the bed.

The visit to the main section of the Potala begins as you enter a doorway on the far side of the roof from the reception hall.

The Upper Floor

The Maitreya Chapel (1)

The main statue here is a large, beautifully made, seated Maitreya. Inside the head of the image is said to be the brain of Atisha. The statue was commissioned by the Eighth Dalai Lama in honour of the recently deceased mother of the Sixth Panchen Lama, Pelden Yeshe, a relative of his. It was also the Eighth Dalai Lama who turned this room into a chapel; from the time of the Sixth Dalai Lama it had served only as a living quarter. The throne facing Maitreya was used by all the Dalai Lamas from the Eighth until the Fourteenth. To the left of the throne is an altar. The image on the far left is of the Fifth Dalai Lama, commissioned shortly before his death by Desi Sanggye Gyatso. In it are some hair clippings from the Great Fifth's head. Many other deities surround the room: Kalachakra, Padmasambhava, the triad of Manjushri, Avalokiteshvara and Vajrapani, Kshitigarbha and Acala. Of particular interest is the wrathful form of Tara to the right of Maitreya. In the far corner is a small wooden mandala of Kalachakra erected at the time of the Eighth Dalai Lama. The scriptures in the upper wall are a complete edition of the Tengyur. The collected works of the Fifth Dalai Lama are in the wall to the left as you go out.

About three years ago this chapel was badly damaged by fire – presumably caused by an electrical fault – and many fine *tangkas* were destroyed.

The Chapel of the Three-Dimensional Mandalas (2)

This chapel was constructed by Kelsang Gyatso, the Seventh Dalai Lama. An image of him sits at the far end of the room next to his throne. The very fine murals also date from his time. Before the three magnificent mandalas were erected, this room used to be Kelsang Gyatso's own personal residence. The mandalas are those of the three principal tantric deities practised in the Geluk order: Guhyasamaja, Samvara and

OPPOSITE *Maitreya, the future Buddha; the main image in the Maitreya Chapel.*

Kelsang Gyatso, the Seventh Dalai Lama, in the Chapel of the Three-Dimensional Mandalas.

Yamantaka. When looking at them from the monk's seat by the window, the mandala of Guhysamaja is in the middle. To the right is that of Samvara – of the Luipa tradition – and to the left that of the thirteen deity form of Yamantaka. To the left of the dark passageway along which you come in are collected about five hundred small statues. In addition to the usual images of the Thirty-five Confessional Buddhas, the Twenty-one Taras and so on are found many of the principal lamas and deities of all four orders of Tibetan Buddhism.

The Chapel Celebrating Victory over the Three Worlds (3)

This room is located in the very middle of the upper storey of the Red Palace. It too was constructed by the Seventh Dalai Lama and the throne in the room was at one time used by him. The most outstanding figure is that of a thousand-armed Avalokiteshvara, commissioned by the Thirteenth Dalai Lama and made from Chinese gold. The glass-covered

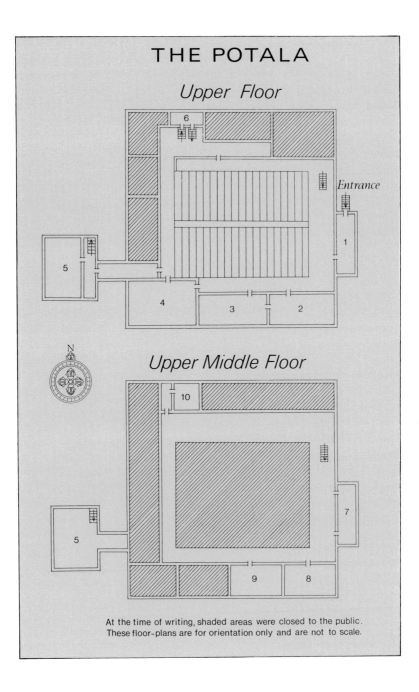

THE POTALA

Upper Floor

6

Entrance

1

5

4

3

2

Upper Middle Floor

N

10

5

7

9

8

At the time of writing, shaded areas were closed to the public.
These floor-plans are for orientation only and are not to scale.

altar by the entrance contains images of Tsongkhapa and the Thirteenth Dalai Lama. A painting of the Chinese emperor Ch'ien-lung (1735-97), the last of the great rulers of the Manchu dynasty and the one responsible for driving the Gurkhas out of Tibet, hangs at the back with an inscription in Chinese beneath. On the wall to the left of the altar is a hundred and twenty volume edition of the Manchu version of the Kangyur. There are three standing cases in a fenced-off part of the chapel containing examples of these texts. The middle case displays an opened volume clearly showing the precise red forms of the jagged Manchu script. The cases on both sides show the ornate wooden covers in which the texts are bound and demonstrate superb craftsmanship: each cover displays embossed gold lettering in Tibetan, Manchu and Chinese and jewel-encrusted images of Buddhas and Bodhisattvas at each end.

The Chapel of Immortal Happiness (4)
Although the Sixth Dalai Lama used this room as his personal residence, he did not convert it during his short reign into a chapel. This was done some fifty years later by the Eighth Dalai Lama. The throne, however, was the one used by the Sixth. The Eighth Dalai Lama dedicated the chapel to Amitayus and a thousand small statues of the deity can be found in niches around the walls. There is also a larger, main image of Amitayus as well as one of Avalokiteshvara and a beautiful red statue of the wrathful principal guardian of Dzog-chen practice, Ekajati.

The Tomb of the Thirteenth Dalai Lama (5)
This chapel is restricted to official tour groups but they allow individual foreigners to join them should they be present when the doors are opened. You enter the chapel through a long corridor that connects it to the Red Palace. This brings you to an ante-room from which you can either descend to enter the chapel from the ground floor or enter it directly at a higher level. A well-executed modern mural adorns the wall to either side of the entrance. It depicts the Thirteenth Dalai Lama surrounded by his teachers, ministers and other contemporary figures. The stupa is two storeys high and well illuminated by sunlight from the many windows (in contrast to the tombs of the other Dalai Lamas). It is a mass of softly glowing gold. The much-depicted pearl mandala is here in an urn on the ground floor.

The Lokeshvara Chapel (6)
This shrine together with the room beneath (10) are the two oldest chapels in the Potala, dating back to the time of Songtsen Gampo in the seventh century. The Tibetans consider it to be the holiest shrine in the Potala. You enter it by climbing a steep wooden staircase beneath a large

An altar dedicated to the Thousand-Armed Avalokiteshvara in the Chapel of Immortal Happiness.

Chinese/Tibetan inscription hanging over the door that reads, 'The Amazing Fruits of the Field of Merit'. The small central statue is a heavily jewelled and gilded standing figure of Avalokiteshvara, which is said to be made of sandalwood and of Indian origin, as are the two accompanying images to either side. They are said to have been found inside a sandalwood tree when its trunk split open. To the left of the main images are the Tenth Dalai Lama and Tsongkhapa; to the right are the Eighth and Ninth Dalai Lamas. Numerous other statues fill the cases to either side. In the case on the left-hand wall as you enter there are three pieces of stone with footprints embedded in them: from the left, these belong to Padmasambhava, Tsongkhapa, and Nagarjuna. A large ferocious figure of Vajrapani stands guard by the opposite wall. To the left of the door as you leave is an old encased image of Atisha.

Also on the upper floor, in locked rooms, are the tombs of the Seventh, Eighth and Ninth Dalai Lamas.

Detail of the three-dimensional Kalachakra mandala.

The Upper Middle Floor

The Kalachakra Chapel (7)

The superb three-dimensional mandala of Kalachakra was erected in this shrine by Desi Sanggye Gyatso. This gold and copper divine mansion, the residence of the deity Kalachakra, is in much better condition than the three similar mandalas upstairs (2). It is about twelve feet in diameter and eight feet high, with every detail accurately rendered. When you stand by the window where the caretaker-monk sits, you can see to the right a life-size statue of Kalachakra and consort. To the left of the statue, in shelves along the wall, are small images of the 176 lamas who have passed the Kalachakra lineage down to the present day. In similar shelves to the right are the seven religious kings of Shambhala and the twenty-five *kalki*, or spiritual presidents, who have been ruling Shambhala since the time of the religious kings. We are now in the reign of the twenty-second *kalki*, Aniruddha. At the far end of the chapel opposite the door is a statue of Manjushri riding a lion, also surrounded by the lamas of his lineage. Hanging from the ceiling above the mandala are *tankas* of the Six Ornaments and Two Supreme Buddhist philosophers of India. A small shrine to Pelden Lhamo is in the right-hand corner by the window. To your left as you leave is an image of Padmasambhava seated on a throne.

The Shakyamuni Chapel (8)

Work began on this chapel at the time of Desi Sanggye Gyatso but it did not reach its present form until the reign of the Eighth Dalai Lama. The main figures are those of Buddha Shakyamuni flanked by the Eight Great Bodhisattvas. The throne is one used by Kelsang Gyatso, the Seventh Dalai Lama. In the wall opposite the throne is a handwritten edition of the Kangyur, above which hang *tankas* of the Eight Medicine Buddhas.

The Amitayus Chapel (9)

Nine statues of Amitayus dominate this small chapel built by the Eighth Dalai Lama. Two Taras are also present. The throne was one used by the Eighth Dalai Lama and the fine murals probably date back to his time.

The Practice Chamber of the Dharma King (10)

As with the Lokeshvara chapel immediately above (6), this cell is one of the very oldest rooms in the Potala. Songtsen Gampo is said to have used this dark, small cell as his meditation chamber. It is now filled with statues, the main one of Songtsen Gampo being behind the central pillar. There are other images of the king as well as similar-looking figures that represent his ministers Tönmi Sambhota and Gawa. On a shelf in the right hand wall is a small statue of the king's mother. Maitreya is to the immediate left as you enter, and behind a pillar at the far end of the room is a somewhat atypical image of the Fifth Dalai Lama. A stove that was supposedly used by King Songtsen Gampo stands at the base of the central pillar.

The Lower Middle Floor

All the chapels and rooms on this floor are closed. It is nonetheless worthwhile studying the many detailed murals on the walls of the

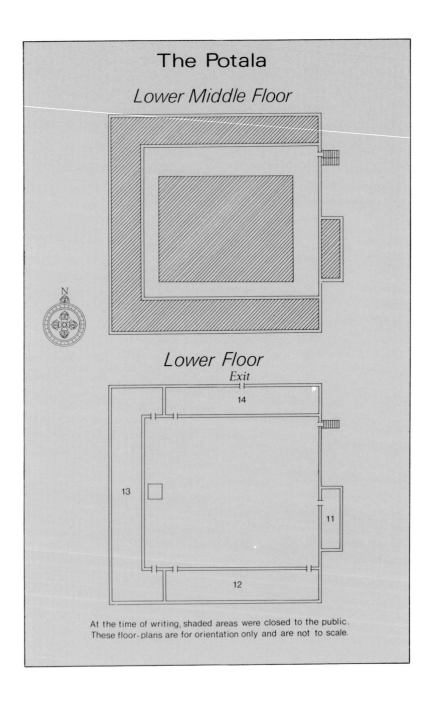

The Potala

Lower Middle Floor

Lower Floor

Exit

14

13

11

12

At the time of writing, shaded areas were closed to the public.
These floor-plans are for orientation only and are not to scale.

The Assembly Hall on the lower floor of the Potala.

quadrangular walkway, which depict many standard subjects such as the construction of the Potala and other major Tibetan monasteries.

The Lower Floor

After climbing down a number of steep dark stairwells you arrive in a spacious assembly hall. Thirty tall solid pillars, draped in thickly woven white material with black markings, rise from the floor to support the roof. A large throne used by the Sixth Dalai Lama alone dominates the area. The subsequent Dalai Lamas from the Seventh to the Fourteenth used a newer assembly hall in the White Palace close by, which is not open to the public.

The Chapel of the Stages on the Path to Enlightenment (11)

The 'Stages on the Path to Enlightenment' *(lam-rim)* is a tradition of instruction detailing all the various steps the meditator needs to take to reach his final goal of enlightenment. For the Gelukpa, this tradition found its definitive statement in Tsongkhapa's major work, the *Great*

Exposition on the Stages on the Path to Enlightenment. Thus this shrine, founded by Desi Sanggye Gyatso, has as its main figure Tsongkhapa, surrounded by the teachers of the *lam-rim* lineages. To the left are the masters of the 'extensive' lineage, starting with Maitreya and Asanga. The 'extensive' teachings deal with the aspects of the path such as compassion, ethics, tolerance and perseverance. To the right are the masters of the 'profound' lineage, who include Manjushri, Nagarjuna and their disciples. The 'profound' teachings are concerned with the contemplative understanding of the ultimate truth of emptiness. To the far right are two Enlightenment Stupas.

The Knowledge Holders' Chapel (12)

The Eight Knowledge Holders (*rig-dzin*) to whom this chapel is dedicated are Padmasambhava and seven more or less contemporary Indian masters. These eight masters are each said to have received a particular tantric practice (*sadhana*) from a cremation ground near Bodh Gaya, the site of the Buddha's enlightenment. Padmasambhava brought these teachings, which belong to the Mahayoga tantric tradition, to Tibet and taught them to the twenty-five adepts of Chimpuk near Samye. The Knowledge Holders are to the left of this long, high room. To the right are the eight manifestations of Padmasambhava himself, which show the richness and diversity of his creative power to appear in whatever form is suitable for a particular occasion. A fine ornate image of him as the Lotus Born Guru sits in the centre in the traditional posture. He is flanked by his two principal consorts, Yeshe Tsogyel and Mandarava.

The Chapel of the Dalai Lamas' Tombs (13)

This is one of the most awesome rooms in the Potala, mainly because of the massive golden stupa of the Fifth Dalai Lama, called the 'Sole Ornament of the World', which reaches all the way to the upper storey. Its spire is lost in darkness while its bulbous base glows softly in the light of silver butter lamps. To the right is a smaller stupa containing the relics of the Tenth Dalai Lama, and on the left, one with the relics of the Twelfth. To either side of the three principal tombs are eight Tathagata Stupas, supposedly housing some relics of the historical Buddha. The shrine was erected by Desi Sanggye Gyatso in commemoration of his master, the recently deceased Fifth Dalai Lama.

The Chapel of the Holy Born (14)

The esteem in which the Fifth Dalai Lama was held by his contemporaries is vividly demonstrated here by his being placed on a joint throne with an identically-sized image of Shakyamuni. To the right and left of these two central statues are numerous other figures seemingly placed in this chapel at random, since no obvious theme unites them all. At the far left, by the entrance, stands a forlorn stupa with the relics of the seventeen year old Eleventh Dalai Lama, who died in 1855. Between this stupa and the main statues are the Eight Medicine Buddhas and the Buddhas of the Three Times (past, present and future). To the right of the Fifth Dalai Lama are Avalokiteshvara, Songtsen Gampo (in an unusual form), Drom Tönpa, and the first four Dalai Lamas. Lined along the bases of these figures are several small statues of Padmasambhava. At the far right of the hall, facing inwards, is a statue of the Sakya lama, Tsarchen Losel Gyatso, the founder of the Tsar sub-order of the Sakyapa.

You leave the Potala from this chapel along a corridor that leads around the back of the statues and finally deposits you in glaring daylight at the back of the huge building. A newly constructed path takes you down to the site of the western gate of Lhasa beneath Chakpori.

A censer at the base of the Fifth Dalai Lama's tomb in the Chapel of the Dalai Lamas' tombs.

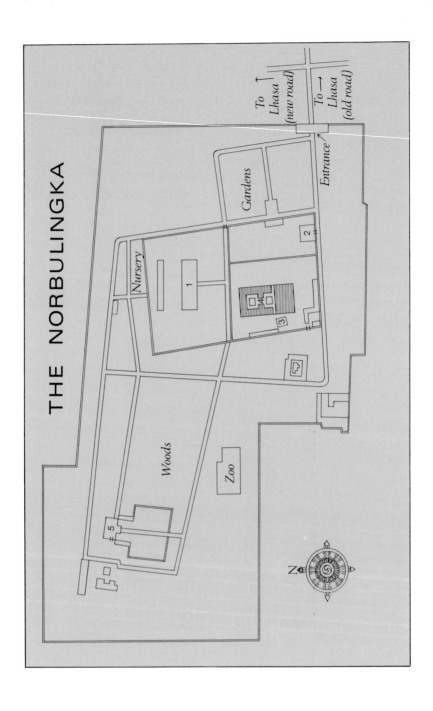

THE NORBULINGKA

Gardens

Nursery

1

2

3

4

Woods

Zoo

5

Entrance

To Lhasa (new road)

To → Lhasa (old road)

4. THE NORBULINGKA

The Norbulingka, the 'Jewel Park', is a large open area about four kilometres to the west of Lhasa. It is sometimes referred to as the Summer Palace of the Dalai Lama. Its official name is now the 'People's Park'. There is no bus and it is a long walk. The best way to go is by bicycle, taking the road that bears off left just after the Chakpori. This is the old, direct route that the Dalai Lama would take each summer when he left the Potala for the bucolic charm of the Norbulingka. Alternatively you can follow the main road to the Lhasa Hotel and turn left at the turning to the hotel. The entrance is about half a mile on your right. There is a 20 Fen charge to park your bicycle outside the main entrance but no charge to enter the park itself. However, it costs 2 RMB to visit the New Summer Palace, 30 Fen to see the Eighth Dalai Lama's Palace and 20 Fen for the Thirteenth Dalai Lama's Palace. No charge was asked for the other buildings.

HISTORY

Since the time of the Eighth Dalai Lama the park has been used as a summer residence, retreat and recreation area for the successive Dalai Lamas. (It is often stated that the Seventh Dalai Lama constructed the first palace here around 1750, but a reliable source informed me that although the Seventh Dalai Lama made use of the area as a recreation garden, it was not until the time of his successor that the construction of a palace began.) Most of the main buildings were constructed during this century by the Thirteenth and Fourteenth Dalai Lamas. It was from here that the present Dalai Lama escaped from Tibet in March 1959. The palaces suffered considerable damage from Chinese artillery fire during the popular uprising that followed his departure. They have now been somewhat repaired, but much of their wealth has disappeared, probably forever, into China and beyond.

THE SITE

The New Summer Palace [Tagtu Migyur Potrang] (1)

This palace was built as the official summer residence of the Fourteenth Dalai Lama. It was completed in 1956. An ornate and opulent building, it contains examples of exquisite Tibetan craftsmanship, several very old images, and a number of incongruous twentieth century objects imported from the West. A Tibetan guide will lead you around the rooms that are open: all those on the first floor.

The New Summer Palace, Tagtu Migyur Potrang.

The first room is the **Audience Chamber** of His Holiness. Three beautiful silver images of Vajradhara, Maitreya and Manjushri are enshrined here. From the ceiling above and to the front of them hangs a fine piece of embroidered brocade depicting the most important thinkers from Buddhist India: these include Nagarjuna, Asanga, Vasubandhu, Dignaga and Dharmakirti. To the right is the Dalai Lama's throne, above which hangs a *tangka* of Yamantaka.

Around the walls is painted a detailed account of Tibetan history from its earliest mythical beginnings until the finding of the Fourteenth Dalai Lama and his return to Lhasa in 1939. It begins at the upper left-hand corner with Shakyamuni Buddha declaring that since there were no human beings in Tibet, his teachings would, for the time being, be restricted to India. He passes the responsibility of teaching the Tibetans to Avalokiteshvara. Avalokiteshvara then assumes the form of a monkey and descends into Tibet on a mountain in Tsetang. He mates with a female demoness and they produce six children – half human and half monkey. These eventually grow into the first Tibetans. The Tibetans are next depicted cultivating the first field in Tibet, again in the region of Tsetang. The first Tibetan king is called Nyatri Tsenpo. According to legend, he was descended from the Shakya clan in India, and thus distantly related to the historical Buddha Shakyamuni.

The history continues with King Songtsen Gampo and the founding of the Jokhang in Lhasa. His minister Tönmi Sambhota is depicted studying Sanskrit in India and returning to Tibet to create the Tibetan alphabet and grammar. This written language enabled Buddhism to be introduced on a wider scale.

The murals on the back wall recount the reign of King Trisong Detsen, the founding of Samye Monastery, and the ordination of the first monks. They conclude with events from the time of the last great Tibetan king, Tri Ralpachen, and the demise of that dynasty with the anti-Buddhist policies of King Langdarma.

On the right of the enshrined deities are images of Lhasa and several of the most important monasteries founded from the eleventh century onwards. There are fine traditional-style representations of Reting, Ganden, Sera, Drepung and Tashilhunpo. It is worthwhile to take note of these paintings and compare them with what remains of the monasteries today.

The wall above the Dalai Lama's throne shows the history of the Dalai Lamas from the First until the Fourteenth. The visits of the Fifth and Thirteenth Dalai Lamas to China are depicted as well as the Thirteenth's brief exile in India. It concludes with the present Dalai Lama being escorted from Amdo to Lhasa as a young boy.

The **Meditation Chamber** of His Holiness is the next room to be visited. This contains images of a thousand-armed Avalokiteshvara, the Gelukpa 'Assembly Tree', and a silk-appliqué *tangka* of Atisha, Drom Tönpa and Ngog Legpa'i Sherab hanging above the Dalai Lama's seat. The square seat to the right is where His Holiness's tutors would sit to

One now enters the **Bedroom** of the Dalai Lama. At right angles to an art-deco bed and radiogram with tape recorder given him by the Indian President Nehru is a small silver shrine containing some very beautiful old images of Vajradhara, Yamantaka, Samvara, Vajrayogini and Manjushri. A small door leads from one side into a very functional, Western-style bathroom.

The **Reception Hall** is the next room. In the very centre is a magnificent, intricately carved golden throne. This throne would be carried outside on special occasions for His Holiness to address the people and give teachings and initiations. Extremely well-executed murals adorn the walls. Famous deeds from the lives of Shakyamuni and Tsongkhapa are shown. Beyond them is a rather bizarre realistic representation of the Dalai Lama and his court circa 1956. Above him sit his tutors, while below are a truly strange assortment of Tibetan officials, members of the Dalai Lama's family, and other dignitaries including the former British representative Hugh Richardson (in a trilby), Indian, Kuomintang and Mongolian ambassadors, and in yellow robes a shaven-headed

Japanese monk who managed to stay illegally in Sera Monastery for three years. The painting was done by Amdo Jampa, an artist who has now returned from exile in India and lives in Tibet. The main statues behind the throne are those of Maitreya, Atisha and Tsongkhapa. On the opposite wall is a group painting of the fourteen Dalai Lamas. Note that the upper four figures have no wheel in their hands whereas the rest do. This shows that only from the time of the Fifth were the Dalai Lamas endowed with political power. To the right Desi Sanggye Gyatso is depicted in conversation with the Mongolian King Gushri Khan.

The guide might now take you to the Dalai Lama's **Dining Room** (this is not always open to the public). Tsongkhapa, Atisha, Manjushri and other deities are depicted on the walls. By the door are a symbolic diagram of the stages of concentration leading to complete mental quiescence, some illustrations of certain monastic customs and rules, and a wheel of life.

Fountain in the courtyard of the Chensek Potrang. The figure is probably a naga.

The **Quarters of the Dalai Lama's Mother** are in the adjoining room. The most remarkable object here is a delightful sandalwood shrine carved at the time of the Thirteenth Dalai Lama. Both the casing as well as the figures inside are of sandal. On the right is an exquisite statue of Milarepa. Smaller images of Shakyamuni and the Six Ornaments and the Two Supreme Ones of Indian Buddhist thought sit to the left of Mila. High on one of the walls a small framed painting done in 1953 shows the procession of the eighteen year old Dalai Lama in an Austin Rover leaving the Potala and heading for the Norbulingka. Being a woman (and the Norbulingka being a monastery), the Dalai Lama's mother would use these quarters only for daytime visits. In the evening she would return to Lhasa.

On the **Landing** above the staircase are four fairly interesting paintings. On the left is a peculiarly Tibetan square diagram divided into many smaller coloured squares. This is called a 'Kunsang Korlo'. Each square has a letter or syllable in the middle. Reading it either horizontally or vertically gives one the names of all the Tibetan kings from Nyatri Tsenpo to Ralpachen. To its right is a picture of the origins and structure of the world according to the *Abhidharmakosha* of Vasubhandu. There then follows another Kunsang Korlo, this one containing the names of all fourteen Dalai Lamas. On the adjacent wall is a symbolic painting of Padmasambhava and the two translators Vairocana and Shantarakshita: at the time of King Langdarma Buddhism was suppressed and it was forbidden to paint images of any Buddhist figure, thus Buddhist artists had to resort to symbols. This painting is an example of that style. Padmasambhava is indicated by the sword, and the two translators by the two-headed duck and parrot. The birds have two heads to show they symbolise translators, that is people capable of speaking two languages.

The Eighth Dalai Lama's Palace [Kelsang Potrang] (2)

There is not a great deal to see here. Only the main audience hall, which you enter from the courtyard, can be visited. This residence was built during the second half of the eighteenth century by Jampel Gyatso, the Eighth Dalai Lama, and was used as a summer palace by all the Dalai Lamas up until the Thirteenth. Judging by what one can see today, it is much more modest than the buildings erected by the Thirteenth and Fourteenth Dalai Lamas. With the morning sun, the audience hall is magnificently illuminated. Rich brocades hang from the pillars and two giant butter lamps stand in the middle of the room. A large throne is raised on a platform at the rear of the chapel, behind which are encased statues of the Eight Medicine Buddhas.

Detail of the Thirteenth Dalai Lama's Palace, Chensek Potrang.

The Thirteenth Dalai Lama's Palace [Chensek Potrang] (5)

This palace was built in 1922 for Tubten Gyatso, the Thirteenth Dalai Lama, by a wealthy lay Buddhist supporter called Chensek Kumbu. It is still known by the Tibetans as 'Chensek Palace'. Normally only the **Main Audience and Assembly Hall** on the ground floor is open to the public. This large and spacious room used to house a superb collection of old *tangkas*, which unfortunately have now been removed. It is thought that the Chinese have taken them to be exhibited abroad, after which they may be returned. Thirty-six silver images of Amitayus, Vijaya and Tara, the triad of deities most strongly connected with longevity, are encased along the rear wall to both sides of the raised platform on which the Dalai Lama's throne is placed. In 1948, when he was thirteen years old, the present Dalai Lama commissioned a statue of his predecessor, the Thirteenth, and had it enshrined behind the throne. The carvings along the tops of the pillars above the throne are worth studying.

Upstairs on the first floor are the private quarters of the Thirteenth Dalai Lama. They consist of a private **Living Room** and adjoining **Bedroom**. The living room is a narrow rectangular chamber barely large enough to contain the three Western-style armchairs that face a small shrine. The bedroom is even smaller, containing a bed that indicates the diminutive stature of its occupant. A beautiful old statue of Tara on the bedside table is the only religious object in the room. It is reputed to have spoken directly to His Holiness on several occasions. Part of a collage of faded black and white photographs collected by the Dalai Lama while he was briefly exiled in India can be seen on the wall opposite the bed.

These rooms have been maintained much as they were left in 1933 when Tubten Gyatso died. The main room is the Dalai Lama's private **Teaching Hall**. This was where the Great Thirteenth would perform monastic ordination ceremonies and tantric initiations and deliver discourses on Buddhist philosophy and doctrine. The two most outstanding images in this room are standing forms of a thousand-armed Avalokiteshvara and a thousand-armed Dugkarma. They are placed side by side and both radiate an indescribable sense of warmth and insight. To their right is a small encased figure of Dorje Drakden, the special protector propitiated by the Tibetan government through the Nechung oracle. Portraits of earlier Dalai Lamas – the First, Second, Third, Fifth and Seventh – adorn the walls along with some paintings of the principal Geluk monasteries. On the wall high above the throne at the back are depicted the seven religious kings and the twenty-five *kalki* of the Shambhala legend.

By going through a sliding door at the back of this room one enters first a bare ante-room and then the small **Prayer Chamber** where the Dalai Lama would perform his daily recitations and other practices. The walls of this tiny cell are richly painted with tantric deities.

Across the courtyard from this palace is a smaller building, the **Kelsang Dekyi Palace**, where the Thirteenth Dalai Lama would retire each night. Most of the main images have been removed but restoration work is now underway to redecorate the rooms. The first main room you enter contains a detailed mural of Tushita (Ganden), the Pure Land where the future Buddha Maitreya now resides. A portrait of Tsongkhapa is beside it. There is a small altar with a fine statue of the Jowo Shakyamuni with two Buddhas seated beside him. The adjoining room, partitioned off by screen doors, has a wonderful mural of the Shri Dhanyakataka stupa of Kalachakra. On the opposite wall is a case with some old statues, including Avalokiteshvara and two images of Tsongkhapa's disciple Khedrup Je. You can see where the golden ornaments have been removed from some of these statues. The one other room on this floor worth visiting (the others are bare) possesses a mural of the Pure Land of Avalokiteshvara (Potala) with a fine thousand-armed representation of the deity in the centre. The wooden carvings on the screen door beautifully depict the Kadampa masters Atisha, Drom Tönpa and Ngog Legpa'i Sherab.

Close by to the Kelsang Dekyi Palace is the **Chime Chokkyil**, the small building in which the Thirteenth Dalai Lama died. This is closed to the public.

Drunzig Palace (3)
This square building facing the usually dry artificial lake to the left of the Eighth Dalai Lama's palace was constructed by the Thirteenth Dalai Lama as a library and personal retreat. To the right of the small palace is a pile of pebbles, each stone having been placed there by the Thirteenth Dalai Lama as he walked around the palace and gardens. Behind this grows an apple tree that he planted. By interpreting the formations of its bark, the Dalai Lama could tell how his meditation was progressing.

The **Library** is on the ground floor. In addition to the thousands of volumes of scripture that are packed into its walls, this dimly-lit study houses a newly-made wooden statue of Avalokiteshvara and a larger image of Amitayus and a thousand smaller ones. A tall glass cabinet that used to contain a silver image of Tara stands empty. The Eight Great Bodhisattvas stand beneath the scriptures at the base of the back wall.

Upstairs are the Thirteenth Dalai Lama's **Retreat Quarters**. The main chamber is a small audience room where His Holiness would occasionally interrupt his retreats to deal with matters of state brought to him by his ministers. No other people were ever allowed in here. The room itself contains a group of very old statues enshrined in a glass case: they include Tsongkhapa and his two chief disciples, Padmasambhava, Samvara, Manjushri, Avalokiteshvara, Amitayus and Shakyamuni. Above the seat is a painting of the five *dhyani* Buddhas, all except the green Amoghasiddhi (bottom right hand corner) having been restored. The meditation cell is reached by passing through a bare ante-room with a single bed where the Dalai Lama would rest and eat. There are also a number of *tsamtors* standing in one corner; these are specially blessed *tormas* aimed at guaranteeing a successful meditation. The cell itself is very small with richly painted walls. A large painting of Yamantaka, the Thirteenth Dalai Lama's personal deity, is on the wall behind the seat. It is said that he spent many years meditating on this deity, receiving visions and words of advice from him.

Behind this palace are a row of rather insignificant buildings that previously served as servants' quarters and kitchens. Visible through the barred window of the room on the far right is a stuffed tiger. The story goes that during the time of the Thirteenth Dalai Lama a tiger was reported roaming the grounds of the Norbulingka. One of the forbidding palace guards (*dzingka*) caught the tiger by its tail and killed it by picking it up and hurling it to the ground.

Painted wooden panel in the wall of the central shrine of the artificial lake.

The Lake and its Shrines (4)

This artificial lake with two shrines was dug at the time of the Eighth Dalai Lama, Jampel Gyatso, during the latter half of the eighteenth century. The whole area was designed primarily for recreation purposes. The central shrine, decorated with playful, lightly coloured images set in panels, has no overtly religious qualities about it and must have been used as a sheltered summer house to entertain friends and drink tea. The second shrine, with the pagoda-style roof, has murals depicting familiar religious figures that still show signs of desecration. Inside are some excellent paintings of some of the main monasteries. This shrine is dedicated to the nagas, snake-like beings believed to inhabit the lake. Various rituals would be performed here as offerings to appease and gratify them.

As you leave this park you will notice a row of long, nondescript buildings to the right of the lake. These locked rooms contain many of the Dalai Lama's possessions not confiscated by the Chinese. The buildings you pass on the left as you leave the entrance courtyard are the stables.

The Zoo (5)

Between the Thirteenth Dalai Lama's Palace and the main entrance to the Norbulingka is a zoo with a small collection of deer, bears, monkeys and other Tibetan animals, none of whom seem particularly pleased to be there.

5. SERA MONASTERY

Sera lies about 5 km to the north of Lhasa along the base of the mountains at the edge of the valley. It is visible from the Potala and several high points in the city. There is a bus from Lhasa every morning at 9 am. It starts from the bus stop opposite the Banak Shöl Hotel and stops at regular intervals along the Dekyi Shar Lam before turning right up the long, straight road to the military hospital close by to the monastery. You can also cycle or walk there. The colleges and chapels of Sera are open daily (except perhaps Sunday) from 9 am to 4 pm (with a long lunchbreak from 12 until 2.30). There is an entry charge of 3 RMB. A bus returns to the city around 5 pm.

If, instead of turning right near the hospital to Sera, you turn left along the base of the hills, you will come to **Pabongka***, a site which served as a meditation place at the time of Songtsen Gampo. The very first seven Tibetan monks also stayed here after receiving their ordination from Shantarakshita in the last quarter of the eighth century. More recently it was the seat of the powerful Gelukpa Lama, Pabongka Rinpoche. An impressive new temple has recently been rebuilt there with eight monks in residence. Nearby is the* **Chub Sang Nunnery** *which is also being rebuilt. A handful of nuns live there.*

HISTORY
Sera is one of the three great Gelukpa monasteries near Lhasa, the other two being Drepung and Ganden. Until the Chinese occupation it served, like its two sister monasteries, as a centre of learning and monastic training to which monks from all corners of Tibet would come to spend as long as fifteen to twenty years methodically studying and debating the meaning of the Buddhist scriptures. Thus for centuries it existed as a small monastic township housing over five thousand fully ordained monks, novices, workers and other functionaries.

Like all other Tibetan monasteries of similar size Sera is divided into colleges (*dratsang*) and houses (*khangtsen*). The colleges are the main units of the monastery, distinguished from each other by the kind of studies the monks follow there. Each college has an abbot (*khenpo*), who is responsible for administrative matters, and a disciplinarian (*ge-kor*), who is in charge of the monks' conduct. Affiliated with each college are a number of houses, where the monk-students live for the duration of their training. The houses are divided according to the regions of the country that the monks come from. Although each college has its own assembly hall and chapels, the monastery often has another 'main

Sera Monastery before 1959.

assembly hall' (*tsog-chen*) where, on important occasions, the monks from all the colleges can gather. In addition to the monks, the monasteries also housed a number of 'lay-brothers' (*dob-dob*), some of whom took care of the upkeep of the buildings, the monastery lands and the kitchens, and others who were little more than hangers-on.

Sera monastery was built below a small hermitage where Tsongkhapa had spent several years in retreat both meditating on and writing commentaries to the Buddhist scriptures. A leading disciple of Tsongkhapa, Shakya Yeshe (1352-1435), started constructing Sera in 1419, the year of his teacher's death. Ten years earlier Tsongkhapa had been invited by Emperor Yung-lo of Ming China to visit his court in Peking. Unable to go himself, Tsongkhapa sent Shakya Yeshe in his stead. A subsequent emperor showed his appreciation of Shakya Yeshe's teachings by giving him the title Jamchen Chöje ('Great Gentle Dharma Lord', the name by which he is best known today) in 1434.

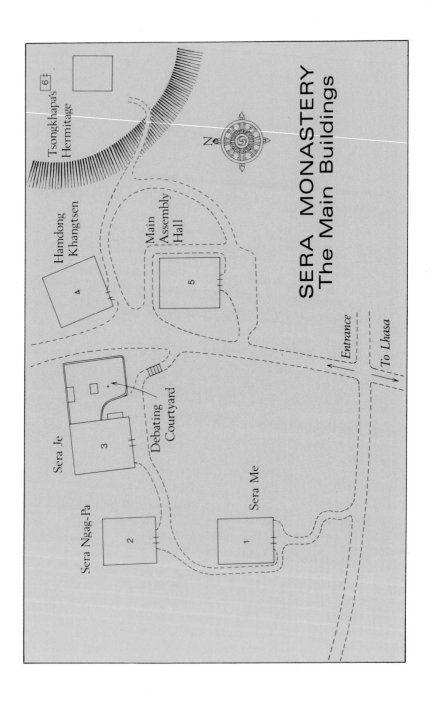

SERA MONASTERY
The Main Buildings

Tsongkhapa's Hermitage

6

Hamdong Khangtsen

4

Main Assembly Hall

5

Sera Je

3

Debating Courtyard

Sera Ngag-Pa

2

Sera Me

1

Entrance

To Lhasa

N

Although many of the outlying residential buildings in Sera were destroyed during the cultural revolution, the principal buildings were left relatively intact. Three hundred monks now live here, many of them recently ordained, and an attempt is being made to recommence the traditional course of study for which the monastery is renowned.

One of the most sacred objects in Sera is the *vajra* (*dorje*) that is the prototype of all other *vajras* in Tibet. It was found by the tantric adept Dacharpa in Padmasambhava's cave in Yerpa, and is now shown to the public only one day a year.

THE SITE

I shall describe the interiors of the colleges and halls in Sera according to the route followed by Tibetan pilgrims. Upon entering the main hall of each building, you turn left and follow the left-hand wall until you reach the first of the chapels that are connected along the back of the building. Only after studying these chapels do we look at the images in the main hall. Finally we visit the shrines on the upper storey.

Sera Me College (1)
The Chapels. The first chapel is dedicated to Ta-og Chögyel, the worldly Dharma protector of the East. He is the wrathful deity to the left of the chapel. The dominant statue is that of Yamantaka and consort; a large, beautiful and fearful image. Numerous old vajras can be seen hanging from one of the beams on the roof. Three iron scorpions are attached to one of the pillars, apparently as a means of warding off the negative influence of the nagas.

The next small chapel contains a stupa with an image of Tsongkhapa inside, with statues of Shakyamuni and Tsongkhapa seated on either side.

Three large Buddhas dominate the following chapel: Shakyamuni, the Buddha of the present, Maitreya, the Buddha of the future, and Dipamkara, the Buddha of the past. Many volumes of the *Perfection of Wisdom Discourses* line the upper walls. Images of the Sixteen Arhats, in Chinese-style pseudo-grottoes, are also enshrined around the room.

The next chapel houses the most sacred image in Sera Me, a statue of Shakyamuni called the 'Miwang Jowo', the Jowo commissioned in the fifteenth century by the influential Miwang family, one of the principal benefactors of Tsongkhapa. Although heavily ornamented, this is a fine piece of work and probably the original. A large figure of Amitayus sits at the rear of the chapel and the Eight Great Bodhisattvas stand along the walls. The wrathful forms of Hayagriva and Acala guard the shrine.

The last of the rear chapels is dedicated to Tsongkhapa, who sits in the company of many important lamas from the Geluk tradition. The

First, Second, Third and Fifth Dalai Lamas are represented, as are Jamchen Chöje, the founder of Sera, and Gyeltsen Zangpo, the monastery's first abbot. Atisha and Drom Tönpa represent the Kadampa tradition. The founder of Sera Me college, Kunkhyen Jangchub Bum, is seated to the right of Drom Tönpa. On the wall near the exit are two, more recent masters: Gyelwa Ensapa and a very expressive Purchok Ngawang Jampa.

The Main Hall. The central figure in the main hall is an image of Shakyamuni with extraordinarily delicate and sensitive features. The workmanship of the halo is worth noting. Maitreya and Manjushri are to either side of the main image. The rest of the long altar running along the front of the hall is occupied by statues of lamas, some more easily recognisable than others. Tsongkhapa and his two chief disciples are there along with lesser-known lamas remembered mainly for their contributions to Sera Me college. A modern image of a portly, smiling Pabongka Rinpoche is found in front of Manjushri.

The Upper Storey. Upstairs are two small shrines. On the left as you come up the stairs is a chapel devoted to Tuwang Tsultrim, a form of Shakyamuni represented here by a small, standing statue with notably aquiline features, suggesting its possible Indian origin. A small stone figure of Tara is to the right of the main image. This used to be the most revered image in Tsang Khangtsen of Sera and has only recently been moved to this shrine. The other figures are modern and for the most part easily recognisable.

On the opposite side of the roof, connected by a small walkway, is a Tara chapel. This used to be the room where an edition of the Kangyur was kept, but all 108 volumes were destroyed during the cultural revolution. In its place a thousand small images of Tara made in China during the last century have been moved up from a smaller *khangtsen*. To the right of the shrine are three larger images of Tara, Amitayus and Vijaya, the longevity triad.

Sera Ngag-pa College (2)
This is the oldest structure in Sera. It is the first building Jamchen Chöje erected and it served as the main assembly hall for the monks until, over the years, Sera expanded to its present size. When it was replaced by the larger assembly hall (5), it became the tantric (*ngag-pa*) college of Sera. The pillar capitals in the entrance hall are some of the finest examples I saw in Tibet.

OPPOSITE *Carved pillar capital at the entrance of Sera Ngag-pa College.*

The Chapels. There are only two chapels to the rear of Sera Ngag-pa. The more interesting is that of the Sixteen Arhats to the left. Seated in niches half-way up the wall are Tibetan images of the sixteen saints. Below them, standing on a ledge, are another sixteen images that are small, lacquered Chinese statues. These were offered by Emperor Yung-lo to Jamchen Chöje when he visited China. A large figure of Shakyamuni is in the centre with a finely carved wooden halo behind him. A small statue of Milarepa is to his right.

The right-hand chapel is the Protector Shrine. The main figure is a single Yamantaka. Dharmaraja, Pelden Lhamo and Mahakala are also present.

The Main Hall. The outstanding image in the main hall is that of Jamchen Chöje, the founder of Sera. The smiling, radiant face of the statue is crowned with a distinctive black hat around which are Sanskrit letters. (Such a hat was probably given to him by the Chinese emperor Yung-lo; it resembles closely the black hat of the Karmapa, also a gift from a Chinese emperor.) It is said that when the new main assembly hall (5) was built, it was planned to move this statue there, but at the moment of departure, the statue declared that it preferred to stay. Therefore, a copy was made and placed in the main assembly hall instead.

Many other Sera lamas sit to either side of Jamchen Chöje. An expressive image of the first abbot of Sera, Gyeltsen Zangpo, sits to the left between Maitreya and Pabongka Rinpoche. He is recognisable by his stern expression and goatee beard. Second from the end on the right is a large figure of Jetsun Chökyi Gyeltsen, the Sera lama who wrote the standard textbooks on philosophy and debate for the college. Next to him is a smaller statue of Lodrö Rinchen, the founder of Sera Je college.

The Upper Storey. The only chapel on the upper floor is dedicated to Buddha Amitabha. A rather unattractive but perhaps ancient statue of this Buddha sits as the central image. To the left is a stupa containing the relics of Gyeltsen Zangpo, and to the right a stupa with the relics of the great debater Chökyi Gyeltsen. The Eight Medicine Buddhas surround the shrine.

Sera Je College (3)

The Chapels. The first chapel is not entered from the rear of the main hall but through a doorway in the left-hand wall. This leads you into a shrine with tall figures of the Buddhas of the Three Times, accompanied by the Eight Great Bodhisattvas. However, this chapel serves more as an anteroom that leads into the most holy shrine in Sera, the Hayagriva Chapel.

You may have to join a long queue of people waiting to enter the

Hayagriva Chapel, circumambulate the deity, and press their heads respectfully to his feet. Hayagriva, the Horse-Headed One', is the main protector of Sera Je. This dark and mysterious shrine was erected by Sera Je's founder, Lodrö Rinchen, and since then has become an important place of pilgrimage. Hanging from the blackened upper walls and ceiling are numerous suits of armour, chain-mail, helmets, swords and other weapons of war. These were offered long ago by Tibetan soldiers as gifts of peace after the sufferings of a long campaign. The beaten bronze front of the deity's shrine is noteworthy for its fine craftsmanship.

The first chapel behind the back wall is a simple shrine to Maitreya: a large image of the future Buddha with Tsongkhapa and his two chief disciples before him adorns the chapel. Scriptures are housed in the surrounding walls.

The following chapel is in honour of Tsongkhapa, a large statue of whom overshadows the two Buddha images seated to either side. A number of other images of the master with his two main disciples are present, as are several other important lamas from the Geluk order. Nagarjuna and other Indian masters are also represented. The chapel is guarded by the ever-watchful Hayagriva and Acala.

The final chapel has as its main figure a delightful image of Manjushri in the posture of 'turning the wheel of Dharma'. You will notice that the smiling head and torso are slightly inclined towards the window on the right. The debating courtyard is immediately outside and it is said that Manjushri is listening eagerly to the discussions taking place beyond the wall. Maitreya and a simple form of Manjushri sit to his sides. Many texts are crammed into the walls around them.

The Main Hall. Since the Hayagriva Chapel houses the holiest image in Sera Je, there is no obviously central image in the main hall. The empty seat reserved for the Dalai Lama has pride of place; beneath it is a smaller throne reserved for the Panchen Lama. To the left is a statue of the Thirteenth Dalai Lama and three stupas containing the relics of lamas from Sera who had reached eminent positions in the Gelukpa heirarchy, such as Ganden Tripa (i.e. Throne Holder of Ganden. See chapter 16, **Ganden Monastery**) or tutor to a Dalai Lama. A row of lamas including Tsongkhapa sit to the right. The founder of Sera Je, Lodrö Rinchen, is fourth to the right. More smaller stupas with the relics of Sera lamas are at the end.

The Upper Storey. The first chapel to the left is again consecrated to Hayagriva, but this time to a small, nine-headed, multi-armed aspect of the deity. Two statues of Padmasambhava also adorn the shrine as does

Interior of the main hall in Sera Je College.

one of the Fifth Dalai Lama. In a row of glass cases in the wall above the Fifth Dalai Lama are many small, well-executed images of various wrathful deities and protectors.

The Debating Courtyard. This large walled courtyard is to the right of Sera Je. Here hundreds of red-robed monks would sit, often in the shade of its many magnificent trees, engaged in philosophical debate, probing the meaning of what they had been taught in their classes. In the centre of the courtyard is a small stone shrine covering a large bare rock. According to tradition, while Tsongkhapa was composing his commentary to Nagarjuna's 'Middle Way' in his tiny hermitage above what would later be Sera, thirteen letter A's hovered in the space above him. When the work was completed, the letters descended to the ground below and embedded themselves in this rock. Because of the offerings thrown onto the rock by devout Tibetans, they are barely discernible today. At the far end of the courtyard is the raised platform where formal examinations are held. The monks may still be seen engaging in this old Indian form of debate.

Hamdong Khangtsen (4)
This residential compound for monks was built by later generations of the Miwang family, who had supported Tsongkhapa and built Sera Je college. It had strong ties with Sera Je, housing many of the monks who would study there.

The Chapels. There are two chapels at the back. The first is a long room containing a central image of Maitreya. To his left is a statue of a recent lama, Tubten Kunga, who died only in 1962 and was responsible for a great deal of restoration work shortly before the cultural revolution undid his labours. Attached to a pillar on the left is an encased statue of Tara. This revered image is said to have spoken on several occasions. She safeguards the spring that supplies Sera with its water. A long train of offered bangles and other items hangs beneath her, a clear indication of the esteem in which she is held by the laity.

The other chapel is a protector shrine dedicated to Gyelchen Karma Tinley, a minor manifestation of Hayagriva who is regarded as the special protector of Hamdong Khangtsen. An assistant deity stands to either side of him and Vaishravana looks on.

The Main Hall. There is no central image here. The Dalai Lama's throne that used to occupy this position has been removed and nothing put in its place. Tsongkhapa and Chökyi Gyeltsen are to the left; Buddha Shakyamuni and the longevity triad of Tara, Amitayus and Vijaya to the right.

The Assembly Hall.

The Assembly Hall [Tsog-chen] (5)

This is the largest building in Sera. Traditionally, it was the place where, on special occasions, all the monks from the three colleges (Me, Ngag-pa and Je) would congregate. Since nowadays there are so few monks, this hall is used for all gatherings of the monastery.

The Chapels. The first chapel is dedicated to the Buddha and the Sixteen Arhats. The second houses a tall, seated Maitreya flanked by the Eight Great Bodhisattvas, with Hayagriva and Acala as protectors. The third chapel contains Tsongkhapa and his two chief disciples, behind whom hangs a very fine silk-appliqué *tangka* of the Fifth Dalai Lama. The protector chapel to the far right is dominated by Yamantaka and consort.

The Main Hall. Of particular note in this huge room are the magnificent appliqué *tangkas* that hang from ceiling to floor along both the left and right-hand walls. This hall also has a more 'lived-in' feel to it: the rows of padded seats on the floor are obviously in daily use. Several times each month (on the special days determined by the lunar calendar) one can participate in the services held here with all the three hundred monks who presently live in Sera.

The main image is that of Jamchen Chöje, the founder of Sera, flanked by the Fifth and Thirteenth Dalai Lamas. Just to the right of centre is a giant and very beautiful seated statue of Maitreya, whose head reaches to the upper storey. To the left is the seventh Dalai Lama, Kelsang Gyatso, in front of whom sit Chökyi Gyeltsen, Tsongkhapa and a small, unusual image of Desi Sanggye Gyatso.

The Upper Storey. On the left at the back of you will find an old and rather appealing chapel dedicated to Avalokiteshvara. The central figure, with a thousand arms and eleven heads, is a small, standing image with delicate features. To the left are two encased images made of stone that are clearly not Tibetan in origin; they must be either Indian or Nepalese. They are finely carved, attractive pieces representing a four-armed Mahakala and Vaishravana.

Crossing over an empty room, which leads out to the ground-level behind the hall, you enter the chapel into which the head of the Maitreya statue below protrudes. It is revealing to observe the features from above as well as from below. A small image of Tsongkhapa can be seen enshrined in Maitreya's heart. Several other images are present, includ-

Rock carving of Tara.

ing, in the far right-hand corner, a Buddha whose bronze or copper halo seems to be Indian in design.

The final chapel contains a simple figure of Shakyamuni surrounded by several lamas.

Tsongkhapa's Hermitage [Chö Ding Khang] (6)

To reach the hermitage you must find the narrow path that leads up the mountainside opposite the assembly hall. (The easiest way is to follow the telegraph wires.) On your way you will pass several interesting painted reliefs on large boulders. The most striking ones are those of Dharmaraja and consort, Tsongkhapa, and Jamchen Chöje. A fine relief of several Taras can also be found a little further up.

The hermitage itself is a simple, ochre coloured, square building. The original was destroyed during the cultural revolution but a replica has been built on the same site. The room inside is quiet and austere with a simple altar bearing an image of Tsongkhapa. It was here that Tsongkhapa composed two of his best-known works: his commentary to Nagarjuna's *Root Stanzas on the Middle Way* and his study of the two principal schools of Buddhist philosophy, *The Essence of True Eloquence*.

The larger building in front of the hermitage used to be a retreat house for the monks of the Tantric Colleges in Lhasa. It is now closed.

6. DREPUNG MONASTERY

Drepung is about 8 km west of Lhasa. It is reached by leaving the city along the Dekyi Nub Lam, and going past the Lhasa Hotel, out towards the airport. It is one kilometre up the hillside to your right. This last stretch has to be walked unless you are with a private tour bus. It is a bit of a haul by bicycle; it is easier to take a bus across the road from the Banak Shöl Hotel (and at other stops along the Dekyi Shar Lam). The first bus leaves around 8.30 am and there seem to be a couple more until 10 am. The bus leaves you by the main road beneath the monastery. Buses returning to Lhasa leave from the same place fairly regularly during the late afternoon. The colleges and chapels are open every day (except perhaps Sundays) from 9 am to 4 pm (with a long lunch-break from 12 to 2.30 pm). There is an admission charge of 3 RMB.

HISTORY

'Drepung' literally means 'rice-mound', a name that well describes the first visual impression one receives of the monastery when approaching it from the main road below. But this aptly descriptive name is the Tibetan translation of 'Dhanyakataka', the Sanskrit name of the magnificent stupa in South India where the Buddha is said to have taught the Kalachakra tantra. When the monastery was founded in 1416 by Jamyang Chöje Tashi Pelden, a disciple of Tsongkhapa, it probably consisted of only a handful of buildings and was yet to resemble a mound of rice.

The abbots and disciplinarians of Drepung Monastery before 1959.

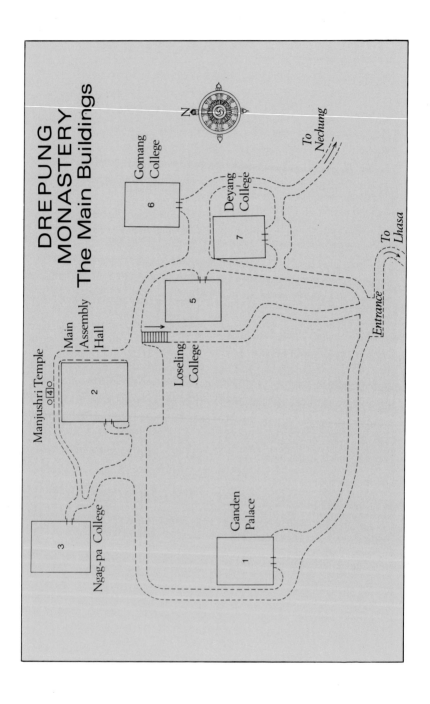

DREPUNG
MONASTERY
The Main Buildings

Manjushri Temple

Ngag-pa College

Main
Assembly
Hall

Loseling
College

Gomang
College

Deyang
College

Ganden
Palace

Entrance

To
Lhasa

To
Nechung

N

Drepung soon grew into the largest of all Gelukpa monasteries, housing more than seven thousand monks. It could well claim to have been the largest monastery the world has known. It soon became a major centre of Gelukpa religious power, as evidenced by the fact that the Second, Third and Fourth Dalai Lamas lived and were entombed here. The Fifth Dalai Lama ruled from here until the Potala was finished. The monastery was particularly renowned for its scholastic learning. It produced many great lamas including Jamyang Zhepa, the founder of Labrang Monastery in Amdo. The Gomang College of Drepung was the main place to which monks coming from Mongolia to Tibet to be trained would go.

Of all the Gelukpa monasteries around Lhasa, Drepung suffered least during the cultural revolution. Although several buildings at the rear of the complex were destroyed, the main colleges and assembly hall were left fairly intact. Since 1982 over four hundred monks have joined the monastery, most of them young men, and an attempt is now being made to begin the courses of study again.

THE SITE

The Ganden Palace (1)

Built by the Second Dalai Lama, Gendun Gyatso, this palace was the home of the Third, Fourth and Fifth Dalai Lamas, and was where the subsequent Dalai Lamas and their entourage of monks would stay when they visited Drepung. Apart from a small retaining staff, the palace would stand empty while the Dalai Lama was not there.

You enter the palace by two flights of stairs and emerge in a spacious courtyard encircled by three to four storeys of rooms and chapels. The main edifice of the palace looms up at the back of the courtyard and at the upper right-hand corner a balcony bedecked with cloth hangings indicates the Dalai Lama's personal quarters (these are not open to the public). The first room you visit is on the opposite side from the Dalai Lama's residence on the ground floor. It is a large, spacious assembly hall, somewhat bare and obviously not used for a long time. This is where the Namgyel Tratsang, the Dalai Lama's personal monastic staff, would gather for their services. Statues of several barely discernible lamas and deities are enshrined behind grilles in dark recesses along the front wall. The assembly hall leads to a protector chapel that contains a formidable statue of Yamantaka and consort flanked by Vaishravana, Mahakala, Dharmaraja and Pelden Lhamo. The Fifth Dalai Lama sits frowning in front.

On the floor above is a room dominated by a large throne used by the Fifth to the Fourteenth Dalai Lamas. It was presumably an audience

The Ganden Palace.

chamber. There are images of Tsongkhapa and his two chief disciples. The walls on both sides are filled with texts, but there is little else of note.

The Main Assembly Hall (2)

The Chapel. Only one chapel is presently open on the ground floor of this gigantic assembly hall. This is a high-ceilinged, spacious room that is one of the oldest structures in Drepung; the assembly hall itself was added on at a later date. The chapel is dedicated to Shakyamuni. Shariputra and Maudgalyayana, his two chief arhat disciples, stand to either side. On a higher tier behind is another image of Shakyamuni but here flanked by Buddhas Kashyapa and Maitreya, thus portraying the Buddhas of the Three Times. Nine stupas modelled on the Kalachakra stupa in India, Shri Dhanyakataka, are arranged along the highest tier at the back. The Eight Great Bodhisattvas line the walls and the wrathful forms of Vajrapani and Hayagriva guard the doorway. Smaller images of King Songtsen Gampo, his queens and ministers are attached to the pillars that support the roof.

The Main Hall. This hall is no longer used as the main assembly hall in Drepung except on special occasions. Instead, the four hundred and fifty monks gather regularly in the smaller but more convenient hall of Loseling College. As you leave the chapel the first object on the long altar at the front of the hall is a stupa containing the relics of the 95th Ganden Tripa. Next is a large seated image of Manjushri in the gesture of turning the wheel of Dharma. He is followed by the female deity Dugkarma; Tsongkhapa; the Thirteenth Dalai Lama; Jamyang Chöje, the founder of Drepung, in a finely carved wood and glass shrine; a youthful Seventh Dalai Lama; the Third and Fourth Dalai Lamas; the Fifth Dalai Lama, on a higher throne; the Ninth Dalai Lama; a boyish Eighth Dalai Lama; and Shakyamuni. The Sixteen Arhats are placed, in two groups of eight, at each end of the altar.

The Upper Storey. The main chapel at the back of the upper storey reveals the exquisite head and shoulders of a giant statue of Maitreya at the age of twelve, the base of which is in one of the closed chapels on the ground floor. In front of Maitreya are three beautiful small images of lamas seated on a bench. To the left is the twelfth century Tibetan lama Togme Zangpo, in the centre is an image of Tsongkhapa, and to the right is Seu Rinzen, the lama who founded the main Tara chapel in the Jokhang. Tsongkhapa sits to the left and an expressive Jamyang Chöje to the right. To the left of the pillar immediately behind Tsongkhapa is a metal stupa containing the relics of Gendun Gyatso, the Second Dalai Lama. The remains of the Third and Fourth Dalai Lamas are also enshrined in stupas in this building but traditionally have never been open to the public. Parallel to the Second Dalai Lama's stupa on the right of Maitreya is another stupa containing the remains of Jamyang Zhepa. On the two sides are eleven other statues representing different incarnations of the Dalai and Panchen Lamas.

To the right is the Tara Chapel, which dates back to the time of the Fifth Dalai Lama. There are three images of Tara side by side encased behind glass. The image on the left is Nartang Chime Drölma, the Tara responsible for preserving Drepung's drinking water; the middle image is Yamdrok Yumtso Drölma, the Tara responsible for Drepung's wealth and prosperity; and the image to the right is Gyeltse Tsechen Drölma, the Tara who empowers Drepung with authority. A superb 114 volume edition of the Kangyur, commissioned by the Fifth Dalai Lama, bound in sandalwood with ivory ends and written in gold ink, is enshrined along the wall. This edition was stolen by the Chinese in 1959 and returned to Tibet only in May of 1985. A statue of Prajnaparamita, the 'Mother of the Buddhas', sits midway between these volumes, holding in her lap an amulet containing a tooth of Tsongkhapa. Three standing

cases down the middle of the room contain examples of the casings and text of this edition of the Kangyur as well as a volume from another edition painted in red ink on a continuous sheet of paper.

It is possible to ascend yet one more storey to the level of the roof, where you will find three more chapels. To the left is a large room containing statues of all the rulers of Tibet, from the earliest kings to the later Dalai Lamas. The Fifth Dalai Lama sits on a raised throne at the centre of the back wall, and there seems to be no particular order in the arrangement of the other images. The statues are nonetheless well-made and expressive. There is also a small Maitreya Chapel, which possesses the conch shell reputedly donated to the monastery by Tsongkhapa, as well as a Shakyamuni Chapel that contains an image of the Buddha surrounded by about fifteen stupas.

Ngag-pa College (3)

The Chapel. This one chapel open at the rear of the main hall is one of the oldest buildings in Drepung. It was erected by Tsongkhapa himself, before the existence of Drepung, as a shrine to Yamantaka. The main image is still that of a single Yamantaka made by Tsongkhapa. According to tradition, Tsongkhapa moulded the body around the relics of the translator Ra Lotsawa, one of the most important figures in the Yaman-taka tradition. When he had finished the neck and was about to make the heads, it is said that they appeared spontaneously. In addition to statues of Tsongkhapa and the Fifth Dalai Lama, the room contains many of the major Gelukpa protectors: Mahakala, Dharmaraja, Vais-hravana, Dorje Drakden and Pelden Lhamo. The prayer wheel in the right-hand corner is consecrated by the mantras of Yamantaka and is regarded as a 'shrine' to the deity's speech.

The Main Hall. The hall and the rest of the Ngag-pa (Tantric) College of Drepung was built on to Tsongkhapa's Yamantaka Chapel at a later date. Along the front of the main hall are a number of texts, some statues of Tsongkhapa and various Dalai Lamas. More interesting are the smaller images of the Indian and Tibetan teachers who make up the lineage of the 'Stages on the Path to Enlightenment'. They are enshrined on both sides of the hall and in the back right-hand corner. Some of the figures, such as Nagarjuna and Asanga, can easily be recognised but most of the lamas are hard to identify.

There are no chapels open on the upper storey of the Ngag-pa College.

OPPOSITE *The Main Assembly Hall.*

The Manjushri Temple (4)

This small temple is situated immediately behind the Main Assembly Hall. The main figure inside is a stone image of Manjushri, the bodhisattva of wisdom, carved on the large boulder around which the

Monk descending an alleyway at Drepung.

temple is built. There are a number of other small stone images including a rather attractive one of Dugkarma. To the left and right of the temple stand white stupas. The one to the left contains one hundred thousand verses of scripture; the one to the right the relics of Lama Umapa, the teacher through whom Tsongkhapa was able directly to communicate with Manjushri.

Loseling College (5)

The Chapels. There are three chapels at the rear of the ground floor in Loseling. The first is dedicated to the Sixteen Arhats, who are arranged on three tiers around the room. In the centre is an Enlightenment Stupa before which sits one of the former abbots of Drepung.

The second chapel is dominated by a large image of Maitreya at the back. Shakyamuni is to the left, the Thirteenth Dalai Lama in front, and Tsongkhapa and his two chief disciples to the right. There are also images of Atisha, Drom Tönpa and Ngog Legpa'i Sherab.

The third chapel houses a small statue of Shakyamuni. To each side of him is a stupa. Texts fill the walls to the ceiling. Many smaller Buddhas are in a glass-cased recess above.

The Main Hall. Starting from the left, the first image on the altar along the back of the hall is the stupa of Legden Rinpoche, the first abbot of Loseling College. Next to his remains are those of the first Kangyur Rinpoche, another famous lama of Loseling, whose third incarnation now lives in India. There then follow statues of the Fifth, Eighth and Seventh Dalai Lamas. A small, old image of Jamyang Chöje sits raised up next to the Seventh Dalai Lama. Beneath him is a mandala of Yamantaka. Sonam Drakpa, the lama who composed the textbooks studied in Loseling, is the next figure (Sonam Drakpa was also the fifteenth Ganden Tripa). Before coming to the Dalai Lama's throne are more images of Tsongkhapa, the Thirteenth Dalai Lama and Sonam Drakpa, this time depicted in debating posture. Beyond the throne is a large stupa containing the relics of the first Dedrup Rinpoche, another renowned Loseling lama. Another stupa of a Loseling lama, statues of Tsongkhapa and his two chief disciples, and Dugkarma complete the arrangement on this long altar.

In niches along both side walls are small images of Amitayus. Originally there were one thousand of them but only about eight hundred survived the cultural revolution.

The Upper Storey. There is only one chapel open on the upper storey of Loseling. This is a protector chapel, the central image being Yamantaka. There are also statues of Guhyasamaja and Chakrasamvara; six-armed and four-faced Mahakalas; the outer, inner and secret aspects of Dharmaraja; Pelden Lhamo; Vaishravana; and Dorje Drakden. A beautiful *tangka* of Yamantaka and consort hangs on the right-hand wall.

Gomang College (6)

The Chapels. The first chapel contains the longevity triad of Amitayus, Tara and Vijaya. Scriptures are stored in the walls.

The second Chapel is the largest and most important of the three chapels on the ground floor of Gomang. A wide assortment of lamas and deities, raised on several tiers, fills the room. The central figure on the uppermost level at the back is Buddha Akshobhya. To the left is Shakyamuni and to the right a smaller Akshobhya. Immediately beneath are three more statues, the central image being Shakyamuni, with Maitreya on the left and Avalokiteshvara on the right. Beneath sits a youthful Tsongkhapa, the principal figure of the thousand other images of the master found in the main hall. Below and in front of Tsongkhapa are a row of five smaller statues depicting the first five incarnations of the famous Gomang lama Jamyang Zhepa. Many other smaller images surround these central figures and there are two stupas containing the remains of the second and third abbots of Gomang.

The third chapel is rather messy. The Twenty-one Taras are arranged in three tiers along the back wall. Along the left wall, in four tiers, are the Sixteen Arhats.

The Main Hall. In the far left-hand corner of this hall are two images of six-armed Mahakala. The first statue past the doorway to the first chapel is of the rarely depicted Tsangyang Gyatso, the Sixth Dalai Lama. Continuing to the right are Tsongkhapa; Dipamkara, a Buddha of the Past; two more images of Tsongkhapa; a thousand-armed Avalokiteshvara; Tsongkhapa; and the Seventh Dalai Lama. Instead of a central image, there is a large opening that leads to the main chapel in the rear (it is presently barred). Further to the right are images of Maitreya, Amitayus, Jamyang Chöje, Tsongkhapa, and an eleven-headed, eight-armed Avalokiteshvara.

The Upper Storey. As with Loseling College, there is just a single protector chapel on the upper storey in Gomang. The main image is a gold-framed Mahakala that is associated with Chankya Rölpa'i Dorje, the second incarnation of Jamyang Zhepa. To either side of it are other aspects of Mahakala and to the far left a statue of Yamantaka. Some minor local deities, converted to protect Buddhism, are also present. *Women are not permitted to enter this chapel.*

Deyang College (7)
The Chapel. The main image in the single chapel of Deyang College is Maitreya. To the left are Jangchub Pelden, a renowned lama of the college, and the Seventh Dalai Lama, while Tsongkhapa, Shakyamuni, Yönten Gyatso – who was the first abbot of Ratö Monastery and the second abbot of Deyang College – and the Third Dalai Lama sit to the right.

View over the Kyichu valley from the roof of Gomang College.

The Main Hall. Old statues of Tsongkhapa and his two chief disciples are the main images in this hall. The female deities Dugkarma, White Tara and Tara Cintamani are also on the altar. The Fifth Dalai Lama is the only other lama present; he is especially important in Deyang College as traditionally the monks have based their philosophical studies on a text composed by him. In the far left-hand corner of the hall is the protector Dorje Drakden, and in the opposite corner Pelden Lhamo.

On the upper storey is a small protector chapel dedicated to Dorje Drakden.

The main doorway of Nechung painted with images of human skins.

7. NECHUNG MONASTERY

Nechung is only a few minutes' walk from Drepung Monastery (see Chapter 6, above). It can be visited either before or after seeing Drepung. It is open daily (except perhaps Sunday) from 9 am to 4 pm with the usual long lunchbreak, when the chapels are closed. There is no admission charge.

HISTORY
Nechung Monastery has an important place in the history of Tibet. Until 1959 the State Oracle of Tibet lived here. The oracle was the medium through whom the special protector of the Tibetan government, Dorje Drakden, would give advice to the Dalai Lamas and leaders of the country. No major decisions of the Tibetan government would be made without first consulting the Nechung oracle.

The Nechung community of monks have always had a special relationship with deity Dorje Drakden. It is believed that this deity was first recognised and propitiated in India, and the Nechung community was initially established somewhere near the Indo-Tibetan border. Because of war it then moved to Samye Monastery, and at the time of the Fifth Dalai Lama came to its present site near Drepung Monastery, where it was given the name 'Nechung' (lit.: 'small place').

In 1959 the oracle escaped to India with the Dalai Lama, settled in Dharamsala, and continued to serve the Tibetan government in exile. He died in 1985 and a successor to his post has not yet been found. (John Avedon's *In Exile from the Land of Snows* has an excellent chapter on the Nechung oracle.) The monastery was severely damaged during the cultural revolution and only during the last couple of years has much progress been made in its restoration. Twelve monks now live here, compared with the sixty or seventy who ran the monastery before the Chinese occupation. The monks are not strictly affiliated to any of the four orders of Tibetan Buddhism.

THE SITE
You enter the monastery through a set of doors macabrely painted with human skins and walk through a dark hall before reaching the first two chapels. The chapel to the left is the protector chapel dedicated to Dorje Drakden. Two images of the protector are found here; on the wall to the left is a large, old *tangka* showing him in his peaceful aspect as a wise old sage; a small statue against the wall at right-angles to the *tangka* depicts

him in his better known wrathful aspect. Between these two images are the remains of a tree-stump. It is believed that when the monastery was founded on its present site, Dorje Drakden took up residence in this tree. Consequently the chapel is called the 'Wrathful Tree-Trunk Chapel'. There is also a life-size statue of Padmasambhava to the left of the chapel.

The adjacent chapel on the ground floor contains a single image of Jowo Shakyamuni. None of the other statues that surrounded this central figure have yet been replaced. Above where the caretaker-monk sits are three very fine *tangkas* of Ekajati, Yamantaka with consort and Tsedrekma. More *tangkas* of various lamas and deities hang from the other walls.

To reach the **upper storeys** of the monastery you must go out the way you came in and enter a small door to the right. This takes you to the first floor, where two adjacent chapels have been restored. The first is a large room that was used as an audience room for the Dalai Lama whenever

Nechung Monastery with a stele and two incense burners in the foreground.

he visited Nechung. The large throne at the back of the room was used by the Fifth to the Fourteenth Dalai Lamas. There are a number of old and beautiful statues along the altar that were recently offered to Nechung by the monks of Drepung. On the far left is a wonderfully expressive image of the Fifth Dalai Lama. Next to him are Tsongkhapa and two Buddhas. Jowo Shakyamuni is enshrined in a glass case. Next to him is Maitreya. To the right of the throne are Tsongkhapa and his two chief disciples and Avalokiteshvara. A fine old *tangka* of Samvara hangs to the far left by the door.

Adjoining this chapel is a smaller room dedicated to Tsongkhapa. A large, newly-made image of the master sits behind glass flanked, as usual, by Gyeltsab Je and Khedrup Je, his two chief disciples. There are also smaller images of the Buddha, Avalokiteshvara, Tara and Tsongkhapa.

Climbing up to the roof you find a single chapel containing a magnificent statue of Padmasambhava, made in 1981 by a Tibetan sculptor living in Lhasa. It is a four-metre-high seated form with an angry expression. The Guru is bedecked in robes of very fine, old Chinese brocade.

Next door to Nechung Monastery is another complex of buildings that has recently been turned into a **Monastic School.** Young monks from different parts of Tibet and from all four main orders of Tibetan Buddhism come here to study Buddhist philosophy and doctrine, using mainly Gelukpa texts. There are at present one hundred and twenty monks training here. One can visit the school but the main chapel-cum-assembly hall is newly and functionally decorated with little that would interest a visitor.

8. RAMOCHE TEMPLE

(GYU-TÖ, THE UPPER TANTRIC COLLEGE)

Ramoche is in the city of Lhasa, to the north of the Dekyi Shar Lam at the end of a narrow street called the Tun Tril Lam. It is easily reached by foot from anywhere in the old city. It is open all day long and no admission is charged, though this is liable to change.

HISTORY

The Ramoche Temple is one of the oldest religious buildings in Lhasa. It was first erected by Songtsen Gampo's Chinese wife in the seventh century and to house the statue of the Jowo Shakyamuni that she brought with her to Tibet. When this statue was moved to the Jokhang after Songtsen Gampo's death, it was replaced by the image of Akshobhya Vajra brought as part of the dowry of Trisun, the king's Nepalese wife. Originally it was built in Chinese style but after repeated damage by fire it was rebuilt in the Tibetan fashion. The Ramoche was always overshadowed by the Jokhang and in 1474 it was taken over by Kunga Döndrup, a second generation disciple of Tsongkhapa, and used as the main assembly hall for the newly-founded Upper Tantric College (Gyu-tö). Up to five hundred monks lived and studied at the Upper Tantric College, their main residential and study area being across the road from the Ramoche (this has now been converted into a school). As with the Lower Tantric College (Gyu-me), some of these monks would enter the college at a young age and specialise in chanting, the construction of mandalas and the performance of complex tantric rituals; others would enter only after having completed their doctrinal training at one of the principal Gelukpa monasteries around Lhasa.

The temple suffered considerable damage during the cultural revolution and was closed until the summer of 1985. Forty monks have now returned and reconstruction work is in progress. The main image of Akshobhya Vajra has recently been replaced; it is said that it was broken in two during the revolution and one part carried off to China. Although Ramoche is reemerging as a place for pilgrimage, any course of study has yet to be resumed.

OPPOSITE *In the space of a year the interior of Ramoche has changed from a 'shrine' to Mao Tse-tung to its present role as a renovated monastery. The first photo was taken in February 1985, the second in April 1986.*

Akshobhya Vajra, the main statue in Ramoche, brought to Tibet in the seventh century. It was badly damaged during the cultural revolution.

THE SITE

Upon entering Ramoche you pass along a hallway that takes you past a protector chapel on the left and a wall painting of Dorje Yu-dru-ma, the special protectress of the Upper Tantric College, on the right. The main hall is adorned with much fresh paint and new brocade, with the long cushions of the monks lined down the centre. To the left a glass cased statue of Guhyasamaja faces you and to the right are three other statues: Tsongkhapa, Kunga Döndrup – the founder of the Upper Tantric College – and Trijang Rinpoche, the late Junior Tutor of the present Dalai Lama.

The main shrine is to the rear of the temple. After passing the Four Guardian Kings you ascend a few steps to face the precious image of Akshobhya Vajra, a representation of Shakyamuni at the age of eight brought to Tibet by Songtsen Gampo's Nepalese wife. As is the Jowo image in the Jokhang, this statue is sumptuously bedecked with brocades and ornaments and seated in an ornate silver shrine. Around him stand the Eight Great Bodhisattvas, and two wrathful protectors guard the doorway. When we first visited this shrine in 1985 the main image was a standing statue of Mao Tsetung, albeit with his ears and fingers tweaked off.

There is an internal circumambulation path around the main shrine as well as a newly constructed circumambulation route around the entire temple. The upper storeys are still being repaired and at the time of writing contain no chapels. From the roof one has a good view of **Tsomoling Monastery** and **Zhide Dratsang**, neither of which are active.

Two old monks who have recently returned to Gyu-me.

9. GYU-ME

(THE LOWER TANTRIC COLLEGE)

Gyu-me is on the Dekyi Shar Lam. If you are walking in the direction of the Potala from the Banak Shöl, it is about three hundred metres from the guest house, on your right. From the street it looks just like any other Lhasa town house, but the doorway can be recognised by the golden Sanskrit lettering painted along the top. You can also see a white cloth showing a Dharma Wheel and two deer hanging in front of the main monastery building inside the courtyard. It is open all day and there is no charge to enter.

HISTORY

The Lower Tantric College was founded in 1433 by Je Sherab Senge, a disciple of Tsongkhapa who vowed to his teacher that he would take responsibility for preserving his Tantric teachings. The college was first known as Se Gyu-pa and was not located in Lhasa but on a mountain called Lhunpo Se in the province of Tsang. It moved to its present site in the city of Lhasa only at the time of the Fifth Dalai Lama. Like the Upper Tantric College it specialised in training young monks in tantric rituals, and elder Geshes in tantric doctrine and practice. There were five hundred and fifty places in the college and the monks would live in the quadrangle of buildings that line the courtyard.

Gyu-me was completely desecrated during the cultural revolution and its buildings turned into houses for the local people. It was reopened in May 1985 but there has been relatively little renovation. The main hall has been cleaned and tidied but is not yet in use (while we were there it was being used as a place to dry sheets of freshly printed editions of the Kangyur). The thirty-five old monks who have returned as well as a handful of novices assemble in a smaller chapel on the upper storey. The reincarnate lama, now a layman, also lives here. The chapel contains no old images and only a few modern ones. The two main statues are those of Tsongkhapa and Je Sherab Senge, the founder of Gyu-me. Smaller images of the Thirteenth Dalai Lama, the Buddha, Yamantaka and two sets of Tsongkhapa and his two chief disciples also adorn the altar.

The monks have revived some of the major monthly ceremonies recited in the college but as yet they have no abbot and give no instructions to the younger novices.

10. PALHALUPUK TEMPLE

A convenient time to visit this small temple, as well as the Tangtong Gyelpo Temple next door, is after you have finished seeing the Potala and return to the main road beneath Chakpori. Just cross the road and turn right down a small street, which leads you around the base of the hill. Palhalupuk is about three hundred yards on your right, and to reach it you must climb a couple of flights of stairs. It is open all day and there is no charge for admission.

HISTORY

This curious and delightfully alive temple is formed from a cave at the base of the Chakpori hill. Its name means the 'Naga's Grotto of the Stone Gods', the slightly dank, subterranean cavern suggesting an abode of the underwater nagas, filled with the wonderful treasures these beings are supposed to possess. The cave is believed to have been used as a retreat by King Songtsen Gampo in the seventh century and is also associated with his Nepalese Queen. Whether this is true or not, the cave is of undoubted antiquity and fortunately has survived the destruction wreaked upon the rest of Chakpori above.

THE SITE

You enter the cave by a staircase that leads you to a small ante-room. Here are sometimes exhibited exquisite butter-sculptures made by the fourteen monks who look after the temple.

Nearly all the images in the Palhalupuk are brightly painted relief stone carvings emerging from the walls and the central column of rock that seems to support the cave. The main image facing you as you come in is that of Shakyamuni. By his shoulders stand Shariputra and Maudgalyayana, his two chief arhat disciples. Maitreya and Avalokiteshvara stand to either side of them. Rows of bodhisattvas greet you from the walls as you circumambulate the central column. On this column you pass larger carvings of three Buddhas: Akshobhya, the Medicine Buddha and Shakyamuni. Along the left-hand wall you may notice a hole with a loose stone inside. Tradition maintains that Songtsen Gampo would beat this stone on the wall whenever it was time for his attendants living above to bring him his meals. At the back of the cave is an uncarved section of the wall behind which are said to be concealed the jewels of the king's Nepalese wife. A small altar stands to the right with an archaic representation of Pelden Lhamo as well as a small Padmasambhava and Yamantaka carved in stone. The final images you see are those of Songtsen Gampo, his two wives and two foremost ministers.

Below the Palhalupuk Temple is another cave but it contains nothing of great note. Niches have been hollowed out along the walls and modern paintings and prints placed in them. Between the two caves is also a small room where the monks perform their daily services.

Close by the Palhalupuk is another small temple built on the side of the same hill. This is the **Tangtong Gyelpo Temple.** Tangtong Gyelpo was one of these remarkable men whose genius and skill made a lasting impression in numerous fields. Born in 1385 he was a contemporary of Tsongkhapa and a lay adept of the Zhangpa Kagyu order of Tibetan Buddhism. He travelled extensively throughout Tibet and in India and

The interior of Palhalupuk.

Pelden Lhamo altar in Palhalupuk. Padmasambhava and Yamantaka are depicted to either side of the archaic representation of Pelden Lhamo. A skull-cup filled with chang, a traditional tantric offering, can be seen in the foreground.

China as well, and everywhere he went he would construct temples and, where needed, his famous iron bridges, remains of which were still observed by travellers vi-siting Tibet in the early decades of this century. He scored a number of operas relating the lives of the early Tibetan kings, which until recently were performed during the A-che festival. He was also a doctor and is attributed with the discovery of two particular medicinal compounds. He died in 1509 at the ripe old age of 125.

Tangtong Gyelpo himself founded a temple on Chakpori. It was renovated in the 1930's by a well-known physician called Khyenrab Norbu but was completely destroyed in the cultural revolution. Only in the last few years has it been reconstructed at its present site on the lower slopes of the hill.

The old sagacious and smiling figure of Tangtong Gyelpo with long white hair, beard and robes is the main statue in the small temple. To either side are a thousand smaller identical images, lined up on shelves along the back wall.

11. LUKHANG: THE NAGA CHAPEL

This chapel is immediately behind the Potala on an island in the middle of a small lake, connected to the shore by a footbridge. It is a part of the Ching Dröl Chi Ling, a small park with trees and paths, which can be reached by turning right by the post office, continuing past the CAAC office to where the road turns sharply right and entering the park through the large wrought-iron gates. This is also a short cut to the Public Security Office and the Bank of China. It is open daily and there is no admission charge.

HISTORY

When the construction of the Potala Palace was finally completed at the end of the seventeenth century, removal of the earth used for the mortar had left a large depression behind the building. This was filled with water and named the 'Lake of the Naga King'. Shortly after, the Sixth Dalai Lama built a small chapel on an artificial mound created in the middle of the lake both as a shrine to the Naga King and as a personal retreat. This 'Naga Chapel' is a square, 'mandalic' building with three floors. At present only the uppermost floor is open and in use as a chapel, although, with the permission of the monks, you can also visit the room on the first floor.

THE SITE

The main image in the chapel is that of the Buddha 'Luwang gi Gyalpo', the 'King of the Nagas', who is dedicated to teaching the nagas and is recognisable by the cluster of snake-like beings (nagas) rising behind his head as a kind of hood, or halo. To the left is a thousand-armed Avalokiteshvara and to the right Tara. In front of the chapel, facing the Potala, is a section separated off by a screen, which the Dalai Lamas would use as a retreat chamber. The Thirteenth Dalai Lama, for example, spent much time meditating here.

Of greatest interest in this chapel, however, are the murals that cover three of the walls, depicting subjects that are rarely seen elsewhere in temples in Tibet today. Unfortunately, but perhaps for the good of the paintwork, they are protected by a chicken-wire grille that somewhat hinders the viewing of the finer details. (Namkhai Norbu's book *The Crystal and the Way of Light* contains photographs and explanations of these images.)

The Lukhang.

If you have just walked clockwise around the main altar, the first wall to your left (west) is illustrated with images of yogis demonstrating the physical postures required for the practice of the 'six yogas of Naropa' and other tantric methods. On the next wall (north) are paintings of the stages of human life, beginning with sexual intercourse and conception and culminating in sickness, ageing and death. Detailed anatomical pictures of the human body with its various inner organs and energy-channels as conceived in the Tibetan medical tradition are also shown to explain how the body is subject to imbalances that result in sickness and decay.

Mahayana Buddhism teaches that after death one enters an intermediate state (Tib. *bardo*) before the next rebirth. The mural now continues with detailed images of the peaceful and wrathful deities that appear as visions to the person passing through this post-death state. These paintings are based on the descriptions found in the *Tibetan Book of the Dead*. At the end of this wall is a picture of Padmasambhava holding a vajra to the head of a horse-riding demon. He is thus shown converting a Bön deity to Buddhism. To the upper left the same demon is shown transformed into the lion-riding protector called 'Mana', a special guardian relied upon by the Dalai Lamas.

The third wall (east) depicts the eighty-four mahasiddhas of India in their eccentric and often provocative poses, their faces expressing the bliss and inner power conferred upon them by their tantric realisations. One can also see the twenty-five adepts who worked with Padmasambhava in the conversion of the Tibetans to Buddhism, as well as the Six Ornaments and Two Supreme Indian philosophers. The old and damaged mural past the window shows the construction of Samye Monastery.

The single room on the first floor immediately below is used as a living and working place by the three monks who are in charge of this chapel. It contains some excellent murals in very good condition (and, as yet, unobscured by chicken-wire). The mural on the west and south walls is an illustration of the story of the mythical youth Pema Öbar. Starting from the left and proceeding clockwise, the paintings recount how Pema Öbar's father is drowned while searching for jewels in the ocean; how the boy is cared for by his mother and protected by taking refuge in the Triple Gem of Buddhism; how he too goes off in search of jewels and returns home with his riches; how the evil king of the country confiscates the jewels and banishes Pema Öbar to the land of the cannibal-spirits; how Pema Öbar converts the cannibal king to Buddhism and is freed to return home; how he is then killed upon his arrival by the evil king; how his ashes are returned to life by the dakinis; how the evil king sees the boy and the dakinis flying through the sky and is tricked into going with them; how they take him to the cannibal king where he is eaten alive by the cannibal-spirits; and how Pema Öbar returns triumphantly to his home country, becomes king and turns the kingdom into a Buddhist state.

The murals on the east and north walls show deeds from the lives of two legendary Indian kings, the 'Northern King' and the 'Southern King'.

12. ANI SANGKHUNG NUNNERY

Although this nunnery can be reached by a short cut through the back streets of Lhasa behind the Jokhang, it is probably easiest to go first to the mosque, which is reached either by the narrow cobbled street that starts at the south eastern corner of the Barkor, or by going down the Ling Kor Lam and then turning right at the last turning before the Tsang Gyu Shar Lam. From the mosque take the small road going west: the nunnery is about two hundred yards on your right but difficult to spot. Ask the local people for the 'Ani Gompa'. It is open all day and as yet there is no entrance charge.

HISTORY

Ani Sangkhung is the only active nunnery in Lhasa today. The foundations for a temple are said to have been laid on this site as early as the seventh century, the place being associated with Songtsen Gampo. Initially it was a monastery and only in the fifteenth century was it enlarged and turned into a nunnery by a disciple of Tsongkhapa called Tongten. It used to house more than a hundred nuns. The building was abandoned during the cultural revolution and began to collapse through neglect. It has been working as a nunnery again only since 1984 and now there are forty-four nuns, most of whom are young. Their main duty is the conducting of rituals, primarily to Avalokiteshvara and Tara.

THE SITE

The assembly hall is newly and brightly decorated. The main image on the altar is a thousand-armed Avalokiteshvara, to the left of whom is a statue of Pabongka Rinpoche, made in 1941, the year he died, and to the far right a well-made figure of Vajra Yogini, the main tantric deity of the nunnery. There are three notable *tangkas* in this room: one of Pelden Lhamo, the torma of whom is in a glass case covered by a red satin cloth on the altar; an old one of Vajrayogini; and one of Padmasambhava mounted in very beautiful brocade. On the upper walls are the only murals surviving from the pre-cultural revolution days. They depict Tsongkhapa and his two chief disciples; the three main tantric deities of the Gelukpa, Yamantaka, Samvara, and Guhyasamaja; a white and a green Tara; Avalokiteshvara; and Vajrayogini.

If you go around the back of the nunnery, on the ground floor there is a long room of unusual shape and design, dedicated to King Songtsen

Four nuns outside the main temple at Ani Sangkhung.

Gampo. He is said to have meditated here and through the force of his concentration diverted the course of the Kyichu river, when it threatened to flood the site where the Jokhang was being constructed. At the far end of the room, covered by a glass canopy, is a sunken pit. At the bottom of this was the king's meditation chamber and there is now a small statue of him there. Tongten, the founder of the nunnery, is also said to have spent time in retreat here.

13. SMALL TEMPLES AND SHRINES

A. **Gongkar Chöde Branch Temple.** This very small temple is immediately behind the Jokhang and entered from the north side of the Barkor. It is on the first floor of a building on the right of a small alley leading off the street. It is a Sakya temple affiliated to the Gongkar Chöde Monastery near the Gongkar (Lhasa) Airport (see Chapter 24, below). At present it is nothing more than a shrine to the protector Pelgön Dramtso, an aspect of Mahakala, a life-size statue of whom dominates the room from the right-hand corner. There are numerous torma and butter sculptures on display but no other images of note. It is an active city temple with apparently a lot of support. Two old monks live here.

B. **Nechung Branch Temple.** This temple is very close to the Gonkar Chöde Branch Temple. It is reached by continuing down the same alley and turning left at the end. This brings you out into a small courtyard facing the entrance of the monastery. It is affiliated to the main Nechung Monastery near Drepung (see Chapter 7, above) and, like its parent temple, adheres to no particular sect. It is primarily involved in the performance of rituals to the various protectors of the Nyingma, Sakya and Geluk traditions. The main protector is Dorje Drakden, the deity who speaks through the Nechung oracle and is relied upon by the Tibetan government. Previously more than a hundred monks lived in this monastery. Now there are about twenty.

The murals in the assembly hall have been badly eroded and only one section, that depicting Dorje Drakden, on the left as you go in, has been restored. Those on the upper wall by the skylight are in better condition. They depict Tsongkhapa and his two chief disciples; Atisha, Drom Tönpa and Ngog Legpa'i Sherab; Padmasambhava, Trisong Detsen and Shantarakshita; Vajradhara and Vajrasattva; and several Buddhas.

The chapel in the slightly raised room at the back of the assembly hall has Padmasambhava as its main image. The three newly-made accompanying images are of the Fifth Dalai Lama, Tsongkhapa and Vajradhara. The chapel is guarded by Dorje Drakden, to the left, and a wrathful Pelden Lhamo, to the right.

On the upper storey there are no chapels but from the rooftop one has an excellent view of the rear of the Jokhang and its roofs. While we were

Unfinished clay statues of the five directional protectors (Nechung Branch Temple).

there clay images of the Five Directional Protectors were being made. These may soon find their way into the chapel downstairs.

C. **Tenggye Ling.** Tenggye Ling is one of the four 'ling' temples of Lhasa, the other three being Tsomo Ling, Kunde Ling (destroyed) and Tsechok Ling. The Fifth Dalai Lama decreed that the regent of a Dalai Lama should be selected from one of these monasteries (although in practice this was not always so). Tenggye Ling is situated to the west of the old city, south of the Dekyi Shar Lam, amidst a maze of old Lhasa town houses. In 1912 it was partially damaged for siding with the Chinese in the conflict of the same year and lost its former prestige. Shortly after the Chinese seized power in 1959, most of Tenggye Ling was turned into living quarters for the army and the local people. During the cultural revolution the last remaining chapels were destroyed. It is still mainly a residential compound converted into numerous small apartments, but a couple of years ago a single chapel was resurrected on the upper storey at the back of this complex. It is in very poor condition and the local residents have been able to afford only a rather ramshackle altar. Padmasambhava is the main image and is surrounded by an assortment of small bronzes and modern prints of different deities. Traditionally, Tenggye Ling was affiliated with Loseling College of Drepung. It was also connected to Samye Monastery, being the Lhasa home for one of Samye's protectors. This affiliation with Samye is still evident in the choice of photographs on the altar.

D. **Kar-nga Dong Shrine**. This small, untidy-looking shrine is built at the base of the Potala, against the easternmost flank of the hill. It is across the road from the CAAC office and can be recognised easily by the rows of prayer wheels outside. It contains a number of relief carvings on large slabs of stone, some of which are supposed to date back to the time of the founding of the Jokhang. The figures portrayed are Shakyamuni, Acala, the Guardian King of the East, Padmasambhava, and Avalokiteshvara. The caretaker-monk said that these carvings,

Two young monks on pilgrimage from Amdo.

which are not engraved on the rock wall of the hill, were taken from the Jokhang and placed here in 1980.

E. Meru Monastery. This large complex is on the Dekyi Shar Lam next door to Gyume, the Lower Tantric College. It has now been turned into a dance and drama school. The main buildings are still intact and you can see the original pillars in the entrance way and the faded remains of some murals. It was first founded by King Ralpachen in the eighth century but destroyed shortly after by Langdarma. After its later reconstruction it became one of the largest and most prestigious Gelukpa monasteries in the city.

F. Tsomo Ling. One of the four 'ling' temples in Lhasa, this temple was connected to Sera Me College and founded by a former tutor of one of the Dalai Lamas. The large residence of this lama stands empty opposite the main entrance to Sera Me (see Chapter 5, above). Several of the Dalai Lama's regents also came from this temple. Tsomo Ling has long ceased to serve as a monastery and is now a rambling compound filled with private dwellings. It is located to the north of the Dekyi Shar Lam, west of Ramoche Temple.

G. Zhide Dratsang. Situated close to Tsomo Ling but further west, Zhide Dratsang was traditionally connected to Reting Monastery. Now it is literally being left to fall down. Although surrounded by apartments and small houses built on its grounds, the roof of the main hall is collapsing. If you climb to the upper storey, you can peer into the empty assembly hall and see some murals of the Buddha and Tsongkhapa smiling at the decay around them.

H. Kumbum Lhakhang. This single large building was a massive shrine to Tsongkhapa. Inside it were kept one hundred thousand images of the master of all different sizes and sculpted from all manner of materials. In the cultural revolution the valuable images were plundered and the less valuable ones discarded. The building was then turned into a granary, which it still is today. It is the first main building on the right as you turn north off the Dekyi Shar Lam and walk towards the Ramoche Temple. It is easily recognisable by the stinking latrine that has been built in front of its main entrance.

I. Tarpa Ling. Tarpa Ling is to the south of the Dekyi Shar Lam to the east of the open market before you reach the Barkor. This used to be the temple in which an oracle who served as a medium for Pelden Lhamo, Mamo and three other deities traditionally lived. It too has been closed as a monastic centre. Its main hall is used as a storeroom and apparently still contains some good murals. The buildings in the courtyard have been turned into dwellings for the people.

J. **Karma Shar Monastery**. This small temple with tall and noble stone walls is behind the Jokhang and can be reached only by a narrow cobbled street in the old city. It has recently been put back into use by a group of local lay Buddhists who assemble there for an hour or so each evening to recite prayers. We were unable to go inside (having come at the wrong time of day) but were told that a few statues and murals remain. It is an old temple of the Gelukpa order.

K. **Trijang Labrang**. This former residence of the Trijang line of reincarnate lamas is situated at the far end of the road that leads from the mosque past the Ani Sangkhung Nunnery. The former incarnation of Trijang Rinpoche, who died in India in 1981, was the junior tutor to the present Dalai Lama. It now houses the offices of the state electricity board and is used as an apartment building by the local people. No trace of any murals is evident.

L. **Tsechok Ling**. Founded by Yeshe Gyeltsen, the tutor of the Eighth Dalai Lama, Tsechok Ling is another of the four 'ling' temples of Lhasa. It is located on the south bank of the Kyichu river. To reach it you must cross the bridge and turn right towards the army encampment. The main building is still standing but is now used as a storeroom. It has been severely defaced and no trace of religious paintings or decoration remains.

14. THE TIBETAN MEDICAL CENTRE (MENTSI KHANG)

The medical centre is easy to find. It is the long white concrete building by the plaza that faces the Jokhang. There is supposed to be a 10 RMB charge for foreigners to be guided around the hospital but this may not be asked. You can receive traditional Tibetan examination and treatment but you have to line up with the local patients. The only charge is for the medicines prescribed and is not likely to exceed 10 to 15 RMB.

HISTORY

Tibetan medicine is an ancient tradition of healing that traces its origins back to the Buddha himself. It is based on four tantras attributed to the Buddha that were translated from the Sanskrit and put into their present form in the eighth century by the father of Tibetan medicine, Yutok Yönten Gonpo (729-854). Yutok was the precocious son of a doctor who studied medicine under both Indian and Chinese physicians, thus assimilating the insights of both traditions. He became the personal physician to two Tibetan kings, Tride Tsukten and Trisong Detsen. Another influential figure in Tibetan medical history was Desi Sanggye Gyatso, the regent of the Fifth Dalai Lama. In addition to being a monk and politician, he also was a doctor who composed two important works on medicine: the *Baidurya Ngönpo*, a word by word commentary to the four medical tantras, and the *Baidurya Karpo*, a treatise on astrology. He also founded the Medical Centre at its original site on Chakpori in the late seventeenth century.

TIBETAN MEDICINE

One of the principles of Tibetan medicine is that the basis of good health is the maintenance of harmony between the three vital humours of the body: energy ('wind'), bile and phlegm. Psychologically, these three humours are related to the 'three mental poisons' described in Buddhism: ignorance, desire and anger respectively. Illness occurs through imbalance of the humours and can be treated by applying remedies that reestablish their harmony. Diagnosis is made mainly through a careful analysis of the pulse, the beat and subtle movements of which can be used by the doctor to recognise the nature and location of the particular imbalance. Treatments vary but the most common is a course of herbal remedies in the form of pills.

Astrology plays a significant role in Tibetan medicine, for when a pulse diagnosis is being made, the doctor must be conscious of the external influences upon its beat. These influences include the season, the budding of certain plants, and the movement of heavenly bodies. If these factors are not detected and accounted for, an exact diagnosis of the patient's ailment is not possible. The study of astrology enables the doctor to understand these influences and recognise them in the pulse-beat. Astrology is also used to determine the course of action to be taken by relatives (i.e. the prayers and rituals to be performed) when a close one dies. By studying a person's chart, a doctor is also able to prescribe preventative treatments to counteract negative astrological influences that are liable to occur at certain times.

THE SITE

The present modern building that houses the Medical Centre was completed in 1980. It serves primarily as an outpatient clinic and its doctors see up to six hundred patients a day. Each of the rooms on the ground and first floors specialises in either certain maladies or certain forms of treatment. There are facilities for treating external wounds, internal ailments, ear and eye disorders, heart problems and gynaecological complaints. There are rooms set aside for minor surgery, 'golden needle' treatment, diagnosis and astrological consultations. A large herbal dispensary is right across from the main entrance. In addition, certain forms of Western and Chinese medication are also available.

There are about two hundred qualified Tibetan doctors presently working in Lhasa. Many work here at the centre, while others are based at the newly opened two hundred and fifty bed hospital in another part of the city. The training school for young doctors is now also housed in a separate building.

On the third floor, at roof level, it is possible to visit two rooms. The one on the left as you climb on to the roof is a kind of shrine in honour of the Tibetan medical tradition. Behind glass at the end of the room are statues of three of the most influential figures in the history of Tibetan medicine: in the centre sits Yutok Yönten Gonpo; to the left is Desi Sanggye Gyatso; and to the right Khyenrab Norbu, a contemporary physician who died in 1962 and was instrumental in establishing the Medical Centre at its present site in the city of Lhasa (the buildings he erected have since been replaced by the present one). Along the side of the room are the Kangyur and Tengyur, the canon of Buddhist scriptures, and at the end of the room near the door, a complete collection of the principal medical treatises studied in Tibet.

Facing this shrine, on the other side of the roof, is another room, which contains a collection of medical *tangkas*. The *tangkas* hanging from the walls are copies of the seventeenth century originals kept in secure wooden boxes on the floor. They depict the anatomy of the body, both its skeletal and organic make-up, and the subtle energy-channels that are described in the medical tantras. They also show the various plants used in the preparation of medicines. If you ask, it is possible to view the very finely painted and technically precise originals. A collection of medical texts is also stored at the far end of this room. Above them hang some more *tangkas* with what seem to be trees painted on them. These are pictorial descriptions of the structure of the medical tantras: the tantra itself is the trunk, which contains chapters (branches), each with its own sub-sections (leaves). Another *tangka* shows the Fifth Dalai Lama surrounded by important figures from the lineage of the medical teachings.

15. THE LHASA MUSEUM

This drab L-shaped building is located directly below the Potala on the corner opposite the main Post Office. It is open only from 10 am to 3 pm on Saturdays and Sundays. There is a 20 Fen entrance fee.

Some years ago this museum was often reported in the foreign press as the place where relics of the evils of the former regime were put on display. Plaster statues of monks torturing small boys and so forth were shown. With the current change in attitude amongst the Chinese, these embarrassing reminders of the cultural revolution were quietly loaded onto the backs of trucks late one dark night and have now disappeared, hopefully into oblivion.

The museum currently displays a wide range of Tibetan cultural artefacts, most of them modern replicas, which gives one an idea of the everyday objects used by Tibetans from different walks of life and regions in their country. The walls display numerous colour and black and white photographs showing the notable historic buildings in Tibet (black and white pictures meaning that the places no longer stand intact). Some interesting photographs of some of the more remote native people in their traditional dress can also be found. There is also a room showing the variety of flora found in Tibet as well as several geological samples.

The historical section begins with photographs of murals depicting the early legends of Tibetan history, such as that of the monkey descending from the sky and mating with the demoness. It continues with the introduction of Buddhism and illustrates this with examples of some early handwritten and printed scriptures, none of which are particularly remarkable. A stele from the time of Ralpachen (a copy?) stands in the corner of the room. In conclusion there are photographs of the 'liberation' showing lorries full of cheering people outside the Potala beneath portraits of Mao, and glass cases displaying the battered enamel mugs and worn socks of the People's Liberation Army.

A mock temple is in the adjoining room. Papier-maché monks sit motionless engaged in a non-existent ritual. A sand mandala and some butter sculptures are displayed in glass cases. Some attractive *tangkas* hang from the walls.

By Western standards the museum is disappointing. It contains virtually nothing of genuine historical interest and far less than the Tibetan sections of the major museums in Europe or America. Moreover, all the accompanying texts to the exhibits are in either Tibetan or Chinese. No information is available in English.

CENTRAL
TIBET

16. GANDEN MONASTERY

Ganden is located about 40 km east of Lhasa. To reach it you must cross the Lhasa bridge and head out along the main road in the direction of Medrogungkar. The monastery, or what remains of it, is on the hillside, hidden from the road itself. About half way to Medrogungkar you turn sharp right, and after a couple of kilometres sharp right again. For the next half hour you climb up a tortuous series of hairpin bends that ends in the ruins of the monastery itself. There is a bus or a truck that leaves Lhasa daily at 6.30 am (or whenever it fills up) from the south-eastern corner of the Barkor. This is a pilgrim bus and may stop in Ganden only long enough for you to race round the chapels and make butter offerings in each one before returning to the city. The driver should not charge more than 5 RMB. If you want to spend the day in Ganden you should get together with some other people and hire a landcruiser or minibus. We paid 170 FEC for a landcruiser from the Taxi Company. The monastery is open daily and an entrance charge of 5 RMB may be asked. The monks claim that all this money goes towards reconstruction and not to the government.

About 15 km out from Lhasa you will pass nearby **Tselgungtang Monastery**. *This is off the road, on the hillside to the right. Tselgungtang was once a very important Kagyu monastery and was founded in 1175 by Tsöntru Trakpa (or Lama Zhang), a disciple of Gampopa's nephew. It became the centre of the Tsel sub-order of the Kagyupa and in the twelfth and thirteenth centuries wielded considerable political influence. Much of the monastery was destroyed in the cultural revolution and what remains stands deserted. The large, impressive assembly hall now seems to be used as a storehouse.*

Further along the road to Ganden you pass through **Taktse Dzong** *(formerly Dechen Dzong), a small town recognisable by the steep hillock around which it is built. It is possible to climb to the remains of the castle on the hill. There is also a small temple there. Shortly after this town is the newly built* **Taktse Zamchen**, *the 'Great Taktse Bridge', where the road crosses the river on its way to the region of Penpo.*

HISTORY

Tsongkhapa was born in 1357 in the north-eastern province of Tibet, Amdo. During the time of the Third Dalai Lama his birthplace was marked by the erection of the Kumbum Jampa Ling Monastery near Xining. While still very young he was recognised as possessing unusual

OPPOSITE *Amitayus (Netang Drölma Lhakhang)*

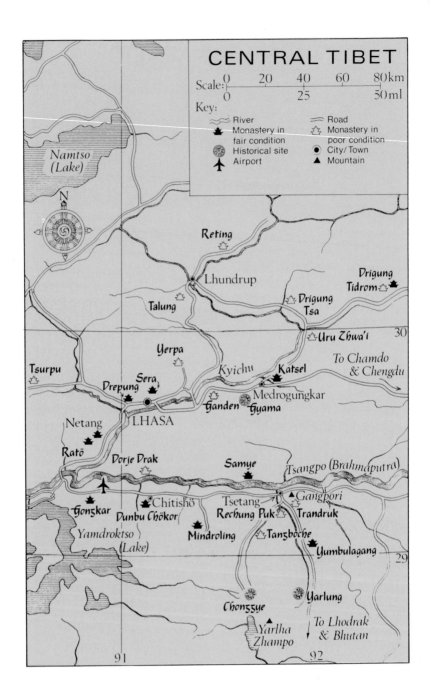

CENTRAL TIBET

Scale:

| 0 | 20 | 40 | 60 | 80 km |
| 0 | | 25 | | 50 ml |

Key:
- ～ River
- ⛰ Monastery in fair condition
- ◉ Historical site
- ✈ Airport
- ～ Road
- ⛩ Monastery in poor condition
- ◉ City/Town
- ▲ Mountain

Namtso (Lake)

N

Reting

Lhundrup

Talung

Drigung Tidrom

Drigung Tsa

Yerpa

Uru Zhwa'i   30

Tsurpu

Kyichu

Katsel

To Chamdo & Chengdu

Drepung Sera

Ganden

Medrogungkar

Netang LHASA

Gyama

Ratö

Dorje Drak

Samye

Tsangpo (Brahmaputra)

Gangpori

Gongkar

Chitishö

Tsetang

Rechung Puk

Trandruk

Dunbu Chökor

Mindroling

Tangböche

Yamdroktso (Lake)

Yumbulagang   29

Chongzye

Yarlung

Yarlha Zhampo

To Lhodrak & Bhutan

91   92

spiritual qualities and as a young man was sent to Central Tibet to further his understanding of Buddhism in the more cultured region of the country. The first monastery he visited was that of Drigung, where he studied the doctrines of the Kagyu lineage and medicine. From here he proceeded to Netang, Samye, Zhalu and Sakya monasteries. He met his main teacher Rendawa at Tsechen Monastery just outside Gyantse. For many years he studied the full range of Buddhist philosophy, including the more esoteric tantric systems. He then retreated to Olka, north of the Brahmaputra downstream from Tsetang, and spent the next four years in intense meditation. Upon returning to society he found himself much in demand as a teacher. One place where he taught was the hill in Lhasa on which the Potala was eventually built. Together with Rendawa he stayed for some time at Reting, where he composed his most famous work, *The Great Exposition of the Stages on the Path to Enlightenment*. After another meditation and writing retreat at Chöding Hermitage (above where Sera Monastery now is), he founded, in 1409, the famous annual Mönlam (prayer) festival in Lhasa, which, after a twenty-five year hiatus, was reinaugurated in 1986.

After the prayer festival he decided to cease travelling from place to place and to found his own monastery. He selected Mt.Drokri, a mountain upstream from Lhasa, and called the monastery 'Ganden', which is the Tibetan name for the Pure Land of Tushita, where the future Buddha Maitreya currently resides. Within a year seventy buildings had been completed but it was not until 1417 that the main hall of the monastery was consecrated.

Tsongkhapa died at Ganden two years later, in 1419, and shortly before his death passed the mantle of succession to Gyeltsab Je, one of his two chief disciples. Gyeltsab Je held the position of Ganden Tripa (Throne Holder of Ganden) until his own death twelve years later, when it passed to Tsongkhapa's other chief disciple Khedrup Je. The post of Ganden Tripa was later given to the senior Dharma Master of one of the two main Ganden Colleges, Jangtse and Shartse. It was a five year post for which to qualify one must first have obtained a *geshe* degree with highest honours (*lharampa*), proceeded to the abbotship of one of the two Lhasa tantric colleges, and from there been appointed Dharma Master of either Jangtse or Shartse college. The tradition has been continued in India and the current Ganden Tripa, Jampel Shenpen, is the 98th in the succession. It is the Ganden Tripa, *not* the Dalai Lama, who is the official head of the Gelukpa order.

During his lifetime Tsongkhapa was regarded as a remarkable spiritual figure whose genius and saintliness held him above the sectarian differences of his times. Although greatly inspired by the example of Atisha, to the point of attributing authorship of his major written

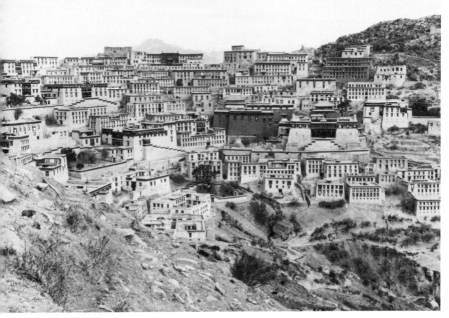

Ganden Monastery, 1949.

work to him, and the spirit of the Kadampa tradition, Tsongkhapa nonetheless studied widely with representatives of all the major orders in Tibet and assimilated their lineages. It is unlikely that he intended to form his own order, though he must have realised it was liable to happen. He could not have foreseen, though, the dimensions this order (the Gelukpa) would eventually assume and the political power it would wield.

Over the following centuries Ganden Monastery grew to the size of a small township, delicately perched along the high sheltered slopes of the mountain. By 1959 this calm, secluded centre of learning and contemplation housed more than five thousand monks, but with the Chinese occupation the monks were forced to scatter, and by the mid-sixties the monastery was nearly deserted. The final blow came with the cultural revolution. Coerced by the Chinese and caught up in the frenzy and terror of the times, the local Tibetans reluctantly demolished the buildings. For many years only jagged ruins remained. The greater religious freedom permitted after the death of Mao Tsetung allowed the laborious and gradual reconstruction of the monastery to begin. One by one the buildings emerged from out of the rubble and monks trickled back to their former home. Yet, perhaps because of its symbolic power as the stronghold of the previous spiritual rule as well as its distance from the capital, Ganden has been rebuilt largely through private funds

View of Ganden Monastery.

and has received scant support from the government. The presence of the two hundred and seventy monks has likewise yet to be officially sanctioned by the Chinese.

THE SITE

Ganden is one of the most spectacular as well as the most tragic of the sacred sites in Tibet. With very few exceptions, everything in the monastery today is new. Nonetheless, great effort has been made to recreate exactly what was there before on the very same sites. The route we will follow through the monastery is somewhat arbitary, but it does allow one to visit all the places of importance in a roughly clockwise direction without having to retrace one's steps.

Ngam Chö Khang (1)

As you enter the monastery along the main pathway this is the second building on your right. It is a small temple built on the site where, in the earliest days of Ganden's history, Tsongkhapa and his monks would assemble for their daily services. As with nearly every temple in Ganden, the main images in the Shrine-room are those of Tsongkhapa himself with his two chief disciples, Khedrup Je and Gyeltsab Je. Before meeting Tsongkhapa both Khedrup and Gyelsab were renowned scholars in their own right, belonging to the Sakya tradition. Convinced of

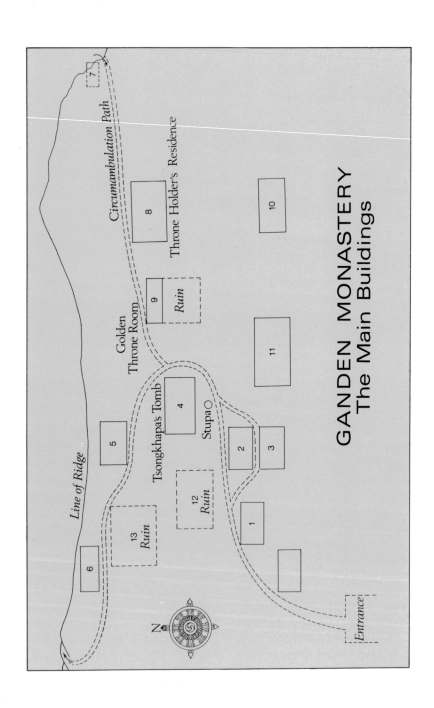

GANDEN MONASTERY
The Main Buildings

Line of Ridge

Circumambulation Path

Throne Holder's Residence

Golden
Throne Room

Tsongkhapa's Tomb

Stupa○

N

Entrance

5

6

13
Ruin

12
Ruin

4

2

3

1

7

8

9

Ruin

10

11

the breadth and depth of their teacher's understanding they remained with him until his death and were responsible for further elucidating his teachings in their own voluminous writings. To the left of this triad is a statue of Shakyamuni and to the right another form of Tsongkhapa, in which he is depicted holding a golden vase. To the left of the shrine-room is a small chapel dedicated to four protectors: Pelden Lhamo, Mahakala, Dharmaraja and, on the far right, a large statue of Yaman-taka.

As with most protector chapels in Ganden, women are not allowed to enter this darkened chamber. This restriction is a fairly recent innovation seemingly introduced because certain monks believed that the wrathful protectors may shock the delicate sensibilities of the fairer sex!

Gom De Khang (2) and Tepu Debating Courtyard (3)

The next building you encounter on your way along the main path is the Gom De Khang (House of Meditation). Although its name suggests that traditionally it was used as a place for meditation, now it is merely a living area for the monks. Immediately below is the Tepu Debating Courtyard. This is a good example of a formal debating courtyard where the monks would meet after their lessons to analyse the meaning of what they had learnt. The raised dais at the back is where examinations would be held.

Tsongkhapa's Golden Tomb [Ser Dung] (4)

This impressive structure is the most prominent building in Ganden. It is easily recognised by its high, inward-sloping, red walls with four small windows at the top. Immediately below it is a recently completed white stupa containing a variety of sacred scriptures and other artefacts, presumably some of the scattered, broken remains recovered after the destruction.

As you enter the Ser Dung from the upper right side you find yourself in a spacious inner courtyard partially open to the sky. Straight ahead of you is a protector chapel dedicated to Dharmaraja. Again, women are not allowed into this room. Inside, the central figure is Dharmaraja. On the black walls around him are painted the Ten Wrathful Beings and above them important lamas who have passed down the teachings pertaining to the protectors.

To the left of the protector chapel is another door leading into a large bare room containing a single copper and gold statue of Shakyamuni. Neatly arranged on shelves around the room are a thousand painted clay images representing the thousand Buddhas of this present aeon.

If you now follow the staircase to the upper storey, you will reach the chapel where Tsongkhapa's remains are entombed. On the left as you enter the chapel is a large assembly room, where rows of monks gather frequently to perform their services. On the right, slightly raised, is the Yangchen Khang where the giant silver and gold stupa stands. It is said that when Tsongkhapa died his body assumed the form of a sixteen year old youth. This was then embalmed and enshrined in a massive stupa. When the stupa was broken into during the cultural revolution, the Red Guards were horrified to discover the body in perfect condition, its hair and fingernails still growing. It was destroyed nonetheless. Only some fragments of the skull were saved and these are now housed in the present stupa. Seated before the stupa are images of Tsongkhapa and his two chief disciples.

The chamber is called the 'Yangchen Khang' on account of a large stone that is believed to have flown miraculously to this spot from the Buddhist city of Yangchen (Sarvasti) in India. The stone is visible, embedded at the base of the wall in the rear, left-hand corner of the room. It is also of interest to study the contents of a small glass case in front of the stupa to the left, which are said to be the begging bowl and wooden tea cup used by Tsongkhapa; a large vajra given to him by his teacher Namkha Gyeltsen; and a small silver stupa in which one of the master's teeth is kept. This tooth is presumably the one a group of his

Tsongkhapa's Golden Tomb, the Golden Throne Room, and the Residence of the Throne Holder of Ganden.

disciples asked for when it fell out shortly before the Tsongkhapa's death. To satisfy them all he placed it on an altar and transformed it into the form of Manjushri. When this apparition faded, he gave the tooth to Khedrup Je.

Amdo Khangtsen (5)
The Amdo Khangtsen is where monks from the north-eastern province of Amdo (now Qinghai) were housed when they came to train in Ganden. Since Tsongkhapa also hailed from Amdo, even today monks from this region consider themselves to have a special affinity with Ganden.

The main chapel in Amdo Khangtsen is richly decorated with brocade hangings and freshly painted murals. On the walls to the left are found paintings of the Thirty-five Buddhas of Confession. The main statues along the back wall are (from the left) Anima Je, a local protector introduced from Amdo by Tsongkhapa and subsequently worshipped in Central Tibet; Jetsun Chökyi Gyeltsen, depicted in the posture of debating; Maitreya; what is believed to be an eye of the protector Dharmaraja in a small glass case on the ground; Tsongkhapa and his two chief disciples; Tara; a small, painted stone image of Tara that is said to have spoken; Lama Para Rinpoche, a famous monk from Ganden; and finally the protectress Pelden Lhamo. A mural depicting the Sixteen Arhats adorns the right-hand wall.

Dreu Khangtsen (6)
There is little of note in this Khangtsen. The main images are again those of Tsongkhapa and his two chief disciples. To their left one can see a small, painted stone image of Manjushri, regarded by the monks as being miraculously formed.

If one walks further along the ridge of the mountain past Dreu Khangtsen, one will find the beginning of a path leading around the back of the hill allowing pilgrims to circumambulate the monastery. The view from this path is quite breathtaking. You look across the wide Kyichu basin at the distant valleys and mountains that recede to the far horizon. The clear, thin air at this altitude allows an extraordinary feeling of spaciousness. All along the path you will notice small, crudely-made shrines covered with prayer flags and other objects of devotion.

Tsongkhapa's Hermitage (7)
This small building suddenly protrudes from the mountainside as the path curves around the hill on its way back to the monastery. This is one of the places where Tsongkhapa stayed in retreat when he first came to Central Tibet. Inside the cave an image of Tsongkhapa is carved in relief

The tomb of Tsongkhapa. Tsongkhapa and his two chief disciples, Gyeltsab and Khedrup, are seated in front of the stupa.

on the stone wall, and to show his particular connection with the Kadampa tradition, carved images of Atisha and Drom Tönpa are placed above his shoulders. Shortly after this hermitage, one can see another shrine built higher up on the mountain slope. This was where Tsongkhapa would worship his protective deities.

The Residence of the Throne Holder of Ganden [Tri Dok Khang] (8)
The Tri Dok Khang is the official residence of the 'Ganden Tripa', the Throne Holder of Ganden, the monk elected to be the titular head of the Gelukpa order. The well-illuminated chapel on the upper storey houses a complete set of the Kangyur. These long, cloth-wrapped texts are set in the rear wall to either side of statues of Tsongkhapa and his two chief disciples. To the far side of the room is one of the thrones used by the Ganden Tripa (the main one being in the Golden Throne Room next door).

On the lower storey there are four shrines worth visiting. The first, at the bottom of the stairs to the left, is a chapel dedicated to Samvara. This typically darkened tantric shrine with black walls covered with ferocious images contains, in addition to the main figure of Samvara, statues of Tsongkhapa's disciple Gyeltsab and Mahakala. To the right of the altar is a small figure of Vajrayogini behind glass. Women are not allowed in this room.

Around the corner from the Samvara Chapel is the Dzom Chen Khang. To the left of the image of Tsongkhapa and his two chief disciples is a statue of Pabongka Rinpoche, and to the left one of Trijang Rinpoche, the late junior tutor to the present Dalai Lama. The throne to the right of this room bears the folded monk's upper robe of Tsongkhapa.

The adjoining room, which is entered by a door to the left of the courtyard and then a corridor, marks the place where Tsongkhapa died. This bare and dimly-lit room contains only a bed and a seat. The walls, however, are richly painted with deities, predominant among which are four aspects of Manjushri: four-armed and two-armed forms on the left-hand wall, and black and lion-mounted forms on the rear wall. Tsongkhapa and Tara are each depicted twice. The other images are those of Guhyasamaja, Vijaya and Amitayus. Dharmaraja and Mahakala guard the doorway.

The next room along is where the Dalai Lamas would stay on their visits to Ganden. In the left-hand corner is an ornate bed where they would sleep. In a case set high in the rear wall are the Thirty-five Buddhas of Confession recently offered to the monastery by lay devotees. The figure to the right of the main image of Tsongkhapa is the Panchen Lama.

The Golden Throne Room [Ser Tri Khang] (9)
This narrow, red building stands between the Residence of the Throne Holder of Ganden and the Golden Tomb of Tsongkhapa. It contains a single, high ceilinged chapel in which the golden throne of Tsongkhapa and the Ganden tradition stands beneath three giant images of the master and his two disciples. The throne itself is said to have been created by one of the horns of Dharmaraja. Lying on it in a grimy cloth bag is the yellow hat of the present Dalai Lama, left behind after his flight to India. Only three lamas have been allowed to sit on this throne: Tsongkhapa, the Ganden Tripa and the Dalai Lama. It faces a large doorway that looks out onto the main assembly area of Ganden. This courtyard is now in disrepair. An edition of the Kangyur is stored in a room on the upper storey that is not open to the public.

Nyare Khangtsen (10)
One of the poorest and least restored buildings in Ganden, Nyare Khangtsen has little to interest the visitor. As usual, Tsongkhapa and his two chief disciples adorn the chapel, but there are no other images or relics of note.

Ngari Khangtsen (11)

The well-maintained chapel in Ngari Khangtsen contains a set of images that distinguishes it from the other *khangtsens*. The main figure is a large image of Tsongkhapa seated alone without the company of his chief disciples. The facial features of this statue are very pronounced, attempting, perhaps, to capture the expression preserved on the images dating from the time of the master himself. To his left are Atisha, Drom Tönpa and Ngog Legpa'i Sherab, founding masters of the Kadampa order, and to his right Panchen Sonam Drakpa, the second Panchen Lama, with Chökyi Gyeltsen and Dondze Drakpa Gyeltsen, a renowned lama from Ganden.

Jangtse and Shartse Colleges (12 – 13)

Jangtse and Shartse were both founded by disciples of Tsongkhapa, the former by Namkha Pelzangpo, and the latter by Neten Ronggyelwa. These two principal colleges (dratsang) of Ganden Monastery are yet to be rebuilt and still lie in ruins. Their approximate location is shown on the plan by dotted lines. Traditionally, monks from the different khangtsens would belong to one of these two colleges, where they would gather for services and engage in their studies. Both these colleges have been re-established in South India, where they continue to train monks. Today in Tibet, all the monks use the building of the Golden Tomb (4) as their common assembly hall.

OPPOSITE *Old monk returning home after completing a circumambulation of the monastery.*
OVERLEAF *View of the Kyichu valley from Yerpa with ruined stupas in the foreground.*

17. YERPA

Yerpa lies about 30 km north-east of Lhasa. The most direct route to it is the road from Lhasa that heads due east out towards the hydro-electric plant along the northern bank of the Kyichu, i.e. the same side of the river as Lhasa itself. Shortly after the hydro-electric plant the road bears left up the mountainside and crosses a pass that leads down into the valley on the other side. A couple of miles further down the road a side valley to the left leads up to Yerpa. Motorised traffic has to stop at the small village at the end of the valley and from there you must walk up for about half an hour towards the ruins you can see from the village. There is no public transport to Yerpa, so you must either hire a vehicle (we rented a Landcruiser from the Taxi Company for 98 FEC for the day) or walk. It takes Tibetans a day to hike from Lhasa, but unless you camp in a cave, there is no accommodation.

HISTORY

Giuseppe Tucci, the Italian scholar, recorded his first impression of Yerpa in 1949 thus: 'Yerpa appeared suddenly before my eyes at a bend of the road, a cascade of small white buildings along steep, green overgrown cliffs. One could have thought one was not in Tibet. Giant junipers and tufts of rhododendron topped a thick tangle of undergrowth, brushwood and grass victoriously fighting the hard barrenness of rocks. The cliffs were riddled with burrows and caves, some of which were so high up on the face of the abrupt hill that it would have been risky to climb them.'

Yerpa was a village of hermits and recluses who lived on a site sanctified by Padmasambhava, Yeshe Tsogyel, Atisha and many of the greatest mystics of the Tibetan Buddhist tradition. Since the seventh century it has been constantly considered as one of the most sacred sites in Central Tibet. Although it suffered terribly during the cultural revolution – its monasteries destroyed and its caves defaced, its trees and shrubs uprooted for firewood – it still retains the incredible natural beauty and dignity of its setting. Drawn by the force of the memory of those who inhabited it before, hermits are slowly returning to its caves and the first building is now being restored. (There were a total of ten monks and nuns meditating in the caves when we visited.)

THE SITE

The view from Yerpa is truly spectacular. Immediately before one is the sacred Lhari, a small domed mountain with OM MANI PADME HUM

View of Yerpa, 1937. The monastery of Drak Yerpa is in the foreground with the caves at the foot of the escarpment.

inscribed with white rocks on its lower surface. Beyond, the valley descends to the Kyichu river and in the far distance snow-capped mountains line the horizon. Towering almost vertically behind you are the ragged, daunting cliffs dotted with tiny caves.

As you climb up to Yerpa from the village at the end of the valley, the first buildings you reach are the ruins of the summer residence of the Upper Tantric College in Lhasa (see Chapter 8, **Ramoche Temple**, above). The five hundred monks of this college would come up here every summer for about two months and continue their study of the tantric doctrines. Not a single chapel remains standing. From this lowest point on the hill one can see another row of ruins slightly higher up to the right. They are all that is left of the **Drak Yerpa Monastery** founded by the disciples of Atisha in the tenth century. Again not a single building still stands.

If you look out towards the distant mountains from the ruins of Drak Yerpa, you can see two isolated ruins down to the left just below the saddle of the ridge that gently rises to the Lhari mountain. The further of these two was the place where Atisha had a small monastery and used to teach, the nearer where the community of his disciples would live. The crumbling remains of two large stupas are also visible to the left and far right of these two temples.

The most important caves are also clearly visible from this vantage point. They lie along the base of the cliff about a hundred and fifty metres from the ruins of the monastery. To the far left is a tall fissure in the rock face. To the left of this is the tiny cave where Atisha once meditated. This is called the **Tendrel Lhakhang** (Relativity Chapel), and, when we visited, was inhabited by a Gelukpa lama from Amdo who had been in retreat there for a year. It is in good condition but devoid of any relics or statues. Continuing to the right, one arrives at the largest cave in this complex, the **Jampa Drup Khang** (Maitreya Practice Chamber). At one time this cave-chapel was filled with a seated statue of Maitreya surrounded by the Eight Great Bodhisattvas. Now three of the disfigured heads of these deities lie in a raised heap on the ground.

Still further along to the right is the **Chögyel Puk** (Cave of the Religious King), where Songtsen Gampo is supposed to have meditated. To the right and slightly below this cave is the first and so far only chapel that is being rebuilt. This marks the entrance to the cave where Lhalungpa, the monk who killed the anti-Buddhist king Langdarma in 842 with a well-aimed arrow shot during the performance of an opera,

Hermit's cave at Yerpa with prayer flags.

The Protectors of the Three Kinds of Beings: Avalokiteshvara, Manjushri and Vajrapani, carved on a boulder at Yerpa.

lived in retreat. The interior of this cave has been badly defaced, but one can still see the central pillar around which sat four of the Dhyani Buddhas, Akshobhya, Amitabha, Amoghasiddhi and Ratnasambhava. The remains of a seated figure of Maitreya can also be discerned to the right of the doorway.

Directly above the cave of Lhalungpa is the **Dawa'i Puk** (Moon Cave) of Padmasambhava. This small, low-ceilinged chamber houses the base of Padmasambhava's throne as well as his footprint set in a rock above the makeshift altar. A Nyingmapa monk was in retreat here when we visited. Higher up the mountain is another cave of Padmasambhava called the **Nyima'i Puk** (Sun Cave).

The best preserved rock-carvings to have survived in Yerpa are a set of the triad of Manjushri, Avalokiteshvara and Vajrapani in a small four-walled ruin beneath the Maitreya Practice Chamber. It is remarkable that these three deities have survived in the midst of the total destruction around them.

18. TSURPU MONASTERY

Tsurpu is about 50 km north-west of Lhasa. You leave the city by the Dekyi Nub Lam, go past Drepung and turn right when the road forks left in the direction of Netang and the airport. This right-hand fork is the paved road leading to a large electricity plant and Namtso Lake. After 24 km (at kilometre stone 1897), you turn left over a small bridge that takes you up the picturesque side valley that ends at Tsurpu itself. There is no public transport to Tsurpu; we hired a land-cruiser from the Taxi Company for 170 FEC, which included, on the return journey, visits to Drölma Lhakhang and Ratö Monastery (see Chapters 22 and 23, below).

If you continue another 50 km up the main road towards Namtso you will come to a junction with the 'Northern' road from Golmud. If you turn left here and continue for 18 km, you will reach the remains of **Yangpachen Monastery**, *the former seat of the Sharmapa Lama. The first Sharmapa was a disciple of the third Karmapa, Rangjung Dorje (1284-1339). 'Sharmapa' means 'One with the Red Hat' (in contrast to the black hat of the Karmapas), and is so called because of the red hat bestowed upon the first of the line by a Mongolian emperor. For more than four hundred years nine Sharmapas lived in Yangpachen. But in 1791, because of the Ninth Sharmapa's implication in the Gurkha invasion, the monastery was confiscated and the line temporarily interrupted. The present Sharmapa lives in exile in Sikkim.*

HISTORY

Tsurpu Monastery was founded in 1189 by the first Karmapa, Dusum Khyenpa, who was born in the eastern province of Kham. He came to Central Tibet to study and at the age of thirty became a disciple of Gampopa. He returned to Kham and founded Karmapa'i Densa, the monastery from which the Karma Kagyu order derived its name. Only towards the end of his life did he return to Central Tibet to found Tsurpu. Shortly before he died he said that he would be reborn in Tibet and gave indications as to how he could be found. He thus became the first lama to introduce the unique Tibetan custom of lines of recognised 'tulkus', a practice that eventually became popular with all the main orders.

Dusum Khyenpa returned in 1204 as Karma Pakshi, the second Karmapa, nine years after his death. Again he was born in Kham and came to Tsurpu only when he was forty-three years old. He stayed there for six years. In 1256 he was invited by Kublai Khan, the founder of the Mongolian Yuan dynasty in China and disciple of the Sakya Lama Pakpa, to the imperial court where, in acknowledgement of his teachings, he was presented with a black hat embellished with gold. He was also given the title 'Pakshi', which means 'Master' (*Acharya*) in Mongolian. However, in 1260, as a result of intrigue and rivalry, he found himself banished from the court and imprisoned. Upon his release four years later he went to Kham. After eight years of teaching he returned to Tsurpu and spent the rest of his life renovating and enlarging the monastery.

Tsurpu was further enlarged during the time of the Fifth Karmapa, Deshinshekpa, in the fifteenth century. During the sixteenth and seventeenth centuries the Karmapas were the spiritual advisors to the kings of Tsang and thus became powerful political figures. They vied with the early Dalai Lamas but when the Mongolian army of Gushri Khan defeated the king of Tsang and enthroned the Fifth Dalai Lama as ruler of Tibet in 1642, they lost their political influence. Although many smaller monasteries belonging to the Karmapa sub-sect of the Kagyu school were then forcibly turned into Gelukpa centres, thus diminishing the power of the Kagyupa in Central Tibet, Tsurpu survived as a stronghold of the Kagyu faith until the Chinese occupation in 1959, at which time there were over a thousand monks living there.

Rigpai Dorje, the Sixteenth Karmapa, went into exile in Rumtek, Sikkim, and directed the Karma Kagyu order from there. A powerful and charismatic figure, he played an important role in preserving the doctrines of the Kagyu tradition and introducing them to the outside world. He died in Chicago in 1981.

As the seat of the Karmapa, Tsurpu was the headquarters of the Karma Kagyu order in Tibet and had numerous other sub-monasteries and temples scattered throughout the country, many of which were in Kham. Monks from the order would travel here for their doctrinal and contemplative training and, once qualified, return to their home province to take charge of their local monastery.

THE SITE

Although now largely in ruins, the outline of the monastery as well as the location of its major buildings can still be clearly discerned. One temple has been rebuilt and work is underway to rebuild the main assembly hall. The hermitage directly above the monastery is also being renovated and it is hoped that retreatants will begin to make use of the facility again in 1987. In 1984 two young incarnate lamas of the Karma Kagyu order, Jamgön Khontrul Rinpoche and Tai Situ Rinpoche, visited

View of Tsurpu.

the monastery and re-established the lineage of monastic ordination. There are currently sixty to seventy monks living here, most of them young.

The only fully reconstructed building is the **Zhi-wa'i Dratsang** and this is the place where the monks now gather from their services. The principal object in the main hall downstairs is a newly constructed throne for the Karmapa, on which stands a photograph of the most recent incarnation, the Sixteenth. To the side of the throne an older black and white picture taken in China in 1958 shows him as a young man. The only ancient statue is one of Nugu Rinpoche, a teacher of the Eighth Karmapa, the great scholar Mikyö Dorje, to the right of the throne. Images of the First, Second and Sixteenth Karmapas sit to the left of the throne. The hall is small and not elaborately decorated. *Tangkas*, most of them modern, depicting various Buddhas, Taras and different incarnations of the Karmapa hang on the walls.

On the upper storey is a protector chapel dedicated to Mahakala, Pelden Lhamo and Dharmaraja, and two residential chambers. The first of these chambers was where Jamgön Kontrul Rinpoche and Tai Situ Rinpoche stayed during their 1984 visit. In a glass case set into the wall are many small bronzes depicting the different Karmapas. These statues are presumably quite old and many may have been cast while their sub-

Monks outside Zhi-wa'i Dratsang.

jects were still living. The second chamber houses four recently comissioned images of the three Tibetan founders of the Kagyu school: Marpa, Milarepa and Gampopa. To the right of Marpa is a statue of Rigpai Dorje, the Sixteenth Karmapa. Hanging from one of the pillars in the room is a photograph of Tsurpu taken in 1967, just before its destruction.

As you walk clockwise around the ruins to the right of Zhi-wa'i Dratsang, you will see a tall, high wall, which used to be one of the sides of the Karmapa's palace. To the right of this palace are the remains of another large building, the palace of Gyeltsab Rinpoche, another important lama of the Karma Kagyu order. In front of these two impressive ruins the assembly hall is being reconstructed on its original site.

If you climb for about half an hour up the steep mountain cliff behind the monastery, you will reach **Drubtra Samten Ling**, the main retreat centre, which is now being reconstructed. Eight small individual cells as well as a temple and kitchen area are being built. Once a major retreat begins, the monks and their helpers will be locked in here for three years. Perched on the cliffside beside this hermitage is another small building, which was built by the Second Karmapa, Karma Pakshi, as his personal retreat. Many other hermitages used to dot this mountainside but sadly they are now destroyed.

From the vantage-point of the hermitage one has an excellent bird's eye view of the entire monastery. The base of the massive stone ramparts that surrounded it are visible, as are the palaces and the smaller buildings where the monks lived. Facing the monastery on the opposite bank of the river is a peculiar, wide staircase-like structure. This is where, on the tenth day of every fourth lunar month, the monastery would hold its most important celebrations. A giant *tangka* would be displayed, and lama dances and other ceremonies performed. Further downriver, where the valley turns slightly to where the monastery is located, is another ruin, the former summer residence of the Karmapa.

THE KARMAPA LAMAS

1.	Dusum Khyenpa	1110-1193
2.	Karma Pakshi	1204-1283
3.	Rangjung Dorje	1284-1339
4.	Rolpai Dorje	1340-1383
5.	Deshin Shekpa	1384-1415
6.	Tongwa Dönden	1416-1453
7.	Chödrak Gyatso	1454-1506
8.	Mikyö Dorje	1507-1554
9.	Wangchuk Dorje	1556-1603
10.	Chöying Dorje	1604-1674
11.	Yeshe Dorje	1677-1702
12.	Jangchub Dorje	1703-1732
13.	Dudul Dorje	1733-1797
14.	Tegchok Dorje	1798-1868
15.	Khakhyab Dorje	1871-1922
16.	Rigpai Dorje	1921-1981

Tashi Gomang Chöten with Siling Götsang Hermitage just visible on the cliffside behind.

19. TALUNG MONASTERY

Talung lies about 65 km north of Lhasa. It is not easy to get to. There are two main routes from Lhasa. The first takes you over the bridge out towards Ganden. You cross the Taktse Zam Chen Bridge past Taktse Dzong and continue north up the long, wide Penpo valley. After about an hour's drive you must turn right up a side valley, which takes you to Chakla Pass (4,873 m) on the way to the town of Lhundrup. The second main route differs in that you enter the Penpo valley via the road that runs along the northern bank of the Kyichu and passes nearby Yerpa. A third route to the Penpo valley, which may not be negotiable by car or bus, runs through the mountains just to the east of Sera. For a two day round trip including visits to Reting and Drigung monasteries we hired a landcruiser from the Taxi Company for 570 FEC.

If you continue further north along the Penpo valley past the turn-off to Talung, you will come to **Nalanda Monastery,** *the most important religious centre of the area, founded by Rongtön Mawa'i Sengge in 1435. Rongtön was an exceptionally learned Sakya lama from Eastern Tibet who composed more than one hundred texts. He named his monastery after the famous Nalanda Monastery in India (in present-day Bihar). The local Tibetans say that the monastery is now 'destroyed' but I do not know exactly what condition it is in. The Penpo valley was also famous for the many Kadampa lamas who lived there.*

Shortly after descending the Chakla Pass you can see the Talung valley to the left with the ruins of the monastery on the left hillside. The monks who look after the monastery will let you visit at any time. There is no charge for admission although donations will be gratefully received. It may be possible to stay in the nearby village. Normally, though, one would spend the night in the nearby town of Lhundrup (see Chapter 20, **Reting,** *below).*

On the road from Talung to Lhundrup you pass a large stupa called the **Tashi Gomang Chöten** *which was built by the old Tibetan government, since it was believed that this was the spot from where water first started to flow into Lhasa. Perched on the hillside above the stupa is the* **Sili Götsang Hermitage,** *founded by Lama Götsangpa in the thirteenth century. This now belongs to Talung Monastery and was where monks would go to do long retreats. It was able to take twenty to thirty retreatants at a time. It was rebuilt about five years ago and there are usually one or two monks living there.*

HISTORY

Talung Monastery was founded in 1180 by the sage Talung Tangpa (or

Partial view of Talung Monastery, 1939 or 1950.

Talung Tashi Pel) on the site where the Kadampa master Potowa lived. Talung Tangpa was a disciple of Lama Pamotrupa in the Kagyu line descended from Gampopa and Milarepa. He was renowned not only for his contemplative insights and powers but also for his austere and simple life. Under the inspiration of its founder, Talung Monastery became well-known for its strict adherence to monastic rules. It grew into a huge monastic establishment, at one time housing up to seven thousand monks. It also became involved in the political upheavals that raged during the thirteenth century and suffered from occasional conflicts with its sister monastery, Drigung, over issues ranging from the theft of Pamotrupa's library by Drigung monks to disagreements regarding timber rights. By the time of the cultural revolution the number of monks had dwindled to about six hundred, among whom were three lines of incarnate lamas (*tulkus*).

The ruins of Talung.

THE SITE

The monastery now lies in ruins. Many of the monks' quarters have been taken over by the village people and are now used as houses and barns. However, reconstruction began on a small scale in 1985 and there is now one restored chapel looked after by six elderly monks. Inside the crudely-made chapel you will find a handful of artefacts that were saved from destruction: some small bronzes, some *tangkas* and a number of texts. The central statue is that of the founder of the monastery, Talung Tangpa.

In front of the chapel are the very impressive ruins of the 'Red Jokhang' of Talung. The four walls remain standing and give a good idea of exactly how huge this building was. Previously it housed a giant statue of Shakyamuni and the roof was supported by eighty massive pillars.

20. RETING MONASTERY

Reting is situated in a juniper forest (which is supposed to have sprung from fallen strands of hair from Drom Tönpa's head) on a hillside overlooking the Kyichu River about 100 km north of Lhasa. To reach it you must first go to the town of Lhundrup, to which there are two routes (see the map of **Central Tibet**)*. The first is the same as that which takes you to Talung (see Chapter 19, above) except that when you descend the Chakla Pass, instead of turning left to Talung, follow the road for another three quarters of an hour, past the* **Tashi Gomang Stupa** *(see Chapter 19), to the Kyichu River, on the bank of which is Lhundrup (also called Lhundrup Dzong). The second route to Lhundrup is along the southern bank of the Kyichu from Lhasa to Medrogungkar to Drigung Chu, where the river turns sharply to the north-west. From here the road may not be passable at all times of the year. From Lhundrup you keep on the road that goes north along the Kyichu for about an hour. Reting is on your left. The monastery is continuously open and there is no charge to visit.*

Four kilometres past Reting is a small nunnery called **Samdrup Ling***, which has three or four nuns in residence.*

It is possible to sleep overnight in Lhundrup in a kind of military truckstop for 3 RMB. Simple Chinese food is also available. Lhundrup itself is an unimpressive place for a regional capital. On one side of the river is a run-down Tibetan village and on the other side a motley collection of Chinese-style, tin-roofed barracks (this is where the truck stop is). However, you cannot fail to be awed by the high conical mountain that soars up opposite the town.

There is supposedly a bus from Lhasa to Lhundrup but I do not know how frequently it runs or from which bus station. We took a landcruiser, rented for two days for 570 FEC, on a round trip to Talung, Reting and Drigung.

HISTORY

Reting Monastery was the first Kadampa monastery to be founded. Drom Tönpa, Atisha's chief disciple, began building it when he settled here in 1057, three years after his teacher's death. He remained here until his own death in 1064, spending most of his time in meditation retreat. Many others who had been similarly inspired by the purity and simplicity of Atisha's teachings joined him in Reting and around them crystallised what came to be known as the Kadam (Spiritual Advice) order of Tibetan Buddhism. These founders of the order were known as the Kadampa geshes. Only later did the Gelukpa, a later outgrowth of the Kadampa ideal, use the term 'geshe' to designate an official degree

The conical mountain at Lhundrup.

of learning. After Drom, the abbotship of the monastery passed to a master called Naljorpa Chenpo (Great Yogin), during whose time the monastery was considerably enlarged. The well-known Kadampa geshe Potowa was also abbot of Reting for three years in the late eleventh century.

Tsongkhapa joined the monastery in 1397, when he was forty years old. While here he received a vision of Atisha, which inspired him to begin composition of his magnum opus, *The Great Exposition on the Stages on the Path to Enlightenment*, and to begin expounding these teachings orally. After Tsongkhapa's time, the monastery ceased to be Kadampa and was taken over by the Geluk order.

In 1738 the Seventh Dalai Lama appointed his tutor Ngawang Chokden as the principal lama of Reting. The successive incarnations of this tutor were then called the Reting Rinpoche. The last Reting Rinpoche served as the regent of the young Fourteenth Dalai Lama, but was caught up in the political intrigues of the times and murdered in 1947 for his role in an attempted coup.

THE SITE

The monastery was very badly destroyed during the cultural revolution and little remains but a mass of ruins spread over the hillside. Reconstruction has begun on the main assembly hall but so far only a quarter of the work has been completed. The small area of the hall that has been repaired contains a small square chapel in which is an old image of an aspect of Guhyasamaja called 'Sangdu Jampel Dorje'. This is considered to have been the main personal tantric deity of Atisha. There is little else of any note in the chapel, although once it contained a statue of Maitreya made by Atisha himself. The murals in the main hall outside the chapel are modern, depicting mainly Tsongkhapa, lamas from the Kadampa and Gelukpa orders, and the main Gelukpa tantric deities.

Higher on the hill is a small protector chapel dedicated to Damchen Garwa Nagpa, a local deity converted to Buddhism at the time of Padmasambhava. In front of the tiny chapel is the tree in which the protector is supposed to live.

Nearby, another quadrangle of ruins is being slowly repaired. One of the most important temples in Reting used to stand here. At the rear of

Reting Monastery in its former splendour, 1950.

the quandrangle one can make out the remains of four thrones. The far right-hand throne is where lamas from Drom Tönpa to Tsongkhapa have taught. It is particularly renowned as the seat from which Tsongkhapa first delivered his teaching *The Foundation of All Excellence*, a versified synopsis of the stages on the path to enlightenment. Next to the throne is the site where the Kadampa Geshe Gönpopa had his meditation cell. On the three thrones to the left stood statues of Atisha, Maitreya and Drom Tönpa.

To the left of the monastery are the crumbling remains of numerous stupas that served as tombs for the remains of many great Kadampa masters. They must have presented a magnificent sight before they were destroyed and allowed to decay. The remaining houses that have been repaired are where the sixty monks who have returned to the monastery now live. Judging by the extent of the ruins, Reting must at one time have housed several hundred more.

The remains of the main assembly hall today.

21. DRIGUNG MONASTERY

Drigung (or Drigung Til) Monastery is about 100 km north east of Lhasa. It rises spectacularly from a high mountainside at the end of the long valley that begins where the Kyichu river makes its last sharp bend before flowing down into Lhasa. It can be approached from two directions, downstream from Lhundrup or upstream from Lhasa. You turn off the Kyichu valley at the town of Drigung Chu and follow the road up the side valley for about an hour until you see the monastery on the left. It is always open and there is no admission charge, although the monks may ask to see your permit from Lhasa (just smile at them).

On the road from Lhundrup to Drigung you will pass another monastery called **Drigung Tsa Monastery.** *This is about 20 km before the turning to Drigung itself. Drigung Tsa, named 'Tsa' ('root') because of the belief that it stands over an important water source, was founded by a lama called Tinley Zangpo. The monastery is situated in the middle of a village high on the river bank past a large roadside stupa, but has now been reduced to one small chapel containing statues of Abchi Drölma, Mahakala, Avalokiteshvara, Manjushri, Padmasambhava, Shakyamuni and Tsongkhapa.*

There is another small valley running due south of Drigung Chu, where the remains of **Uru Zhiwa'i Temple** *can be found. This is an important site for the Nyingma Dzog-chen tradition, founded in the eighth century by the minister Ting-nge-dzin Zangpo. It is where the Kashmiri teacher Vimalamitra, invited to Tibet by Trisong Detsen shortly before Padmasambhava, composed and concealed one of the root texts of the Dzog-chen school,* The Inner Essence (Nying Tik). *Only the foundations of the monastery survive today.*

About one kilometre to the east of Medrogungkar, visible from the road, is **Katsel Temple.** *This is one of the four Tadul (Extremity Subduing) Temples of Tibet associated with King Songtsen Gampo (see Chapter 29,* **Trandruk***). It contains the stone that used to be where Songtsen Gampo kept his prayer wheel.*

8 km to the west of Medrogungkar, about half a kilometre from the road, is the **Gyama Valley,** *where Songtsen Gampo was born. There are now a couple of reconstructed buildings that mark the site. Further up this pleasant valley there are three or four small temples.*

HISTORY

A small monastery was first founded on this site by Minyak Gomrin in 1167, but only in 1179 was it established as the base of the Drigung Kagyu order by Jigten Gönpo, a disciple of Lama Pamotrupa and a former abbot of Densatil Monastery. More accurately known as

Katsel Temple near Medrogungkar, 1949.

'Drigung Til' Monastery, it quickly grew in size and reputation and by the thirteenth century was vying with the Sakya order for political power under the sponsorship of the Mongolians. It lost this struggle in 1290 when the Sakyas burnt the monastery to the ground. Although it was never again involved in national politics, it continued to be a monastery renowned for training monks in the contemplative tradition. In 1959 there were about three hundred monks living here.

THE SITE
Although the monastery was badly damaged during the cultural revolution, it has recovered remarkably well. Several buildings have been restored and now ninety monks live here, about twenty of whom are in long-term retreat in hermitages on the top of the mountain.

The main assembly hall is on top of a high, white building which rises straight out of the sheer rock face. The central image is that of Jigten Gönpo, the founder. Below him is a slab of rock bearing his footprint and to the right a small stupa containing his remains. A statue of Vajradhara is to the right of the stupa. Along the right-hand wall is an

image Abchi Drölma, a wrathful form of Tara who is the main protector of the Drigung Kagyu. There are also two high thrones with the robes and red hats of the two incarnate lamas of Drigung Monastery, both of whom are currently in exile.

A little higher up the mountainside is a protector chapel dedicated to Abchi Drölma. A white peaceful and a golden wrathful image of the protectress sit side by side in the chapel. To their left are encased images of the Buddha, Padmasambhava and Nagarjuna. Below Padmasambhava is another footprint of Jigten Gönpo. A number of small bronzes that were saved from destruction are placed in no particular order around the chapel. A pair of horns hangs from one of the pillars in the room. These are the horns of the *dri* (a cross between a yak and a cow) that acted as the basis for a vision that inspired Jigten Gönpo to build his monastery here: hence the name *Drigung* (the exact meaning of which is unclear).

Tidrom Nunnery

In 772 King Trisong Detsen offered his wife of two years, Yeshe Tsogyel, to the Indian tantric guru Padmasambhava. This caused such an uproar among the king's Bön ministers that the couple were forced to flee the royal court. They took refuge at Tidrom, where they lived alone practising tantric yogas in a cave. When the Guru departed, Yeshe Tsogyel remained in this cave for several years perfecting her meditation.

Shortly before you reach Drigung Monastery there is a small valley to the left. Tidrom Nunnery, built on the site of Yeshe Tsogyel's cave, is located at the point where this valley divides into two above some hot springs. About fifty nuns live here in a couple of poorly renovated buildings. The main images in the shrine-room are of Padmasambhava and his two consorts, Yeshe Tsogyel and Mandarava.

PREVIOUS PAGE *View of Drigung monastery and valley.*

22. NETANG: DRÖLMA LHAKHANG

Netang is the name of the area about 20 km south-west of Lhasa where the Kyichu valley broadens out into a small plain. When driving from Lhasa along the paved road in the direction of the airport, it is the region immediately after the large seated Buddha you see carved on a cliff to your right. Drölma Lhakhang, the Tara Temple, is easy to spot: it is the small monastery that stands all alone about 25 metres from the road on the right (or on the left when coming from the airport or Gyantse). We visited it as well as Ratö Monastery after seeing Tsurpu. The cost for the day's hire of the landcruiser was 180 FEC. It should be easy to arrange to visit it separately. One could always try

The Kyichu valley as it winds into Netang shortly before reaching the Brahmaputra.

and take a bus in the direction of either Gyantse or Tsetang, get off here and hitch a ride back to the city, or else visit it on your way either to or from the airport. It is open daily. The caretaker monks here respond in unpredictable ways to visitors. Sometimes they charge you 3 RMB to go in; sometimes they simply refuse you entry at any price; and sometimes they let you in free. The price for taking photos can also be negotiated. There used to be at least two other major religious sites in Netang but none of them survived the cultural revolution.

HISTORY

Atisha is the honorific name given to Dipamkara Shri Jnana, the Indian Buddhist master from Bengal who was instrumental in the 'Second Dissemination of Buddhism' in Tibet. Atisha, or Jowoje ('Precious Lord') as he is called by the Tibetans, was born to a noble family in Bengal in 982. He renounced his home and wealth at an early age and dedicated himself to the extensive study of Buddhism. He even travelled as far as Java (probably to the region of the Borodobur temple) to receive instructions on the development of the compassionate resolve to attain enlightenment (*bodhicitta*). Upon his return to India he taught widely and became one of the most revered Buddhist teachers of his time, probably settling at the Vikramashila monastery.

In the early decades of the eleventh century Buddhism started to undergo a revival in Tibet. The communities of monks who had been living in the east of the country since the time of Langdarma began to return to Central Tibet. In the west the Tibetan Rinchen Zangpo had returned from eighteen years' study in India and was actively teaching and translating Buddhist scriptures. It was also from the western kingdom of Gu-ge that the local king, Yeshe Ö, sent out repeated invitations to the greatest Indian teacher of the time, Atisha, to visit Tibet. After much supplication and personal sacrifice from the Tibetans, Atisha finally accepted and arrived in Western Tibet in 1042, aged sixty.

His teaching aimed at resolving the conflicts that were present within the Buddhist community of Tibet at that time. Above all he emphasised the need for a sound ethical basis before engaging in the more advanced tantric practices. He composed a short text, *The Lamp of the Path to Enlightenment*, which became the basic writing of the Kadampa school, which formed after his death under his chief disciple, the layman Drom. He spent a total of twelve years in Tibet, of which three were in Ngari (Western Tibet) and six in Tsang and Central Tibet. He spent his last years in Netang and died here in 1054. Since his death, the Drölma Lhakhang, dedicated to the female deity Tara, with whom he had a particularly strong connection, has been preserved as a shrine in his memory.

The Drölma Lhakhang was one of the few religious sites to have escaped much damage during the cultural revolution. The temple (or at least the statuary) was spared because of a request from the Bengali government that no harm be caused to the most sacred site of Atisha, even today a revered national figure in Bengal. Consequently, the images preserved in the temple are fine examples of the Tibetan religious art and craftsmanship of the eleventh century, often reflecting a distinct Indian influence that is no longer so evident in more recent works.

THE SITE
Protecting the small temple are life-size statues of the Four Guardian Kings, quite different from the customary Tibetan representations of them. Less ornate and stylised, they possess a simplicity and power that other versions often lack. Two recently repainted murals adorn the front of the building, the one on the left showing Atisha flanked by Drom Tönpa and Ngog Legpa'i Sherab.

The first of the three chapels you visit is dominated by a large Vijaya Stupa. To the left are other metal stupas containing relics of Kadampa teachers and to the right a larger bronze stupa that is supposed to contain some relics of the Indian master Naropa, who was a teacher of both Atisha and Marpa, the father of the Kagyu order. A statue of a reflective Atisha is the main image and to either side of him are the Eight Medicine Buddhas.

The middle chapel used to house Atisha's own statue of Tara, which he brought from India. This has been lost over the course of time. On the main altar one can still see two of Atisha's other possessions: on the left, a small Indian stupa, and on the right, an Indian statue of Shakyamuni. Above the altar is another Buddha Shakyamuni. To the left of the Buddha sits a fine statue of Tara, the main image among the twenty-one statues of her that fill both sides of the room. To the right of the Buddha is a statue of Guru Suvarnadvipa, the teacher Atisha visited in Indonesia in order to receive special instructions on the development of compassion. To the left of the altar is an urn that used to contain the remains of Atisha. (These were returned to Bengal during the sixties.) The five Dhyani Buddhas sit by the right wall above the Taras and to the left, concealed among the lower row of Taras, is a small standing statue of Maitreya called the 'A-tsa Jampa', so called because he is said to have once exclaimed 'A-tsa!' (Ouch!) upon being pricked by a needle.

The third room is where Atisha used to teach. In the middle of the room is the solid back of what used to be his throne, immediately in front of which is a small statue of Atisha that is said to be one of only

two such images made during his lifetime. Around the walls of this room one meets the gaze of three huge seated images. At the back is Amitayus. Tradition maintains that Atisha blessed thousands of small lumps of clay with the mantra of Amitayus and the statue was then constructed out of them. To the right is Buddha Kashyapa and to the left Buddha Dipamkara, both Buddhas of the distant past. The Eight Great Bodhisattvas stand noble and erect between them. All these statues give the room a sense of exceptional lightness and purity.

As you leave the final chapel you will see two white stupas to either side of the doorway. The one to the left contains the monastic robes of Atisha and the one to the right the leather jerkin of Drom Tönpa (a layman). It is also possible to circumambulate the shrine along a tall, inner corridor containing several old prayer wheels.

OPPOSITE ABOVE LEFT *One of the Twenty-one Taras.*
ABOVE RIGHT *Head of one of the Twenty-one Taras.*
BELOW LEFT *Atisha.*
BELOW RIGHT *Two of the Eight Great Bodhisattvas.*

23. RATÖ MONASTERY

Ratö is in Netang, about 5 km behind Drölma Lhakhang. It is reached by a small road that turns right off the main road into a side valley shortly after Drölma Lhakhang (when coming from Lhasa). Since there is not a great deal to see, it is ideal to combine a visit here with a visit to Drölma Lhakhang (see Chapter 22, above, for travel details). It is open daily and no admission charge is asked.

HISTORY

Ratö Monastery was founded by a lama called Tak-tsang, who was born in 1045. It was an important early centre of philosophical learning in Central Tibet and was eventually taken over by the Geluk order. Ngog Loden Sherab, the great translator, lived in the monastery and later Tsongkhapa spent some time here and in hermitages in the surrounding mountains. Latterly it was renowned as a centre for the specialised study of logic and debate. The three incarnate lamas of the monastery all live in exile abroad, Ratö Rinpoche in India, Ratö Kyongla Rinpoche in the United States, and Dagyab Rinpoche in Germany. Photographs of them are on display on the altar.

What is now the village of Ratö used to be part of the monastery, housing up to four hundred monks. Now the monastery retains only the main temple building and a small chapel higher on the hill behind. About fifty monks live here today.

THE SITE

The most revered image in the temple is a small Indian figure of Tara, now enshrined in a glass case to the left of the throne. It is said that Atisha himself paid homage to this image and it spoke to him. The statues along the rear wall depict a variety of lamas connected to the monastery. Mukchok Rinpoche is the lama to the far left; next to him is Ngog Loden Sherab. Then follow Manga Trakzang, a disciple of Tsongkhapa; Atisha; Chokla Ösel, the writer of the logic tests studied in Ratö; Ngog Legpa'i Sherab; and Yönten Puntsok, a scholar from the monastery.

To the left and right of these lamas are three intriguing statues of Tse-drek-pa, a Bön deity converted into a Buddhist protector specially worshipped in Ratö Monastery. He is usually depicted riding a horse. The small encased image on the right is of exceptionally fine workmanship.

At the rear of the temple, behind the statues, is a large empty chapel

The Fifth Dalai Lama (mural at Ratö Monastery).

that formerly contained statues of Shakyamuni and Tsongkhapa. You can see where the images have been torn from their supports on the wall.

But without doubt the most impressive images in Ratö Monastery are the beautiful murals that cover all four walls of the temple. Unlike those in so many other temples, these paintings are not restorations and the monks claim that they date back to the thirteenth or fourteenth century. Unfortunately water seepage is causing some damage to them now but they remain surprisingly intact. As you enter the temple and turn left, the first images are of the local protector Tse-drek-pa (his face covered with a cloth), Yamantaka, Dharmaraja, Vijaya and Maitreya. On the left-hand wall are Tara, Avalokiteshvara and Maitreya. On the back wall are the lamas of the *Stages on the Path to Enlightenment* lineages, Tsongkhapa, the Fifth Dalai Lama, and the early kings of Tibet and their ministers. The right-hand wall starts with Desi Sanggye Gyatso, and continues with the Thirty-five Buddhas of Confession, the Medicine Buddha, Manjushri, Avalokiteshvara, Dugkarma and Vajrapani. On the front wall as you head back to the entrance are Tara, Vaishravana, Pelden Lhamo and another protector, Drong-dzin.

As you head up through the village to visit the small Maitreya chapel on the hill, you pass on your left an enclosed area with trees and a small shrine. This is where the local protector Tse-drek-pa is supposed to live. The Maitreya Chapel contains nothing of any historic or artistic value, and is simply a good example of an active village temple.

Manjushri (mural at Ratö Monastery).

24. GONGKAR MONASTERY

Gongkar is the name of the administrative region 100 km south of Lhasa. When you cross the Brahmaputra after leaving Lhasa, you can see the Chuwori, the mountain that looms up on the south bank of the river, directly above the bridge. Chuwori is one of the four sacred mountains of Tibet. The castle of Gongkar Dzong, the former centre of the area, now lies in ruins. To visitors Gongkar is best known as the site of the Lhasa airport, and because the monastery is only a few kilometres down the road to Lhasa, a good time to visit it is on your way to or from the airport. When going towards Lhasa, it can be seen about one hundred metres to the left of the road. We visited it as part of a four day trip to Tsetang, the Yarlung Valley and Samye by landcruiser, which cost 570 FEC. The monastery is open daily and there is no entrance charge.

HISTORY
Gongkar Monastery, whose full name is Gongkar Chöde Monastery, was founded by Dorje Denpo Kunga Namgyel and belongs to the lesser known Zung tradition of the Sakya order. It used to house about 160 monks and now has thirty. The main temple building remains more or less intact. During the cultural revolution all the statues were removed and the two upper storeys with their gilded roofs taken down. The surrounding monastic buildings were either destroyed or turned to other uses.

THE SITE
The murals that survive in the assembly hall and elsewhere in the monastery are well worth seeing. Covering the two side-walls of the spacious assembly hall are some excellent scenes from the Buddha's previous lives, as told in the *Paksam Trishing*. Each scene is shown in minute detail, having been painted with very careful and delicate brushstrokes, and bears a short numbered text in Tibetan beneath it. Before entering the chapel at the rear, there are two other older-looking murals to either side of the doorway. The one on the left is a beautiful representation of the Sakya lama Kunga Nyingpo, with smaller images of Drakpa Gyeltsen to the left and Sonam Tsemo to the right. This Sakyapa triad is traditionally called the Three White Ones. To the right of the doorway is a mural in a similar style of the Two Red Ones. Sakya Pandita is the main figure and is accompanied by his nephew Pakpa. The newly-made statues in the assembly hall depict the founder

Front-view of Gongkar Chöde.

of the monastery, Kunga Namgyel (in the centre), Sakya Pandita and Padmasambhava (to the left), and two Buddhas (to the right). The Sixteen Arhats are depicted on the upper wall by the skylight.

There are two dimly-lit protector chapels through a door to the left of the assembly hall. The walls are black and, with a flashlight, fearful animal-headed demons and other deities can be discerned traced in gold, red and white. The further of these two chapels (mind your head on the doorway!) is dedicated to the Sakya protector Gönpo Guru.

The large, high-ceilinged chapel to the rear of the assembly hall is now completely empty, its walls coated in whitewash to obscure the murals. It used to house a tall image of Shakyamuni, which was destroyed during the cultural revolution. If you look at the panelled ceiling you can make out lotuses with the mantra OM MANI PADME HUM written in Sanskrit on their petals. There is an inner circumambulation corridor around this chapel and it is just possible to recognise the twelve deeds of the Buddha painted on the inner wall and the Thousand Buddhas of the aeon on the outer wall. All the walls on this ground floor were whitewashed in the sixties. One can now appreciate the careful and painstaking efforts the monks have made to remove this coat of wash so successfully, especially in the assembly hall.

The **Upper Storey** of the monastery is largely empty and unused but contains the most remarkable **Yidam Chapel**. The walls of this small room are entirely covered with extremely well-painted images of the main tantric deities *(yidams)* of the Sakya tradition. The main image, which faces you as you enter, is that of Hevajra, in front of which used to be a life-sized statue of the deity. The colours of all these murals have been well preserved and the attention to detail is exceptional. Not only the main figures but also all the smaller attendant deities and dakinis associated with their mandalas are shown, the artwork indicating a craftsman of considerable spiritual sensitivity. The deities depicted include Yamantaka, Manjushri (in several forms), Kalachakra and Samvara. There were several I could not recognise.

At the front of the upper storey is a series of rooms, in fairly good condition, reserved for both visiting dignitaries and the principal lamas of the monastery. Although largely devoid of religious images and furniture, the rooms give a good impression of the kind of surroundings in which a high lama would live.

About ten miles from Gongkar Chöde, further along the road to Tsetang, you reach another Sakya monastery called **Rawame**. This temple is easily recognisable by the tall radio mast that protrudes incongruously from its roof. Founded by two Sakya lamas, Kunga Lhundrup and Sherab Pelden, this monastery used to have 120 monks. There are now thirty. It was badly defaced during the cultural revolution and nothing of note, not even one mural, remains. It has only recently been turned back into a monastery and the assembly hall is still used to store sacks of grain.

25. DUNBU CHÖKOR MONASTERY

Dunbu Chökor is a Sakya monastery situated in the village of Chitishö along the southern bank of the Brahmaputra between Gongkar and Tsetang. When coming from Lhasa, you turn right into the village and continue for about three hundred metres until you come to a medium sized monastery surrounded by high walls. Inside there is a large, spacious courtyard. We visited it as part of a four day trip to Tsetang, the Yarlung Valley and Samye by landcruiser, which cost 570 FEC. It is open daily and there is no charge for admission.

HISTORY

Dunbu Chökor was founded in the eleventh century by a *tertön* called Drapa Ngonshe (1012-1090), who came from the nearby village of Dranang. He was a Nyingma lama who served as the abbot of Samye and was the first teacher of the female Tibetan mystic Machik Lachi Drönma. As a *tertön* he was responsible for revealing the *Four Medical Tantras*. He died during a medical operation while having lymph drawn out of his heart with a golden straw. During his lifetime he is reputed to have established 128 temples and shrines. Dunbu Chökor was his principal monastery, as indicated by its name, which means 'Foremost of the Seven (Main) Places where the Dharma is Taught'. It was later taken over by the Sakya order, and was expanded to its present size in the fifteenth century by the Sakya Lama Shedrong Panchen, a disciple of Gorampa Sonam Sengge. The present Dalai Lama stayed here briefly during his flight into exile in 1959. Previously the monastery must have consisted of many more buildings, since it housed one hundred and thirty monks. There are now only twenty.

THE SITE

The main temple building is in fairly good condition in spite of the fact that all its images were removed and have not yet been replaced. The murals, too, are in good repair. In the entrance porch are two interesting paintings, one of the wheel of life and another of the world according to traditional Buddhist cosmology. On the wall to the left immediately as you enter are painted four protectors. The first is Pekor She, a Bön deity converted to Buddhism. Next follow Gönpo Guru – the principal protector in the Sakya tradition, easily recognisable by the short staff he holds horizontally in his two hands – Mahakala and Pelden Lhamo. Down the left-hand wall are shown the twelve major deeds of the Buddha, with three large Buddha figures in the foreground. Just before you enter the chapel at the rear of this assembly hall you can see a beautiful old wall-painting of the famous Sakya lama Kunga Nyingpo.

The chapel itself contains a large altar with several bronzes and many large butter lamps. Previously the main images were a Tara that had been worshipped by the Indian Pandit Chandragomin and a large Maitreya surrounded by the Eight Great Bodhisattvas.

As you leave the chapel, the mural on the left shows the five major Sakya lamas, a group known as the Five Great Ones of the Sakya. These include Sakya Pandita (at the centre), Kunga Nyingpo, Pakpa, Drakpa Gyeltsen and Sonam Tsemo. Through an opening in the right-hand wall can be seen an empty chapel which, judging by the murals, must have been very impressive at one time. It used to house a statue of Buddha Vairocana made by the monastery's founder Drapa Ngonshe. Murals of Hevajra and Dugkarma are painted on the right-hand wall, and on the front wall, just before you reach the entrance, are three more protectors: Vaishravana, the local protector Shalö and Vajrapani. On the upper wall by the skylight are ten more murals. These depict the Sixteen Arhats, the Six Ornaments and Two Supreme Indian philosophers, Padmasambhava and his lineage, the Sakya lineage starting with the *mahasiddha* Virupa, and the Eight Medicine Buddhas. There are two well-executed *tangkas* on the central pillars: one of the Hevajra and one of the Sakya lineage of teachers.

Dorje Drak

From the village of Chitishö it is possible to visit the renowned Nyingma monastery of Dorje Drak. It is situated on the far bank of the Brahmaputra almost directly across from Chitishö. A good view of Dorje Drak can be had just before you arrive in Chitishö from the Lhasa road. It is picturesquely located on the river-bank at the base of a towering mountain. The near bank of the Brahmaputra is about half an hour's walk from the village and a small ferry or coracle can be rented for the crossing.

Dorje Drak was founded in the sixteenth century by the Nyingma lama Tashi Tobgyel. Together with Mindroling it is one of the most important Nyingma monasteries in Central Tibet. Also like Mindroling it was burnt to the ground in the early eighteenth century by the invading Dzungar Mongols but was rebuilt. It is considered as the principal monastery of the 'Northern Tradition' of the Nyingmapa.

It was reduced to ruins during the cultural revolution and only in the last couple of years has restoration work begun. A couple of buildings have been erected but they are yet to be put into use. Apart from a handful of small bronzes, no images of note remain. Eight monks currently live there.

26. MINDROLING MONASTERY

Mindroling is in a small side valley to the south of the road between the village of Dranang and Tsetang. When coming from Lhasa, you turn right off the road shortly after Dranang (which is about 10 km east of Chitishö). It is a couple of kilometres up the valley to the right and does not come into view until you are directly below it. We visited it as part of a four day trip to Tsetang, the Yarlung Valley and Samye by landcruiser, which cost 570 FEC. The monastery is open daily and there is no admission charge.

HISTORY

Mindroling is one of the largest and most important Nyingma Monasteries in Central Tibet. It was founded by the *tertön* Terdak Lingpa (1646-1714) in 1676. Terdak Lingpa was a renowned teacher who included among his disciples the Fifth Dalai Lama. Another important disciple of his was Lochen Dharmashri, a monk who was master of a wide range of subjects including medicine, poetry and painting. Mindroling became a centre of learning where officials from the lay government in Lhasa would traditionally be sent to study. It also attracted a great number of monks from the smaller Nyingma monasteries in Kham and Amdo, who would come there to be trained in Buddhist philosophy and medicine. In 1718 it was burned to the ground by the Dzungar Mongols but was reconstructed and grew into a sizeable monastery housing around three hundred monks. Hermitages and a nunnery were built in the hills behind it, and just below it there used to be a massive thirteen-storey stupa (*kumbum*). The monastery was badly damaged during the cultural revolution but has been partially rebuilt. A small community of twenty or so monks now live here.

THE SITE

The main temple is made out of the characteristic brown stone of the local area and stands out impressively on the higher reaches of a small valley overlooking the village below. A hundred years ago the Indian scholar Chandra Das remarked that 'the neatness of the stonework and the finish of all the masonry about the temple were very remarkable'. This is still true today and can be observed on the ruined walls of the buildings that stood to the right of the main temple.

The central statue in the main hall of the temple is that of Terdak Lingpa, a large figure with a white beard, seated in a glass case. The

throne in the centre of the room is reserved for the incarnate lama of the monastery, a monk called Kunsang Wangyel, now in exile in India. By the throne there is a small, finely-made stupa containing the relics of a lama from Mindroling who was jailed in 1959 and released only twenty-five years later. He spent the last years of his life in Lhasa and died in 1980. After death he sat meditating on the Clear Light for ten days. Murals depicting numerous images of Amitayus cover the walls. These are still being painstakingly restored by carefully peeling off the white paper pasted over them during the cultural revolution.

To the left of the main hall is a small chapel with five Kadampa stupas of different sizes dominating the altar. Two excellent statues of Shakyamuni and Padmasambhava stand among them. Finely painted images of Manjushri cover the walls.

At the back of the main hall is a chapel dedicated to Shakyamuni. The head of the main Buddha is original but the body was destroyed in the cultural revolution and has been remade. Shariputra and Maudgalyayana stand to either side of the Buddha and restored statues of the Eight Great Bodhisattvas stand along the walls. Hayagriva and Vajrapani guard the chapel. There are also two stupas: an Enlightenment

OPPOSITE *The Assembly Hall of Mindroling.*

RIGHT *Stonework at Mindroling.*

Stupa and a Stupa of the Two Purities. Portraits of the present and former Panchen Lamas hang from the central pillars.

There are two chapels open on the upper storey. On the left is the **Dewachen Lhakhang**, dedicated to the memory of Lochen Dharmashri, the main disciple of Terdak Lingpa. The small room used to contain a statue of the master, but there is now just one *tangka* hanging from one of the walls. On the altar stand many Kadampa stupas and small bronzes of lamas from all four orders of Tibetan Buddhism. Portraits of the three Tibetan kings Songtsen Gampo, Trisong Detsen and Nyatri Tsenpo are painted on the rear wall.

Next door is the **Lama Lhakhang**, a bare room with exceptional and highly original murals of the lamas in the Nyingma lineage. Each figure has its own peculiar posture and expression, giving a strong sense of the vitality of the Nyingma tradition. The central image is a new painting of Samantabhadra and consort, considered, in the Nyingma tradition, as the 'Primordial Buddha'. Originally there was a statue of this deity but it was destroyed. The small altar houses a number of bronzes recently returned to the monastery by local people. There are figures of two *tertöns*, Tara, Vajrasattva and Padmasambhava. To the right of the altar is a rock bearing what is supposed to be the hoofprint of Terdak Lingpa's horse, Spontaneous Tara. A *tangka* of Terdak Lingpa commissioned by the Fifth Dalai Lama hangs from one of the pillars. The hand- and footprints of the master are clearly visible on the painting.

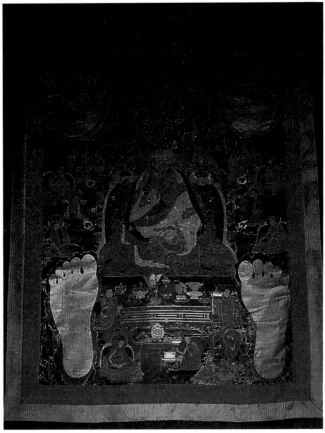

Tangka of Terdak Lingpa, the founder of Mindroling, in the Lama Lhakhang.

A passageway from the roof of the main temple leads you to an older part of the monastery that has not yet been restored. Here you can see the original assembly hall, which now stands empty. The murals around the upper walls were reputedly painted by Lochen Dharmashri. As you leave this building, you may see a striking portrait of Padmasambhava painted on the wall by the side of the entrance to the former assembly hall. This was also painted by Lochen Dharmashri and represents the Guru as he appeared in a vision to Terdak Lingpa.

27. SAMYE MONASTERY

Samye is located on the north bank of the Brahmaputra about 40 km west of Tsetang. To reach it you need to take a ferry – a locally built, flat-bottomed boat powered by a small tractor engine – that leaves from the opposite shore by the main Lhasa-Tsetang road, slightly upstream from the monastery. The ferry ride takes an hour and a half since it has to meander across to avoid the sandbanks. (A friend who crossed with a group of Tibetan pilgrims related how when the boat got stuck on a sandbank in midstream the immediate response of the passengers was to whip out their prayer wheels and start frantically spinning!) It is nonetheless a beautiful journey. The ferry will leave whenever it has enough people willing to pay the 25 RMB it costs to hire it. When full you pay 1-2 RMB each (foreigners usually end up paying more than the Tibetans).

On the other bank a tractor and a cultivator wait with trailers attached. The tractor charges 25 RMB to the monastery, the cultivator 12 RMB, again this is divided by the number of people on board. The journey takes about forty minutes through a sandy terrain in which the vehicles tend to get stuck. There is a guesthouse at Samye itself in a fairly congenial courtyard. You pay 3 RMB in a five-bed room. A small and very rudimentary restaurant can be found on the opposite side of the monastery to the guesthouse, where they will fill your thermos with hot water and provide tukpa for 50 fen. We visited Samye as part of a four day trip to Tsetang, the Yarlung Valley and Samye by landcruiser, which cost 570 FEC. The monastery is open from 9 to 12 in the morning and 3 to 5 in the afternoon. There is no admission charge. It is good to arrange the return journey with the tractor driver beforehand. Trekkers can hike to Samye from Ganden in two or three days.

As you approach Samye along the road that leads from the ferry-stop to the monastery, you will notice on the ridge of the hillside two small white stupas, carved out of the very rock itself, a few feet apart from each other. They mark the spot where King Trisong Detsen came to meet Padmasambhava, who had just arrived from India.

HISTORY

Samye was the first monastery to be built in Tibet. It was probably founded during the 770's under the patronage of King Trisong Detsen, with the work being directed by Padmasambhava and Shantarakshita, the two Indian masters the king had invited to Tibet to help consolidate the Buddhist faith. The monastery was designed on the plan of the Odantapuri temple in present-day Bihar, India, and mirrored the basic

Samye Monastery, 1949.

structure of the universe as described in Buddhist cosmology. The central temple represents Mt. Sumeru, the mythical mountain at the centre of the cosmos. Around it are four temples called 'ling', which represent the four continents (*ling*) situated in the vast ocean to the north, south, east and west of Sumeru. To the right and left of each of these temples are two smaller temples called 'ling-tren', representing the sub-continents (ling-tren) of the Buddhist universe. There are even two chapels representing the sun and the moon. The entire monastery was surrounded by a circular wall topped with numerous small stupas, and four great stupas in four colours (white, red, blue and green) stood facing the south-east, south-west, north-west and north-east corners of the main temple respectively.

Samye is located at the foot of one of Tibet's four holy mountains, Hepori, on which, in ancient times, Trisong Detsen was supposed to have had his palace. The king was born in the nearby village of Drakmar further up the valley, where a small shrine still marks the spot. The surrounding landscape consists of barren mountains and sand dunes, with the monastery and village occupying a small fertile patch of land in a valley leading to the mountains in the north.

PREVIOUS PAGE *The barren landscape around Samye. On the right are the two stupas marking the place where Trisong Detsen first greeted Padmasambhava.*

Samye is an especially important monastery because it was here, towards the end of the eighth century, that the first Tibetans were ordained as monks by the Indian Abbot Shantarakshita. Seven men from noble families were tested by Shantarakshita to see if they were suitable for the monastic life and then ordained, presumably in the company of other Indian monks accompanying the abbot. They are known even today as the 'Seven Examined Men'.

When the monastery was first built, both Indian and Chinese monks were invited there to work on the translation of Buddhist scriptures from their respective languages into Tibetan. (The Indians lived in the Aryapalo (Hayagriva) Ling temple to the south, while the Chinese lived in the Jampa Ling to the west.) Conflicts arose between the two factions concerning doctrinal interpretation and the king had to call for a public debate to settle the matter. This took place around 792 between a representative of Indian Buddhism, the scholar Kamalashila (a disciple of Shantarakshita, one of the founders of Samye) and a Chinese Ch'an teacher called Hoshang Mahayana. The debate was presided over by King Trisong Detsen and was intended to establish which form of Buddhism should prevail in Tibet: the Indian tradition of systematic study, firm adherence to ethical rules, and a practice that entails the gradual ascendance of stages leading to enlightenment; or the Chinese tradition of Ch'an (Zen), which emphasises the possibility of 'sudden', 'instantaneous' bursts of enlightenment and the following of a spiritual life that lays itself open to these possibilities. The records of the outcome of the arguments pursued in the debate are ambiguous: both sides claim that they won. The actual outcome, though, is beyond doubt: the Indian view was favoured and from then on the Chinese influence waned. Mahayana had to leave Tibet and the Ch'an tradition was effectively proscribed. The place where the debate took place was the Jampa Ling, the residence of the Chinese monks.

At the time of the founding of Samye there were no separate schools of Tibetan Buddhism, but because Padmasambhava is so closely connected with the creation of the monastery it has always been strongly associated with the Nyingma tradition. The monks who returned in the eleventh century from Kham and Amdo, where their predecessors had gone into exile during the suppression of Buddhism by Langdarma, established Samye as an important Nyingma monastery. It was later taken over by the Sakya tradition and more recently came under the influence of the Gelukpa. But this holy, ancient shrine has always been rather eclectic. Even today the monks insist that the monastery does not belong to any particular school although it is inhabited primarily by adherents of both the Nyingma and Sakya traditions.

In the course of its history the monastery has been repeatedly damaged by fire and then restored. The original buildings erected in the eighth century were burned down in 986 and rebuilt by the famous translator Ra Lotsawa. Other restoration work was carried out by the Sakya lama Kunga Rigdzin, Demo Ngawang Jampel Delek Gyatso (a teacher of the Third Dalai Lama), and the Tenth Dalai Lama, Tsultrim Gyatso.

The monastery was damaged during the cultural revolution but not totally destroyed as is sometimes suggested. The greatest harm it suffered was the removal of the magnificent upper storeys of the main temple, whose glittering golden rooftops and spires were once a beauty to behold. The four *ling* and most of the eight *ling-tren* temples are still standing but are either empty or used as storerooms. No trace remains of the four giant stupas, and the encircling wall has partially collapsed. The village has now encroached on the monastery grounds to the extent that the whole place seems like a farmyard, with cattle, yaks, pigs and chickens roaming everywhere.

The main temple of Samye.

Trisong Detsen's stele proclaiming Buddhism as the state religion of Tibet.

THE SITE

As you stand in front of the entrance to the main temple in Samye, you will notice an ancient stele on the left. This is the record of an edict made in 779 by King Trisong Detsen, officially proclaiming, for the first time, Buddhism to be the state religion of Tibet. An old bell hanging from the roof right above the entrance might also date back to the times of the early kings. Two attractive stone elephants also stand by the entrance.

The main temple is renowned for each storey's being designed in a different architectural style. Unfortunately, my sources (the monk who looks after the temple, Giuseppe Tucci and my Tibetan encyclopedia) disagree as to which storey is in which style. On visiting the temples one will see that it is not at all obvious; stylistic differences can be observed but none of them is clearly Chinese, Tibetan or Indian. And since the third storey no longer exists, no comparisons with it are possible. Since two sources (the caretaker-monk and Tucci) agree that the ground floor is Chinese in style, I will assume that to be the case. But since all three sources disagree about the first floor, you can make your own decision!

The large, cavernous ground floor is divided into two main sections: an **Assembly Hall** and, connected to it, the **Main Chapel**, dedicated to Shakyamuni. The murals around the walls of the assembly hall date back to the time of the Thirteenth Dalai Lama. A fine portrait of Hevajra surrounded by attendant dakinis on one wall suggests a strong Sakyapa influence. At the front of the room, to either side of the entrance of the Chapel, are a series of eleven superb statues of identical size representing famous personages associated with the monastery. The five figures to the left are the translator Vairocana, Shantarakshita, Padmasambhava, Trisong Detsen and Songtsen Gampo, most of whom were instrumental in the early phases of Samye's history. To the right, on the other side of the chapel entrance, are Drom Tönpa, Atisha and Ngog Legpa'i Sherab – the familiar Kadampa triad. Atisha is recorded as having visited Samye, discovering in the library there many Sanskrit texts no longer extant in India. Longchenpa, Sakya Pandita and Tsongkhapa – a less common triad known as the Three Incarnations of Manjushri – sit next to the Kadampa masters. This grouping is noteworthy for its non-sectarianism: Longchenpa was a famous Nyingma lama, Sakya Pandita a Sakya lama, and Tsongkhapa founder of the Geluk order.

The entrance to the chapel is unusual in that it consists of three tall doorways, a feature rarely found in other Tibetan temples and supposedly a characteristic of Chinese temple architecture. The three doorways symbolise the 'Three Doors of Liberation', which are emptiness, signlessness and wishlessness. This beautiful and impressive chamber has as its centrepiece a large stone statue of Shakyamuni, apparently at the age of thirty-eight. This statue is supposed to have appeared miraculously on Hepori at the time of King Trisong Detsen when the monastery was being built. During the cultural revolution the head was damaged but has been well restored. Since the image is covered in drapery, it is impossible to study the stonework. Lining the walls on each side of the room are five tall bodhisattva figures. These images, which are newly made, depict the Buddhas of the Ten Directions, in the aspect of bodhisattvas. They consist of the Eight Great Bodhisattvas plus two others: Drimamepa and Kawa'i Pe. Behind each of the standing figures is a painted mural of the corresponding Buddha. These paintings are

Carved animals above the entrance to the main temple.

presumably quite old. Two giant wrathful deities, Khamsum Namgyel and Acala, guard the shrine. The high, panelled ceiling depicts, in each panel, a tantric mandala. It is difficult to identify them but the monks explained that they are the mandalas of the main supreme yoga tantra deities as well as some from the lower three classes of tantra. The throne reserved for the Dalai Lama is to the right of the entrance.

It is possible to follow an inner circumambulation path around the chapel. Murals of the deeds of the historical Buddha and some *jataka* tales adorn the wall.

A doorway in the right-hand wall of the assembly hall leads you into the **Protector Chapel.** This dark and eerie room evokes a strong feeling of the pre-Buddhist, shamanistic culture of Tibet. There are none of the commoner, more explicitly 'Buddhist' protectors here, only some of the older Bön deities that were converted by Padmasambhava. The main figure is Pehar, almost unidentifiable because of the great number of clothes and scarves draped over him. To the right are Tsemar, Peldön Masung Gyelpo (with a stuffed fox hanging from his belt and a horn and a lasso above him), and the truly scary Nöjin Chiyungbum. Tied to one of the pillars are a gigantic stuffed snake, an old musket and a sword. Not a room for the fainthearted!

To the left of the main assembly hall and chapel is an **Avalokiteshvara Chapel**, which is entered from the front of the building. This small shrine was built by the Sakya lama Sonam Gyeltsen on the death of his mother. It contains in relief on the back wall a wonderful thousand-armed Avalokiteshvara made of clay. An old statue of Padmasambhava is in the right hand corner and next to him an unusual image of Songtsen Gampo. The remains of Kunga Zangpo, a disciple of Tsongkhapa, are enshrined in a glass case to the right. On the wall by their side is the walking stick of the translator Vairocana. Smaller images of Padmasambhava as well as seven relief carvings on slabs of stone (depicting Milarepa, Atisha, Tara and Padmasambhava) can also be seen. The relief carvings were taken from the large white stupa to the south-east of the monastery. Lamas from all four Tibetan Buddhist traditions are painted around the walls.

There are two chapels open on the **upper storey** of the temple. The main chapel, directly above the Shakyamuni chapel below, is dedicated to Padmasambhava. A large, imposing and slightly wrathful statue of the Guru is the central figure in this spacious and rather bare, square room. To his immediate left and right are images of two of the most important Nyingma lamas to succeed him, Longchen Rabjampa and Jigme Lingpa. An ancient and miraculously undamaged statue of Amitayus is to the far left and an old Buddha figure to the far right. As with the chapel downstairs, paintings of the Buddhas of the Ten Directions are found on the walls, but the accompanying statues have been removed. An interior circumambulation path surrounds the room and its walls are also decorated with images from the Buddha's previous lives.

Some detailed murals worth studying are found by the entrance to this chapel. On the left are numerous scenes from the life of Padmasambhava as described in the *Padma Ka Tang*, a well-known biography of the master discovered in Samye and Sheldrak by Ogyen Lingpa in the thirteenth century. To the right are the Seventh Dalai Lama, surrounded by the early kings and former Dalai Lamas, and the Fifth Dalai Lama, surrounded by more images of Padmasambhava.

If you pay the caretaker-monk 20 fen, he will also let you in to the **Quarters of the Dalai Lama**. These are located to the left of the main chapel at the front of the upper storey. There are three rooms, the first of which is a completely bare ante-chamber. You then enter the throne room, which presumably served as a small audience chamber. Of greatest note here is a very fine old mural of Samye protected by a cloth drape. It is worthwhile comparing the details of this painting with what remains of the monastery today. The bedroom also has some beautiful old murals depicting the Buddha, Maitreya and Tara. Among the bronzes, a standing Padmapani (Avalokiteshvara) is of note.

The main temple can be circumambulated by a covered cloister that runs around the inside of the courtyard. It is lined with prayer-wheels on one side and extensive, though partially defaced, murals on the other. Large images of the Thirty-five Buddhas of Confession are depicted at regular intervals, surrounded by scenes from a *jataka* text that describes the 500 pure and 500 impure previous incarnations of Buddha Shakyamuni. The pure incarnations refer to the times that he was born as a human or a god, the impure to the times that he was born as an animal. On the front wall (to the left and right of the entrance) paintings of the country of Shambhala, the world as conceived in Buddhist traditional cosmology, and Samye itself can be seen.

Of the four *ling* temples, the only one we were allowed to visit was the **Aryapalo Ling**, which is located about a hundred and fifty metres to the south of the monastery. This renowned temple is frequently mentioned in the *Padma Ka Tang*. Although the exterior of the temple is in very good condition, it has been desecrated inside and now stands empty. It used to house a statue of Hayagriva. Murals, probably of this century, can be seen but they are in a poor state. The most interesting ones are found by the balcony on the first storey. These depict strange deva creatures riding dragons, scorpions, elephants and bears.

Detail of mural in the Aryapalo Ling depicting beings riding scorpions.

To the left of Aryapalo Ling you can see a yellowish, single storey building, which is the library where much of the translation work of Buddhist texts by Indian pandits and Tibetan scholars was performed. This is one of the 'ling-tren' temples.

The *ling* temple to the west, **Jampa Ling**, was where the Chinese monks lived before the great debate. It is a reddish building recognisable by its peculiar red apse. It marks the place where the debate between Kamalashila and Hoshang Mahayana was held. This temple is now unused but the throne of Kamalashila, the Indian participant in the debate, is apparently still preserved inside.

About a quarter of a mile to the south of Samye is a large compound with high walls called **Kamsum Sanggak Ling**. This impressive, multi-storey structure has now been converted into living quarters for the local people. The main temple is used as a storeroom and apparently several murals still survive (we were unable to go inside).

It is well worth climbing **Hepori**, the small mountain behind Samye. It affords an excellent view of the monastery and valley and the vast Brahmaputra basin. There are also several carvings on the rocks and the remains of some fortifications and stupas.

Yamalung and Chimpuk

Two retreat centres can be reached in several hours by foot from Samye. The first is **Yamalung**, off the path over the mountains to Ganden. There are now only two small buildings looked after by an old monk who spends his time in retreat there. Padmasambhava and Yeshe Tsogyel are both supposed to have meditated there.

The other retreat site is **Chimpuk**, a warren of caves that dates back to very early times. In 776 it was the place where Padmasambhava initiated the 'Twenty Five Adepts of Chimpuk' (among whom were included the King Trisong Detsen) into the secrets of the Mahayoga tantras. Both he and Yeshe Tsogyel lived there for extended periods. It is located up a smaller valley to the north-east of Samye and can be reached by foot in about four hours. There are several hermit nuns and a couple of monks living there.

28. TSETANG

*Tsetang is the largest town in the Lhoka region, an area south of Lhasa along the banks of the Brahmaputra river. By road it is 170 km from the capital. Although originally overshadowed by the neighbouring town of Netong, it slowly gained prominence and is now a kind of regional capital with a typically drab and functional Chinese 'new town' added on to the cluttered, filthy but more homely Tibetan quarter. There is a daily bus service from Lhasa to Tsetang, which leaves at 8 am and usually arrives in the late afternoon. We visited it as part of a four day trip to Tsetang, the Yarlung Valley and Samye by landcruiser, which cost 570 FEC. There are two hotels in Tsetang, situated next to each other at the south end of town. The first is a fancy, modern place, which reminded me of a sunken ocean liner. Its ugly white and red form stands out for miles around and is a good landmark. This is presumably where tour groups are put up. Next door is the thoroughly utilitarian **Tsetang Guest House**, which is scrupulously clean but utterly devoid of feeling. We were charged 5 RMB per bed in a two-bed room which, in terms of comfort and value, was the best we had in Tibet. A filling Chinese meal can be bought in the adjoining dining hall for 1.15 RMB, but you have to buy meal tickets beforehand from the desk.*

*Tsetang is not so interesting in itself but it serves as a base for visiting the surrounding area. Tibetan civilisation began around here and some traces of those times are still visible. From Tsetang one has easy access to Samye, as well as to the valleys of **Yarlung** and **Chonggye**. Until 1959 these wide, fertile valleys were studded with numerous temples, shrines and stupas. Very few indeed have survived the cultural revolution. Of most there is not even a trace remaining. The famous **Yumbulagang**, the earliest building in Tibet, and the ancient **Trandruk Monastery** are all that have been reconstructed in the Yarlung Valley. The **Tombs of the Ancient Kings** can still be seen in the adjoining Chonggye valley but only a couple of temples, **Tangboche** and **Rechung-Puk**, are in any sense still intact. These sites are described separately below (see Chapters 29-33).*

*About 17 km to the east of Tsetang on the opposite bank of the Brahmaputra lie the ruins of **Densatil Monastery**, founded in 1158 by the renowned Lama Pamotrupa, a disciple of Gampopa. Densatil was the first great Kagyu monastery and from here disciples of Pamotrupa went forth to establish the monasteries of Drigung, Talung and Ralung. The monastery is located high above the valley but only one dilapidated chapel and a single monk remain, perhaps on the site where Pamotrupa's meditation hut used to be. The monastery also used to house the tombs of the powerful Pamotrupa kings, who seized control of Tibet from the Sakyapas in the fourteenth century.*

*Further along the river from Densatil is the side valley leading to **Olka**, a place where Tsongkhapa spent many years in retreat and built his famous Maitreya Chapel. There is still a small monastery here with a handful of monks in residence. By going north up the valley and over the mountains from here it is possible to reach the renowned **Lhamo'i Latso**, the 'Oracle Lake' of Pelden Lhamo, formally consecrated as a Buddhist site by Gendun Gyatso, the Second Dalai Lama. This is a hard climb and there are no facilities at the lake, so do not attempt this trek without sufficient preparation.*

*By travelling south of Tsetang along the road through Yarlung that eventually brings you to Bhutan, you will arrive at the region of **Lhodrak**. This is where Marpa, the teacher of Milarepa, lived. A day's journey by landcruiser will bring you to **Sekargutok**, the nine-storey tower that Milarepa built for his teacher to prove his sincerity and atone for his former evils. Although the roof has been damaged, the basic structure still stands and it is a popular place for pilgrimage.*

HISTORY

The old town is built along the base of the **Gangpo Ri**, one of the four sacred mountains of Tibet, where Avalokiteshvara descended into the country in the form of a monkey and mated with a demoness to produce the first member of the Tibetan race. The name 'Tsetang' literally means 'playground', i.e. the place where the children of the monkey and the demoness, the first Tibetans, came down to play. A shrine in honour of this progenitor and his mate can still be found at the top of the mountain, but is was considerably damaged during the cultural revolution. Behind the hospital is the site where the first cultivated field in Tibet is said to have been. The town itself was established in 1351 by Jangchub Gyeltsen, the powerful leader of the Pamotrupa dynasty who overthrew the Sakyapa in 1354 to become ruler of Tibet.

SITES

If you walk up the main street of the old town, you will arrive at a sort of square with a large old crumbling monastery to the left. This is what remains of Tsetang's foremost monastery, **Ganden Chökor Ling**, founded by a monk called Sonam Topgyel, and previously home to several hundred monks. It is now deserted and is used as a storeroom. To its left is a single-storey, white building in good condition, which used to be **Ngachö Monastery**. It has now been turned to other uses.

By turning to the right and continuing to the upper edge of town, you reach a small temple called the **Sang-ngag Zimche Nunnery**. This was founded on the site of a cave where Kyerong Ngawang Trakpa meditated and is reputedly one of the first Gelukpa nunneries. Above the nunnery are found the ruins of a Kadampa monastery called Chözom Ling. Six nuns, most of whom are young, live there at present.

Ganden Chökor Ling in Tsetang, 1935.

The main chapel of the nunnery has as its central image an old statue of Avalokiteshvara supposedly dating from the time of Songtsen Gampo. Other images of several Buddhas, Tsongkhapa, Tara and Tangtong Gyelpo are lined alongside it. In small niches in the wall behind are the Sixteen Arhats and the Thirty-five Buddhas of Confession. There are two other chapels around the back of this main room, which are entered through the kitchen. One contains an image of Kyerong Ngawang Trakpa, to the left of whom sits Avalokiteshvara on a lion and to the right Manjushri. This room is half shrine and half dwelling for two monks. The adjoining room is a chamber reserved for visiting lamas. The main images are of Tsongkhapa and his two chief disciples, Tangtong Gyelpo, and Atisha. An interesting photograph of Trijang Rinpoche at the age of twenty hangs from one of the roof beams.

As you leave the nunnery and stand outside you may notice on the hillside to your left in large letters the mantra OM MANI PADME HUM outlined in white stones. The inscription of such mantras on hillsides was quite a common practice in Tibet. Nowadays it is fairly rare to see them.

Sheldrak

Looking across the town and valley to the west you can see a high, pointed mountain standing out from the surrounding hills. Higher up near the summit is the **Sheldrak (Crystal Rock) Cave** of Padmasambhava. This highly revered site is about a six hour walk from Tsetang. One monk lives there as caretaker of the rather bare shrine. The ruins of an old monastery can be seen and the view is spectacular. Yeshe Tsogyel concealed several texts here among which was the *Padma Ka Tang*, the biography of Padmasambhava, rediscovered in the thirteenth century by Ogyen Lingpa.

OPPOSITE *View of Padmasambhava's cave at Sheltrak,* BELOW *the caretaker reciting prayers.*

29. TRANDRUK TEMPLE

Trandruk is situated in the middle of a village about 7 km south of Tsetang on the road leading into the Yarlung valley. In its present dilapidated state it is somewhat difficult to spot from the road, but the local people will point it out to you. We visited it as part of a four day trip to Tsetang, the Yarlung Valley and Samye by landcruiser, which cost 570 FEC. It is open daily and there is no charge for admission.

HISTORY

Trandruk is considered to be one of the first Buddhist temples built in Tibet. Together with the Jokhang and the Ramoche temples in Lhasa, its founding is attributed to King Songtsen Gampo in the seventh century, who is said to have erected it to house a spontaneously formed image of Tara that miraculously appeared on the site. It is regarded as one of the four Tadul (Extremity Subduing) temples built by Songtsen Gampo to subdue a demoness who was threatening the peace and stability of the land. These four temples are located at places that are said to correspond to the shoulders and hips of the demoness. The Katsel Temple near Medrogungkar (*see Chapter 16*) is another of these Tadul Temples. (The other two are the Buchu Temple in Kongpo and the Dram Temple in Tsang). It was repaired and enlarged by King Trisong Detsen and further expanded in the fourteenth and seventeenth centuries. It was also damaged at the beginning of the eighteenth century by the Dzungkar Mongols and subsequently repaired by the Dalai Lamas. The buildings suffered considerable damage during the cultural revolution and now only a few of them remain intact and only a handful of artefacts survive. Previously it was famous for its large bell inscribed with the name of King Trisong Detsen, a kitchen containing the implements of the king's Chinese queen, and a statue of the queen. Its most precious piece in recent times was a *tangka* of Avalokiteshvara embroidered with pearls, but even this has just been moved to Lhasa for 'safe-keeping'.

THE SITE

To the right of the main gate as you enter the monastery is a small room containing a large prayer wheel. Around the walls are some old and attractive murals of Avalokiteshvara, a Vijaya Stupa, Amitayus, Tsongkhapa and a fine eleven-armed Avalokiteshvara at the back.

The temple at the rear of the main courtyard is currently being rebuilt

Trandruk Temple, 1949.

and the only chapel open to the public is a small shrine entered through the left of the courtyard and round the back. The central image here is a beautiful piece-work *tangka* of Shakyamuni, composed in soft and balanced colours. An ornate wooden altar contains small statues of Padmasambhava, Tara and the Medicine Buddha. *Tangkas* of the Sixteen Arhats, eight along each side wall, and two *tangkas* of the Karmapa also adorn the room.

30. YUMBULAGANG

Yumbulagang is about 12 km down the road due south of Tsetang. You cannot miss it. We visited it as part of a four day trip to Tsetang, the Yarlung Valley and Samye by landcruiser, which cost 570 FEC. It is also possible to hitch or walk from Tsetang. It is open daily and there is no charge for admission.

HISTORY

Yumbulagang is reputedly the oldest dwelling place in Tibet, being associated with the first, quasi-mythical king Nyatri Tsenpo, and situated in the historical Yarlung valley. This tall, dignified building rises erect on the spur of a hill, commanding an impressive view of the entire valley. It was destroyed during the cultural revolution and the present building is a replica of the original, rebuilt in 1982. Scholars aver that the structure that stood on the site until the mid-sixties probably dated back to the seventh or eighth century and may well have been built by one of the Great Tibetan kings, Songtsen Gampo or Trisong Detsen. Tibetan murals suggest that the building found its final form during the time of the Fifth Dalai Lama.

THE SITE

Yumbulagang has long ceased to be used as a dwelling or fortress and has been turned into a chapel. The ground floor is a shrine in honour of the ancient kings. The central figure is a Buddha called 'Jowo Norbu Sampel', who presides over the assembled kings and ministers. To the left of the Buddha is King Nyatri Tsenpo and to the right King Songtsen Gampo. Along the left-hand wall are lined Songtsen Gampo's minister Tönmi Sambhota and the kings Trisong Detsen and Tori Nyentsen. Facing them along the right-hand wall are the kings Tri Ralpachen and Ö Sung, followed by Songtsen Gampo's minister Gawa.

The upper storey houses a delightful chapel built around a balcony from which you can look down into the shrine of the kings below. The main images on the altar are Avalokiteshvara and Shakyamuni. The statue of Avalokiteshvara is a replica of the one originally here, which was in the same style as the one enshrined in the Lokeshvara Chapel in the Potala. An old, faded *tangka*, recovered from the ruins of the original building, is framed behind glass to the left of the altar. The murals are newly painted in a naive, folkloristic style. On the left of the room the mural depicts the earliest events of Tibetan history. Nyatri Tsenpo is shown descending from the heavens and settling in an early form of the Yumbulagang. A Buddhist scripture is seen descending from the sky at the time of King Latotori and falling onto the tower of the Yumbulagang. Padmasambhava is also shown meditating in a cave. The murals on the opposite wall depict the Twenty-one Taras, Padmasambhava, and Shakyamuni with the Sixteen Arhats. A collection of small, old bronzes is also housed in a case in the corner by the altar. These include statues of Avalokiteshvara, Padmasambhava and his consorts, and the triad of Padmasambhava, Trisong Detsen and Shantarakshita.

The Yumbulagang is presently cared for by five elderly Gelukpa monks.

31. RECHUNG PUK MONASTERY

Rechung Puk can be reached from either the Yarlung or Chonggye Valleys. Its ruins can be seen from afar on the ridge of the mountain that separates the two valleys. From Yarlung you turn west off the road between Trandruk and Yumbulagang to the village at the base of the ridge. From Chonggye you go to Tangboche and then along the base of the hill until you reach the same village. It is a steep half-hour walk up a precipitous, shale-covered slope to the monastery itself. We visited it as part of a four day trip to Tsetang, the Yarlung Valley and Samye by landcruiser, which cost 570 FEC. It is open daily and there is no charge for admission.

HISTORY
One of Milarepa's foremost disciples was a yogi named Rechungpa (1083-1161). He was only eleven years old when he met Milarepa and spent many years practising under his guidance. He travelled twice to India, where he also studied extensively with Indian teachers. It was to Rechungpa that Milarepa dictated his famous biography shortly before he died. Rechung Puk is one of the caves where Rechungpa spent some time meditating; it literally means 'Rechung's Cave'. Originally just a humble cave on the ridge of the mountain that divides the Yarlung and Chonggye valleys, its association with the renowned Rechungpa encouraged the building of a large monastery around it which, in its heyday, housed about a thousand monks. By 1959, however, the population had dwindled to sixty.

THE SITE
Today all that remains of Rechung Puk is a small cluster of white buildings, which have been rebuilt around the site of the cave, below the ruins of the main monastery. There are now nine monks living here, including a young incarnate lama from Kham, who acts as the abbot and teacher. The monastery belongs to a tradition called the Rechung Nyinggyu, in which teachings from both Nyingma and Kagyu sources are combined.

There are three small chapels to visit. On the left, immediately upon arrival at the monastery, is a room that serves as the assembly hall for the monks. While we were there, they were in the process of consecrating two new images that had just arrived from Lhasa. One was of Padmasambhava and the other of Tsang-nyang Heruka. The latter is

ABOVE *Rechung Puk, 1949.*

BELOW *Rechungpa's cave, now housing an altar with images of (from left to right) Milarepa, Marpa and Rechungpa. The dakini Dorje Pagmo is at the front of the altar.*

OPPOSITE *The remaining buildings of Rechung Puk clinging to the hillside.*

regarded as the reincarnation of Rechungpa's speech. Tsang-nyang Heruka is perhaps another name for Gyare Yeshe Dorje (1161-1211), the founder of Ralung Monastery and one of the main figures in the Drukpa Kagyu lineage.

As you climb up the narrow stairway leading to Rechungpa's cave you will pass another tiny room on your right, which serves as the protector chapel. It is so small that only two monks can fit in at any one time.

The chapel built around the cave itself is a low, dark room: the 'cave' is little more than an indentation in the cliffside. Presumably Rechungpa, too, built a little hut for additional protection. An altar is set into this niche in the wall and bears a statue of Marpa (in the centre), Milarepa (to the left) and Rechungpa (to the right). A small statue of the dakini Vajravarahi (Dorje Pagmo), the personal deity of Rechungpa, stands below them. Also on the altar is a rock with the footprint of Tsang-nyang Heruka. To have this rock rubbed on your back is thought to be remedial.

32. TANGBOCHE MONASTERY

Tangboche is about a third of the way down the Chonggye valley from Tsetang. Keep a careful lookout for the square temple building at the base of the hillside in a village, on the left of the valley if you come from Tsetang, on the right if you come from the tombs. Then follow the rough track from the main road to the village. We visited Tangboche as part of a four day trip to Tsetang, the Yarlung Valley and Samye by landcruiser, which cost 570 FEC. It is open daily and there is no charge for admission.

HISTORY
Tangboche means 'great plain'. This area in the lower Chonggye valley derives its name from the time when the vast forest on the hillside burned down and showered the valley below with ash and charcoal, causing people to call it 'solnak tangboche', the 'great plain of coals'. It is believed that a monastery was founded here as early as the seventh or eighth century by a disciple of the famous Indian Master Chandragomin. It was revived in 1017 by a monk called Tsultrim Jungne, a disciple of Lumpa Lume-pa, one of the main figures responsible for the re-establishment of the monastic order in Central Tibet and Tsang after the suppression of Buddhism by Langdarma. During the eleventh century the abbot of Tangboche, Tsöndru Yongdrup, invited Atisha to live in the monastery. The Indian master accepted and for some time resided in a small hermitage on the hillside facing the main temple. Two relics from the time of Atisha were cherished by the monastery: a statue of the master and a set of twelve texts brought by him from India. These were lost during the cultural revolution and efforts are still being made by the monks to retrieve them. In writings of the Kadampa masters, Tangboche is mentioned as possessing a rare Indian statue of the Buddha, purportedly made during the time of the Buddha himself. This too has been lost. Fifty monks used to live here in dwellings surrounding the main temple but now only eleven remain.

THE SITE
The altar in the main hall of Tangboche contains very few images, most of them small bronzes recently offered to the monastery by the government to replace what has been lost. There are several Buddhas, a fine red dakini, and Atisha. To the right of the altar is the throne of the incarnate lama of the monastery, Jampa Kelsang, who is now in exile in Germany.

Although the hall is rather low on statues it possesses some extremely beautiful murals, which cover all four walls. These were commissioned in 1915 by the Thirteenth Dalai Lama and are still in good condition. Starting from the left as you enter through the main doorway, the deities depicted are as follows: Pelden Lhamo, accompanied by two lion-headed beings and painted with extraordinary attention to detail; Vaishravana; Manjushri; Vajrasattva; Vajrapani; Kun-rig; Vairocana; Samvara and consort surrounded by the four principal dakinis of the mandala; Buddha Shakyamuni; a two-armed Yamantaka with consort, an unusual representation associated with the advanced 'Stages of Completion' phase of tantric practice; and Atisha. Going past the altar over to the opposite wall you will find the triad of Padmasambhava, Trisong Detsen and Shantarakshita; the Eight Medicine Buddhas; an exquisite Avalokiteshvara mounted on a lion (Chenrezi Sengge Dra); the Eight Taras who Dispel Fear; Mahakala; and Dharmaraja.

A small and bare protector chapel can also be entered from this main hall. Again there are no statues, only the murals having survived. These are painted in gold, white and red on black and depict the protectors of the five directions, Padmasambhava, the Lion-Faced Dakini and Vaishravana.

From the upper storey one can study the fine murals of Buddha and the Sixteen Arhats, and the Fifth and the Thirteenth Dalai Lamas painted along the back of the raised, sky-light section of the main hall.

OPPOSITE *The deity Sarvavid (*Tib. Kun Rig*), an emanation of the Buddha Vairocana. A mural at Tangboche Monastery.*

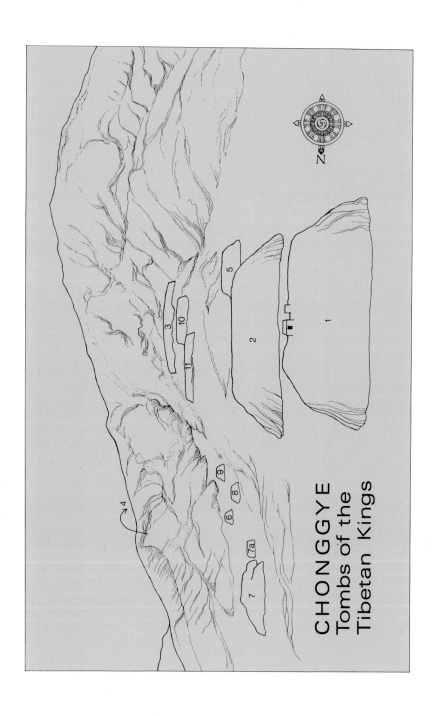

CHONGGYE
Tombs of the
Tibetan Kings

33. CHONGGYE: THE TOMBS OF THE TIBETAN KINGS

Chonggye is the name of the valley south of Tsetang at the end of which are the tombs of the early great Tibetan Kings. It is a straighforward 25 km drive from Tsetang to the tombs. Shortly before you enter the valley itself you can see a small hill (Yarlha Zhampo) not far from the road that marks the place where the first Tibetan king Nyatri Tsenpo is supposed to have descended into Tibet from the skies. We visited the tombs as part of a four day trip to Tsetang, the Yarlung Valley and Samye by landcruiser, which cost 570 FEC. There is no charge for admission.

THE SITE

Chonggye was the site chosen by the early Tibetan kings as their burial ground. The large, eroded tumuli that mark the tombs are found at the end of the valley. The biggest and most easily recognisable tomb – with the small temple on top – belongs to King Songtsen Gampo. It is probable that his two queens were also buried with him here. There are conflicting accounts as to the identity, and even the number, of the other tombs. I will follow here the description given to me by one of the monks responsible for the temple atop Songtsen Gampo's tomb; the numbers correspond to those on the accompanying plan.

1. Songtsen Gampo (617-649), reigned from 629.
2. Mangsong Mangtsen (646-676), the grandson of Songtsen Gampo, enthroned 650.
3. Dride Tsugten [Me Agdzom] (704-754), enthroned in the year of his birth.
4. Trisong Detsen (742-797), reigned from 754.
5. Mune Tsenpo (d.800), a son of Trisong Detsen, reigned from 797.
6. Tride Songtsen [Se–na-lek], a son of Trisong Detsen, (776-815), reigned from 800.
7. Tri Ralpachen [Tritsug Detsen] (805-836), reigned from 815.
7a. Stele erected by Tri Ralpachen.
8. Langdarma (803-842), reigned from 836.
9. Ö Sung (843-905), the son of Langdarma.
10. Lhe Bön (d.739), the son of Dride Tsugten.
11. Luna Trukyi Gyelpo (n.d.), the son of Lhe Bön (?).

With the exception of Dusong Mangpoje, the successor of Mangsong Mangtsen, all the kings of the powerful 'Yarlung' dynasty are buried here. Songtsen Gampo (1), Trisong Detsen (4) and Tri Ralpachen (7) occupy the prominent positions in early Tibetan history. It was through their efforts that Tibet was transformed from an insignificant border area into a major Central Asian power and Buddhism introduced and established as the religion of the land. The stele (7a) erected by Tri Ralpachen at the side of his tomb is sunk into the ground and enshrined in a small, bare chapel. The rune-like inscriptions on it are hard to decipher. Apparently the notorious Langdarma (8), who brought the dynasty to an end through his factionalism and anti-Buddhist policies, is also entombed here, albeit in a rather insignificant tumulus. His son Ö Sung (9), who established the kingdom of Gu-ge in the west of Tibet, lies beside him. Some distance away, about one kilometre further down the valley, is another barely visible tumulus in which, the Tibetans claim, are the remains of the first king of Tibet, Nyatri Tsenpo.

ABOVE *The tomb of King Ralpachen.*

OPPOSITE *The valley of the kings, 1949. The tomb in the foreground is that of King Ralpachen. On the hillside behind the tomb are visible the Chingwa Tagtse Castle, birthplace of the Fifth Dalai Lama, and Riwo Dechen Monastery.*

The small chapel on the top of Songtsen Gampo's tomb is reached by a flight of stone stairs from the road below. From the tumulus one has a clear view of all the other tombs except that of Trisong Detsen, which is out of sight on the back of the mountain. The chapel was destroyed during the cultural revolution and rebuilt only in 1983. The main figure is a statue of King Songtsen Gampo flanked by his two wives and his two chief ministers, Tönmi Sambhota and Gawa. The newly painted murals depict the Eight Taras who Dispel Fear, the Thirty-five Buddhas of Confession, Padmasambhava and his eight main manifestations, and the protectors Mahakala, Ekajati, Pelden Lhamo and Vaishravana. Another chapel behind the main room is dedicated to the Buddhas of the Three Times: Maitreya is the central figure, to the left is Dipamkara and to the right Shakyamuni. Amitayus sits to the far left and Padmasambhava to the far right. Vajrapani and Hayagriva stand on guard.

Riwo Dechen Monastery

Just before arriving at the tombs of the ancient kings in Chonggye you pass through the village of the same name, above which are clearly visible the ruins of the **Chingwa Tagtse Castle** *(dzong)*, a series of ramparts climbing up the ridge of the hill. This castle was originally built by King Shatri, the tenth ruler of the Yarlung line. It was in this castle, many hundreds of years later, that the Fifth Dalai Lama was born. Also visible, beneath the ramparts, are the remains of the once magnificent Riwo Dechen Monastery. The mighty, crumbling walls of the great assembly hall are all that still stand of this monastery, whose buildings formerly covered the upper part of the hillside. This main assembly hall of Riwo Dechen was founded by Lodrö Pelzang according to a design of one of Khedrup Je's disciples, Gartön Chöje, at the time of the Fifth Dalai Lama and was affiliated with Drepung Monastery. The monastery grew in size and by 1959 it housed about six hundred monks. Last year a few of the monks returned and started to rebuild one small chapel. This is still under construction and as yet no images or paintings have been installed. Seven monks live here while another fifty live in houses in the village below waiting for the opportunity to return.

TSANG

34. SAMDING MONASTERY

Samding is located 8 km to the east of Nangartse, a small town reached after you have descended the Kamba La Pass and left the shores of Yamdrok Lake when travelling the main road from Lhasa to Gyantse. Nangartse is 173 km from Lhasa and 91 km from Gyantse. When you get to Nangartse ask the villagers for Samding and go the way they point. Leading off the highway is a narrow dirt road that takes you across a strange, marshy terrain to the hills on the far side of the valley. Samding itself is on the spur of a ridge overlooking this wide, marshy plain and the distant mountains. The edge of Lake Yamdrok can be seen a couple of miles further to the east.

Between Lhasa and Nangartse is the marvellous **Yamdrok Lake**, *the 'Turquoise Lake of Yamdrok'. When coming from Lhasa, the first view you have of this breathtaking body of deep blue-green water is when you reach the top of the Kamba La Pass at 4,794 metres (15,724 ft). The lake is only a few hundred metres below. The road continues for several kilometres along the shoreline. It is a 'dead' lake with no constant flow of water into or out of it, which perhaps accounts for its colour. The Chinese plan to build a hydro-electric plant in the valley beneath it and tunnel through the mountain to drain off the water. Understandably, many Tibetans, who regard the lake as a sacred site, are not very happy about this project.*

Between Nangartse and Gyantse is another pass, the Karo La, at 5,045 metres (16,548 ft). A glacier hangs off the mountainside only a few hundred metres from the road.

HISTORY

Samding Monastery was probably founded by Khetsun Zhönu Drup during the later part of the thirteenth century, but is best-known for its association with the eminent lama Bodong Chokle Namgyel (1306-1386). Bodong was an immensely learned scholar, a poet, and a prolific writer. He composed a total of a hundred volumes of writings. He studied with Sherab Gyeltsen of the Jomonang Monastery and at one time gave instruction to Tsongkhapa, but the order he founded, the 'Bodong Tradition', was soon overshadowed by the Geluk and never gained any widespread acceptance or prominence. The Bodong order was a synthetic school based on the Nyingma and Sakya teachings. It survived until 1959 as a small sect based at Samding, with thirty sub-temples in the nearby regions affiliated with it.

Samding was most noted for its being headed by the only female

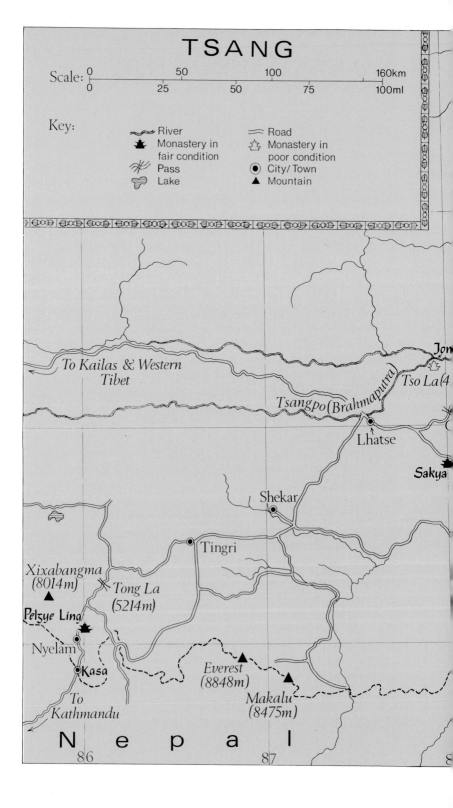

TSANG

Scale:

Key:
~~ River   ≈ Road
🏯 Monastery in fair condition   ☆ Monastery in poor condition
彡 Pass   ◉ City/Town
🐚 Lake   ▲ Mountain

To Kailas & Western Tibet

Jon

Tso La (4

Tsangpo (Brahmaputra)

Lhatse

Sakya

Shekar

Tingri

Xixabangma (8014m)

Tong La (5214m)

Pelgye Ling

Nyelam

Kasa

To Kathmandu

Everest (8848m)

Makalu (8475m)

N e p a l

86   87   8

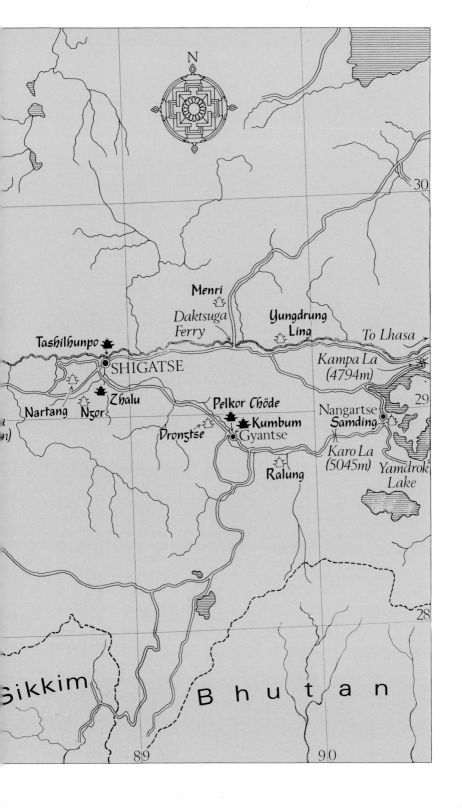

N

Menri

Daktsuga
Ferry

Yungdrung
Ling

To Lhasa

Tashilhunpo

SHIGATSE

Kampa La
(4794m)

Nartang   Ngor

Zhalu

Pelkor Chöde

Nangartse

Samding

29

Drongtse

Kumbum
Gyantse

Karo La
(5045m)

Yamdrok
Lake

Ralung

30

28

Sikkim

B h u t a n

89

90

incarnate lama in Tibet, Dorje Pagmo, named after the female tantric deity Vajravarahi (Adamantine Sow), the *yidam* of Bodong Chokle Namgyel. The rest of the community, however, were monks. Chandra Das, in his *Journey to Lhasa and Central Tibet*, recounts that 'in 1716, when the Dzungar [Mongol] invaders of Tibet came to Nangartse, their chief sent word to Samding for Dorje Pagmo to appear before him, that he might see if she really had, as reported, a pig's head. A mild answer was returned him; but, incensed at her refusing to obey his summons, he tore down the walls of the monastery of Samding, and broke into the sanctuary. He found it deserted, not a human being in it, only eighty pigs and as many sows grunting in the congregation hall under the lead of a big sow, and he dared not sack a place belonging to pigs. But when the Dzungars had given up all idea of sacking Samding, suddenly the pigs disappeared to become venerable-looking monks and nuns, with the saintly Dorje Pagmo at their head. Filled with astonishment and veneration for the sacred character of the lady abbess, the chief made immense presents to the monastery'.

ABOVE *Dorje Pagmo (seated), abbess of Samding, in July 1935.*
OPPOSITE ABOVE *View of Yamdrok lake from the Kamba La Pass.*
OPPOSITE BELOW *The Karo La Pass.*
OVERLEAF *View from Samding of the surrounding landscape with a subsidiary lake of the Yamdrok complex.*

Samding Monastery before 1959.

The peculiar arrangement of having a community of monks under the direction of an abbess has spawned a number of fictitious tales in the West, best-known of which is Lionel Davidson's entertaining but scurrilous novel, *The Rose of Tibet*. There the monastery is called 'Yamdring', a compound of 'Yamdrok' and 'Samding'. The present incarnation of Dorje Pagmo is a woman in her late forties who has renounced the religious life and now apparently supports the communist regime. She lives in Lhasa and does not visit the monastery.

THE SITE

The monastery was entirely destroyed during the cultural revolution and reconstruction began only in 1985. Eight of the former seventy monks have returned to oversee the building work and re-establish religious services and so forth. So far one chapel has been rebuilt and houses a number of small bronze images recently donated by people in Lhasa. The view from the monastery is superb, and for this alone it is worth making the side trip from the main road.

RALUNG MONASTERY

Ralung is located between Nangartse and Gyantse, 205 km along the road from Lhasa (at kilometre stone 195). You turn left into a dry riverbed opposite a group of three houses (the first buildings you see after the Karo La Pass). A four-wheel drive vehicle can theoretically negotiate the 'road' all the way to the monastery. A more reliable route takes you past this turning for another five kilometres to Ralung Village, from where you walk.

The ruins of Samding Monastery.

Local people unearth an old three-dimensional mandala at Ralung Monastery. Like many such religious objects, it was hidden at the time of the cultural revolution.

Ralung was founded in 1180 by Tsangpa Gyare Yeshe Dorje, while he was still a young man. Yeshe Dorje was a disciple of Ling-repa, who in turn was a disciple of the famous Kagyu lama Pamotrupa. Ling-repa is considered as the spiritual founder of the Drukpa Kagyu sub-order and Yeshe Dorje as the one who established the order's main monastery. Ralung grew into one of the largest and most influential Kagyu centres in Central Tibet. Today the Drukpa order is still very strong in Ladakh and Bhutan.

Little remains of Ralung today. The impressive ruins of two old colleges and several other monastic buildings were all that was left until recently. In 1984 a handful of monks returned and started the daunting task of reconstruction. A few hermits' caves can be seen on the mountainside above the monastery.

35. GYANTSE

Gyantse is a small, friendly town on the eastern side of the province of Tsang, 264 km south-west of Lhasa. It is situated on the northern bank of the Nyang River, which flows into the Brahmaputra at Shigatse. Not having suffered from modern expansion it still retains the charm of a traditional Tibetan town. There are two hotels: The **Gyantse Hotel***, a large truckstop on the left as you come into town from Lhasa, and* **The Hotel** *(sic), which is further into town just before the Kumbum. There is also a Chinese guesthouse on the edge of town but this is not recommended. We stayed at the Gyantse Hotel in one of their 'luxury' rooms for 5 RMB per bed (six beds per room). The cheaper rooms, with thinner mattresses and less gloss paint on the woodwork, cost only 3 RMB. Tolerable Chinese-style food is served in the dining room downstairs. There is a daily bus service from Lhasa to Gyantse for 23 RMB and from Shigatse to Gyantse for 7 RMB. Make sure you stop at Gyantse if you are on your way to Shigatse.*

HISTORY

Gyantse first came to prominence during the fifteenth century, when it served as the capital of a small kingdom established by a series of enterprising warlords from the region. The exquisite Kumbum and the daunting castle still bear witness to the powers that ruled at the time. It became the main centre for Tibet's wool trade with India and the border countries of Nepal, Bhutan and Sikkim, since it was suitably located at the junction of the trade routes from Lhasa and the east, Shigatse and the west, and India and the south. Nine major monasteries were built in the vicinity of the town.

In 1904 it became the focal point of the British expedition to Tibet under Colonel Younghusband. The British approached Tibet by the trade route leading to Gyantse and close to the town took place a battle in which several hundred Tibetans were shot dead by the superior British firepower. After storming the castle, Younghusband and his troops billetted here for a month before proceeding to Lhasa. The ensuing agreement reached between the British and the Tibetans resulted in a British trade agent being stationed at Gyantse. The British also opened a small school here.

Until recently Gyantse was the third largest town in Tibet, after Lhasa and Shigatse. But because a sprawling Chinese new-town has not yet grown up around it, it has since been overtaken by other places. It is situated in a crescent of hills that rise up out of the wide valley that sur-

ABOVE *Archers preparing for a contest in a folk festival at Gyantse.*

BELOW *The monastic complex at Pelkor Chöde, circa 1935.*

rounds it. Nestling at the foot of this natural amphitheatre are the closely packed, whitewashed houses and narrow, winding streets of the old town, along the western side of which a new, straight main road has been built, leading to the main entrance of the monastery complex. The town is dominated by a high, barren peak, along whose ridge sprout the forbidding walls and turrets of the castle.

THE MONASTERIES

The famous Kumbum (see the following section for a full description) is at the far end of the town. The area in which it is located is surrounded by a high wall that runs along the ridge of the hill behind and round to the front of the remaining religious buildings, thus effectively sealing off the monastic section from the town itself. Although this area seems rather bare today, it used to contain a complex of sixteen monasteries – not including the Kumbum and the Pelkor Chöde, the assembly hall beside it (see Chapter 37 for a full description). Nine of these monasteries, including the Norbu Ganden Monastery founded by Tsongkhapa's disciple Khedrup Je, belonged to the Geluk order, four were Sakya, and three were affiliated to the Bu Order, a small tradition established by Butön Rinpoche, the founder of Zhalu Monastery near Shigatse (see Chapter 39, below.) Now only two remain: a large,

View of the old town of Gyantse with the Kumbum and Pelkor Chöde from the top of the fort.

deteriorating Sakya monastery in the courtyard in front of the Kum-bum, where many of the monks now live, and Riting Monastery, a small Bu monastery on the hillside behind Pelkor Chöde. The high-walled structure up by the ramparts is where on ceremonial occasions a large *tangka* would be displayed.

THE CASTLE
You can enter the castle by climbing the hill from the opposite side of the main town. (You have to get the keys from the old lady who lives in the last house on the right at the point where the path begins to ascend to the castle. She will give you keys and a ticket for 2 RMB). The path leads you through a huge gateway and brings you to a number of deserted, gloomy buildings with dark rooms and maze-like corridors. There is a temple about half-way up to the top. Although it is in poor repair, some attempt at restoration has begun: three new Buddha images have been installed in the main chapel downstairs, murals of Avalokiteshvara and Padmasambhava have been crudely repainted, and two white stupas stand by the doorway. In the upper storey there are no statues but some interesting, though badly damaged, murals remain, especially the three large mandalas of Guhyasamaja, Kalachakra and Samvara on the back wall. In two of the smaller buildings higher up you can also find rooms with traces of religious murals. From the uppermost turret there is an unrivalled view of the town and Kumbum. In a cleft in the hills immediately behind the town are visible the extensive remains of **Ritrö (Hermitage) Monastery**, where monks would go for solitary retreat.

OPPOSITE *View of the Gyantse fort from Pelkor Chöde.*

GYANTSE KUMBUM

N

Entrance

36. GYANTSE KUMBUM

The Kumbum is at the far end of the old town of Gyantse, about a fifteen minute walk from the Gyantse Hotel. It is open from 9 am to midday and 2 pm to 5 pm. There is no charge for admission. For places to stay, buses, etc., see Chapter 35.

HISTORY

The Kumbum (or Pango Chöten) at Gyantse is one of the most magnificent buildings in Tibet. Gold-capped, it greets you with two bewitching eyes painted high on its circular upper wall above the ascending symmetrical storeys, which house one hundred and twelve chapels. Of the statues and murals that inhabit the chapels, Tucci wrote: 'Now peaceful, now terrific, [they] seem to jump up alive before your eyes, to crowd on your subconscious so as to haunt your dreams as well. You would think that the painters have by some wizardry conjured up living forces and driven them into their work, and that these could float out of the walls, force their way into your soul and take possession of it by a magic spell.' Many of these paintings are the work of fifteenth century Newari (Nepalese) craftsmen and are among the best preserved examples of that style to have survived in Tibet.

The Kumbum was built in 1440 by Rabten Kunzang, the second in a line of chieftans who made Gyantse the capital of a small kingdom carved out of the surrounding regions. Nearly all the monasteries around it are now destroyed, but the Kumbum has withstood all the battles and revolutions that have taken place since. Although many of the statues were somewhat defaced during the 1960's, they remain fairly intact. However, only twenty-three of the chapels are currently open and it is hard to judge the condition of the others. The innermost contents of the stupa, the relics and so forth enshrined in its core, were untouched.

THE SITE

The description of the Kumbum will follow the plan of the stupa on the opposite page. Only the ground floor, the fourth floor (by the eyes) and the uppermost chapel at the top can be visited. The ground floor consists of four principal chapels, one in each of the cardinal directions, separated by sixteen smaller shrines. The descriptions are taken from the brief Tibetan text pasted to the wall of each chapel.

1. **Shakyamuni Chapel.** This is the first chapel you visit. It faces you as you enter the Kumbum through the main doorway and climb to the top of the stairs. Buddha Shakyamuni is shown seated in the posture of 'turning the wheel of Dharma'. At his sides his two chief arhat disciples, Shariputra and Maudgalyayana, are gracefully depicted. To the far left and right are two of the Eight Medicine Buddhas. Padmasambhava is also visible on the left. As with many of the larger statues in the Kumbum, the writhing animals and gods who populate the 'halo' behind the Buddha are exceptionally well made.

2. **Özer Chenma Chapel.** The eight–armed female deity Özer Chenma (She who Radiates Light) is the principal figure here. Three slightly different aspects of her are painted on the walls, surrounded by about

Gyantse Kumbum and OPPOSITE *its intricate construction.*

ABOVE *Detail of a sculpted* garuda *and* devas *at the top of an elaborate halo.*

BELOW *Buddha Amitabha in the Sukhavati Chapel.*

one hundred minor deities. An Enlightenment Stupa is also found in this shrine.

3. **Jung Dul Chapel.** A form of Vajrapani peculiar to the charya tantras called 'Jung Dul' is the main figure here. Three painted images showing different aspects of him are on the walls, surrounded by numerous minor deities from the same tantric cycle.

4. **Dag Je Chapel.** 'Dag Je' means 'purifying'. The main deity is a smoky-coloured Me Tsek (He who Purifies by Fire), with six arms and three heads. In front of him stand two smaller attendants. The Ten Wrathful Ones and sixty-four diamond angels (*dorje po-nya*) are depicted in the murals.

5. **Dok Je Chapel.** 'Dok Je' means 'dispelling' and the main deity is a three headed, six armed seated Dugkarma in the aspect of She who Dispels Planetary Influences. She is attended by four wrathful female deities. Five more images of her are painted around the walls.

6. **Sukhavati Chapel.** 'Sukhavati' means 'Land of Bliss' and is the name of the Pure Land in the west presided over by the Buddha Amitabha. A giant seated statue of the red Amitayus, a bodhisattva aspect of Amitabha, is the central image. Two attendant bodhisattvas stand to his sides and two other bodhisattvas, facing inwards and seated on remarkably constructed lotus thrones, are beside them. Colourful paintings of the Pure Land are found on the left and right–hand walls. The Thirty-five Buddhas of Confession are also depicted.

7. **Lo Gyunma Chapel.** Lo Gyunma is the first of several deities described in the accompanying work as 'appearing in the *Collection of Tantric Rites (Trubtab Gyatsa)*', a basic Sakya liturgical work that assembles a number of different *sadhanas*, each used as a guide for the practice of a particular deity. This obscure female deity is the main figure in this chapel. She is yellow, with six arms and three heads, and kneels in a strange posture, with her right leg buckled beneath her. Two wrathful attendant deities stand beside her. The mural shows three more aspects of her in the company of numerous minor figures.

8. **Hayagriva Chapel.** A red, four-armed form of Hayagriva as found in the *Collection of Tantric Rites* is the main image. Two smaller attendants stand at his sides. Murals of Hayagriva adorn the walls as do two paintings of Avalokiteshvara and about eighty minor figures.

The female deity Lo Gyunma in the Lo Gyunma Chapel.

9. Acala Chapel. Also from the *Collection of Tantric Rites*, this statue of the wrathful Acala (Immovable One) stands accompanied by two smaller deities. Two blue and one white forms of Acala surrounded by twenty-two minor figures are painted on the walls.

10. Za Yum Chapel. 'Za Yum' means 'Mother of the Planets'. She is depicted as a white female deity with six arms and three heads, sitting cross-legged. Two attendant female deities stand to her sides. Most of the murals are badly faded and in poor condition. The triad of Manjushri, Avalokiteshvara and Vajrapani can be made out above the door.

11. Dipamkara Chapel. Dipamkara, the Buddha of the Past, is shown here in a large, very delicately sculpted form, reminding one of a Thai Buddha image. Four bodhisattvas, two standing and two seated, accompany him. Approximately two hundred smaller Buddhas and deities adorn the walls.

12. Nor Gyunma Chapel. Another figure from the *Collection of Tantric Rites*, the female deity Nor Gyunma, is depicted in a beautiful peaceful

Hayagriva in the Hayagriva Chapel.

form with five female attendants, all six figures displaying the same hand gestures. On the wall opposite the deity is a painting of her in a strange pose, holding a smaller male figure on her lap. The murals also show about fifty other deities, some of them with elephant heads.

13. *This chapel is not open.*

14. **Tobpoche Chapel.** Tobpoche (One of Great Strength) is vaguely described as 'appearing in the tantras', whereas the appearance in the *Collection of Tantric Rites* of the other wrathful deities on the walls is mentioned explicitly. The lamas depicted on the walls are probably from the Sakya tradition.

15. **Gyeltsen Tsemo Chapel.** This red, standing female deity with four arms and three heads is accompanied by two smaller attendant figures. The murals are in poor condition but one can make out a painting of Gyeltsen Tsemo, above whom sit Atisha and Drom Tönpa. A fine red dakini can also be discerned.

16. **Tushita Chapel.** A large seated image of Maitreya is the central

figure, accompanied by, as in the other chapels of the cardinal directions, two standing and two seated bodhisattvas. Tushita, like Sukhavati (6), is a Pure Land. It is the place where Maitreya, the future Buddha, now resides prior to his appearance in this world. Thus in three of the four cardinal chapels we have seen the Buddhas of the Three Times: Shakyamuni, Dipamkara and Maitreya.

17. Vaishravana Chapel. A rather peaceful, solitary figure of Vaishravana, the god of wealth, is seated here on a lion. This newly-painted statue stands in contrast to the two old murals of the deity on the walls.

18. Four Guardian Kings Chapel. The four familiar kings stand by the wall of this room, which serves more as the entrance-way to the upper storeys of the Kumbum than a chapel.

From here one climbs up a series of dark, uneven staircases, which bring you out onto the fourth floor. Although this is the route taken by pilgrims on their visit to the Kumbum, we shall continue with descriptions of the two remaining chapels on the ground floor before proceeding to the chapels above.

19. Guru Gönpo Chapel. This is the protector chapel of the Kumbum. It is dedicated to the principal Sakya protector Guru Gönpo, who is accompanied here by two local protectors. The walls are black, with several gruesome paintings on them.

20. Vijaya Chapel. A striking, white Vijaya Stupa stands at the far end of this small room. Inside the stupa is a statue of the six-armed female deity Vijaya. Two golden bodhisattvas stand on lotuses to each side, while two goddesses hover in the sky above.

The Fourth Floor

Around the entrance to each of the four chapels on this level is some colourful stucco work depicting various animals and divine beings. Also, from here the view over the town and castle is excellent.

21. Shakyamuni Chapel. A beautifully ornamented seated figure of Shakyamuni is the main image in this first chapel on the fourth floor. A white and a golden bodhisattva stand to his sides. Around the walls, enclosed in artificial grottoes, are the Sixteen Arhats. The Buddhas of the Ten Directions sit above them at a slightly higher level. As in each of the four chapels on this floor, the walls are covered with extraordinary mandalas, varying in size from eight feet to two feet in diameter. They probably represent tantric cycles practised in the Sakya tradition.

22. Buddha Sengge Ngaro Chapel. This large seated Buddha, whose name means 'Lion's Roar', is flanked by two bodhisattvas, one white and one gold. Ten superb, large mandalas belonging to the charya tantra are spread over the walls, with many smaller mandalas in between them.

23. Prajnaparamita Chapel. 'Prajnaparamita' means 'Perfection of Wisdom', a quality of the enlightened mind here personified in the form of a female deity. She has four arms, the upper two holding a scripture and a vajra, the lower two showing the gesture of turning the wheel of Dharma. A red bodhisattva stands to each side. Again, the murals are an intricate profusion of mandalas.

24. Vairocana Chapel. A single bronze statue of the Buddha Vairocana (One who Illuminates Things) sits in this less ornate chamber. Metal grilles seal off sections of the chapel. Here, somewhat concealed at the back, is the staircase that leads up to the last chapel, at the very top of the Kumbum.

The Pinnacle

As you climb up even more steep and dark staircases to reach the top of the Kumbum, you pass walls covered with paintings of the main wrathful deities of the supreme yoga tantra. The predominance of Hevajra and Samvara indicate the strong influence of the Sakya school, the Tibetan Buddhist order under whose spiritual guidance the Kumbum was designed. Other deities depicted on the two small landings where you can pause on your ascent are Yamantaka, Vajrayogini, Kalachakra and many lesser known dakinis. Lamas from the lineages of these tantric teachings are also shown.

25. Vajradhara Chapel. The main image in this small, circular room in the pinnacle of the Kumbum is the tantric aspect of Shakyamuni, Buddha Vajradhara. A bronze statue of him on the altar is flanked by the bodhisattvas Avalokiteshvara and Manjushri. Another smaller Vajradhara is attached to the central pillar that supports the ceiling.

OVERLEAF *Doorway on the fourth floor of the Kumbum embellished with fine stucco work.*

37. PELKOR CHÖDE MONASTERY

Pelkor Chöde is the central monastic building in the complex by the Kumbum at the far end of the old town of Gyantse. It is about a fifteen minute walk from the Gyantse Hotel. It is open from 9 am to midday and 2 pm to 5 pm. There is an entrance charge of 2 RMB, which some of the monks enforce strictly and others ignore. For general information on Gyantse, see Chapter 35.

HISTORY

Pelkor Chöde Monastery was founded by Rabten Kunzang in 1418, under the spiritual guidance of Tsongkhapa's disciple Khedrup Je. It has been remarkably well preserved and many of the statues and paintings inside date back to the time of its founding. Although the shrines are predominantly Sakya, the monastery was traditionally unaffiliated, being used as a common assembly place for the monks from all the nearby monasteries. At present it is looked after by Gelukpa monks. In former days, 'Pelkor Chöde' sometimes referred to entire complex of monastic buildings in the walled section of Gyantse.

THE SITE

The Ground Floor

The first room on the left before you enter the assembly hall is the **Protector Chapel.** The three huge figures in this blackened room are barely visible because of the mountains of offering scarves etc. draped over them. The main protector is the principal Sakya guardian, Guru Gönpo. To the left is the goddess of concentration, Ekajati, and to the right Pelden Lhamo. But apart from Pelden Lhamo's mule, little else can be made out. Tantric *tangkas,* gold lines traced on a black background, hang on the walls, depicting Dharmaraja, Yamantaka, Pelden Lhamo and Vaishravana. The murals show the fearful entourage of Guru Gönpo. Antique weapons, chain-mail and masks are attached to the pillars.

There is little of note in the large **Assembly Hall** itself. The woven tangkas that hang in rows from the ceiling around the skylight were commissioned from Hangzhou in China in the early part of this century by the previous Panchen Lama.

The **Main Chapel** is at the back of the assembly hall. Before entering it you can see a fine appliqué *tangka* of Tsongkhapa and his two chief disciples on its front wall, and murals of Dugkarma and Avalokiteshvara to•the left and right of the entrance way. Shakyamuni is the central figure in the chapel, with Avalokiteshvara to the left and Manjushri to the right. Further to the left is Dipamkara, the Buddha of the Past, and further to the right Maitreya, the Buddha of the Future. Sixteen standing bodhisattvas are around the walls, representing the Eight Great Sons and, in female aspect, the Eight Great Daughters. Also on the left is a pyramid-shaped square shrine covered by a canopy. This houses numerous small bronzes, the central figure being Akshobhya, surrounded by many other Buddhas and bodhisattvas. The workmanship of the pillars and beams is noteworthy; two delightful peacocks can be seen perched on one of the beams. There may also be fine butter sculptures on the altar. You can walk along an inner circumambulation path around the chapel but the murals there are in poor condition. It is just possible to make out the forms of the thousand Buddhas of this present aeon.

To the left of the main chapel is a **Vairocana Chapel**. This contains some superb old lacquered clay statues of the Five Dhyani Buddhas. The central Buddha is a four-headed aspect of Vairocana. Along the back wall sit the other four Dhyani Buddhas, Ratnasambhava, Akshobhya, Amitabha and Amoghasiddhi. The subtlety and gracefulness of expression revealed through the craftsmanship of these figures is truly exceptional. Various bronzes of bodhisattvas, Buddhas and lamas cover the altar. Sixteen goddesses are also portrayed at the back, and to the right are images of the thirty-seven deities associated with the practice of Vairocana. A gigantic scripture, bound in wooden covers and written in gold ink on black paper, lies to the right of the altar. It is a copy of the *Eight Thousand Verse Perfection of Wisdom Discourse*.

To the right of the assembly hall is a **Maitreya Chapel.** In addition to a statue of Maitreya, there is also a line of other figures (from the left): Atisha, Kamalashila, Padmasambhava, Shantarakshita, the triad of Manjushri, Avalokiteshvara and Vajrapani, the Kashmiri Pandit Shakya Shri, and the three great Tibetan kings, Songtsen Gampo, Trisong Detsen and Ralpachen. A painting of Avalokiteshvara in the Newari style is on the wall, and a large embroidered *tangka* that formerly would have been displayed outside on special occasions is in a long box on the floor.

A small room to the right of the Maitreya Chapel contains a large Vimala Stupa surrounded by shelves bearing an edition of the Kangyur. The smallish statues at the back are (from the left): Amitabha, Shakyamuni, Khedrup Je, the Panchen Lama Losang Chökyi Gyeltsen and the Fifth Dalai Lama.

The Protectors of the Three Kinds of Beings: Avalokiteshvara, Manjushri and Vajrapani in Pelkor Chöde.

The Upper Storey

There are five chapels on the upper storey, all of which are worth visiting. We shall start from the first chapel on the left as you climb up to the roof from the main entrance, and go around clockwise.

The Samvara Chapel. The most striking feature of this chapel is the impressive three-dimensional, gold and bronze mandala of Samvara erected by Khedrup Je himself. This has pride of place in the centre of the room. It represents the sixty-two deity mandala of Samvara belonging to the tradition of that tantra that traces itself back to the Indian mahasiddha Luipa. Khedrup Je's personal vajra and bell are supposedly still kept in the monastery by the abbot, but it is not possible to see them.

However, the gilded mandala draws attention (and daylight) away from the exceptionally fine figures of the Sakya *lam-dre* lineage lined along the side and back walls. 'Lam-dre' means 'the path and its fruit', referring to the teachings received from the Indian mahasiddha Virupa that describe the stages along the path to enlightenment, combining both the sutric (exoteric) and tantric (esoteric) elements. All the statues are lacquered and probably made of clay. Like the Five Dhyani Buddhas downstairs and the Sixteen Arhats across the way, they are of exceptional quality, perhaps even made by the same artist. Vajradhara is the central figure in the line, seated in the middle of the back wall. To the left sit the Indian teachers, many of them mahasiddhas, and to the right the Tibetan teachers, concluding with the thirteen Sakya holders of the lineage up to the founder of the monastery, Rabten Kunzang. The mural on the wall to the left by the doorway depicts Pakpa in conversation with the Mongolian emperor Kublai Khan who, in 1260, appointed him as the temporal and spiritual head of Tibet. Another painting of Pakpa is nearby, surrounded by various scenes from his life. All around the upper part of the side and back walls are very well-executed paintings of the eighty-four Indian mahasiddhas.

Next is a **Maitreya Chapel**. The main figure of Maitreya is accompanied by a number of smaller bronzes, some of which may be Nepalese or Indian in origin. There are stupas, Buddhas and tantric deities, as well as lamas from the Butön, Sakya and Geluk traditions. The most highly revered image on the altar is the small figure of Tara in the middle, buried beneath offering scarves. The chapel also contains a Vijaya Stupa, an edition of the Kangyur written in gold ink, and some *tangkas*, one of which is an old Nyingma painting of the peaceful and wrathful deities depicted in the *Tibetan Book of the Dead*.

The chapel at the centre back of the upper storey is a shrine dedicated to **Tsongkhapa**. Two Buddhas are seated to the left of the central figure of Tsongkhapa. To the right, in descending size, are the Seventh Dalai Lama (in the form of a scholar), a Buddha, Butön Rinpoche (with white hair), Sakya Pandita and Padmasambhava. To the far right are images of the lamas of the Sakya *lam-dre* lineage. The murals in this chapel are very fine and must have been commissioned some time during the reign of the Thirteenth Dalai Lama, a portrait of whom adorns one wall. The longevity triad of Amitayus, Tara and Vijaya is shown on another wall, surrounded by numerous smaller images of Amitayus. The back wall depicts the Buddha with various scenes showing his twelve major deeds. The mantras of Manjushri, Avalokiteshvara and Vajrapani are written above the door.

Directly opposite the Samvara Chapel is a **Chapel of the Sixteen Arhats**. Again the lacquered, clay images of these sixteen saints are quite exceptional. Two small attendants stand to the side of each figure, while behind them are picturesque little cliffs with grottoes, stupas and monks. Unfortunately, these slightly smaller than life-size statues are screened off by metal grilles. To the left, in front of the first arhats, is a set of five statues known as the Five Families of Manjushri. The central

LEFT AND OPPOSITE
Mahasiddhas of the
lamdre *lineage in*
the Samvara
Chapel.

figure of these five is an exquisite image of Manjushri seated on a lion. The four surrounding figures depict four earthly representatives of the bodhisattva of wisdom who served as kings of China, Mongolia, India and Tibet. Four fine Guardian Kings protect the chapel.

Finally, just before you take the staircase downstairs, you will find another smaller **Chapel of the Sixteen Arhats,** much simpler than the other one. Shakyamuni stands on a small altar with Shariputra and Maudgalyayana at his sides. The arhats are seated in individual grottoes along the walls, with smaller Buddhas and Taras in little niches above them. The statues of the arhats are made of a special kind of clay that looks exactly like wood.

The Uppermost Storey

The **Zhelye Tse Chapel** is the sole shrine on this floor. 'Zhelye Tse' means 'Peak of the Celestial Mansion', an apt name for the most tantric chapel in the monastery, which caps the profusion of deities housed in the shrines below it. There is a single, newish-looking altar in the centre

of this rather bare and spacious room. One has the impression that it once contained rather more than it does now. The central image on the altar is Jowo Shakyamuni, with Maitreya to the left and Manjushri to the right. Above sit Tsongkhapa and his two chief disciples. Below are Amitayus, Padmasambhava and Tara, and further to the right Amitayus, Dugkarma and a peculiar little statue of Padmasambhava. The masterpieces of this chapel, though, are the awesome eight-foot-diameter mandalas of the principal tantric deities of the Sakya tradition depicted along all three walls. Although they are sealed off by a wooden barrier, the caretaker-monk will let you go closer if you ask. The mandalas are all from the class of the supreme yoga tantra. The central mandala (immediately behind the altar) is that of Kalachakra. Among those to the left are the mandalas of Guhyasamaja, Samvara, and Yamantaka. To the right are three of Hevajra as well as of different aspects of Guhyasamaja and Samvara. Formerly this chapel used to house many volumes of the collected writings of the main Sakya lamas.

38. DRONGTSE MONASTERY

About five kilometres outside Gyantse on the road going west to Shigatse, you will see on the left a steep little hill crowned with the tall, stubborn ruins of an old monastery. This was **Tsechen Monastery**, *the home of the Sakya lama Rendawa, the principal teacher of Tsongkhapa. Another four kilometres down the road you will see, perched up on the hillside on your left, the newly built assembly hall of Drongtse Monastery. It is best to have your own transport to get here, but it would also be possible to hitch-hike from Gyantse. The monastery is open daily and there is no charge for admission.*

HISTORY

While Tsongkhapa was staying at Tsechen Monastery with his teacher Rendawa he met a small boy called Rinchen Gyatso, the son of a prosperous and devoted family in the nearby village of Drongtse. Tsongkhapa prophesied that in the future the boy would build a monastery above his home. Many years elapsed and the boy grew into a young man who became something of a recluse. He would spend most of his time away from towns and villages, living in the mountains like the yogi Milarepa. One day, however, he had a vision of the deity Tara, who told him that now it was time to leave his retreat and build a monastery. So he returned to his home village and started work on what was to be known as the Drongtse Monastery.

The monastery was erected on the hillside above the village of Drongtse in 1442. It consisted of a main assembly hall and two colleges, one specialising in the study of philosophy and the other in tantric rituals. It eventually became a sub-temple of Tashilhunpo Monastery in Shigatse under the jurisdiction of the Panchen Lamas. Sarat Chandra Das spent a lot of time here during his visit in 1881 and gives a good description of life in the monastery at that time (see his *Journey to Lhasa and Central Tibet*).

During the cultural revolution it was completely destroyed. Only this year, largely through the efforts of the head lama of the monastery, who holds a high post in the religious affairs department of the government in Lhasa, was it granted sufficient funds to start restoration. Work proceeded rapidly and in three months the main assembly hall was rebuilt in stone, wood and mortar. The villagers retrieved some of the original pillars, which they had stored since the destruction, and returned them. Now two elder monks and eight young novices live here.

THE SITE

Although the main image of Shakyamuni was desecrated during the cultural revolution, it was not totally destroyed. The body was saved and repaired and the statue now stands in the main chapel behind the assembly hall. The other principal statue of the monastery, a Jowo Shakyamuni, is currently being repaired in Lhasa and is due to be reinstalled shortly. Upstairs there are two old statues of Manjushri and Maitreya. These did not originally belong to the monastery but were recently returned from China and given to Drongtse.

About a hundred yards behind the monastery is a small shrine built over a large rock on which are carved several images: Amitayus, Padmasambhava, a number of Taras, Vajrapani and Avalokiteshvara. Piled up beside the shrine are many images carved in relief on slabs of slate. Some of these are of exceptionally high workmanship.

OPPOSITE *Fine relief carvings preserved at Drongtse.* UPPER LEFT *a Buddha,* UPPER RIGHT *Agni – the god of fire,* BELOW LEFT *an unidentified figure spinning wool, and* BELOW RIGHT *a lama called Mi-chepa. Each carving is approximately 40 cm in height.*

A monk working on the site of the old monastery of Zhalu, which now lies in ruins.

39. ZHALU MONASTERY

19 km south east of Shigatse, in a valley near the main road, is Zhalu Monastery. It can be visited conveniently on a side trip when travelling between Gyantse and Shigatse. The rooves of the monastery can be seen in the distance to the left of the road as you come from Gyantse. If you are staying in Shigatse you can easily hitch out to it. It is open daily and there is no admission charge. This might change once the restoration work is completed.

HISTORY

Although Zhalu was founded in the eleventh century by a Sakya/Kagyu lama called Sherab Jungne, it came to prominence only during the fourteenth century with the rise of its most famous abbot, Butön Rinchen Drup. From then on it was the centre of the small but influential order, the Butön or Zhalu Luk, founded by Butön and his followers.

Butön was a brilliant scholar who played an important role in bringing Tibetan Buddhism to a state of full maturity. He was responsible for organising all the diverse scriptures that had been translated from Sanskrit in the preceding centuries into a coherent whole. Although the Kangyur, the translated discourses of the historical Buddha, had largely been put into order, the Tengyur, the far more numerous translations of the commentaries written by the later Indian masters, was still in disarray. Thus Butön's main contribution was to gather all these texts together, classify them, and write them down in a single series of volumes. That these volumes amounted to two hundred and twenty-seven thick tomes and that Butön wrote them all out by hand indicate both the amazing powers of mental synthesis and the sheer strength of dedication he must have possessed. Until the cultural revolution these handwritten volumes as well as his metal pen were kept in Zhalu. The Red Guards burnt them all. He also composed a history of Buddhism in India and Tibet, a text that is still used today and has been translated into English. His own collected writings on subjects such as the *Perfection of Wisdom* and the Kalachakra tantra amounted to a further twenty-six volumes, the hand-written originals of which were kept in his personal residence nearby until they too were destroyed during the cultural revolution.

Butön lived in Zhalu for most of his life. It may have been during his time that the monastery was divided into two sections: the older buildings on the hillside to the west, which are now in ruins, and the newer

Chinese-style structure (the Serkhang) lower in the valley, which is still intact. Atisha is said to have spent some time in the older part of the monastery. Among the ruins is a small pool associated with him, perhaps marking the spot where he retrieved twelve texts that had supposedly found their way there after being deposited in a lake in India. These would have been the twelve texts previously enshrined in Tangboche Monastery in the Chonggye Valley (see Chapter 32). Butön also had his quarters in this older part of the monastery and the original twenty-six volumes of his writings were kept up there. Traditionally, the monks would spend the five summer months on the hillside and the seven winter months in the large temple complex in the valley. Once there were 350 monks in Zhalu; today there are only twenty-three. The monastery is currently undergoing extensive restoration under the direction of the 'Cultural Repair Committee' of the government in Lhasa.

Through his immediate disciples Butön's influence extended to Tsongkhapa, who was seven years old when Butön died. Tsongkhapa held Butön in high esteem and traced many of his teachings back to him.

THE SITE

The green-tiled Chinese roof of Zhalu contrasts vividly with the traditional design of Tibetan temple roofs. This architectural style is the result of the offerings of Chinese supporters of the monastery, who sponsored the construction of the main temple. The assembly hall, which is entered from the courtyard in front, is presently closed. It is devoid of images although some murals remain. There are only two chapels currently open and these are both on the upper storey, which is entered by a gateway and a flight of stairs on the right of the main building.

The West Chapel

Immediately in front of the West Chapel, before you climb the stairs to the entrance, is a worn stone basin. This is the basin over which Sakya Pandita shaved his head in order to receive ordination from the Kashmiri Pandit Shakya Shri at the beginning of the thirteenth century.

The most revered image in the West Chapel is that of a stone Avalokiteshvara, called the 'Indian Jowo' because it was brought to Tibet from Bodhgaya in 1027 by the founder of the monastery, Sherab Jungne. It is actually *two* images, having a figure of Yamantaka carved on the back (which you cannot see). The most prominent statue, though, is one of a gaunt, austere-looking Butön Rinpoche. A silver and gold stupa on the same altar contains his cremated remains. A conch shell in a glass case also dates back to the time of Butön, endowed, as

The distinctive green roof-tiles of Zhalu.

usual, with mysterious properties such as being able to sound without human agency and possessing a naturally formed Tibetan letter 'A' inside. A black stone with a perfectly formed OM MANI PADME HUM mantra standing out of it in white provides another puzzle.

Numerous statues line the back wall. Among those to the left are the Eight Medicine Buddhas. To the right are Amitayus, Maitreya, Padmasambhava, Butön, a very fine old Kalachakra, Vajrasattva, a standing Maitreya, several tantric deities and some Kadam Stupas. *Tangkas* hang around the upper walls. From the left, as you enter, they depict the seven kings of Shambhala, the Thirty-five Buddhas of Confession, and the Sixteen Arhats. On the opposite wall is a *tangka* of Dorje Rabdenma, the special protectress of Zhalu Monastery, above a small shrine to her in the corner. Further along are depicted the Pure Land of Manjushri, a circular map of Shambhala, White Manjushri, the Pure Land of Padmasambhava (Ogyen), the Pure Land of Amitabha and the twenty-five *kalki* of Shambhala. You can also just make out some badly worn mandalas, which used to adorn the front wall.

The South Chapel
In the entrance hall of this chapel there are three murals. One is an astrological map designed by Butön to show the correlations between the movement of the planets and the days of the year. The one to the left

of the doorway shows the stages of concentration one must ascend in order to attain complete mental quiescence. A monkey and an elephant are seen climbing a winding path. They represent the excitement and heaviness of mind that hinder the development of clear, calm concentration. As one progresses in meditation, these hindrances are gradually overcome, symbolised here by the animals' being caught and then tamed by the monk. Eventually the monkey (excitement) is left behind and the elephant, (heaviness) is brought under control. The monk then mounts the elephant, and in the final stage is seen flying in the sky, free of any trace of hindrance. The picture to the right of the door shows details of the monastic rule, reminding the monks how to dress and behave properly and under what circumstances they can relax the rule. In the summer, for example, one can remove one's upper robe and cool oneself in the branches of a tree (two things normally prohibited).

All four chapels on this upper storey of the monastery were once famous for their rare murals of mandalas from the yoga tantras, the third class of tantra. The mandalas one sees elsewhere usually belong to the supreme yoga tantras, the fourth class, which was the class most commonly practised in Tibet. Today only the South Chapel contains well-preserved examples of these images. The original mandalas were traced onto the walls of this chapel in the fourteenth century, but the large ones that you see on the back wall were repainted in the late nineteenth century. Those on the side and front walls, however, have not been restored. From the left, the mandalas belong to the yoga tantra cycles of Peljor, Doying, Tsemo and Kamsum Namgyel. These four mandalas are about four metres in diameter and are extremely well-painted, showing the artist's great precision and delicate sense of colour. The remaining mandalas in the chapel are in poorer condition and belong to the minor deities within the Peljor cycle (within which there are four divisions and twenty-eight sub-divisions).

Seated in front of the Tsemo mandala is Butön Rinpoche with copies of the twenty-six volumes of his collected works beside him. To the left sits his chief disciple Rinchen Namgyel and, about six statues further to the left, the portly figure of the Zhalu translator Dharmabhadra (a Tibetan with an Indian name). A fine statue of Kalachakra, made at the time of Butön, is to the right of the texts along with two Kadam stupas that may be of Indian origin. The other figures depict, among others, Amitayus, Shakyamuni and Tara.

40. SHIGATSE

Shigatse, the capital of the province of Tsang, is 354 km west of Lhasa. It is located 90 km west of Gyantse on the south bank of the Brahmaputra at the point where the Nyang Chu River flows into it. It can be reached by two routes from the capital: by the Northern Road, which runs from Golmud and reaches Shigatse via the Daktsuga ferry over the Brahmaputra, or the Southern Road via Gyantse, which is the usual route for those travelling into Nepal. There is a daily bus from Lhasa, which costs 27 RMB (although this price seems to vary widely). It is an all-day ride and quite gruelling. A landcruiser can make it in about seven hours. It is also possible to hitch. West of Shigatse there is no public transport.

Recently a 'modern' hotel has been built at the southern end of town, presumably for upper-level cadres and foreign tour groups. Most individual travellers, however, stay at the small Tibetan truckstop/guesthouse, which is directly opposite Tashilhunpo Monastery and thus easy to find. It charges 5 RMB for a bed in a scruffy dorm. Hot water is provided morning and evening but the food situation is very bad. Nevertheless, its convenient location outweighs the disadvantages. The other guesthouse is the Chinese hotel in town, opposite the cinema. The price is the same and the facilities better, but the atmosphere is deadening.

THE TOWN

Shigatse has long been the commercial and political centre of Tsang Province. Formerly it was dominated by a massive castle built on the hillock above the old town. Only the bases of the ramparts are visible today, suggesting nonetheless the grandeur of the building. This is where the powerful kings of Tsang lived during their rule in the late sixteenth and early seventeenth centuries. Until the Chinese occupation it was the home of the provincial governor.

Most of the town consists of a singularly unattractive sprawl of functional Chinese buildings, with only a couple of pockets of traditional–style housing left. It has a population of about 40,000 and after Lhasa is the second biggest town in Tibet. It possesses a bank, post-office, public security office (rumoured as a good place to get visa extensions and permits even after they have been refused in Lhasa), and a department store. The open market lacks the charm of others in Tibet but offers a fairly wide range of items old and new.

Since the time of the Fifth Dalai Lama, the town has been the seat of the Panchen Lama, and his monastery, Tashilhunpo, is the only place of genuine interest left (see the following chapter for a full description).

ABOVE *The Castle (dzong) at Shigatse, 1938.*

BELOW *Aristocratic ladies from Sigatse, 1938.*

The town of Shigatse with the ruins of the old castle.

Recently the Panchen Lama built a new palace, the Dechen Potrang, but this is a building with little attraction.

NEARBY PLACES OF INTEREST

Twenty-seven kilometres to the south west of Shigatse along the main highway to Lhatse and Nepal is **Nartang Monastery**, founded in 1153 by Tumtön Lodrö Drakpa, a disciple of the Kadampa master Drom Tönpa. It became famous for housing the woodblocks of the 'Nartang' edition of the entire Buddhist canon, which were carved between 1730 and 1742. This formerly noble monastery now stands in ruins, its high mud-brick walls visible behind the roadside village.

About twenty kilometres south of Shigatse, on a small road between Nartang and Zhalu, is the important **Ngor Monastery** of the Sakya order, which was founded in 1429 by Ngorchen Kunga Zangpo, the monk who established the Ngor sub-order of the Sakya. Extensive rebuilding is underway.

East of Shigatse, on the northern bank of the Brahmaputra near the town of Daktsuga (where the ferry connects the main road from Shigatse to Golmud), are two Bön monasteries: **Yungdrung Ling** and

Menri Monastery, one of the few surviving centres of Bön, on the northern banks of the Brahmaputra near Daktsuga.

Menri Monastery. Both are being renovated and a number of Bön monks live there. Because of the degree to which the native animistic Bön religion has been influenced by Buddhism, it is hard to distinguish these places from Buddhist temples.

To the west of Shigatse along the Brahmaputra is the **Jomonang Monastery,** founded in the thirteenth century by Kunpang Tukje Tsöntru and built on the plan of Shambhala. This was the centre of the Jonangpa school who, under the guidance of Sherab Gyeltsen (1292-1361), a disciple of the founder of the monastery, formulated an original philosophy of emptiness that was condemned as heretical by Tsongkhapa and his Geluk followers. The last famous representative of this school was the lama Taranata, a prodigious writer and historian. In the seventeenth century the Fifth Dalai Lama closed down all Jonangpa monasteries and forbade the publication of their texts. I was unable to visit the monastery and have no reliable information about its present condition.

41. TASHILHUNPO MONASTERY

Tashilhunpo is situated on the western edge of Shigatse, at the base of the Drölma (Tara) Mountain. It is a vast monastic complex about fifteen minutes' walk from the town centre, impossible to miss. The monastery is open every day except Sunday from 9 am to midday and 2 pm to 5 pm. In the afternoon, however, some of the chapels may be closed. There is an entrance charge of 3 RMB and the monks are very strict in prohibiting photography. Tashilhunpo is often felt to be a mere showpiece for foreigners. Yet while this may be partially true, a genuine course of study is nonetheless pursued. For information on accommodation etc. in Shigatse, see Chapter 40.

HISTORY

Tashilhunpo Monastery was founded in 1447 by Gendun Drup, a nephew of Tsongkhapa, one of his foremost disciples, and the First Dalai Lama (recognised retrospectively, as described earlier). Gendun Drup was entombed in Tashilhunpo, the only Dalai Lama (except also the Sixth) whose remains are not enshrined in Lhasa.

Shortly after his assumption of power in 1642, the Fifth Dalai Lama declared that his teacher, Losang Chökyi Gyeltsen, then the abbot of Tashilhunpo Monastery in Shigatse, was a manifestation of Buddha Amitabha and the fourth in a line of incarnate lamas starting with Khedrup Je, one of the two chief disciples of Tsongkhapa. Since the abbot of Tashilhunpo was already referred to by the title 'Panchen' (Great Scholar), these incarnate lamas were called the Panchen Rinpoches. Losang Chökyi Gyeltsen thus became the Fourth Panchen Lama. But in humbly proclaiming his teacher, and henceforth all the head lamas of Tashilhunpo, as an incarnation of Buddha Amitabha, the Dalai Lama seems to have opened the way for trouble. In 1728 the Chinese bestowed Losang Yeshe, the next (Fifth) Panchen Lama, with sovereignty over the western province of Tsang (of which Shigatse is the capital). Although this was seen by both Tibetan parties at the time as a merely nominal gesture, it marked the beginning of a continuing Chinese attempt to divide the Geluk church by playing the two lamas off against each other.

In 1774 a young Scotsman called George Bogle was sent to Tibet to establish contact with the Sixth Panchen Lama, Pelden Yeshe, as the result of a letter sent by the Panchen to the British Governor of Bengal. This was the first official contact between the British and the Tibetans

and apparently was conducted independently of the Lhasa government. Bogle became good friends with the Panchen Lama and even married a noble lady from his court, but their relationship was unable to mature since both men died prematurely only a few years later. Descendants of Bogle and his Tibetan wife may still be found in Scotland today.

Tashilhunpo became the official seat of the Panchen Lama, who in turn became, in varying degrees, the chief spiritual and temporal authority of Tsang. The greater the estrangement from Lhasa, the more absolute this power became. But in 1922 the powerful Thirteenth Dalai Lama, in attempting to bring Tashilhunpo firmly back under the jurisdiction of Lhasa, inadvertently caused the Ninth Panchen Lama to flee to China, where he spent the remaining years of his life. His successor, the Tenth and present Panchen Lama, was born in 1938 in Amdo close to the Chinese border. Whether this incarnation was ever officially acknowledged by Lhasa remains unclear, and he has remained in the hands of the Chinese ever since. He presently lives in Peking and only rarely visits Tibet. In 1986 he travelled to Australia as part of a Chinese government delegation, and later to Nepal.

THE SITE

Architecturally, Tashilhunpo presents a wonderful sight: a line of imposing red buildings of varying height crowned with gleaming, golden rooftops. Before them is a sprawling mass of single-storey white monastic dwellings. A high wall surrounds the complex and at the north-eastern corner rises a mighty white wall on which a giant *tangka* was ceremoniously displayed on special occasions. Surrounding the monastery is a circumambulation route, along which are prayer wheels, carved rock inscriptions and the occasional small shrine.

Extensive building was done during the time of the Fifth Dalai Lama and his teacher the Fourth Panchen. Further additions were made by the next two Panchen Lamas and also the Ninth. Between them, the Fourth and Fifth Panchen Lamas supplied the monastery with eight thousand religious images. It suffered relatively little damage during the cultural revolution although many buildings fell into disrepair due to inadequate maintenance. There used to be five (or by some accounts six) colleges (*dratsang*) in the monastery. Now there are only three: a Philosophy College, a Tantric College and the Dronggo College (no jokes, please), all of which, however, are in use. At its height Tashilhunpo is said to have housed up to four thousand monks; at present there are six hundred, with a fairly high proportion of elderly monks and teachers.

OPPOSITE *Side view of Tashilhunpo. The white windowless building at the back is used for hanging large* tangkas *during religious ceremonies.*

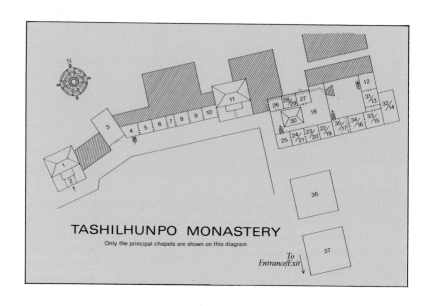

TASHILHUNPO MONASTERY

Only the principal chapels are shown on this diagram

To
Entrance/Exit

THE PANCHEN LAMAS

1. Khedrup Je	1385-1483
2-3. *Dates not known*	
4. Losang Chökyi Gyeltsen	1570-1662
5. Losang Yeshe	1663-1737
6. Pelden Yeshe	1738-1780
7. Tenpai Nyima	1781-1853
8. Tenpai Wangchuk	1854-1882
9. Chökyi Nyima	1883-1937
10. Chökyi Gyeltsen	1938-

Although Tashilhunpo impresses one with the size and number of images seen in its chapels, there are relatively few statues or paintings of particular note. Many of the chapels are designed on a similar plan and after a while it becomes hard to remember one from another. The altars in the chapels are usually three to four levels of stepped shelves packed with numerous small bronzes surrounding a larger bronze figure.

The Maitreya Chapel

This high building at the far left of the monastery was erected in 1914 by Chökyi Nyima, the Ninth Panchen Lama. The **Maitreya Chapel** (1) itself is several storeys high and contains one single, enormous seated image of Maitreya, which reaches to the roof. The figure is coated with gold and impresses not merely by its huge size but also by the delicacy of the workmanship and the sublimity of its facial expression. A thousand images of Maitreya are painted in gold outline on the surrounding red walls. Tsongkhapa and his two chief disciples are also depicted on the left wall, and just before you leave the chapel, after circumambulating the metal base of the main image, you pass paintings of the Geluk yidams, Guhyasamaja, Samvara and Yamantaka. Next to them are the Kadampa triad of Atisha, Drom Trönpa and Ngog Legpa'i Sherab. Unfortunately it is not possible to climb to the higher storeys to view the Maitreya statue from other angles.

There is one other chapel in this compound: on the first storey facing the entrance to the Maitreya Chapel, is a **Tushita Chapel** (2) containing one thousand small statues of Tsongkhapa, also built by the Ninth Panchen Lama.

The Victory Chapel

The **Victory Chapel** (3) is now used as a school for the monks to study philosophy and is often closed to the public. If you get a chance to go in, the central figures are huge gold images of Tsongkhapa and his two chief disciples. Tall figures of the bodhisattvas Maitreya and Manjushri stand to either side.

The Panchen Lama's Palace

The main, residential section of the palace is the high white building that rises behind the long red front wall containing the series of chapels to be described here. It is not possible to visit the interior of the actual palace since it is still used occasionally by the Panchen Lama. Seven connected chapels line the first floor, a doorway leading from one to the next.

The first is called the **Chinese Chapel** (4) because of its decorative

Chinese-style altar built by the Sixth Panchen Lama, Pelden Yeshe, in honour of his disciple Ch'ien Lung, the Chinese Manchu emperor. Vajradhara, clasping a vajra in each hand, is the central figure on the altar. Other statues include Amitayus, the Medicine Buddha, Tsongkhapa and his two chief disciples, and Tara. A *tangka* of the Sixteen Arhats surrounding the Buddha also hangs here.

The next room is the **Lhen Dzom Zim Puk** (5), the chamber in which the Panchen Lamas would receive the official Chinese representative, the Amban. Two thrones of equal height dominate this room, the one on the left being used by the Panchen Lama. A series of seventeen of the woven Hangzhou *tangkas* that were commissioned by the Ninth Panchen Lama and are seen everywhere in Tashilhunpo, hang from the right-hand wall. The seventeen *tangkas* show *seventeen* incarnations of the Panchen Lamas. Normally the present Panchen is considered to be the Tenth, that is, the tenth dated from Khedrup Je. When seventeen are spoken of, the seven incarnations prior to Khedrup Je are counted, including five Indian masters, starting with Arya Rabjor, and two Tibetan masters, one of whom is recognised as Sakya Pandita.

The next room is an **Amitayus Chapel** (6), with a statue of this Buddha of Limitless Life on the left as you enter. The other two larger figures are Shakyamuni and Manjushri. Between the main images are many smaller bronzes. Editions of the Kangyur and Tengyur are also kept here. Note the exquisite Chinese brocade on the ceiling and the series of yellow cloth *tangkas* printed with a detailed woodblock from Nartang.

You must climb a few stairs to reach the next chapel. At their top is a landing and on the left a small **Shrine to Dzegya Chökyong** (7), the red, wrathful standing deity who is the special protector of Tashilhunpo.

A **Tushita Chapel** (8) is next. Tsongkhapa and his two chief disciples are the central figures. Beside them sits Khedrup Sanggye Yeshe, the tutor of the Fourth Panchen Lama. Avalokiteshvara, Tara, Shakyamuni and numerous other Buddhas, bodhisattvas and deities line the shelves of the long altar.

Since there is no main image in the next chapel, it is called the **Synoptic (Kundu) Chapel** (9). It houses a multitude of Buddhas, bodhisattvas and deities but none are of particular note.

This long line of chapels ends with a **Tara Chapel** (10). The central figure of Tara is accompanied by two female bodhisattva attendants and surrounded by her twenty-one major manifestations.

The Tomb of the Fourth Panchen Lama (11)

This tall red building crowned by a golden roof is, with the Maitreya Chapel, the most prominent structure in Tashilhunpo and can be

View of Tashilhunpo from the circumambulation path behind the monastery.

reached by an inner flight of stairs leading from the Tara Chapel (10) or, alternatively, by a front entrance. It houses a large silver stupa in which is the intact, embalmed body of Chökyi Gyeltsen, the Fourth Panchen Lama. A small statue of the lama can be made out in a rainbow-enclosed niche in the stupa. The longevity triad of Amitayus, Tara and Vijaya are shown in fine statues before the stupa. As you circumambulate the stupa you can just make out the images of the thousand Buddhas of this aeon in the faded mural around the high walls.

The Kelsang Temple

This, the largest and most intricate complex in Tashilhunpo, is to the far right of the main set of buildings. Upon leaving the Tomb of the Fourth Panchen Lama, turn left and continue along the base of the high red wall until you reach a passageway on the left. If you follow this dark, stone alley, you will emerge on the flagstones of the inner courtyard of the Kelsang Temple. Images of the thousand Buddhas of this aeon are painted around the walls of this courtyard. Beneath each of these fresh, radiant figures is a small text with a verse describing each Buddha. The throne of the Panchen Lama is at the rear of the courtyard.

The complex of buildings consists of two sections of different periods.

The older part is the assembly hall (18), which dates back to the fifteenth century when the monastery was founded by Gendun Drup. The other buildings enclosing the courtyard were added on in the seventeenth century by the Fourth Panchen Lama.

In visiting this complex I shall follow the somewhat circuitous route taken by most Tibetan pilgrims.

On the first floor, on the far side of the courtyard facing the assembly hall, is a **Jokhang** (12), dedicated to Shakyamuni. The youthful form of the Buddha here is surrounded by a thousand smaller Buddhas, each dressed in a yellow cloth.

Next door to it is the **Silver Tomb Chapel** (13), a small room that houses two silver stupas in niches amongst all the Buddha images that fill the shrine. The main figure is Vajradhara.

The **Printing Room** (14) is entered through a corridor to the left. It is a larger room lined with shelves containing the wood-blocks of a complete edition of the Kangyur and several texts from the Tengyur. Monks can often be seen at work printing, usually for the benefit of passing visitors.

Another **Shakyamuni Chapel** (15) follows. The main image of the Buddha is surrounded by a thousand smaller figures. The paintings on the wall depict a form of Samvara with a white-coloured consort and Pelden Yeshe, the Sixth Panchen Lama.

Next door is a **Tara Chapel** (16), in which a larger figure of Tara is surrounded by a mass of smaller bronzes. Copies of the seventeen Hangzhou *tangkas* showing the incarnations of the Panchen Lamas hang from the walls.

The final chapel in this section is a **Tushita Chapel** (17). Two sets of statues of Tsongkhapa and his two chief disciples are on the altar accompanied by various Buddha figures, Taras and other deities.

Descend to the **Assembly Hall** (18), which was built at the time of Gendun Drup and is one of the oldest and most atmospheric buildings in Tashilhunpo. The giant, undecorated pillars are worn with centuries of bodily contact; on four of the main ones, facing south, are mounted fine golden statues of Vijaya, Tara, Dugkarma and Avalokiteshvara. In contrast to the main Gelukpa monasteries in Lhasa, the rows of cushions on which the monks sit are raised about two feet from the ground, giving you the feeling that you are caught in a maze of knee-high corridors. The centre of the room is occupied by the massive throne of the Panchen Lama. Woven Hangzhou *tangkas* illustrating the seventeen incarnations of the Panchen hang around the room.

Two chapels can be entered from the Assembly Hall. The larger of the two is dedicated to Shakyamuni. Shariputra and Maudgalyayana stand to his sides and the Eight Great Bodhisattvas are around the walls. High on the two pillars facing the doorway are Gendun Drup, the founder of the monastery, and Chökyi Gyeltsen, the Fourth Panchen Lama. Two images of seated Manjushris are immediately beneath them. A small statue of one of the Panchen Lamas is seated in a small glass case on a pillar to the right and a standing Tara on a pillar to the left. The smaller chapel next door is a dark and rather dismal shrine to Tara. Three large images of Tara, which reputedly date back to the time of Gendun Drup, are seated in the centre of the room. Unfortunately, they lack the soft, feminine quality usually associated with Tara. The murals have been erased, probably by time.

The row of chapels *at the front of the first floor* begins with the **Chapel of Great Joy** (19). The main image is a Kadam Stupa. Numerous smaller stupas and statues of the Buddha are lined along the shelves around it. A beautiful embroidered *tangka* of Yamantaka hangs on the wall.

Next door is a **Chinese Chapel** (20) housing a Jowo Shakyamuni. To either side of him are the Sixteen Arhats and slightly in front a statue of the Ninth Panchen Lama. As usual, the shelves are packed with many smaller images.

The final room is the **Precious Chapel** (21), which enshrines a heavily bedecked, standing Maitreya. Other prominent figures are Vajradhara, Avalokiteshvara and Tara.

Continuing *up a flight of stairs to the next storey*, immediately above the three previous chapels, you reach a **Tara Chapel** (22). The main figure is a standing Tara surrounded by numerous Buddhas and bodhisattvas. The walls are covered with *tangkas*.

The **Pandrup Chapel** (23) follows. This shrine is dedicated to the Fourth Panchen Lama, a statue of whom sits with great dignity in the cente of the altar. To the left is a beautiful image of Dugkarma and to the right a thousand-armed Avalokiteshvara. A number of small, lithe standing Buddhas line the shelves. Two exquisite and apparently very old circular images of Tara and Manjushri surrounded by concentric rings of mantras and texts in tiny script are painted on the wall.

The next room is the **Chapel of 'Gadong' Maitreya** (24). It contains a tall, noble Maitreya statue surrounded by many minor figures. *Tangkas* hang from the walls.

In the end room of this row is the **Chapel of Miscellaneous Lamas** (25). Tsongkhapa and his two chief disciples are the most prominent and easily recognisable figures. Numerous other Geluk lamas surround them.

To reach the next chapel, it is necessary to *descend again to the first floor* and go to the back. On the left is a **Protector Chapel** (26). There are no statues in this room, only painted murals of the protectors Dharmaraja and Pelden Lhamo.

Further along is a **Maitreya Chapel** (27), founded by the Sixth Panchen Lama. This large room allows you to see a wonderful statue of the Maitreya seated on the ground floor below, his head and shoulders rising into this chapel. To the left is a standing image of Manjushri and to the right, Avalokiteshvara. Both of these finely made deities are said to have been sculpted by the Sixth Panchen Lama himself.

Taking another flight of stairs *up again to the next storey* brings you to a strange **Shakyamuni Chapel** (28) in which the Buddha, in the pristine company of Shariputra and Maudalyayana and the Sixteen Arhats, sits in the midst of many macabre tantric hangings and motifs including two long, stuffed snakes. To the right is a small shrine to Pelden Lhamo. The monk who was showing us around explained that these two apparently incompatible aspects of Buddhism, which in most monasteries are

A collection of slates carved with mantras and images of lamas.

enshrined separately, are mixed here to emphasise the unity of sutra and tantra taught in the Tibetan Buddhist tradition.

Returning downstairs you reach the **Chapel in which You Can See the Face** (29), from which you can look down into the main chapel on the ground floor (see 18) and see clearly the face of the Jowo Shakyamuni there. *Tangkas* of the Six Ornaments and the Two Supreme Philosophers of India are on the walls, along with a beautiful modern painting of Amitabha. On the right is a small mandala of the Medicine Buddha beneath a roofed canopy. On the altar is a black stone with the perfectly formed letters OM MANI PADME HUM protruding from it in white, similar to the one in Zhalu Monastery.

If you are not lost by now, *go upstairs again* to visit one of the most sacred shrines in Tashilhunpo. This is the **Tuwang Dönden Chapel** (30), in which is enshrined the stupa containing the relics of the First Dalai Lama, Gendun Drup, the founder of the monastery. The other two stupas in the room contain the remains of two former abbots of Tashilhunpo: Samdrup Yeshe and Lungrig Gyatso.

To complete the visit to the Kelsang Temple you leave the assemby hall the way you came in, cross the open courtyard and *climb to the second storey of the building opposite*. There are five chapels on this level. The first is an **Amitayus Chapel** (31) with three main statues of Amitayus. To the left of the central figure is a Tara and to the right a somewhat unusual seated form of Samvara with consort. A number of cymbals are placed along the altar.

The **Kangyur Chapel** (32) next door seems to be directly above the Printing Room (14) on the floor below. Copies of the Buddhist sutras line the walls of this room and cushions and reading tables are placed in rows on the floor. Each morning the room is filled with monks reciting the texts aloud. Images of the Buddha with Shariputra and Maudgalyayana are enshrined on an altar in one wall and a statue of Amitabha in another. The same woven Hangzhou *tangkas* depicting the Panchen Lamas hang from the walls.

The next room is a **Sukhavati Chapel** (33) and the main figure is Amitabha, the Buddha who rules over the Pure Land of Sukhavati. To the left is Manjushri and to the right Maitreya. Numerous smaller Buddhas and bodhisattvas fill the shelves around.

Another Pure Land is celebrated in the adjacent room, a **Tushita (Ganden) Chapel** (34). The main figure is that of Tsongkhapa. To the right are medium-sized images of the Eighth and Sixth Panchen Lamas. The other statues depict the teachers of the 'Stages on the Path to Enlightenment' lineage, including both Indian masters and their Tibetan successors. To the left of Tsongkhapa is a statue of the Fifth Dalai

Lama. This is remarkable in that it is the only image of a ruling Dalai Lama in the whole of the Tashilhunpo Monastery. One would have expected at least some other images of the Fifth Dalai Lama, since it was he who inaugurated the line of Panchen Lamas. One cannot help but wonder whether this absence is a sign of the rivalry that seems tragically to have beset relations between these two spiritual leaders.

The final chapel is a **Tara Chapel** (35). A small standing Tara is in the centre of the room, surrounded by numerous other seated and standing Buddhas and bodhisattvas. Some of these are images of exceptionally high standard. A somewhat defaced but recently restored mural of the twelve major deeds of the Buddha adorns the walls.

The Tantric College

To reach the **Tantric College** (36) you leave the Kelsang Temple by the passageway that goes under the chapels at the front of the complex, then turn right and shortly after take a left down the main alley, which leads downhill to the main entrance of the monastery. Only recently has this quadrangle of buildings been converted into the Tantric College; previously it was a monastic residential area (*khangtsen*). There is only one chapel of the college open to visitors. This is on the first floor and is the room the monks use for their daily services and assemblies. There are only a few images here; Tsongkhapa and his two chief disciples and the Fourth Panchen Lama are the main figures. The throne used by the tantric abbot and the Panchen Lama is prominently placed in the centre of the room. Next to it is a Yamantaka mandala beneath a small roofed canopy. Images of some of the protectors can also be seen. Rows of the peculiar high cushions used by the monks cover the floor.

The Philosophy College

The **Philosophy College** (37) is also a coverted monastic residential area. The assembly hall on the ground floor has statues of six lamas beside the entrance to the main chapel at the rear: the three figures to the left resemble but are not Tsongkhapa and his two chief disciples; the central figure is Tsongkhapa, but Gendun Drup is on the left and the Fourth Panchen Lama on the right. The other three figures, to the right of the doorway, are the important Tashilhunpo lamas who composed the philosophy textbooks studied in the monastery. The main chapel, reached through the doorway, houses a large seated Buddha with Shariputra and Maudgalyayana. The Sixteen Arhats and the Eight Great Bodhisattvas are also on display. In front of the Buddha sits the Ninth Panchen Lama.

Upstairs are three protector chapels. The one on the far left is closed. The middle chapel contains no statues and its walls are covered with hangings and drapes concealing behind them, perhaps, murals of wrathful protectors. A small doorway in the right-hand wall leads you into the third chapel, a small shrine-room dedicated to Tashilhunpo's special protector Dzegya Chökyong, the red, standing, wrathful deity already seen in Chapel 7.

In 1987 it is planned to open another large building, which is presently under construction on the hillside immediately above the courtyard of the Kelsang Temple. This will be used to house the stupas containing the relics of the Fifth, Sixth, Seventh, Eighth and Ninth Panchen Lamas. These were formerly kept in separate chapels but suffered damage during the cultural revolution and are now being stored elsewhere for restoration.

Monks at prayer in Tashilhunpo.

42. SAKYA MONASTERY

Sakya is 143 km to the south-west of Shigatse, along the upper reaches of the small, fertile valley carved out by the Trom River. There are two high passes between Shigatse and Sakya: the Tso La (from where you can see Everest on a clear day) and the Gyatso La, which is 117 km from Shigatse. When coming from Shigatse, you turn left after the Gyatso La Pass and drive up the valley for a further 26 km until you come to the massive structure of the monastery. There is a small guesthouse across the road, which charges 3 RMB per bed. A rudimentary kitchen provides bread and tea but not much else. The monastery is open only from 10 am to midday and 2 to 4 pm. There is a 3 RMB entrance charge and strict control over photography.

HISTORY

Sakya Monastery, the centre of the Sakya order of Tibetan Buddhism, was founded in 1073 by Könchok Gyelpo of the powerful Khön family. Probably in retrospect, descendants of the Khön lineage created a myth of the distant, divine origins of this family, beginning with the descent from the sky of the three 'brothers of luminosity'. Nonetheless, the influential position of this family can be reliably traced back to the times of the early kings of Tibet, when Khön Palpoche appears as a minister of King Trisong Detsen. At the same time, a son of Palpoche called Lu'i Wangpo was a disciple of Padmasambhava one of the seven 'examined men' who, having been tested by Shantarakshita, were chosen to be the first Tibetans ordained as Buddhist monks.

Könchok Gyelpo, who lived during the latter half of the eleventh century, is regarded as the progenitor (in a quite literal sense) of the Sakya order. As a young man he became a monk and studied with the famous Tibetan mystic and translator Drokmi. Drokmi was also a teacher of

The Northern Monastery at Sakya, circa 1935.

Marpa, a founder of the Kagyu school, and a devotee of the Hevajra Tantra, which he translated from Sanskrit into Tibetan. It is because of Drokmi that Hevajra figures so greatly in the Sakya tradition and is prominently depicted in Sakya monasteries. Later in life, in accordance with a prophecy, Könchok Gyelpol disrobed, married, and in 1092 fathered Kunga Nyingpo (or Sachen, the Great Sakyapa).

Although Könchok Gyelpo is credited with the founding of Sakya Monastery, it was his son Kunga Nyingpo who, through his reputation as a scholar, meditator and powerful leader, firmly established the place as the spiritual centre of a newly founded Tibetan Buddhist order. Kunga Nyingpo also started construction of the Northern Monastery, a complex of buildings along the north bank of the Trom River by a peculiar patch of tawny hillside, which gave the order its name 'Sakya', 'Tawny Ground'. He was posthumously recognised as a manifestation of Avalokiteshvara.

Kunga Nyingpo had four sons, two of whom, Sonam Tsemo and Trakpa Gyeltsen, became renowned monks in the Sakya tradition. Another, Kunga Bar, was also a monk but died young while studying in India. The fourth remained a layman and continued the family line. To this day, the Sakya hierarchy has remained very much a family affair. Unlike the other Tibetan orders, it does not rely greatly on the recognition of incarnate lamas to provide it with spiritual leaders. Instead, its hierarchy is continued through a system of heredity, the mantle of the heads of the order passing from father to son. A celibate monastic order is also preserved but is subordinate to the non-ordained line of leaders.

One of the greatest Sakya lamas was Kunga Gyeltsen, better known simply as Sakya Pandita, who was to usher in the most glorious epoch of the dynasty's history. He was the grandson of Kunga Nyingpo and ordained as a monk. Revered as one of the greatest lamas of his generation, he was also recognised as a worthwhile ally by the Mongols, who were the dominant political force in Central Asia and China at that time. The Mongolian emperor Godan Khan 'invited' him to the royal court in 1244 and after a three year journey in the company of his two young nephews he arrived in Mongolia in 1247. He stayed there for the remaining four years of his life, during which time he disseminated Buddhism throughout the land and established a close relationship with the ruler. After the death of both Sakya Pandita and Godan Khan in the same year, their relationship bore further fruit under their respective successors. Sakya Pandita's nephew, Pakpa, became the personal spiritual teacher of Godan Khan's heir Kublai Khan. The Khan heaped many rewards upon Pakpa, culminating in 1264 with Pakpa's being granted virtual sovereignty over Tibet as its 'imperial preceptor'. Sakya thus became the de facto capital of the country and it continued to be ruled from there for nearly a century.

Pakpa died in Sakya in 1280 after a peripatetic life divided between stays in Mongolia, China and Tibet. Power remained in the hands of the Sakyapa although other Buddhist orders vied with it for the backing of the Mongols. In 1290 the Sakya army destroyed Drigung Monastery to end that order's political ambitions. However, internal feuding and the collapse of the Mongolian Yuan dynasty in China allowed another powerful Tibetan family, the Pamotrupa – descendants of the famous Kagyu lama of the same name – to gain control of the country in 1354.

Although the Sakyapa never again achieved national prominence, they remained overlords of the immediate region and were still a quasi-autonomous 'principality' in 1959. The line of religious teachers flourished, creating two main sub-sects, the Ngor and Tsar traditions, in the fifteenth century.

THE SITE
What first strikes one about Sakya today is the peculiar colouring of its buildings. They are painted dark grey, with white strips along the tops of the walls and red and white vertical stripes from top to bottom. Both the village houses in the valley and the monastery are painted in this dismal, uniform scheme, apparently to indicate that they lie within the area governed by Sakya and are therefore taxable.

The ruins of the Northern Monastery at Sakya. The one intact building is the Vijaya Chapel. Kunga Nyingpo's white stupa is also visible.

Because of the region's proximity to the Indian border, the two spiritual heads of the Sakya order along with many monks and other people fled the country in the 1950's. Now there are only fifty or so monks left, whereas five hundred lived here before. The Northern Monastery built by Kunga Nyingpo was completely destroyed during the cultural revolution. Only one small chapel has managed to reappear from the ruins. The imposing Southern Monastery, on the opposite bank of the river, alone remains standing. This massive, daunting enclosed compound was erected by Pakpa in the thirteenth century. With its huge unscalable walls it resembles a fortress or a prison more than a monastery.

The Northern Monastery

There used to be one hundred and eight chapels contained in the monastic complex that stretched along this hillside. The only one rebuilt is the **Vijaya Chapel**. It was founded by the translator Bari about nine hundred years ago and the present building (reconstructed in 1981) is on the site of the original, which must have been one of the earliest chapels in Sakya. It houses the restored Vijaya stupa that was originally enshrined here by Bari and is said to contain relics of the historical Buddha. A portrait of the white-haired translator holding a golden vase in his hand is on the left of the altar. The central statue is Shakyamuni and by his side is a very fine image of Vijaya. Recently woven cloth images of Shakyamuni are pinned to the four walls.

Higher on the hillside, not far from the Vijaya Chapel, is a large white stupa reconstructed on the site where a stupa was originally built in the twelfth century to house some of the remains of Kunga Nyingpo.

The Southern Monastery

This complex of buildings is surrounded by a huge, thick square wall, with turrets at the four corners and a pathway on the top, along which you can walk. The central monastic building inside is also square and enclosed between four high, windowless walls. Painted around these walls, about two yards from the ground, is a continuous yellow and white band. Some smaller monastic dwellings and other buildings are scattered around the central structure but one has the impression that several others must have been destroyed.

You enter the monastery through a tall gateway in the eastern wall and arrive in a courtyard facing the entrance of the large, reddish central building. To the right is a building that used to serve as the 'kashag' of Sakya, i.e. the centre of local government. Nowadays it is used for receiving and entertaining official guests.

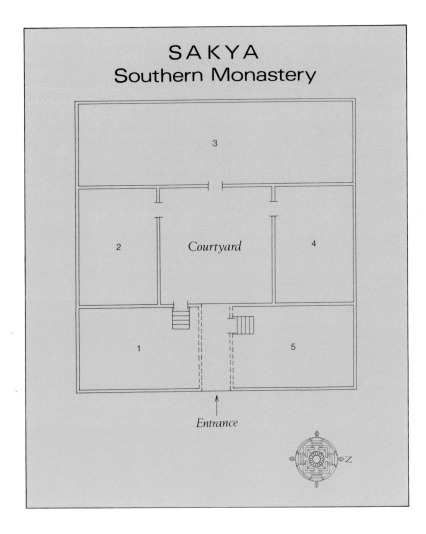

1. The Puntsok Palace

The Puntsok Palace is entered through the first doorway on the left when you reach the inner courtyard. It is on the first storey. This palace is the residence of one of the two principal lamas of the Sakya school, who is now in exile in Seattle. The only room you can visit is a spacious, high-ceilinged chapel with exquisite statues lining two of the walls. The figure you encounter first nearest the door is White Tara. Next to her are two statues of Amitayus, one of Sakya Pandita and one of Vijaya. This brings you to the main and most ornate statue, Manjushri, who is seated on a slightly higher throne. Vajrasattva and Vajradhara are the other deities along this wall. Another Tara is in the corner.

Continuing along the back wall you then pass two stupas containing the relics of prominent Sakya lamas before reaching a most imposing figure of Kunga Nyingpo, which dates back to the founding of the monastery. This tall statue is excellently crafted and highly expressive, showing the lama, with white hair in old age, smiling gently down upon you. In front of him is a small statue of Tangtong Gyelpo. The wall on the right shows murals of the longevity triad of Amitayus, Tara and Vijaya. Surrounding each of the major figures are smaller identical images of all three deities, extending to cover the entire wall.

2. The Manjushri Chapel
Entered from the left (south) of the courtyard, this high, spacious, rectangular chapel is overlooked by two principal figures. To the left is a very fine Jowo Shakyamuni and to the right, Manjushri. Both statues were designed and sculpted by Sakya Pandita. An edition of the Ten-

The entrance to the Southern Monastery at Sakya.

Detail of the entrance to the Southern Monastery.

gyur is stored between the two images and to the left of it are shelves filled with volumes of the Kangyur. The faded murals on the far left wall depict some of the Sakya tantric deities, the predominant one being Hevajra. The murals on the back wall show the longevity triad of Amitayus, Tara and Vijaya, the Medicine Buddha and two versions of Shakyamuni, the one on the far right being in a rather ancient style. Set in the right-hand wall are a mass of glass cases in which are housed several thousand small bronze statues around a central figure of Tara. It is hard to identify the smaller statues but they are said to be mainly Sakya tantric deities and prominent lamas and numerous other Buddhas and bodhisattvas. Another Tara and the Protector of the West are in separate glass cases in front. The five principal Sakya protectors are painted around the doorway.

3. The Great Assembly Hall

This magnificent room is situated directly ahead of you as you enter the courtyard. To the left of the doorway are painted Acala and Brahma and to the right Hayagriva and Indra, thus ensuring both mundane and supra-mundane protection. Huge tree trunks converted into pillars support the roof of this immense hall and rows of high cushions for the monks line the floor. Scenes from the Buddha's former lives as recounted in the *Paksam Trishing* are depicted in the murals covering the thick, front wall. To the far left are stacked copies of the Kangyur and Tengyur.

The statues that dominate the room are mainly huge bronze Buddhas set against elaborate, wide bronze haloes. Not only is the style of the Buddhas unique but they also serve the unusual purpose of being reliquaries for the remains of prominent lamas and rulers from the Sakya tradition.

The first Buddha along the left-hand wall contains the relics of Shakya Zangpo, Pakpa's second regent (the person authorised by him to take care of temporal matters in Tibet), who is remembered for having carried out one of the first censuses in Tibet. Next to this statue are a smaller Buddha, Avalokiteshvara, the reliquary of a minister and finally a small Padmasambhava.

The first giant Buddha along the back wall contains some of the relics of Sakya Pandita. This is followed by a stupa that houses the remains of Ngawang Tutob Wangchuk, the previous throne-holder and father of the Sakya hierarch who now lives in Seattle. The central and largest Buddha contains some of the relics of the founder of the Southern Monastery, Pakpa himself (half of Pakpa's remains were taken to Mongolia and enshrined there and the other half kept in Sakya). Several important Sakya lamas sit in front of this Buddha: Kunga Nyingpo, in a red hat, is to the left; Sakya Pandita is immediately in front. After the statues of the longevity triad of Amitayus, Tara and Vijaya are three thrones reserved for the heads of the Sakya order. The next large Buddha contains more relics of Sakya Pandita, followed by the Sakya triad of The Three White Ones, that is Kunga Nyingpo (centre) and his two ordained sons, Sonam Tsemo and Drakpa Gyeltsen. Next are statues of the 'Unconquerable' Manjushri and a seated Maitreya, the latter housing the relics of the Sakya lama Pe Jungma. The remains of the Sakya Imperial Preceptor Dharmapala, a nephew of Pakpa who ruled from 1279 to 1286, are enshrined in the beautiful, adjacent figure of Vajradhara. The stupa that follows is called the 'Heart Stupa'. It contains miscellaneous relics of Sakya lamas dating back to the foundation of the monastery a thousand years ago. A Buddha with the relics of Pakpa's minister Aklen, a statue of Manjushri with the relics of Lama Dukhor (a disciple of Sakya Pandita), a stupa and a final Buddha complete the impressive series of figures on this long altar.

Also of note are the thirty-seven small deities from the Kunrig tantric cycle lined along the base of the Buddhas to the right of the central figure, and the glass cases lined along the base of the entire altar containing cups and other Chinese porcelain objects that were the personal possessions of the previous Sakya lamas.

The right-hand wall starts with a Buddha in which are contained the relics of another of Pakpa's ministers, Kungawa Rinchen Pel. Numerous smaller statues of tantric deities and lamas are clustered along a dark altar, above which is a mural depicting the Five Great Ones: Kunga Nyingpo (centre), Sonam Tsemo, Drakpa Gyeltsen, Sakya Pandita and Pakpa. The large metal bowl by the corner (now filled with rice and offering scarves) was offered to the monastery as a water container at the time of Pakpa by a man from Derge called Rabten.

4. The Chapel of the Silver Stupas
This chapel is named after the eleven tall silver reliquaries that line it and contain the remains of the eleven Imperial Preceptors, or Throne Holders, of the Sakya line who ruled during the golden era, beginning with Pakpa and ending in the middle of the fourteenth century. On the wall behind the stupas are large paintings of the Five Dhyani Buddhas. Above the head of each of these Buddhas is a smaller figure of one of the Five Great Ones of the Sakya order. By the left-hand wall are shelves filled with copies of the Buddhist canon and the collected writings of major Sakya scholars. Behind them is an unusual depiction of the triad of Manjushri, Avalokiteshvara and Vajrapani: the three bodhisattvas are shown standing, with Vajrapani in a peaceful aspect instead of the more common wrathful one. Of particular note by the right-hand wall is a fine sand mandala of Hevajra encased in glass.

Five more stupas are found in a small chapel that is reached through a door in the back wall. An interesting image here is that of Sakya Pandita in conversation with Manjushri, the bodhisattva of wisdom, of whom Sakya Pandita is considered to be a manifestation. This image portrays how they communicated with each other as one person to another. Around the walls of the chapel are paintings of mandalas. It is not possible to examine closely those at the side and back of the room, but the mandalas on the front wall belong to the charya tantra cycles of Vairocana and Amitayus (to the right) and the supreme yoga tantra cycles of Guhyasamaja and Samvara (to the left). None of them is in particularly good condition.

Drakshul Trinle Rinchen, a former Throne Holder (Trichen) of the Tara Palace, with his entourage, circa 1935, shortly before his death.

5. Tara Palace

You reach the Tara Palace by a flight of stairs that leads off from a doorway in the entrance corridor. Like the Puntsok Palace on the opposite side of the corridor, it is on the first storey. It too is part of the residence of one of the two chief Sakya lamas, the present incumbent being in exile in northern India. This majestic chapel contains five stupas of different heights, the largest of which contains the relics of the father of the incumbent lama. Superb murals cover the walls. On the left are scenes from the life of Padmasambhava, the central portrait of the Guru being framed by an exceptional transparent rainbow halo. The chapel is also called the 'Tenth Day Chapel', a reference to the day of the lunar month when special ceremonies are performed throughout Tibet in honour of Padmasambhava. On the opposite wall is the longevity triad of Amitayus, Tara and Vijaya. Here (in contrast to the Puntsok Palace), each of the main figures is surrounded by smaller images of that same figure alone, that is Tara is surrounded by many smaller Taras, and so forth. The front wall shows various Sakya lamas and protectors.

There is also a library somewhere in the monastery that contains a renowned collection of ancient manuscripts and texts, some of them in Sanskrit. At present it is not possible to visit the library without special permission from Peking.

43. SHEKAR DZONG

Shekar is 238 km south-west of Shigatse, 7 km off the main road going to Nepal. It is a convenient place to spend your last night in Tibet before driving to the border the next day, or your first night in Tibet when coming up from Kathmandu. There is only one place to stay, a spacious Chinese truckstop-cum-hotel that charges 10 RMB per bed (three beds to a room). Meals are also available at around 5 RMB. It is located to the right of the road shortly after you enter the town.

61 km further south-west is the village of Tingri, renowned as the place where the Indian master Padampa Sanggye lived and taught for a while. Just before you reach Tingri the road passes through a long, wide valley, offering an excellent view of Mt. Everest: it is the mountain to the far left of the range.

HISTORY

Shekar Dzong, literally the 'White Crystal Castle', was traditionally the provincial capital for the wider area of Tingri. The governor lived in the castle on the summit of the steep hill that rises above the old Tibetan part of town. Shekar Dzong has now become the Chinese administrative centre for this part of Tibet and is sometimes referred to as 'New Tingri'. In recent years a scattered complex of official, modern buildings has grown up about a mile from the old town. Despite its small population and remoteness, it is used as a starting point for expeditions to the Mt. Everest base camp.

SHEKAR CHÖDE

If you walk from the new town through the cluster of old Tibetan houses at the base of the hill, you will reach a small temple called Shekar Chöde, or simply Shekar Monastery, which was founded in 1266 by a Sakya lama called Sindeu Rinchen. 'Sindeu' is a Chinese name that he was given during one of his visits to China. Although originally Sakya, it later became a Geluk monastery affiliated to Sera in Lhasa (*not* Tashilhunpo, the monks will hasten to add!). Formerly it covered a wide area at this point mid-way between the village and the castle, housing up to three hundred monks. It was completely destroyed during the cultural revolution and only recently has reconstruction work begun. There are now eleven monks living here. The sole chapel to have been rebuilt contains nothing remarkable. The main images are those of Tsongkhapa and his two chief disciples. Above them sit Vajradhara and

The ruins of the old fort at Shekar.

a small Padmasambhava in a glass case. Several smaller bronzes recently donated by Sera are also on the altar. However, the construction is somewhat unusual in that there are two curved flights of stairs that join at the back of the main room, at an upper level shrine, thus giving a circular effect to the shape of the room.

From the monastery you can gaze up at the ruins of the castle, which cling to the very steep, shale-covered mountain-side. The castle itself, partially intact, is balanced incredibly on the very summit, which can be reached only by going around to the back of the mountain once you are about a third of the way up. From here you can see Mt. Everest.

PREVIOUS PAGE *The valley of Shekar. Shekar Chöde is the monastic building visible to the left of the picture.*

44. NYELAM PELGYE LING

(MILAREPA'S CAVE)

Forty kilometres north of the Nepalese border crossing is a small temple that can only just be seen clinging to the hillside beneath the main road. When coming from Lhasa and Shigatse it is about 40 km after the spectacular Nyelam Tong La pass, about 10 km before you reach the village of Nyelam. Nyelam is, in a sense, the last (or first) town in Tibet, since from here one descends rapidly from the plateau to the lush Himalayan valleys leading into Nepal. The temple is open daily (provided one of the two caretakers can be found) and a 20 Fen entrance fee is charged.

HISTORY

Milarepa, probably the most widely revered Tibetan Buddhist mystic, never founded any monasteries or centres of practice. His life was an itinerant one that led him from one remote area to another throughout Central Southern Tibet. For most of his adult life he lived in caves, surviving on whatever he was offered by local villagers or grew roundabout. He was known and loved for the songs he composed and sang to the people, which poetically and succinctly expressed his insights into the truths of Buddhism.

As a young man he was robbed of his inheritance by a wicked uncle. In order to seek revenge for his now destitute mother, he studied the arts of black magic, in whose methods he became sufficiently adept to cause his uncle's house to collapse, thereby killing all those inside. Eventually, remorse for his misdeeds led him to the Buddhist teacher Marpa, a farmer in the Lhodrak region of Southern Tibet. To atone for his murders and prove his sincerity, he was ordered to build singlehanded a series of stone towers. One of these, the final, nine-storeyed tower called the 'Sekargutok', still survives today and can be reached from Tsetang by road (see Chapter 28, **Tsetang**, above).

Marpa then gave him religious instruction and initiated him into the secrets of the tantras. For several years he stayed with his teacher and practised meditation under his guidance, until he was finally told to leave and continue his training in the solitude of the mountains. His yogic training in the Six Yogas of Naropa, for example, enabled him to endure and transform the hardships of the elements.

Milarepa attracted a growing number of disciples, who would live around him and listen to his teachings. The best-known of these were Gampopa, through whom the Kagyu lineage was established in a

definitive form, and Rechungpa. He died after being poisoned by rival teachers jealous of his achievement and popularity.

The small temple of Nyelam Pelgye Ling overlooks a delightful mountain valley, at the end of which the soaring white peaks of the Himalayas rise into the sky. 'Pelgye Ling' (Place of Increase and Expansion) was the name Milarepa himself suggested for this temple, which was to be built around a cave where he and Rechungpa had meditated but was not built until after his death. At first it belonged to the Kagyu school but it was eventually taken over by the Gelukpa, who have been running it ever since. Once the surrounding buildings housed seventy monks; now there are only two, who serve as caretakers. The original temple was destroyed during the cultural revolution, but in 1983 on the same site a new building was erected with the help of Nepalese supporters and craftsmen.

THE SITE

The main chapel, the central section of the temple, contains an image of Padmasambhava and several protectors. The principal shrine, however, is the **Namkha Ding Cave**, which is entered through a doorway to the left of the foyer to the chapel. 'Namkha Ding', which means 'hovering in space', is the name Milarepa gave to this cave, in which he spent several years. Before going into the cave itself you will see on the ground a curious impression in the rock. This mark, blackened with the pious fingers and hands of Tibetan pilgrims, is said to have been made by Milarepa's buttocks, thigh and foot as he sat in meditation. Next to it is another impression, the hoofprint of Pelden Lhamo's mule, which appeared after Milarepa once received a vision of the protectress. The tiny, low-ceilinged cave lies beneath a large overhanging rock, which has been prevented from falling to the ground by a smaller rock resembling and serving as a pillar. Legend relates how Milarepa held the overhanging rock aloft with his mystical powers (the monks will show you his handprints in the rock, made while he accomplished this feat), while Rechungpa moved the smaller rock into position. On the upper side of this main rock you can see where Milarepa used to keep his bowl and barley flour (tsampa). There is now a statue of him in the place where he used to meditate. This statue and those of Tsongkhapa and his two chief disciples were rescued from the original site; the statue of Pelden Lhamo and the other images lining the altar are new.

If you now go out of the chapel and walk up behind the cave, you will come to another small cave, which is used as a protector chapel. On the altar are two small stone images, one of Yamantaka and the other of the

Tibet's great yogin Milarepa.

special Geluk protector Shukden. Wrathful masks depicting Yaman-taka, Mahakala, Pelden Lhamo and Shukden hang to the left of the altar.

A little higher up is the cave of Rechungpa, Milarepa's disciple and attendant. This cave, even more cramped than that of Milarepa, has few images inside. A modern picture of Milarepa is on the makeshift altar. To the right are some older, damaged figures of Avalokiteshvara, the Buddha and several lamas. These were retrieved from the rubble of the former monastery. Also rescued were the stone carvings and the hands of a large Buddha that are beside them. The bamboo staff of Rechungpa is attached to the left-hand wall.

WESTERN
TIBET

WESTERN TIBET (NGARI)

BRIAN BERESFORD AND SEAN JONES, *edited by the author*

By 'Western Tibet' we refer primarily to the area around Mount Kailas, includ-ing the lakes of Manasarovar and Rakshas Tal, and the towns of Shiquanhe, Purang, Töling (Zada) and the ruined city of Tsaparang. There are three possible ways of entering this region: (1) with an organised tour group departing from Peking or Kathmandu, (2) by crossing the Karakoram highway from Pakistan, going to Kashgar in Xinjiang and arranging individual transport from there south via Yecheng to Shiquanhe (although at the time of writing permits are rarely given to undertake this difficult journey), and (3) by going to Lhasa via any of the routes mentioned (see pp 389) and from there travelling by truck, jeep or landcruiser to Shiquanhe. Since it is at least a six day journey to reach Western Tibet from any of these departure points, it is not worth even considering a visit to this region for any time less than three or four weeks. It is vital that one's budget adequately covers the expenses for the entire journey, which average between 30 to 50 RMB per day ($10-15). May to November is the only time that weather conditions are tolerable and it is possible to circumam-bulate Kailas. The winter is extremely cold.

At the time of writing (1986) the whole region of Western Tibet is restricted to travellers who have obtained permits as members of bona-fide CITS travel tours. Individuals are unable to obtain permits in either Lhasa, Shigatse or Pek-ing. However, the Chinese and Tibetan authorities in Western Tibet itself strongly dispute this prohibition and welcome any tourists who manage to make their way there.

From Lhasa to Shiquanhe *(known to the Tibetans as Senge Tsangpo, or simply Ali). In Lhasa, the place to arrange transport to Western Tibet is the* **Baizhou Guest House**, *situated about 3 km north of the city, two-thirds of the way to Sera Monastery, on the left-hand side of the Ching Drol Lam. The hotel is located in a compound known as the Ali Truck Depot ('Ali' is the Chinese pro-nunciation of the Tibetan 'Ngari', the name of the western province of Tibet of which Shiquanhe is the administrative capital). It is possible to stay there for 10-15 RMB per night not including meals. Starting in 1987, the management of the Baizhou Guest House intend to provide a regular travel service (every ten days) from Lhasa to Purang via Shiquanhe by Chinese jeep for around $320 one way. The price for this nine day journey will include accommodation in hotels and truckstops along the route, but food will be provided only in the Baizhou Guest House, Shiquanhe and Purang. There will also be a one-day stop in Shigatse. In general, facilities in Western Tibet are very primitive and food, water and fuel are in short supply, so it is essential to stock up in Lhasa. The Baizhou Guest*

House may also be able to arrange a 'seat' on the back of a truck to Ngari, travelling with local Tibetans for about 300 RMB (negotiable). Permits, if necessary, will be arranged through the Baizhou Guest House.

The road to Western Tibet starts at **Lhatse**, a small town to the west of Shigatse on the main road to Nepal. 6km west of Lhatse you cross the Brahmaputra by ferry and head for **Raga**, where the road divides into southern and northern routes to Western Tibet. The only passable road during the summer months is the northern route. From Raga you continue north, passing some beautiful lakes and a geothermal area of geysers and hot springs, to **Tsochen (Coqen)**, the largest town before the western region proper. From here it is a full day's journey to **Gertse (Gerze)**, one of the least attractive towns in Central Asia but the centre for a large nomadic population. It is possible to reach Shiquanhe in one day from Gertse, but this long empty stretch may be broken by a night in **Chagtsaka (Qakcaka)** or **Getsai (Gê'gyai)**, small towns in the Indus valley. Apart from the panoramic views, the empty vastness, endless stony plains surrounded by rocky hills and finally the Indus river, there is nothing of note remaining in any of these places on the route.

Shiquanhe is a modern Chinese town, the administrative capital of the region and the only shopping centre for literally hundreds of miles in all directions. Here you can stock up on tinned and dried foods, and buy some fresh fruit and vegetables. There are two truckstops near the crossroads in the middle of town, which charge about 5 RMB per night, although, strictly speaking, you are supposed to stay at the recently built **Ali Hotel**, which costs 80 RMB for a fully furnished room including food. The Ali Hotel boasts the best restaurant in town, serving good Sichuan food.

Although Shiquanhe is the regional capital, when visiting Kailas and the other places of interest in the area, it is best to base yourself at **Purang (Pulan** or, for the Indians, **Taklakot)**. If your trip does not already include transport to Purang, it is possible to hire a jeep or landcruiser from the Ali Hotel. The journey (435 km), which takes one and a half to two days depending on weather, road conditions etc., takes you through **Menjir (Mencir** or **Moincer)**, a seedy coal-mining town and usually your first night stopover. A guesthouse here costs 5 RMB per person and for those who really want to rough it there is one very basic eating house-cum-doss house for even less. The road, which now becomes a deeply rutted track, goes down the open plain south of Kailas, passes between the two lakes of Rakshas Tal and Manasarovar, and skirts round the western flanks of the other major mountain of the area, Gurla Mandhata (7,728 m.). In Purang you can stay at the well-appointed **Pulan Guest House** for 50 RMB per night including food (hot showers are also available), or in one of the less expensive truckstops near the Tibetan market. Purang itself is a small but regionally important market town where, for centuries, Tibetan nomads have come to trade wool, barley, salt and livestock amongst themselves as well as with the Nepalese who bring rice and wood over the passes on the backs of porters, sheep, goats and *yaks. There is also a small Nepalese encampment nearby where Nepalese traders live in the summer and where it is possible to replenish your stocks of colour film.*

There are also a number of cave-dwellings carved into the riverbank above the town, including a monastery, **Tsegu Gömpa***, situated nine storeys up from the base of the cliff, where, according to legend, Sudhana, the hero of the Buddhist epic recounted in the Gandhavyuha Sutra, once lived. High above, on the peak of the hill, was a fortified castle and monastic complex called* **Simbiling,** *where the governor of the area formerly lived. This was all destroyed in 1966.*

OVERLEAF *The marketplace at Purang with cave-dwellings in the background.*

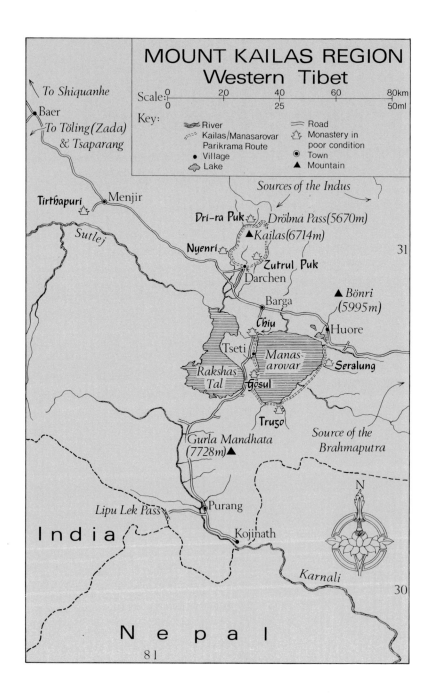

MOUNT KAILAS REGION
Western Tibet

Scale: 0 — 20 — 40 — 60 — 80km
0 — 25 — 50ml

Key:
- River
- Kailas/Manasarovar Parikrama Route
- ● Village
- Lake
- Road
- Monastery in poor condition
- ◉ Town
- ▲ Mountain

To Shiquanhe
Baer
To Töling (Zada) & Tsaparang

Tirthapuri
Menjir

Sutlej

Sources of the Indus

Dri-ra Puk
Drölma Pass (5670m)
▲ Kailas (6714m)
Nyenri
Zutrul Puk
Darchen

Barga

▲ Bönri (5995m)

Chiu
Huore

Tseti
Manas-arovar
Seralung

Rakshas Tal
Gosul

Truzo

Source of the Brahmaputra

Gurla Mandhata (7728m)▲

N

Purang

Lipu Lek Pass

India
Kojinath

Karnali

Nepal

31

30

81

45. MOUNT KAILAS

(TIB. GANG RINPOCHE; CH. KANGRINBOCHE FENG)

Mount Kailas is remarkable in that four of the largest rivers in Asia have their sources within 100 km. of it: the Indus flowing to the north, the Brahmaputra to the east, the Karnali, one of the main tributaries of the Ganges, to the south, and the Sutlej to the west. As a mountain in this part of the world it is not particularly high, a mere 6,714 m., yet it is striking in the way it rises high above the surrounding range and always remains snow-capped (thus its name in Tibetan 'Gang Rinpoche', which means 'Jewel of Snow'). Traditional Buddhist cosmology has often connected Kailas with Mount Meru, the great mythological mountain that forms the axis of this world system. The power of this strange, domed peak has gripped the imagination of the people of India and Tibet since time immemorial. Being a central watershed of Asia, it has always been the most sacred of mountains for Hindus, Buddhists, Jains and 'Bönpos'. Hindus believe it to be the throne of Shiva, while Buddhists revere it as the abode of Samvara (a tantric Buddhist transformation of Shiva). The Jain faith, founded at the time of the Buddha in India, regards it as the place where the very first Jain saint gained emancipation, and followers of the Bön religion in Tibet worship the mountain as the spiritual centre of the ancient country of Shang-shung and as the place where their founder, Shenrab, descended to earth from the sky. Because of the religious associations, many Hindu and Buddhist ascetics, hermits and pilgrims have been drawn to the area of the mountain for the past two thousand years or so to see it, circumambulate it, and to practise austerities and meditation. This is where, in the eleventh century, the Tibetan Buddhist saint Milarepa defeated his Bön opponent, Naro Bön-chung, in a famous contest of magical powers. Mila is associated with the valley on the eastern side, where he is said to have lived for eleven years. Padmasambhava is also associated with the mountain, particularly the valley on the western side, where he stayed in a cave.

Although Kailas has been a popular place of pilgrimage for Indians, Tibetans and Nepalis for many centuries, only a small handful of Western travellers have succeeded in visiting the area until the last few years. The mountain itself was reopened for Tibetan and Indian pilgrims at the beginning of the eighties, but it was only in the autumn of 1984, when the Chinese began to open Tibet to the outside world, that a few Western visitors, the first since Lama Govinda in 1949, began making their way into the area in trucks, landcruisers and even by foot and on horseback. It is still an extremely difficult area to reach and the obstacles that people meet in trying to get here are readily attributed to the power of the mountain itself, which allows only those with sufficient spiritual preparation a glimpse of its magical presence.

Circumambulation (Parikrama) of Kailas. Before undertaking this trek it is essential to be properly equipped and prepared. Warm clothing, waterproof raincoat/jacket, strong shoes, sleeping bag, groundsheet, fuel, cooking pot and sufficient food for at least three days are essential. Although in the summer months tents may be found at two points along the route (Dri-ra Puk and Zutrul Puk), since they are provided specifically for the official parties of Indian pilgrims, you are strongly recommended to take your own. If space is available in the official tents, the charge is 1 RMB per person. Rain, hail and even snow storms can be common, especially from June to September. Binoculars and copies of *The Sacred Mountain*, by John Snelling, and *The Way of the the White Clouds*, by Lama Govinda, will greatly enhance your perception and appreciation of what you see and experience during your trip around the mountain.

Although many hardy Tibetan pilgrims complete the circumambulation (51 km/32 miles) in one day, less robust visitors who wish to contemplate the ever-changing scenic beauty of the place and absorb the various subtle moods and charging atmosphere of the mountain cannot possibly hope to do this. Even at a good pace, the circumambulation takes two full days, staying overnight at Dri-ra Puk. (The Tibetan one-dayers leave at 4am and arrive back at midnight.) Three days enable you to enjoy the trek at a reasonable pace, with stopovers at Dri-ra Puk and Zutrul Puk; four to five days allow you to stop when and where you wish and take a few side detours.

Formerly there were four small monasteries around the circumambulation route: Gyangtra in the southern interior, Nyenri to the west, Dri-ra Puk to the north and Zutrul Puk to the east. All four were badly damaged during the cultural revolution but three (Gyangtra, Dri-ra Puk and Zutrul Puk) are now being restored. Along the route are footprints and handprints in the rock, supposedly left by great saints and Buddhas. Many of the minor peaks around Kailas are dedicated to bodhisattvas and other divine beings. Several natural rock formations are seen as Padmasambhava's *torma*, the Hindu god Hanuman, Shiva's bull and so forth. There are many other extraordinary formations; on the peaks and ridges are needles, points and protuberances, some of which look as if they are stupas.

The western valley of the Kailas circuit.

The staging point for the circumambulation is the sheep-trading station and tent-town of **Darchen**, situated 6 km off the main Shiquanhe-Purang road, north of Barga, nestling at the foothills of Kailas. You can either go straight here from Shiquanhe or take the Indian pilgrimage bus from Purang, which costs 30 RMB and takes about five to six hours. It is also possible to rent a jeep from Purang for about 320 RMB per day. Once at Darchen, the place to stay is the **IP (Indian Pilgrim) Guesthouse** for 15 RMB per night. It is possible to hire yaks (with yakherder) for about 20 RMB a day to carry your luggage. You can leave your excess baggage at the IP Guesthouse. The IP Guesthouse will also tell you whether the tents at Dri-ra Puk and Zutrul Puk are currently being used by Indian pilgrims or not and can grant you the written permission needed to use them. Supplies of food and drink can be bought at some of the tent-shops in the encampment. There is also a small Bhutanese temple, now used as a rest-house, and a poor-quality restaurant there. By 1987, the third building at Darchen should be completed. This is a new guest-house and restaurant designed to cater for Western travellers. At the time of going to press we are unable to give the rates, although they may be comparable to those at the Pulan Guest House.

From Darchen you head west, skirting the base of the foothills rising up to your right from the plain. After a couple of hours you come to a pile of mani-stones with prayer flags. Here you turn northwards into the valley that runs along the western side of the mountain, down which flows the Lha-chu, or 'Divine River'. A little further on you will see a tall flagpole streaming with prayer flags in the middle of a wide, grassy valley. This place is called **Tarpoche**; in former days it was where the local people would gather to celebrate Buddhist festivals. These may have resumed, since 1982, on the full-moons of April and August. From here, instead of heading straight down to the river, better views are obtained by climbing for a while up to the east side of the valley and skirting the base of the mountain, before coming down to the valley bottom on your left. Along this trail you will pass across a ledge covered in huge mani flagstones, marking a place where the Buddha himself is supposed to have taught.

One hour north of Tarpoche, directly opposite on the west bank of the river, are the ruins of **Nyenri Monastery** and the **Langchen Bepuk**, the 'Hidden Elephant Cave' associated with Padmasambhava. On the east bank the path passes by the destroyed stumps of a line of large stupas near the river. This place is called **Chugu** and is a good place to camp. Just before the path reaches Chugu there are hundreds of mani stones and, on a cliff above the stupas, the hard-to-spot **Pemapuk**, a cave associated with the historical Buddha, in which it is possible to stay. From Chugu one has the first good view of Kailas from the cirumambulation path, best seen from a huge boulder on the river's edge. It towers above a high sandstone escarpment dedicated to and associated with the Sixteen Arhats.

As you proceed further up the valley, you see ahead of you on the right-hand side in the distance, a squat, domed outcrop of rock, which is known as 'Padmasambhava's Torma'. When you get nearer, it appears as one wing of a huge, sweeping arc of rock-face. Shortly before reaching this outcrop you pass three peaks towering above the western bank of the river, which are associated with the longevity triad of Tara, Amitayus and Vijaya. The Tara peak to the south is remarkable for the peculiar stupa-like formations that protrude from it.

The valley now widens out and starts to curve round to the east. Marmots have made this area their territory, showing little fear and sharing the paddocks with the nomads. There is a large boulder here with a carving of and offerings dedicated to the protector Mahakala. You will then reach the area north of the mountain, with its pleasant green terrain and, across the river, **Dri-ra Puk Monastery**. Although the monastery has been rebuilt, it is usually difficult to reach because there is not yet a bridge across the often fast-flowing river. However, the tents for the Indian pilgrims, possibly your first day's destination, stand in an open area on the south side of the river close to the path, a half-hour walk short of Dri-ra Puk. Dri-ra Puk faces southwards straight up a narrow valley, at the end of which looms the impressive northern face of Kailas itself, a vertical wall of six thousand feet. If you have time and the

OPPOSITE *Buttresses of Kailas to the north-west.*

The summit of Kailas.

weather is clear, it is well worth making a detour up this valley to the edge of the moraine at the base of the peak. This takes about two hours each way. Three lesser peaks surround Kailas, those of Jampelyang (Manjushri), Chenrezi (Avalokiteshvara) and Chana Dorje (Vajrapani), the triad known as the Protectors of the Three Kinds of Beings. Jampelyang is to the west of the valley looking up to Kailas, Chenrezi and Chana Dorje to the east.

About three kilometres east of Dri-ra Puk you cross the Lha-chu river on a newly constructed bridge and then begin a steady and physically taxing climb to the south-east towards the highest point on the *parikrama*: the **Drölma (Tara) Pass** (5,670 m). Half way up to the pass is the Vajrayogini Cemetery, a place where the bodies of pilgrims who die while visiting Kailas are still deposited. Tibetan pilgrims usually will leave a piece of clothing, a lock of hair or other personal mementos at this site. To the left of the path and above the cemetery is the Vajrayogini Peak, on which devout pilgrims have piled countless small heaps of stones. Before reaching the pass itself, you will see a small lake; from here you turn right to struggle up the last slope to the pass. Because of the altitude the ascent of the pass is one of the most arduous stretches of the circuit around Kailas. The air becomes increasingly thin as you climb and it is important not to over-exert yourself.

Shortly after the Drölma Pass, to the south of the path is another very large lake, the **Tukje Tso**, 'Compassion Lake' (called 'Gouri Kund' by the Indians); it takes half an hour to climb down to it from the path. The scenery around the lake is particularly dramatic, with soaring cliffs rising a thousand feet up from the turquoise or frozen water. Indian pilgrims often make a detour to this lake to perform their ritual ablutions, even though the water is extremely cold. After the lake there is a steep descent of several thousand feet down a rock 'staircase'. At the bottom of the staircase you meet the eastern valley. This begins with a stretch of marshy, boulder-strewn terrain, where it is easy to make the mistake of crossing the river by a stone causeway towards which the path at one point leads. Instead, make sure to keep on the west bank of the river, hugging the mountain itself. At this point, depending on the amount of daylight left, you should decide either to make camp here or proceed to **Zutrul Puk**.

Although some maps may suggest otherwise, the eastern stretch of the route from the base of the staircase of Zutrul Puk, though fairly level and straight, is a good five hour walk, the entire stretch from Dri-ra Puk to Zutrul Puk taking ten to twelve hours.

Zutrul Puk (Miracle Cave), is where part of the magic contest between Milarepa and Naro Bön-chung took place. Having displayed his superior magical powers at Lake Manasarovar and other points around Kailas, Milarepa suggested to his opponent that they build a shelter against the rain that had started to fall. Mila split a stone to use for the roof but it was too heavy for Naro Bön-chung to lift. So he manoeuvred it into place himself, leaving impressions of his hands and head in the rock as he did so. These imprints are still visible in the roof of Zutrul Puk today. Still more contests took place between the two, the final and decisive one being the race to the summit of Kailas on the day of the full moon. Early in the morning Milarepa's disciples saw the Bön priest riding through the sky towards Kailas on a drum. Milarepa was unconcerned and patiently waited for the first ray of sunlight, which he miraculously alighted to reach the summit in a fraction of a second. Naro Bön-chung was humiliated and conceded defeat. As a gesture of his compassion Milarepa stated that the followers of Bön could continue circumambulating the mountain in their traditional, anti-clockwise fashion and bestowed upon them Bönri mountain, between Barga and Huore, so that they might have a place from which they could see Kailas.

During the summer months, tents for the Indian pilgrims are erected here and a caretaker provides hot water and Tibetan tea. The small monastery of Zutrul Puk has recently been renovated and is currently looked after by a monk of the Drukpa Kagyu order. Unfortunately, the rebuilding has obscured the cave itself by making it into an altarpiece. Photography is strictly forbidden inside the cave. Around the monastery are a vast collection of mani stones and huge piles of rocks with mantras and scriptures carved into them. There are also the remains of several large stupas. Above it are a number of small caves where hermits used live. Now they are only occasionally used by nomads and pilgrims and when empty can be used as shelters for the night. Below Zutrul Puk, at the bottom of the valley, are some fine examples of mani walls. If you have time, you can visit the beautiful waterfall that is in a small side valley to the south of the monastery.

It is a leisurely four- to six-hour walk from Zutrul Puk back to the starting point of Darchen. You continue to the end of the eastern valley, then turn westwards across the edge of the plain, passing many huge mani-walls, until you arrive at Darchen.

Either before or after completing the circumambulation, it is possible to make a short but outstanding excursion from Darchen into the centre of the Kailas massif. By proceeding uphill due north over the foothills

The eastern valley of the Kailas circuit.

from Darchen for about two hours, you will reach the small monastery of **Gyangtra.** This has just been rebuilt by monks of the Drigung Kagyu order, to which sect the monastery has traditionally belonged. It is located high on the wall of a natural amphitheatre. Descending west to the bottom of the amphitheatre, you follow a path that takes you to the ruins of **Seralung Monastery**. Although all pilgrims are allowed to proceed this far into the massif, to go any closer to the mountain you must first have qualified by completing thirteen circumambulations by the route described above. If you are thus qualified to continue north from here, you will finally reach the moraines that lead to the base of the south face of Kailas. To cross this terrain can be dangerous for those who are inexperienced or ill-equipped. Originally there were thirteen stupas erected at this spot, containing the relics of great lamas from Drigung Monastery in Central Tibet (see Chapter 21). They are now being slowly rebuilt. Tso Kapala, a complex of two tiny lakes, is somewhere off this route, but is difficult to locate. Those with less time are strongly encouraged at least to climb up onto the western ridge behind Darchen. It takes only a couple of hours to walk to the tops of these hills, from where there is an utterly spectacular view of the great south face of Kailas and the plains below Darchen, with the lakes of Manasarovar and Rakshas Tal lying at the base of Gurla Mandhata.

Sadly, as with many other 'tourist features' in Tibet, you must be prepared to pay a fee for the privilege of circumambulating Mount Kailas. The charge dictated by the government authorities for all Westerners in 1986 was 60 RMB. This was negotiable if you did not complete the full circuit.

46. LAKE MANASAROVAR

South of Mount Kailas, across the great plain of Barga at the base of the majestic Mount Gurla Mandhata, are the two lakes Manasarovar (Mapam Yumtso) and Rakshas Tal (Lhanag Tso). They are the highest bodies of fresh water in the world, with Manasarovar, at 4,558 metres, about fifteen metres higher than Rakshas Tal. The two lakes are connected by a channel called 'Ganga Chu' which, although it has been flowing in increasing volume for the past three years, was dry for the thirty-five previous years. Traditionally, it is believed that water flowing in this channel augurs well for the Tibetan people. Manasarovar is the larger of the two lakes (330 sq km as opposed to 224 sq km) and considered by both Buddhists and Hindus to be the more worthy of veneration. Buddhists believe that Queen Maya, the Buddha's mother, was carried here by the gods and washed prior to giving birth to the Buddha. Hindus regard it as the mental creation of the god Brahma, specially made so that pilgrims to Kailas would have a place to perform their ablutions. In 1948 some of Mahatma Gandhi's ashes were carried here from India and scattered on the lake. Although Manasarovar is traditionally circumambulated as part of a Kailas pilgrimage, Rakshas Tal is usually ignored, and whereas Manasarovar was formerly surrounded by eight Buddhist monasteries, Rakshas Tal had only one. Manasarovar's character or aspect is often clear and bright, whereas Rakshas Tal's is frequently moody, overcast and dull. Because of its shape and mood, Manasarovar is likened to the sun and the forces of light, whereas Rakshas Tal is compared to the moon and the forces of darkness.

Before setting out on the circumambulation of Manasarovar, it is necessary to have sufficient supplies for three to four days since it is generally not possible to buy much food along the route. Only noodles and beer can be bought at Huore. Seralung and Trugo monasteries may be able to supply you with rice and vegetables, tea and tsampa. In the summer make sure to bring a surgical mask to protect yourself against the swarms of flies and mosquitoes that may plague the trekker at various points. The walk itself is longer than that around Kailas but completely flat.

The starting point for the circumambulation of Manasarovar is the village of **Huore** (near the site where Bönri Monastery used to be). To reach Huore, you leave Darchen and go to Barga, a small settlement of three compounds and a military post, at the junction of the road connecting

Shiquanhe and Purang with the so-called southern route to Central Tibet. The old site of Barga is a few kilometres away from the present, Chinese-built town. From New Barga you continue east along the southern route for a further 18 km, passing to your left Bönri (5,995 metres), the snow-capped mountain given by Milarepa to his vanquished Bön opponent in the magic contest. The only regular transport between Darchen and Huore is the Indian pilgrim bus, which leaves once every four days during the pilgrimage season, and costs around 10 RMB. It is also possible to hitch a ride on a truck or jeep.

At Huore you can stay the night at a small guest house (5 RMB per bed) before starting off for the lake itself the following morning. From Huore you can also hire horses to ride or carry your baggage around the lake as far as Tseti Guest House. The charge is likely to be between 20-30 RMB per day. The body of water you see to the south of Huore is not Manasarovar but a small independent lake. Make sure to keep it to your right as you cross the deserted landscape, heading south-west to Manasarovar. When you first reach the north-east shore of the lake, there is a short stretch where peculiar egg-shaped balls of weed and other debris and 'Karmapa' stones, which are small pieces of highly polished jet, can be found. Both objects are venerated by Tibetans as precious relics. From here you head south for about three hours until you reach **Seralung Monastery**. The original Seralung Monastery, which housed up to one hundred monks, was located a couple of kilometres up the

The eastern shore of Manasarovar with Seralung Monastery in the foreground.

valley from the lake. It was destroyed during the cultural revolution but in 1982 a modest temple was rebuilt at its present site on the lakeside. Seralung is traditionally a Drigung Kagyu monastery, at present cared for by monks of the Geluk order, with a married Nyingma *ngak-pa* lama acting as caretaker. It has a single shrineroom. If you feel like sleeping here, it may be possible to either stay in the kitchen or tents nearby. On the lakeside by the monastery one can find layers of five-coloured sand – black, red, gold, green and silver – which is also venerated by the Tibetans.

From Seralung it is a seven hour walk to **Trugo Monastery** on the southern shore of the lake. Most pilgrims walk from Huore to Trugo in one day. Trugo has also been rebuilt on the lakeside instead of its original site, at a place where both Ra Lotsawa and Atisha spent time in meditation. Atisha is also associated with Yer-ngo Monastery, the ruins of which are four kilometres east of Trugo. The long walk down the eastern shore takes you through diverse and beautiful landscapes, often cutting through areas of desert instead of following the shoreline. You can picnic at the Ta-ge River, where there is a footbridge. Several kilometres up this river are hot springs and geysers. There is a government-built Pilgrim's Guest House at Trugo, where you can spend the night for a small sum. Trugo is also a trading point for Tibetan nomads, who come down from the northern plains (Jangtang) to sell wool and salt to Nepalese traders. Many Nepalese Hindus from north-west Nepal also come here to bathe and perform ablutions in the lake but rarely continue to Kailas.

The next stretch of the circumambulation entails a full day's walk from Trugo to **Tseti Lake** on the western shore. As you turn round the south-west corner of Manasarovar, you will notice that this is the nesting place for many wild geese that migrate to the region. Also near this corner is a cairn made up of several peculiarly shaped rocks, upon which Tibetans make offerings of scarves, sweets and *chang*. This act of devotion is done to recall the time that a spirit visited the tantric adept (*mahasiddha*) who was living at the spot and transformed cakes of brown sugar into these rocks (which explains their strange shape). A couple of hours further round the shore you will pass by some tall cliffs in which are several blackened caves. A small monastery, **Gösul Gömpa**, has just been rebuilt on top of the cliffs. A climb up affords a magnificent view of the entire lake. From here you can peer down into the clear blue water and see giant fish swimming in its depths. Unfortunately, Kailas itself is obscured from this point, even though it is visible directly before you along most of the western shore. The only building at Tseti is another rest-house, where it is possible to spend the night (the charge for Westerners is 15 RMB per bed but there are no cooking facilities). From here

Proceeding north towards Kailas from the western shore of Manasarovar.

you can wait to meet the pilgrim's bus or try your luck hitch-hiking on the road nearby, either back to Purang or on to Darchen and Shiquanhe.

The final part of the full route takes you the short distance, about two hours' walk, to **Chiu Monastery** at the north-west corner of the lake. This small monastery is on a hill and it marks the place where Padmasambhava spent the last seven days of his life on this earth. This is the point where the connecting channel between the two lakes, the Ganga Chu, passes. Hot springs are found nearby, a short distance down the channel.

The northern shore of the lake is not usually covered as part of the circumambulation because of marshes and cliffs that prevent one from approaching the shoreline. One can only traverse the marshy section in winter when the ground is frozen.

Pilgrims must now make their way back to either Darchen via Barga or Purang. From Chiu Monastery you can walk to Barga in about four hours, or hitch a ride with a truck on the nearby road. From Barga it should be possible, though not necessarily easy, to arrange transport back to Shiquanhe. You would probably have more success at Darchen. It is 104 km from Chiu to Purang, which has to be hitched unless you have pre-arranged transport. Remember that hitching in Tibet means stopping a truck and negotiating with the driver how much you will pay for the journey. Because there is no public transport, all travellers (Tibetans included) pay for lifts. During the summer months the Indian pilgrim bus picks up groups of Indians here every few days and takes them to Darchen and then back to Purang. If seats are available, it will take other passengers for a small charge.

Tirthapuri

The only other point of pilgrimage considered essential to the traveller in the Kailas region is Tirthapuri. This is a sacred place of Padmasambhava and his consort Yeshe Tsogyel. A cave where they both meditated and a granite rock with their embedded footprints can be seen here. Tirthapuri is also known for its hot springs and a geyser with pink and white limestone terraces, a favourite picnic spot for Tibetans. It is best visited as part of your return journey to Shiquanhe. To reach it turn south-west off the main road at Menjir and continue for 13 km. Despite the excuses your driver may make to avoid going there, be assured that it is an easy, quick and enjoyable side-trip.

47. TÖLING AND TSAPARANG

After the breakup of the Yarlung dynasty in Central Tibet that followed the assassination of Langdarma in 842, the entire country was divided into small regions under the control of one or another local prince or lord. One of Langdarma's sons, Ö Sung, retreated from the central part of the country and established a small state in Western Tibet, in the upper Sutlej valley, called Gu-ge. Nothing much is known of the early history of Gu-ge but it came into prominence with the ascendency of King Korde, who is better known as Yeshe Ö, the name the king took in later life as a Buddhist monk. Yeshe Ö was a key figure in the second period of the dissemination of Buddhism in Tibet. Around 970 he sent the young and gifted monk Rinchen Zangpo to India to study. Rinchen Zangpo spent a total of seventeen years in India and became possibly the greatest Tibetan translator of Sanskrit scriptures. He was responsible for the invitation of a number of Indian scholars to Tibet, and the construction of over one hundred monasteries in Western Tibet. Towards the end of his life King Yeshe Ö was captured and held for ransom by a rampaging Turkic army. His grand-nephew Jangchub Ö, also a Buddhist monk-ruler, raised the gold for Yeshe Ö's release but was told by his grand-uncle to use it instead to invite the renowned Indian master Atisha to Tibet. In this way Yeshe Ö sacrificed himself for the sake of Atisha coming to Tibet. In 1042 Atisha, already sixty-one years old, arrived in Gu-ge. He stayed for three years at Töling, the capital of Gu-ge at that time, giving teachings and composing his most famous work, *The Lamp for the Path to Enlightenment*. He also met the eighty-five year old Rinchen Zangpo, who had founded two of the main temples at Töling, and exhorted him to spend his remaining years in solitary meditation. From Gu-ge, Atisha made his way to Central Tibet, where he died in 1054.

The kingdom of Gu-ge, with its two main centres of Töling and Tsaparang, continued to prosper for another five hundred years or so, but Tsaparang, the capital at the time, was suddenly abandoned around 1650, probably because of factional conflicts as well as a drop in the water table. Töling remained active as a religious centre until the 1960's. Despite the inevitable desecration that subsequently took place during the cultural revolution, several buildings and temples remain and many works of art are still preserved in both sites. Today a few farming families live in the formerly fertile and prosperous valley, eking a living out of the dry, eroded soil.

The valley of Töling. The Red Temple is just visible among the buildings.

Gu-ge is a two-day journey by jeep or truck from either Purang or Shiquanhe. There is *no* public transport. During the wet season (June to August) the road can become completely impassable and no driver will agree to take you. Although it is theoretically possible to get there in one day from Purang, it is wisest to break the journey at Menjir (perhaps taking this opportunity to visit Tirthapuri) and stay overnight at the truckstop there. The next day you continue for about 40 km, crossing a high pass, to Baer. At Baer you turn left onto the newly built road, which takes you the remaining 180 km to **Zada**, the new Chinese name for Töling. About three hours after leaving Baer and crossing the two passes that lead into the northern plateau above the upper Sutlej basin, you reach an elevated section of the road from which can be had one of the most spectacular views of the Himalayan range possible: a wide arc of mountains stretching hundreds of miles from the Dhaulagiri/Annapurna massif in the south-east to the Karakoram peaks in the north-west. The focal point of this extraordinary landscape is Mt. Nanda Devi, directly south of your vantage point. The distance to Zada from Shiquanhe is about 100 km less than from Purang, but still would be an arduous one-day drive. At Zada, your base, is a primitive guesthouse and a simple Sichuan restaurant.

Formerly there were three main temples at Töling (Zada), which operated as a monastery until 1966. The Temple of the Three-Dimensional Mandala (referred to by Lama Govinda as the 'Golden Temple') is badly destroyed and now used as a corral. Only the remains of the mandala's structure and a few surviving statues are visible among the rubble. The **Red Temple**, where both Rinchen Zangpo and Atisha worked and lived, now serves as the main temple. Although normally closed and inactive as a place of worship, it has been partially restored

White Tara; mural at Tsaparang.

The remains of the monastic buildings at Töling.

and was recently reconsecrated. Many of its extensive murals are partly obscured by a layer of grime and mud, yet it is still possible to discern their extremely fine workmanship. Hopefully, the superficial coating of dust will soon be cleaned away. A powerful torch is an indespensible item in these dim interiors. In the **White Temple** (now the colour of the earth) next door, however, most of the paintings are not so obscured. This temple has not been reconverted in any way and is still derelict. You have to ask specially to be let inside. Here the scene before you is one of extraordinary contrast. All the paintings along the left-hand wall have been badly damaged by water seepage. They depict life-size images of the main male peaceful tantric *yidams*, or meditational deities. Those along the right-hand wall, however, are in immaculate condition and represent a corresponding selection of female deities such are Tara and Prajnaparamita. Their colours seem as fresh as when they were painted, possibly around three hundred years ago. Since Tsongkhapa is depicted in the murals, they must date back to the fifteenth century at the earliest but are nonetheless outstanding examples of religious art. To enter both these temples you have to track down the caretaker, who lives in the village, and pay an entrance fee of 20 RMB per temple. An additional charge of 50 RMB is made to take photographs.

The stupa of King Yeshe Ö near the village of Töling.

Other points of interest include the citadel of Töling, now just ruined walls and caves, which can be reached by climbing to the top of the cliff behind the town up a dangerous staircase and precipitous tunnel. From this vantage point you have a superb view of the immediate Sutlej valley as far west as Tsaparang. Also worth seeing is the large stupa attributed to King Yeshe Ö on the far bank of the small stream south-west of the Tibetan village.

Tsaparang, which is the older of the two ancient capitals of Gu-ge, is a one hour journey by jeep down winding roads, west of Zada. All that remains of the abandoned city is a mass of ruins and crumbling walls. There are five surviving temples there, four in the main part around the lower ramparts of the deserted town, and one on top of the citadel in the midst of the ruins of the ancient summer palace of the kings. The **White Temple**, in the lower complex of buildings, contains some of the earliest examples of Tibetan Buddhist tantric art, probably about one thousand years old. The paintings have been executed in a dynamic, less-stylised manner than most later works. Although the statues on the pedestals have been badly damaged, these incredibly detailed murals remain intact. The roof-panels too present a magnificent array of classical decorative motifs. Directly above the White Temple is the **Red Temple**.

This also abounds with very well preserved examples of tantric images, though of a later period, depicting the five Dhyani Buddhas, the Eight Great Bodhisattvas, and some protectors. The statues in this temple have all been recently destroyed. Near the Red Temple is the smaller **Yamantaka Temple**. Previously this housed a statue of the wrathful, bull-headed deity, but sadly it too has been destroyed. However, there remain on the walls gold images on a black background of Guhyasamaja, Samvara, Hevajra, Tsongkhapa, Maitreya, Tara and several protectors. The fourth temple in this part of Tsaparang is a small building below the White Temple near the entrance dedicated, it seems, to Tsongkhapa, and hence later in date. It contains rather more seriously damaged paintings, stylistically similar to those in the Yamantaka temple.

To reach the actual citadel of the kings, an impregnable fortress above the city, you have to climb via a tunnel and staircase, up through the centre of the pinnacle to a small plateau on the top of the sheer cliffs that rise above the ruins below. The eroded walls of the king's summer palace and temple complexes stand stark against the sky. In the middle of these ruins is another red-walled temple, the **Demchok Mandala**. This once contained a three-dimensional mandala of Samvara (Demchok), which has now been smashed to rubble. The murals, however, have hardly been damaged at all and are exceptionally beautiful.

OPPOSITE *The eastern elevation at Tsaparang. The Demchok Mandala is at the top right-hand corner of the picture.* BELOW *View of Tsaparang.*

Detail of a deity's knee and an unidentified figure, showing the fine workmanship of the artists who painted the murals at Tsaparang.

On the front wall are depicted two forms of the protector Mahakala and the dakinis of the mandala; on the left-hand wall, the five forms of Samvara; on the back wall, five aspects of Guhyasamaja; and on the right-hand wall, five forms of Hevajra. Being the chapel of the king, they must have been painted by the greatest craftsmen of the age and are possibly five hundred years old. The ceiling, panels and carved beams are also covered with finely painted patterns and motifs, likewise in excellent condition.

The king's winter palace is also in the citadel. This is a complex of rooms, chambers and passageways, carved deep down into the very heart of the mountain. Take care as you descend the very steep staircases into this area.

To visit the temples in Tsaparang you must pay a fee of 20 RMB per person. You must also leave your camera with the attendant at the main gate: photography is strictly prohibited for both Chinese and Western tourists. To take pictures it is necessary to obtain a special permit from Peking and, in addition, pay up to 1000 RMB. The charge for film or video is at least 10,000 RMB! These extremely high prices are perhaps an indication of the high regard in which these works of early Buddhist art are held by the Chinese.

TRAVEL TO TIBET

The first point to make is that by the time you read this (or any other) book about travel in Tibet, the details may already be out of date. In a place like Tibet, which is only just beginning to cater for foreign visitors, rapid and unpredictable changes in regulations, prices, routes and accommodation are inevitable. Likewise, it should be understood that these things are in any case not fixed, in the Western sense. Even within a period of hours or days, different people will have considerably different experiences in the same place. Depending upon their own approach to the situation or the whims and moods of the people they are dealing with, they may end up paying different prices, following a different route, being allowed to see different things, staying in a different place and eating different quality food.

The lesson, then, is this: if you travel to Tibet (even with an officially organised tour), do not expect things to conform to your preconceived notions of what the journey will or should be like or to information read in books. Otherwise, frustration is virtually guaranteed. To enjoy Tibet it is necessary to be as open-minded and as tolerant of 'inefficiency' (that is things being done in a way other than that to which you are accustomed) as possible.

The information given below was true of the Summer of 1986, and updated before going to press in the Spring of 1987.

Tour Groups

With certain exceptions, these tend to be unduly expensive and excessively controlled. Often an itinerary that boasts of a visit to Tibet will entail spending most of the time in China with a short side trip to Lhasa. Some tours offer merely three days of their itinerary in Tibet, which, for most people, is not even long enough to get used to the altitude. If you want to have the security of going with a tour group, make sure that at least two weeks are spent in Tibet itself and, ideally, that the group is accompanied by a non-Chinese guide provided by the agency in the West. Most tour groups will automatically find themselves with a standard Chinese CITS guide who is almost certain to repeat the official government line on Tibet and to have a very poor and biased understanding of Tibetan religion and culture. Recently, certain tours have become more imaginatively and intelligently organised by companies in the West, though the cost still remains very high. It is also reported that some native Tibetans are being trained as tour guides by CITS.

Individual Travel

Although travelling by yourself may involve certain delays and inconveniences that tour groups are spared, it is by far the more preferable way to visit the country. You have the freedom to see Tibet at your own pace and on your own terms. As long as you are prepared to rough it, it is easy, enjoyable and offers the chance to meet Tibetan people without restrictions. The official policy towards individual travellers is ambiguous. There is a persistent rumour that the Chinese intend to tighten up on individuals by being more restrictive in giving visas, increasing the cost of staying in Lhasa and enforcing the rule prohibiting unguided travel outside Lhasa. But the reality of the situation seems to indicate the opposite: new borders are opening up, people are travelling further and further afield with increasing impunity, and rarely is anything done to hinder them. Tibet is so large and remote that it is nearly impossible for the Chinese to police all but the most sensitive areas effectively.

Visas and Permits

If you are with a tour group, these arrangements will be taken care of by the agency organising the trip. As an individual this procedure will give you your first taste of the vagaries of Chinese bureaucracy. Embassies in different countries will tell you different things. Since it makes it easier to arrange the visa before you travel, it is worth applying at the nearest embassy or consulate of the People's Republic of China and seeing what happens. When we applied in February 1986 at the embassy in London we received three-month visas within a week by post. Other embassies may still tell you that you cannot travel to Tibet as an individual or must apply through an officially approved travel agency. The regulations may also vary according to the season of the year. The Chinese embassy in Kathmandu now issues three-month visas for individual travellers although until June 1986 it consistently refused to give anything. The surest and quickest place to obtain a visa is Hong Kong, where its issue is merely a formality.

A charge of about £20 ($35) is made and two photographs must accompany the application. Visas are typically valid for stays of one to three months but can be extended for up to six months when you are in China or Tibet.

Once you have a valid tourist visa for China it is not necessary to obtain an 'Alien's Travel Permit' to visit Lhasa. Since January 31st, 1986. Lhasa has been an 'open city', that is it can be visited with a standard Chinese tourist visa alone.

Unless you have an exit permit to Nepal and are en route to the Nepalese border, it is officially forbidden to travel anywhere in Tibet outside of Lhasa. In practice, though, this restriction is simply not enforced. Do not even bother to inquire at the Public Security Bureau in Lhasa for a permit to visit a particular place; just go there. Again, other travellers will keep you informed about the current regulations. While we were in Shigatse, for example (in April 86), permits were suddenly being issued for Kailas and Western Tibet.

Nepalese visas and exit permits from Tibet to Nepal can be obtained in Lhasa. The Nepalese visa costs 35 FEC (plus two photos) from the Nepalese embassy (near the Norbulingka) and the exit permit 5 FEC from the Public Security Office.

Customs

Foreigners these days are generally not subjected to more than perfunctory baggage checks both upon entering and leaving Tibet and China. Be careful, though, to conceal anything that may be interpreted as 'harmful to the State Security of the People's Republic of China', such as critical literature, Dalai Lama pictures, Tibetan national flags, etc. When you enter the country you will be asked to fill in a form declaring whatever valuables (cameras, tape recorders, watches etc.) you are bringing in. The customs officials are quite strict about checking this form when you leave the country and making sure that you have not mislaid anything en route. You may have difficulty bringing out objects such as statues, jewellery etc. that were made before 1959 and are therefore classified as part of the 'Chinese Cultural Heritage'.

Weather

Tibet is *not* as cold as most people imagine. In Lhasa, even in winter, snow will never lie for more than a few hours and it is unpleasantly cold only during the night. During the day it can be quite hot. Rather than the cold, the most characteristic feature of Tibetan weather is dryness. There is very little rain except during a couple of months in the summer. Snow settles only above five thousand metres. There is generally very little precipitation and a great deal of direct, strong sunlight.

Otherwise the weather patterns are seasonal and regular. The spring comes late, with blossoms and leaves not appearing until mid- to end-April. But by March the cold edge of winter has already gone and as it moves into summer, the weather gets progressively hotter and the atmosphere dustier. When combined with winds, which can be strong, very unpleasant dust storms can occur. The rains come in mid-summer and last intermittently for a couple months. The autumn is clear and it gets gradually colder until December, when the first chill of winter can be felt. Although winter can be cold and rather bleak, it is also extremely clear and bright. During winter, travel is made more difficult because passes are blocked by snow. Western Tibet is much drier and Eastern Tibet is more subject to the wetter Chinese weather patterns.

Currency

Two forms of money are used in China and Tibet. Foreign Exchange Certificates (FEC) are what you will be issued with when you change cash or travellers cheques at banks. These are supposedly the only legal tender for non-Chinese. The local money, Renminbi (RMB), is what the Chinese and Tibetans use. As a foreigner you are not supposed to possess or use it. Theoretically, FEC and RMB have the same value. It is impossible legally to obtain either form of currency outside mainland China. The rate of exchange is about 4.50 FEC to £1 sterling and 3.30 FEC to US$1.

The difficulties of this system become evident as soon as you enter China or Tibet. Most shops in the towns will accept FEC but give you change in RMB. But although you start accumulating RMB you cannot use it to pay for most hotels, transport, or anything connected with the government. In smaller villages, people very often refuse FEC outright since they don't know what it is.

Inevitably, a black market has arisen to exploit this situation. In every major town in China, and Lhasa as well, you will be approached by furtive money changers offering you RMB for your FEC, often at very advantageous rates (as much as 1.70 RMB for 1 FEC). The rate fluctuates constantly. Likewise, when purchasing goods on the open market, remember to take this discrepancy into account when bargaining.

In practice, then, you find yourself dealing in both forms of money, keeping RMB for daily expenses and FEC for hotels, plane tickets and so forth. Make sure you are not left with too much RMB when leaving the country. You cannot change it back into anything. Also, keep all bank receipts for money changed into FEC. You will need these to reconvert whatever excess FEC you have when leaving.

In Lhasa and Shigatse all major currencies in either cash or travellers cheques can be changed into FEC at the Bank of China. When travelling further afield take sufficient cash, particularly RMB. At present in Tibet, black market money changers are not interested in changing US dollars or other foreign currency directly into RMB.

Credit cards are not accepted in Tibet, although the availability of such facilities may not be far off. Do not have money sent to the Bank of China in Lhasa unless you want a good excuse for having your visa extended. It may take up to a month to arrive.

For further details of the monetary system see **Useful Words and Phrases** (pp. 428).

Postal Services

The post to and from Lhasa is amazingly efficient. Friends in England received postcards from Lhasa in a mere six days. A surface-mail package I sent from Lhasa took only six weeks to reach England. To receive mail in Tibet, have it addressed to Poste Restante, Main Post Office, Lhasa, Tibet, China. Incoming mail also arrives in good time and unopened. Since the post office is now insisting that foreigners pay all charges in FEC, it may be worth asking a Tibetan or Chinese friend to mail things for you (and thus pay in RMB).

International telephone calls can be made from Lhasa from either the Telecommunications Office on Dzuk Trun Lam (on the junction of the road going north from the Banak Shöl) or even your hotel. Expect some delay. The lines can be remarkably clear.

What to Bring

Strong, resistant clothing and good walking shoes or boots are essential. Windproof down jackets and thermal underwear are necessary for trekking, travelling on trucks, and in winter. Bring at least one set of light clothes.

Dark glasses, a hat to protect you from the sun, suntan lotion, lip salve, a water flask, a good penknife (with bottle opener, can opener, screw-driver and scissors), toilet paper, a mug and a torch (flashlight) are indispensable. Torch batteries are available in Lhasa but it is best to bring a supply from the West. Adhesive tape, plastic bags, drawing pins, nails (cheap hotels do not have hooks on the walls!), and an ample supply of ballpoint pens are recommended. Trekkers should have a compass, binoculars and a tent.

A sleeping bag is useful but not essential unless you are trekking or travelling through remote country. All hotels and guesthouses provide thick, warm quilts.

Basic first aid equipment is always useful. Lozenges or anything for sore throats are especially necessary. It is also worthwhile to take a supply of multivitamins or at least vitamin C.

Concentrated and dried foods that are rich in vitamins and protein are the most valuable dietary supplements you can bring with you. Instant coffee, teabags and powdered soups are also worth bringing. They can always be used with the hot water provided in all guesthouses and hotels. Powdered milk is available in Lhasa (see **Food**).

As gifts for the Tibetans colour photographs of the Dalai Lama are best. (Cards of the Dalai Lama are available in quantity from Wisdom, and you may be able to get others through a nearby Tibetan Buddhist centre.) Photos of the heads of the Kagyu, Sakya and Nyingma orders are also much appreciated, especially in the monasteries of those schools. Likewise, photos of any Tibetan Buddhist religious figures – historial lamas, deities, etc. – are welcome as well (you can obtain most of these through Wisdom). When bringing such pictures into the country, make sure to conceal them well. Ballpoint pens are also much in demand, especially by children.

Photography

Tibet offers wonderful opportunities for the photographer but it is necessary to be equipped with not only the right lenses and film but also the right attitude.

To maintain cordial relations between foreign visitors and Tibetans it is most important to respect the local customs, regulations (however annoying) and people's feelings. Always try to put yourself in the place of the person you would like to photograph. How would you feel if Asian tourists constantly tried to photograph you while you were out shopping? Worse still, how would you feel if a group of strangers tried to photograph your grandmother's funeral? Tibetans are no less disturbed by the invasion of their privacy than anyone else. So either ask permission to take someone's photograph or at least take such shots discreetly with a telephoto lens.

Many Tibetans have heard of Polaroid cameras and expect that if you ask to take their picture, you will be able to produce an instant photograph of them. Thus always make it clear whether or not you will be able to do this. Others will ask you to send a copy of the picture to them by post. Elderly people and many women will refuse outright to be photographed. Although we would perhaps consider their reasons superstitious, their wishes have every right to be respected. Some believe, for example, that a photograph of them left on earth after their death will somehow bind a part of them to this world.

In most monasteries and temples the monks will ask you to pay to take photographs. The charge is often as high as 20 RMB per chapel. This is a regulation imposed on the monasteries by the Chinese. Many of the monks selected to enforce this rule seem to be chosen for their officious bent of mind and get very upset if they catch you trying to snap something secretly. Others, however, will go out of their way to spite the Chinese by breaking the regulation and will keep watch at the door while you take your pictures.

Film supplies in Lhasa are very unreliable, so it is necessary to bring with you all the film you need. The very strong sunlight makes film above 100 ASA impractical. But the dark shadows require at least 100 ASA to expose without flash. If you have two camera bodies you can get around this problem by loading one with 25 ASA film for bright outdoor shots and the other with a higher speed film for shadow shots and interiors. I used 100 ASA film with a single camera for all occasions and that was quite satisfactory for my needs.

A flashgun and a tripod are useful. Skylight filters are essential and a polarising filter can produce some stunning results. Because of the dust make sure to bring a good case for your camera and a lens brush.

Getting Around

Public Transport in Tibet is very limited. There are more or less regular bus services from Lhasa to Tsetang, Gyantse, Shigatse, Golmud and Chamdo. Although these are slow, uncomfortable and liable to break down, they get you to your destination at a cheap price.

For remoter regions you can try travelling on trucks. These can be picked up either at truck stops in the towns or by hitch-hiking. This can be a very slow and unreliable way of travelling but to get to certain places you may have no choice. You will often have to stand in the back of an open truck, squeezed in with numerous Tibetans, for hours on end. It is therefore important to be equipped with sufficient warm clothing and a dust mask. The cost of travelling by truck is very low. Even when hitchhiking you should be prepared to pay something to the driver. It is sometimes reported that the Chinese intend to forbid truck drivers to carry foreigners.

The most comfortable, and most expensive, way of travelling is by jeep or landcruiser. These can be hired, with a driver, quite easily in Lhasa. The companies who rent these vehicles are increasingly willing to take you to more remote areas. Try to ensure that you have a Tibetan rather than a Chinese driver. Different companies charge different rates and you should try to bargain. However, the cheaper companies often use less reliable vehicles. And there is a great difference between an old Chinese army jeep and a modern Japanese landcruiser. The official rate for renting such a vehicle is 2.8 FEC per kilometre. This charge is calculated for the outward journey alone and *includes* the return journey. Remember that the charge is per vehicle and not per person. Depending upon how many people the company will accept (usually between 6 and 8), the price per person will vary.

For those with more time and a greater sense of adventure, it is possible to trek. There are many routes over the mountains that can only be done on foot. This is certainly the best way to experience the countryside. But do not go trekking without sufficient preparation. Maps, compass, binoculars, sleeping bag, first aid and survival rations should be carried at all times. Since trekking is not officially permitted, avoid towns with evidence of a Chinese presence and, above all, anything that looks like a military base. Nomad camps are usually hospitable but beware of their dogs.

Mountain bicycles are another possibility. Several people have brought them into Lhasa by plane and cycled out to the Nepalese border. Others have gone even further afield. People have been reported carrying kayaks into the country and a French team have even hang-glided over Lhasa!

Accommodation
Only in Lhasa, Shigatse and Tsetang is there anything remotely resembling Western hotel accommodation. As an individual traveller you will spend most of your time in either Tibetan-style or Chinese-style guesthouses, which typically charge between 3 and 5 FEC (sometimes RMB is accepted) for a bed. The quality of these places varies considerably but at the very least you will be supplied with enough quilts, a vacuum flask of hot water and a wash basin. When travelling further afield you can stay in truckstops. Where there are no truckstops, the local people will usually take you in for the night.

Food
Tibet is not noted for its cuisine. The food tends to be coarse, heavy and rather bland. Since the Chinese occupation wheat, rice and vegetables have become more common, but outside Lhasa are often hard to find. The standard Tibetan dish in restaurants is *tukpa*, a noodle and meat soup with a sprinkling of vegetable. Occasionally *mo-mo* meat dumplings and eggs (usually already boiled) can be found. In the countryside *tsampa* (roasted barley flour), butter, tea, curd, cheese and meat are what most people live on. Local fruit is rarely available.

In most towns with a Chinese presence, you will find a small restaurant with Chinese food. This rarely resembles what is called Chinese food in the West. It is characteristically very greasy (cooked in pork fat) and unappetising.

Most restaurants nowadays will let you see what they have available and select the food you would like them to cook. If you can make yourself understood, you can also ask for the food to be cooked as you wish.

Lhasa now stocks a fairly wide range of canned and bottled food imported from China. This includes meats, fish, green vegetables, preserved fruit and jams. Powdered milk (even 'Kerrygold' from Ireland!) can be purchased quite cheaply. Imported fruits and vegetables, nuts and dried fruit are also available in the market in Lhasa.

The restaurants in the towns will rarely serve you traditional Tibetan butter tea or *chang*, barley beer: the standard drinks are weak sweet tea or bottled Chinese beer. It is nearly impossible to find soft drinks. In the countryside you will be served the more traditional drinks or plain

Chinese tea. It is not advisable to drink the water unless it comes from a spring or has been boiled.

For specific information on restaurants etc., refer to the relevant chapter.

Health
Compared to the Indian subcontinent Tibet is a relatively disease-free place. This is largely due to the cold, dry atmosphere and the small concentrations of people. However, Tibetans have little conception of hygiene so there is always the danger of infection from dirty cooking utensils etc. Periodic stomach upsets resulting in diarrhoea should be expected. Mild food poisoning is not rare. Colds, flu and vicious sore throats are particularly common. The biggest problem is altitude sickness, which is discussed below. For the lesser problem of rabies, see **Dogs**, below.

Altitude Sickness
Most people will suffer from the effects of altitude. (Although one of the lowest places in Tibet, Lhasa is four thousand metres (12,000 ft.) above sea level.) The degree varies from person to person and depends upon how gradually one has made the ascent to Tibet. Obviously, acclimatisation is more difficult if you fly in than if you enter by bus.

'Early mountain sickness' usually develops slowly during the first two or three days at high altitude. Its symptoms include headache, nausea, loss of appetite, sleeplessness and difficulty in breathing. People will be affected in different ways and not all the symptoms need be present. This is the body's way of warning you not to go any higher until these symptoms have disappeared. Thus you will find that you may have to rest for your first three days in Tibet. Aspirin and direct intakes of oxygen can help alleviate these symptoms, but there is no medicine to prevent them. Most people get over the initial symptoms quite soon but it takes about six weeks before complete adaptation occurs. Climbing stairs too quickly, even after a month in the country, can leave you gasping for breath.

Early mountain sickness can develop into pulmonary or cerebral oedema, that is waterlogged lungs or brain. These are serious complaints that can result in death. They are liable to occur only if the symptoms of early mountain sickness are ignored and you continue to ascend. The symptoms of pulmonary oedema are as follows: weakness, tiredness, shortness of breath, increased respiratory and heart rates, dry cough at first followed by cough with watery or bloody sputum later, noisy and bubbly breathing, congested chest, and dark blue fingernails and lips. If pulmonary oedema is diagnosed (not all the symptoms need be present), you must descend immediately. Since this is not possible if you are in Lhasa, you must go straight to a hospital. From there it is probable that you will have to fly out of the country.

Cerebral oedema can occur together with pulmonary oedema or follow it. Its symptoms are extreme tiredness, vomiting, severe headaches, difficulty in walking, abnormal speech and behaviour, drowsiness and unconsciousness. If this is diagnosed (again, not all the symptoms need be present), you must descend immediately and stay down. Descent should not be delayed for any reason and the patient should be accompanied. No medication is a substitute for descent. If in Lhasa, go straight to a hospital, from where descent by air will be arranged.

Although early mountain sickness is common, pulmonary and cerebral oedema are not. The greatest risk is for those with heart or lung diseases. It is advisable that before leaving for Tibet such persons, the elderly and people with chronic illnesses consult their doctor.

Dogs

Tibetans are the only Asian people who are genuinely fond of dogs. In the towns they are kept as pets and in the country as protection against wild animals and thieves. The streets and monasteries abound with half-wild mongrels that are surprisingly well cared for and generally good-natured. However, you must always be careful of the occasional dog with a penchant for human calves and ankles. Be especially wary when walking through back streets or visiting Tibetan homes. Before entering a courtyard or house, first inquire if there are any dogs (kyee). In the countryside the danger of dogs is greater and it is advisable always to carry a stick or a stone to ward them off. Most dogs will retreat merely upon being threatened with an upraised arm.

If you are bitten, there is apparently little danger of rabies. Nonetheless, in Lhasa at least, Tibetans receive inoculation against the disease every October. Otherwise no treatment is available for a case of suspected rabies in those not inoculated. The only solution is either to rely on traditional Tibetan medicine or, to leave the country by air (I would advise the latter.) It may be worth considering inoculation before leaving for Tibet.

GETTING TO LHASA

There are currently several ways of getting to Tibet. If you are with a tour group, the journey will be arranged for you. As an individual you can try one of five routes, some of which are straightforward, others more difficult.

By Air – Chengdu to Lhasa
The easiest, quickest and most expensive way is to fly in. At present the only city in China with a regular service to Lhasa is Chengdu, the capital of the western province of Sichuan. (A flight from Xian to Lhasa via Golmud is another possibility but this is somewhat infrequent and unreliable.) Chengdu can be reached by a direct flight from Hong Kong. This is a CAAC flight that leaves every Saturday at 11 am and costs HK$1180 (US$150). Alternatively, you can take a train from Hong Kong to Guangzhou and fly to Chengdu from there for 250 FEC. There are flights every day except Wednesday and Sunday. Chengdu can also be reached by air and rail from most other major cities in China.

Another way of reaching Chengdu that has only recently become possible is to fly from Rangoon, Burma, to Kunming, a city in the south-western province of Yunnan in China. There is a CAAC flight every Wednesday for US$240. From Kunming you can fly directly to Chengdu or take the twelve-hour picturesque train ride.

From Chengdu there are daily (except Sunday) flights to Lhasa that leave at 7 am. During summer there may be two flights a day. The cost is 400 FEC. No matter what you may be told to the contrary, there is a bus shuttle service to the airport from behind the CAAC office in Chengdu that starts every morning at 5.30 am.

There are a number of hotels in which you can stay in Chengdu. The official tourist hotel is the Jinjiang, located opposite the CAAC office, which is where the bus from the airport leaves you. From the railway station it can be reached by the No. 16 bus. Unless you can persuade the management to let you sleep in a dormitory, you have to pay 60 FEC for a double room. Another tourist hotel is being constructed opposite the Jinjiang and should be open in 1987. Cheaper hotels can also be found. The Rong Feng, for example, charges 16 FEC. It is off the same road as the Jinjiang, closer to the town. The cheapest place is the curiously named Black Coffee, also down the road from the Jinjiang, but not recommended.

If you are staying in Chengdu for the day you should visit the **Wen Shu Yuan Monastery**, located between the Jinjiang Hotel and the Railway Station. This complex is an active city temple with several chapels, gardens and a delightful vegetarian restaurant and traditional teashop run by the monks. It can be reached by the No. 16 bus, four stops north of the Jinjiang (ask the conductress to tell you when to get off).

The internal Chinese airline is known by the acronym CAAC, jokingly but not without reason interpreted as 'Cancel At Any Cost'. This airline is notorious for suddenly declaring that your flight has been cancelled, the usual reason being 'bad weather'. Such heavy cloud cover usually turns out to be no more than a hazy bureaucratic smoke-screen. Informed sources explain that CAAC habitually cancel flights if they are not full enough to cover their costs and then wait until they are. This happened to us in Chengdu (and the year before in Lhasa). After much arguing, the airport officials finally confessed that 'China does not have enough aeroplanes today'. Having admitted this, they were then obliged to cover most of our hotel and food bills while we waited for the next flight. With further persistence, we actually wheedled the money out of the CAAC office in the city. The airport officials were also able miraculously to materialise a room for us at the 'completely full' Jinjiang Hotel.

The flight from Chengdu to Lhasa takes an hour and a half and proceeds over Kham, the Eastern Tibetan province now partly incorporated into the Chinese province of Sichuan. As the sun rises on the morning flight you are greeted with the spectacular sight of massive white mountain ranges extending to the horizon in all directions. The highest peak of one of the first ranges you see to the south is the Minya Gongkar, which stands at 8,200 metres (24,900 ft.) Traversing these mountains further to the west are three of the largest rivers in Asia, all of which have their sources in the high wasteland of North Central Tibet called the Jangtang: the Yangtse, the Mekong and the Salween. Having flown over these valleys, the plane heads for the Brahmaputra valley, along the banks of which is the Gongkar Airport, which is used for all commercial traffic to Lhasa.

It is 110 km from the airport to Lhasa. The road connecting the two was finished only in 1985 and now the airport bus takes but two hours to complete the journey. You ride along the banks of the Brahmaputra, passing Gongkar Monastery before reaching the bend in the river where you cross the bridge leading to the last 60 km of road running along the Kyichu river to Lhasa. The small temple stands alone in the sand to the left of the road about 25 km before the city is the Drölma Temple of Netang, where Atisha spent the last years of his life (see Chapter 22).

The first glimpse of Lhasa is of two tiny hillocks protruding from the vast valley basin to the north. On the hillock to the left you can just make out the white of the Potala. As you approach the more built-up area around Lhasa you pass Drepung Monastery on your left. A few minutes later you are in the city itself, coming to a stop in the yard of the CAAC office at the foot of the Potala. The truck carrying your luggage (which does not come with you on the bus) may not arrive for several hours, so while you are waiting you can check into a hotel or take a *slow* stroll around the city.

Overland – Chengdu to Lhasa

An alternative way of reaching Lhasa from Chengdu is to take a bus or a truck. This is a gruelling journey of ten days that takes you through the spectacular mountains and countryside of Kham to Derge, where the still intact monastery contains the woodblocks of the most authoritative edition of the Buddhist canon in Tibet. From Derge you continue to Chamdo, the third largest town in Tibet (after Lhasa and Shigatse). The main monastery there is the Jampa Ling Temple, founded during the fifteenth century by a disciple of Tsongkhapa. After leaving Chamdo you enter the region of Kongpo before reaching Central Tibet and Lhasa. A less travelled overland route runs south from Chengdu via Litang, Batang, Markam and Nyingchi to Lhasa (or Tsetang).

Overland – Lanzhou/Xining/Golmud/Lhasa

The other principal overland route from China to Tibet is from the city of Lanzhou, a large industrial town to the north of Chengdu in the province of Gansu. Lanzhou can be reached by air or rail from most major cities in China. It is located on the western border of China and shortly beyond it to the west begins Amdo, the north-eastern region of Tibet.

If you pass through Lanzhou, you should definitely visit **Labrang Monastery**. This can be reached by an eight hour bus ride to Xiahe, the town near the monastery. The bus leaves Lanzhou at 6.30 each morning. This large, impressive and still active complex was founded in 1709 by Jamyang Zhepa, a renowned abbot of Drepung Monastery, who in the last years of his life returned to his home province and founded this monastery, whose full name is Labrang Tashi Khyil. It now houses about six hundred monks and nuns. There are a couple of cheap Chinese hotels near where the bus leaves you, or you can stay at the mock Tibetan Guest House on the far side of the monastery in a double room for 50 FEC per night.

From Lanzhou you can take a train to Xining, the capital of the neighbouring province to the east, Qinghai, which now includes the Tibetan province of Amdo. Twenty-five kilometres to the south-west of Xining is the famous Tibetan monastery of **Kumbum** (full name: Kumbum Jampa Ling; in Chinese, Taer Si). A regular bus service from Xining leaves you in Huangzhong, about one kilometre from the monastery. Kumbum was built in 1588 by Özer Gyatso in accordance with the wishes of the Third Dalai Lama, Sonam Gyatso, to honour the place where the founder of the Gelukpa order, Tsongkhapa, was born (the present Dalai Lama, Tenzin Gyatso, was also born near this monastery, in 1935). It grew into a sizeable complex with four colleges, including a Kalachakra and a medical college, many chapels, tombs and stupas. It was a centre of study for both Tibetan and Mongolian monks. It is still active, with several hundred monks in residence. The monastery is also renowned for its exquisite butter sculptures. It is sometimes possible to stay in the traditional guesthouse within the monastery itself.

From Xining you can take either a morning or an evening train to Golmud in central Qinghai, the route of which passes by the northern shore of Lake Kokonor. Depending upon the kind of train, this journey takes between thirteen and twenty-two hours. From Golmud a thirty- hour (if you are lucky) bus ride through mountainous regions and open, barren country will bring you to Lhasa. Try to take the modern Japanese bus for around 80 FEC. The local bus is cheaper but much slower and colder. Make sure you have warm clothing for either journey. If you are weary of overland travel, it is sometimes possible to get a flight from Golmud to Lhasa for 230 FEC.

Overland – Kathmandu to Lhasa
You can now enter Tibet easily through its southern border with Nepal. This route will probably become the most economic and popular as soon as a regular and reliable bus service is established between Kathmandu and Lhasa. It is a wonderful way to enter the country since you climb from the lush valleys of the Himalayan foothills to the barren plateau of Tibet within the space of a single day.

The route from Nepal to Lhasa takes you through the border at a town called Kasa, which can be reached by bus from Kathmandu for less than US$1. A taxi will take you from Kathmandu to Kasa for about US$20. However, there is as yet no public transport from the Tibetan side of the border to Lhasa. Thus you must either find a truck or hire a jeep or land-cruiser that is returning to Lhasa after bringing other travellers from Central Tibet. The price for such a vehicle is negotiable and payable in RMB. It costs much less than the journey from Lhasa to the border, and can be as little as 1000 RMB.

The road to Lhasa passes through Nyelam, Tingri, Shigatse and Gyantse and can be done in two days of continuous driving. I will not describe this route here since it is covered in detail in Chapters 34-44.

Overland – Pakistan/Xinjiang/Kailas/Lhasa

The final and most adventurous overland route into Tibet is through Pakistan and the recently opened Kunjirab Pass, the highest road in the world, which traverses the magnificent Karakoram mountains. Officially opened on May 1st, 1986, this border can be crossed from May to November. From Pakistan you enter the province of Xinjiang, in the far north-west of the Chinese empire. The road takes you north-east to the city of Kashgar, from where the Silk Road leads you into China proper.

The Pakistan/China border has been opened to encourage trade between the two countries and to allow Chinese Muslims from Xinjiang to reach Pakistan, from where they can make the pilgrimage to Mecca. It has *not* been opened to allow Western travellers to enter Tibet. At present all foreigners will be turned back at the checkpoint in Yecheng, 250 kilometres south of Kashgar. Even if you are lucky enough to get past the officials at Yecheng, you will still face considerable difficulties in reaching Tibet. There is no public transport from Kashgar to Tibet and the only way to traverse this great distance is to hire a jeep or go by truck.

Assuming you can find transport and avoid being turned back, the road will take you to the main Chinese outpost in Western Tibet, Shiquanhe. The main Xinjiang-Tibet highway continues east from here through Chagtsaka (Qakcaka), Gertse (Gerze), Tsochen (Cogen) to Raga and Lhatse. However, it is worthwhile to go south from Shiquanhe to Baer, where you can turn off into the ancient Tibetan kingdom of Gu-ge. Further south from Baer is Purang, the name of another ancient Tibetan kingdom of Western Tibet. From the town of Purang you can go to Barga, where you are only a few kilometres south of the sacred **Mt. Kailas** and the two holy lakes of Manasarovar and Rakshas Tal. The southern route from Purang to Lhatse and Central Tibet is little travelled and it is best to return to Shiquanhe and take the northern route via Gertse and Tsochen to Lhatse. From Lhatse you are only a half-day's drive from Shigatse.

For details of travel in this area see the section **Western Tibet**.

If you find yourself in Kashgar and unable to proceed south to Tibet via Kailas, then your only alternative is to continue by bus to Urumqi. From Urumqi you can travel to Golmud via the delightful **Dunhuang Caves**, which contain some of the finest examples of Central Asian Buddhist art. The journey from Golmud to Lhasa is described under the section **Overland – Lanzhou/Xining/Golmud/Lhasa**.

Leaving Tibet

Any of the above routes can be chosen to leave Tibet. It is generally easier to leave the country than to enter it and transport from Lhasa in any direction can be arranged without difficulty. If you plan to leave by going overland to Pakistan or Nepal it is essential that you have an exit permit. These cost 5 FEC and can be obtained only at the Public Security Bureaus in Lhasa and Shigatse. The Xinjiang route via Shiquanhe to Kashgar and Pakistan is less problematic when leaving. If you do go this way, it is necessary to have your Pakistan visa (most people from Western countries do not need one, but check anyway) before you arrive in Tibet. Lhasa has no Pakistani consulate. Nepalese visas can be obtained in Lhasa at the Nepalese consulate, near the Norbulingka, for 35 FEC.

Probably the most popular way of visiting Tibet, and that upon which the information in the book is based, is to fly in from Chengdu and leave overland through Nepal (or vice versa). This has the advantages of being relatively quick and allows you to visit nearly all the major historical sites in Central Tibet and Tsang.

It is necessary to book your flight out of Lhasa several days in advance, especially in summer. This can be a rather laborious procedure since, in good Chinese bureaucratic fashion, you cannot actually buy the ticket until two days before the flight. This usually means lining up twice (once to book, once to pay). With sufficient advance warning, the airline office in Lhasa can also book your onward flight from Chengdu to Guangzhou, Peking or another destination in China. To be on the safe side, give yourself a day's layover in Chengdu in case 'bad weather' prevents your plane from leaving Lhasa on schedule.

At present it is possible to take a bus westwards from Lhasa only as far as Shigatse. Getting from Shigatse to the Nepalese border or the Xinjiang highway can be quite a hassle since there is little traffic on that route and it is therefore difficult to hitch a ride. Hopefully a bus service will soon be provided between Lhasa and Kathmandu (or at least the Nepalese border). There is a daily bus service from Lhasa to Golmud which leaves about 7 am each morning. A less frequent service is available to Chamdo (this also depends upon the condition of the treacherous roads).

There are two bus stations in Lhasa, the old and the new. The old bus station is just up the road from the CAAC office but may soon be phased out. The new bus station is south of the Norbulingka on the Tsang Gyu Nub Lam. For all journeys out of Lhasa it is necessary to buy tickets two to three days in advance. Try both bus stations and talk to other foreign travellers for the latest details.

If you want to have the freedom of selecting your own route, stopping wherever you wish and doing the journey in your own time, then you have to hire a jeep or a landcruiser (unless you are willing to walk or cycle). The going rate from Lhasa to the Nepalese border is 1500 FEC, although this varies according to the company and the vehicle. This is the flat price for two full days' driving, with an overnight stop in Shigatse – not the ideal way to see the country. For each additional day spent visiting sites along the route, you must pay 100 FEC. We paid 2000 FEC for a landcruiser and driver for six days plus the charge for the extra kilometres to Sakya. Divided between six people this worked out at just over US$ 100 each.

Postscript
According to plans announced by the Vice-Chairman of the Government of the Tibetan Autonomous Region on April 29, 1986, it may eventually be possible to fly directly to Lhasa from Kathmandu, Hong Kong and several major cities in Southern China. The same official disclosed that the Tibetan Autonomous Region also intends to start its own airline to serve these routes. He stated that 'the planned aviation company aims at meeting the needs of Tibet's expanding tourist industry, around which the region's economic development will centre'. He added that by 1990, Tibet plans to receive 100,000 tourists a year. A sobering thought.

1. *Shakyamuni*

ICONOGRAPHICAL GUIDE

DRAWINGS AND TEXT BY ROBERT BEER

It is impossible to depict here all the deities you will see in Tibet because they are far too numerous. We have chosen the most commonly seen Buddhas, bodhisattvas, tantric deities, historical figures and protectors, and hope that the following drawings and descriptions will help you recognise them as statues or paintings. The symbolic significance of the various deities and their postures and implements can be given only in the broadest outline. Full understanding would require much deeper study with qualified teachers. Most of the names are given in Sanskrit with their Tibetan equivalents in brackets. Where no bracketed equivalent is given the name is Tibetan. The colours mentioned below are those traditionally used in paintings and on statues.

1. Shakyamuni (Tib.: Shakya Tubpa)
Shakyamuni is the historical Buddha Gotama, who lived in India in about 500 BC and founded Buddhism. He is shown sitting in the full lotus posture on the discs of sun and moon, which are on a lotus blossom supported by a lion throne. His body is gold in colour, he wears the three robes of a monk, his hair is dark blue, and the golden emblem of enlightenment rises above the protuberance on his head. In his left hand he holds the blue iron begging bowl of a monk, while his right hand touches the earth in the 'earth witness' gesture, invoking the earth as a witness to his realisation.

2. Maitreya (Tib.: Jampa)
Maitreya is the bodhisattva who will be the next Buddha to appear in this world. He is shown here as a Buddha seated in the 'Western' posture, with his feet resting on a moon disc and a lotus. His hands are held to his heart in the gesture of teaching, or 'turning the wheel of Dharma'. Maitreya may also be depicted as a bodhisattva with a yellow body, wearing the clothing and ornaments of a bodhisattva and holding the stems of two lotus blossoms that bear his emblems: a vase and a Dharma-wheel. He can be shown seated either in the full lotus posture or with his legs extended down to the floor. Maitreya may also be recognised by a white or golden stupa in his hair.

3. Amitabha (Tib.: Öpagme)
Amitabha, the 'Buddha of Infinite Light', is one of the five Dhyani Bud-

2. *Maitreya*

dhas, the personification of the five Buddha energies. He represents the
Lotus energy, which transmutes passion into spiritual purity. His family of emanations includes Avalokiteshvara. He is the Buddha of the
Pure Land of the West called Sukhavati (Dewa Chen). He is red in colour, wears the monastic robes of a Buddha, and with his hands in the
meditation gesture holds a begging bowl. He is sometimes shown seated on a peacock throne.

4. The Medicine Buddha (Skt.: Baishajyaguru. Tib.: Sanggye Menlha)
The Medicine Buddha is the Buddha of healing, who is invoked to care

for the sick. He wears the monastic robes of a Buddha and sits on a lotus blossom upon a lion throne. His body is dark blue and he holds an iron bowl in his left hand containing the medicinal plant *arura*. He may also hold a stem of the arura plant in his right hand. Eight Medicine Buddhas are often depicted in the company of Shakyamuni.

5. Four-Armed Avalokiteshvara (Tib.: Chenrezi Chak-zhi-pa)

Avalokiteshvara (Chenrezi), the bodhisattva of compassion, sits in the full lotus posture on sun and moon discs supported by a lotus blossom. His body is white and he wears the five silk robes and jewelled ornaments of a bodhisattva. Two of his hands hold a wish-fulfilling gem to his heart and the other two hold a crystal rosary and the blue flower of compassion. Avalokiteshvara has many forms, but he can always be identified by a green/grey deer skin draped over his left shoulder.

3. *Amitabha*

4. *The Medicine Buddha*

6. Thousand-Armed Avalokiteshvara (Tib.: Chenrezi Chak-tong Chen-tong)

The bodhisattva Avalokiteshvara once took a vow to save all beings from suffering, but when he realised the magnitude of his task his head exploded into countless pieces. His body was reassembled by Buddha Amitabha and the bodhisattva Vajrapani into a much more powerful form with eleven heads and a thousand arms. Each of his hands has an

5. *Four-Armed Avalokiteshvara*

eye in the centre of the palm, symbolising the union of wisdom (eye) and skilful means (hand). In this form he has a white body and stands on a moon disc and a lotus flower. He has eight main hands, the first two of which hold a wish-fulfilling gem, the next five hold a lotus, bow and arrow, vase, rosary, and wheel, and the eighth is held in the open-palmed gesture of generosity. He has three rows of three faces coloured red, white and green, symbolising the three principal aspects of Buddhahood, while above these nine heads are the blue wrathful face of Vajrapani and the red face of Amitabha.

7. Manjushri (Tib.: Jampelyang)
Manjushri, the bodhisattva of wisdom, is shown as a beautiful youth with a golden yellow complexion. In his right hand he holds aloft the

6. *Thousand-Armed Avalokiteshvara*

7. *Manjushri*

flaming sword of wisdom, which cuts through ignorance, while in his
left hand is the stem of a lotus blossom bearing a *Perfection of Wisdom*
scripture. The sword and the scripture are the emblems of Manjushri.
He is often depicted in a triad with Avalokiteshvara and Vajrapani (Tib.:
Rig-sum-gön-po) symbolising the compassion (Avalokiteshvara), wisdom (Manjushri) and power (Vajrapani) of Buddhahood.

8. Vajrapani (Tib.: Chana Dorje)
Vajrapani is the bodhisattva of energy and power. Here he is represented in his wrathful aspect, standing on a sun disc and wielding a
vajra in his right hand. His body is dark blue in colour and he wears a

8. *Vajrapani*

tiger skin around his waist and a snake around his neck. In his peaceful aspect Vajrapani is represented as a dark blue bodhisattva holding a lotus flower on which rests his principal symbol, the vajra.

9. Green Tara (Tib.: Drölma Jang)

Green Tara, the 'Green Saviouress', is the patron goddess of Tibet and represents the motherly aspect of compassion. Her body is green and she sits in the royal posture on a moon disc and lotus flower, her right leg extended, with its foot resting on a small lotus blossom. Her two hands hold the two blue lotuses of compassion. Sometimes there may be an image of Amitabha in her tiara.

10. **Amitayus** (Tib.: Tsepame)

Amitayus is the bodhisattva of longevity. His body is red and he wears the clothing and ornaments of a bodhisattva. His hands rest in his lap in the meditation gesture, and in them he holds a golden vase containing the nectar of immortality and a sprig of the myrobalan plant (bell fruit). Amitayus is invoked for long life, health and happiness, and is often depicted in a trinity together with White Tara and Vijaya.

11. **White Tara** (Tib.: Drölma Kar)

White Tara represents the fertile aspect of compassion. Her body is white and she sits in the full lotus posture on moon and sun discs

9. Green Tara

10. *Amitayus*

11. *White Tara*

12. Vijaya

upon a lotus flower. In her left hand she holds the stem of the blue lotus of compassion, while her right hand makes the gesture of generosity. White Tara may be easily recognised by her seven eyes: three in her face, two in the palms of her hands, and two in the soles of her feet. She was born from a tear of compassion that fell from the eye of Avalokiteshvara.

12. **Vijaya** (Tib.: Namgyelma)
Vijaya is a goddess of longevity, often represented in a triad with Amitayus and White Tara. She has eight arms and three faces and is seated in the full lotus posture upon a lotus throne. Her body is white, her right face is blue and her left face yellow. She holds a double vajra,

13. *Vajrasattva*

a hook and a snare, a bow, an arrow, an image of the Buddha, and a
vase containing the nectar of immortality. Her two other hands display
the gestures of generosity and fearlessness. Her image is often shown
on Vijaya (long life) stupas.

13. **Vajrasattva** (Tib.: Dorje Sempa)
Vajrasattva is the bodhisattva of purification and thus personifies the
purity of the awareness of ultimate reality. He is also known as the
primordial Buddha of all mandalas since he is a reflection of all Buddha-
qualities. He is white in colour and wears the robes and ornaments of
a bodhisattva. He has one face and two arms, and his hands hold a
vajra to his heart and a bell to his left hip. Sometimes Vajrasattva is
represented in the form and aspect of Vajradhara.

14. *Vajradhara*

14. **Vajradhara** (Tib.: Dorje Chang)

Vajradhara is the tantric manifestation of Shakyamuni Buddha and, for the Kagyu order, the primordial Buddha. He is dark blue in colour and sits in the full lotus posture on moon and sun discs upon a lotus and lion throne. He has one head and two arms, which are crossed at his heart holding a vajra and a bell, symbolising the enlightened union of bliss and emptiness. He is often depicted embracing his consort, who is also dark blue and holds a skullcup and a curved knife.

15. **Yamantaka** (or Vajrabhairava. Tib.: Dorje Jigje)

Yamantaka, the 'Destroyer of Death', is a wrathful manifestation of Manjushri. He belongs to the supreme yoga tantra division of the Vajrayana and is a special protector of the Geluk order. He has nine

heads, thirty-four arms and sixteen legs. His main head is that of a
buffalo and his uppermost head is that of Manjushri. His body is dark
blue, he wears bone ornaments, and around his neck hangs a snake
and a garland of fifty-one freshly severed human heads. He holds a
skullcup and a curved flaying knife in front of him, and stretches an
elephant skin across his back. His other hands are outstretched holding
various symbolic implements. Underfoot he tramples upon eight
Hindu deities, eight mammals and eight birds. He is shown here as a
single figure but is often depicted with his consort Rolangma in the
'yab-yum' posture.

16. **Samvara** (or Chakrasamvara. Tib.: Demchok)

Samvara also belongs to the supreme yoga tantra division of the Vajrayana. He is usually represented in either his two- or twelve-armed
forms embracing his consort Vajravarahi (Tib.: Dorje Pagmo). Together
they symbolise the union of emptiness and bliss. His body is dark

15. Yamantaka

16. *Samvara*

blue, he wears a tiger skin around his waist and holds an elephant
skin across his back. He wears bone ornaments, a tiara of skulls, and
a necklace of fifty-one freshly severed heads. He has four faces coloured
yellow, blue, green and red. In his hands he holds a vajra and bell, a
skullcup, a snare, the head of Brahma, a tantric staff, an elephant
knife, a flaying knife, a trident and a drum. He is enhaloed in flames
and stands on a sun disc trampling the Hindu god Bhairava and his

17. *Vajrayogini*

consort. His consort, Vajravarahi, is red and has two arms and one face. She holds a skullcup and curved knife. In his two-armed form Samvara has only one face and embraces his consort with crossed arms holding a vajra and a bell.

17. **Vajrayogini** (Tib.: Dorje Naljorma or Naro Kachöma)

Vajrayogini personifies the female wisdom energy of emptiness. Here she is depicted in the form of 'Naropa's dakini'. She is red in colour and stands on a sun disc crushing underfoot the Hindu god Bhairava and his consort. She is naked and wears bone ornaments, tiara and skirt, and a necklace of fifty-one skulls. She holds a curved knife in her right hand and a skullcup from which she drinks blood in her left. A tantric staff rests on her left shoulder symbolising the essence of bliss. Vajrayogini can also be depicted standing in the 'bow and arrow' posture dancing upon a corpse. Another form is that of Vajravarahi, the 'Vajra Sow', where she has a small pig's head above her right ear.

18. Guhyasamaja (Tib.: Sangdu)

Guhyasamaja also belongs to the supreme yoga tantra. He has three faces and six arms and sits in full lotus posture on a moon disc upon a lotus throne. His body and central face are dark blue, his right face is white and his left face red. He embraces a light blue consort who also has three faces and six arms. They both carry the same emblems: a vajra, bell, sword, jewel, wheel and lotus.

18. Guhyasamaja

19. Hevajra

19. **Hevajra** (Tib.: Kye Dorje)

Hevajra is another important supreme yoga tantra deity and is particularly practised in the Sakya order. He is dark blue in colour with eight faces, sixteen arms and four legs. He embraces his consort Nairatma and together they dance on four lesser deities, who symbolise the four demonic forces. Hevajra wears bone ornaments, a tiara of five skulls and a necklace of fifty-one severed heads. In each of his sixteen hands he holds a skullcup. The skullcups in the right hands contain eight animals and those in the left hands eight Hindu gods. His consort is also dark blue. She has one face and two arms, and holds a skullcup and a curved knife. She wears bone ornaments, a tiara of five skulls, and a necklace of fifty-one freshly severed heads. They are encircled by flames and dance in the 'bow and arrow' posture on a sun disc resting on a sixteen-petalled lotus. Hevajra may also be portrayed in a two-armed form.

20. *Kalachakra*

20. Kalachakra (Tib.: Dukor)

Kalachakra, the 'Wheel of Time', is the most complex of all the supreme yoga tantra deities. He has four faces, twenty-four arms and two legs. He wears a tiger skin around his waist, golden ornaments, vajra ear-rings, bracelets, belt and necklace. His torso and central face are dark blue or black, his right face is red, and the two left faces are white and yellow. His right leg is red and his left leg is white. His two feet trample on the Hindu deities Ananga and Rudra and their respective consorts. Kalachakra's eight lower arms are dark blue/black; the eight middle

21. *Hayagriva*

22. *Songtsen Gampo*

arms are red; and the eight upper arms white. Each hand holds a symbolic tantric implement. He embraces his consort Vishvamati with his two principal arms, whose hands hold a vajra and bell. She is golden in colour with four faces, eight arms and two legs. Together they stand on four discs symbolising the astrological planets of the sun, moon, Rahu and Kalagni. Kalachakra is sometimes depicted in a simple two-armed form.

21. Hayagriva (Tib.: Tamdrin)

Hayagriva, the 'Horse-necked One', is a wrathful emanation of Avalokiteshvara. He has several forms, and functions as both a powerful protector who destroys evil spirits and a deity (*yidam*) in tantric practice. He is represented here as a deity. He has three faces, six arms and four legs. His body is red, his right face is white and his left face green. He wears a tiger skin around his waist, a tiara of five skulls, and a necklace of fifty-one freshly severed heads. Across his back are an elephant skin, a human skin and the unfurled wings of a *garuda* (a large

23. Trisong Detsen

mythical bird). He holds a lotus, a skullcup, a snare, a sword, an axe, and a club. He embraces a blue consort, who wears a leopard skin and holds a skullcup and lotus. Together they stand on a sun disc and trample underfoot male and female corpses. Hayagriva can most easily be identified by the one or three horse heads that protrude from the top of his head.

22. Songtsen Gampo

Songtsen Gampo, the king who unified Tibet in the seventh century and introduced Buddhism, is considered to be a manifestation of Avalokiteshvara. He is depicted with a white or flesh-coloured complexion, seated on a throne, wearing the royal attire of a king. He is usually represented holding a wheel and a lotus flower. On his head he wears a white turban, which is folded around an image of a red Amitabha Buddha. He is often accompanied by his Chinese queen Wen Cheng (to his left) and his Nepalese queen Trisun (to his right).

23. Trisong Detsen

Trisong Detsen, the second great religious king of Tibet, who ruled during the eighth century, is represented in a similar form to Songtsen Gampo but without the image of Amitabha in his turban. He is a manifestation of Manjushri, the bodhisattva of wisdom, and holds lotus flowers that bear the emblems of Manjushri, the sword and the scripture. Songtsen Gampo, Trisong Detsen and Ralpachen are often portrayed in a trinity as the three great religious kings of Tibet.

24. *Padmasambhava*

25. *Milarepa*

24. Padmasambhava (Tib.: Lopön Rinpoche or Guru Rinpoche)

Padmasambhava the 'Lotus Born One' was the Indian tantric master invited to Tibet by King Trisong Detsen in the eighth century. He is usually represented wearing royal robes and seated on a lotus blossom that rises from a lake, his right foot resting on a smaller lotus blossom. His body is flesh-coloured and his face has a stern and regal expression. His right hand holds a vajra and his left hand a skull-cup containing a vase of the nectar of immortality. He carries a tantric staff (*khatvanga*) surmounted with a trident in the fold of his left arm. He wears the folded red hat of the Nyingma order, of which he is the founder. There are eight principal forms of Padmasambhava and these are often found together in a single chapel or set of *tangkas*.

25. Milarepa

Milarepa was a founding figure of the Kagyu order and a greatly loved saint throughout Tibet. He is usually depicted sitting on a yogin's antelope skin in a cave. He wears a single white cotton robe and a red meditation belt around his body. His skin is either flesh-coloured or has

26. *Atisha*

a light green hue on account of the many years he spent eating only net-
tle soup. His left hand holds a skullcup and his right hand presses his
ear forward in the attitude of singing his songs of realisation.

26. **Atisha** (Dipamkara Shrijnana. Tib.: Jowo-je)

Atisha, the Indian Buddhist master who helped revive Buddhism in
Tibet in the eleventh century, is depicted with a gold or flesh coloured
body seated on a lotus throne in the full lotus posture with his two

27. *Tsongkhapa*

hands in the gesture of teaching. He wears the robes of a monk with a blue under-jerkin, and a red hat. He can be identified easily by the stupa and basket of scriptures placed beside him.

27. **Tsongkhapa** (or Je Rinpoche)

Tsongkhapa, the fourteenth century reformer of Tibetan Buddhism and founder of the Geluk order, is considered to be a manifestation of Manjushri. His body is either golden- or flesh-coloured. He wears the robes of a monk and a yellow hat. His two hands are in the gesture of teaching and hold the stems of two lotus blossoms that bear a sword and a scripture, the emblems of Manjushri. He is often depicted in a triad with his two chief disciples, Gyeltsab Je (to his right) and Khedup Je (to his left).

28. The Dalai Lama

Among the fourteen incarnations of the Dalai Lama, here we show the 'Great Fifth' Dalai Lama, Lobsang Gyatso (1617-1682), who built the Potala Palace and established the system of government that lasted until 1959. He is seated on a cushioned throne, wearing monastic robes and a yellow hat. He holds a Dharma-wheel and lotus flower and wears a ritual dagger (*purbu*) in his belt. All the Dalai Lamas are represented in a similar form but with variations in their hand gestures and the symbols they hold.

29. Pelden Lhamo (Skt.: Shri Devi)

Pelden Lhamo, the 'Glorious Goddess', is one of the most important protectors of the Geluk order and the guardian of Lhasa. She is dark blue in colour and has one face and two arms. In her right hand she holds a club and in her left a skullcup full of blood. She wears a tiger skin around her waist and a human skin over her shoulders. In her mouth she holds a corpse, and hanging from her earrings are a snake and a

28. *The Dalai Lama*

29. *Pelden Lhamo*

lion. Her hair streams upwards and she is shaded by a canopy of
peacock feathers. The moon rests in her hair and the sun in her navel.
Around her ankles she wears broken chains, and at her waist she carries
a baton bound with a snake belt. She sits astride a mule on a cannibal
skin saddle and rides across a sea of menstrual blood. The reins of the
mule are snakes and a single eye is on the mule's rump. From her saddle
hangs a skull, a skin bag of poisons and two divination dice. She is usually attended by her two companions: the blue 'lion-headed one' and
the red 'crocodile-headed one'. She sometimes has four arms instead of
two.

30. **Vaishravana** (Tib.: Namtöse)

Vaishravana, also known as Kubera and Jambhala, is the Guardian King of the North and the Buddhist god of wealth. As the god of wealth he is shown here riding a white lion, which stands on a moon disc and a lotus. He is golden yellow in colour and has a large, rounded body. In his right hand he holds a silk banner of victory and his left hand holds a mongoose that vomits jewels. The sun and moon are usually shown resting on his right and left shoulders.

31. **The Four Guardian Kings** (Skt.: Lokapala. Tib.: Chok-kyong)

The Four Guardian Kings are the protectors of the four cardinal directions and are almost always found at the entrance to monasteries and

30. Vaishravana

31. One of the Four Guardian Kings

temples. They each have two hands and one face and are dressed in the ornate armour and clothing of a warrior king. They may be depicted either sitting or standing. Illustrated here is **Dhritarashtra**, the Guardian King of the East; he is white in colour and plays a lute. **Virupaksha**, the King of the West, is red in colour and holds a small stupa in his right hand and a serpent in his left. **Virudhaka,** the King of the South, is blue in colour and carries a sword and scabbard. **Vaishravana**, the King of the North, is yellow in colour and carries a banner of victory in his right hand and a mongoose that vomits jewels in his left.

The Eight Auspicious Symbols (Skt. *Astamangala*, Tib. *Tashi Targye*).

The Eight Auspicious Symbols, or Glorious Emblems, represent the offerings that were presented to Shakyamuni Buddha after he attained enlightenment. They may be represented either singly or grouped together to form a vase-shaped motif.

1. The Precious Parasol. The silk canopy that is held above the Buddhas and gives protection from all evil influences.
2. The Banner of Victory. The silk banner that proclaims victory of the Buddhist teachings over ignorance.
3. The White Conch Shell. It spirals to the right and is blown as a horn to announce the Buddha's enlightenment.
4. The Two Golden Fishes. They represent spiritual release from the ocean of *samsara*.
5. The Vase of Great Treasures. It contains the spiritual jewels of enlightenment.
6. The Knot of Eternity. This is also known as the Lucky Diagram and represents unending love and harmony.
7. The Eight Spoked Golden Wheel. This is also known as the Wheel of the Law (Dharma) and represents the Noble Eightfold Path of the Buddha's teachings.
8. The Lotus Flower. It represents spiritual purity and compassion.

USEFUL WORDS AND PHRASES

The Tibetan language belongs to a small independent language group called 'Tibeto-Burman'. It bears no structural similarities with either of the main language groups of its neighbours, China and India. Apart from occasional words that have been borrowed from Chinese and mantras, which are recited in Sanskrit, it is an independent form of speech peculiar to the Tibetan people.

The written Tibetan script is alphabetic and consists of thirty letters. It was invented in the seventh century by Tönmi Sambhota, a minister of King Songtsen Gampo, and based upon a form of Sanskrit. Certain letters can be placed above or below others to denote particular sounds and give spelling variations for words of the same sound but different meaning. Other letters can be used as prefixes and suffixes, some of which affect the sound and some of which do not. Most Tibetan words consist of either one or two syllables. There are only three main grammatical particles, each of which serves a number of functions. The word order of a sentence is always 1) Subject, 2) Object, 3) Verb. The verb must be placed at the end.

There are three forms of the script: **U-Chen**, capitalised letters, which are used in all printed texts and on most signs; **U-me**, a more flowing cursive script often used in inscriptions and in formal letter writing; and **Kyu-yig**, the common cursive script used by Tibetans in non-formal letter writing and daily business. An example of each script is given below.

U-chen: བཀུ་ཤིས་བདེ་ལེགས་ཕུན་སུམ་ཚོགས་

U-me: བཀྲ་ཤིས་བདེ་ལེགས་ཕུན་སུམ་ཚོགས་པ།

Kyu-yig: བཀྲ་ཤིས་བདེ་ལེགས་ཕུན་སུམ་ཚོགས་པ།

Like many Asian languages Tibetan has a structure and system of pronunciation very different from our own. Since making yourself understood depends a great deal upon intonation and inflexion, you may find it difficult and frustrating to get even the simplest words and phrases across. There are also many different regional dialects in Tibet and ways of pronouncing the same word can vary wildly. The pronunciation given here follows approximately the Lhasa dialect, which scholars consider to be the 'standard' form.

Basics

Unfortunately there is no simple way of saying 'yes' and 'no' in Tibetan. It is done by repeating the auxiliary verb ending (of which there are many) in which you have been addressed, in either the affirmative or negative form. However, nods and shakes of the head are universally understood.

Hello!	*tashi deleg!*	བཀྲ་ཤིས་བདེ་ལེགས།
How are you?	*kusu debo yinbay?*	སྐུ་གཟུགས་བདེ་པོ་ཡིན་པས།
I'm fine	*la, debo yin*	ལགས། བདེ་པོ་ཡིན།
Goodbye (to the person leaving),	*kallay pay ronang*	ག་ལེ་ཕེབས་རོགས་གནང་
Goodbye (to the person staying),	*kallay shu ronang*	ག་ལེ་བཞུགས་རོགས་གནང་
Thank you	*too-jay-chay*	ཐུགས་རྗེ་ཆེ།
Sorry, excuse me	*gonda*	དགོངས་དག
Okay? All right? Is this allowed?	*diggi rebay?*	འགྲིག་གི་རེད་པས།
It's okay/all right/allowed	*diggi ray*	འགྲིག་གི་རེད
That's good!	*yappo doo!*	ཡག་པོ་འདུག
That's not good	*yappo mindoo*	ཡག་པོ་མི་འདུག
This	*dee*	འདི
That	*day*	དེ
What is this?	*dee karray ray?*	འདི་ག་རེ་རེད
How much does it cost?	*gong ka-dzö ray?*	གོང་ག་ཚོད་རེད
When?	*kadoo*	གདུས
Where?	*kaba?*	ག་པར
Who?	*soo?*	སུ
Why?	*karray yinna?*	ག་རེ་ཡིན་ན
Today	*dering*	དེ་རིང
Yesterday	*kesang*	ཁ་སང
Tomorrow	*sang-nyin*	སང་ཉིན

Now	*danta*	དལྟ་
I/me	*nga*	ང་
You	*keerang*	ཁྱེད་རང་
He/she	*korang*	ཁོ་རང་
Hot	*tsa-bo*	ཚ་པོ་
Cold	*drangmo*	དྲང་མོ་
New	*sar-pa*	གསར་པ་
Old	*nyingma*	རྙིང་པ་
Near	*ta-nyay-bo*	ཐག་ཉེ་པོ་
Far	*ta ring bo*	ཐག་རིང་པོ་
Mountain	*ree*	རི་
Pass	*la*	ལ་
Road	*lam-ka*	ལམ་ཀ་
Rain	*char-ba*	ཆར་པ་
Snow	*gaang*	གངས་
Where are you from?	*keerang kanay ray?*	ཁྱེད་རང་ག་ནས་རེད་
I'm from England	*nga Inji nay ray*	ང་དབྱིན་ཇི་ནས་རེད་
America	*a-may-ri-ga*, or (Chinese) *may gwo*	ཨ་མི་རི་ཀ་
Germany	*jur-men*	ཧར་མན་
France	*pu-ran-see*	ཕུ་རིན་སི་
Tibetan (person)	*bö-mee*	བོད་མི་
Chinese (person)	*gya-mee*	རྒྱ་མི་
What is your name?	*keeranggi ming karray ray?*	ཁྱེད་རང་གི་མིང་ག་རེ་རེད་
My name is	*ngay ming .... ray*	ངའི་མིང་ རེད་
Where's the toilet?	*sang-chö kaba doo?*	གསང་སྤྱོད་ག་པར་འདུག་
I'm not well	*nga naggi doo*	ང་ན་གི་འདུག་
Where is the hospital?	*men-kaang kaba doo?*	སྨན་ཁང་ག་པར་འདུག་
Is there a doctor?	*em-chi doo gay?*	ཨེམ་ཆི་འདུག་གས་
What is this called?	*dee ming karray ser gi ray?*	འདི་མིང་ག་རེ་ཟེར་གི་རེད་

Numbers

one	chik	གཅིག	chu-drook	sixteen	བཅུ་དྲུག
two	nyi	གཉིས	chup-doon	seventeen	བཅུ་བདུན
three	soom	གསུམ	chob-gyay	eighteen	བཅོ་བརྒྱད
four	shi	བཞི	chup-goo	nineteen	བཅུ་དགུ
five	nga	ལྔ	nyi-shoo	twenty	ཉི་ཤུ
six	drook	དྲུག	soom-choo	thirty	སུམ་ཅུ
seven	doon	བདུན	shib-choo	forty	བཞི་བཅུ
eight	gyay	བརྒྱད	ngap-choo	fifty	ལྔ་བཅུ
nine	goo	དགུ	drook-choo	sixty	དྲུག་ཅུ
ten	choo	བཅུ	doon-choo	seventy	བདུན་ཅུ
eleven	chup-chik	བཅུ་གཅིག	gyay-choo	eighty	བརྒྱད་ཅུ
twelve	choo-nyi	བཅུ་གཉིས	goop-choo	ninety	དགུ་བཅུ
thirteen	chup-soom	བཅུ་གསུམ	gya (tampa)	hundred	བརྒྱ་ཐམ་པ
fourteen	chup-shi	བཅུ་བཞི	nyi-gya	two-hundred	གཉིས་བརྒྱ
fifteen	cho-nga	བཅོ་ལྔ	dong	thousand	སྟོང

Counting Money

The basic monetary unit in Tibet nowadays is the Chinese *yuan*. It is worth about 30 American cents or 20 English pence. One *yuan* is divided into ten *mao* (or *jiao*) and one *mao* into ten *fen*.

Yuan	gormo	སྒོར་མོ
Mao	mo-tsi	མོ་ཚི
Fen	ping	ཕིང
One yuan	gormo chik	སྒོར་མོ་གཅིག
Two yuan etc.	gormo nyi etc.	སྒོར་མོ་གཉིས་སོགས
Two yuan and five mao	gormo nyi dang mo-tsi nga	སྒོར་མོ་གཉིས་དང་མོ་ཚི་ལྔ
Two yuan, five mao and three fen	gormo nyi, mo-tsi nga dang ping soom	

སྒོར་མོ་གཉིས། མོ་ཚི་ལྔ་དང་ཕིང་གསུམ

Food and Drink

Restaurant	sa-kang	ཟ་ཁང
Where is a/the restaurant?	sa-kang kaba doo?	ཟ་ཁང་ག་པར་འདུག
food	kala	ཁ་ལག
Please give me some *water*	nga-la choo *nang* ronang	ང་ལ་ཆུ་གནང་རོག་གནང
hot water	choo tsa-bo	ཆུ་ཚ་པོ
tea	so-ja	གསོལ་ཇ
Tibetan tea	pö-ja	པོད་ཇ
beer	piju (Chinese)	པི་ཇུ
Tibetan barley beer	chang	ཆང
yoghurt	sho	ཞོ
bread	pallay	པག་ལེབ
rice	dray	འབྲས
butter	mar	མར
milk	o-ma	འོ་མ
meat	sha	ཤ
egg	gong-a	སྒོང
vegetables	tsay	ཚལ
noodle soup	tookpa	ཐུག་པ
dumplings	mo-mo	མོག་མོག
salt	tsa	ཚ
pepper (chili)	see-bin	སེ་པན
This is delicious	dee shimbo doo	འདི་ཞིམ་པོ་འདུག
I don't want this	dee moggo	འདི་མི་དགོས
I don't eat meat	nga sha saggi may	ངས་ཤ་ཟ་གི་མེད

Visiting Monasteries

monastery	gompa	དགོན་པ
chapel	lha-khang	ལྷ་ཁང

protector chapel	*gön-khang*	མགོན་ཁང་
monk	*trapa*	གྲ་པ་
nun	*ani*	ཨ་ནེ་
deity	*lha*	ལྷ་
What is this deity called?	*lha dee tsen karray ray?*	ལྷ་འདིའི་མཚན་ག་རེ་རེད་
Can I go in here?	*dee nang la dro choggi rebay?*	འདིའི་ནང་ལ་འགྲོ་ཆོག་གི་རེད་པས
Can I go upstairs?	*yar la dro choggi rebay?*	ཡར་ལ་འགྲོ་ཆོག་གི་རེད་པས
Can I take a photograph?	*par gyap choggi rebay?*	པར་རྒྱབ་ཆོག་གི་རེད་པས
What religious order is this?	*chö-luk karray ray?*	ཆོས་ལུགས་ག་རེ་རེད་
How many monks are here?	*drapa ka-dzö doo?*	གྲ་པ་ག་ཚོད་འདུག
I am a Buddhist	*nga nang-pa yin*	ང་ནང་པ་ཡིན་
I am on a pilgrimage	*nga nekor drogi yin*	ང་གནས་སྐོར་འགྲོ་གི་ཡིན་
Sorry, I don't have any Dalai Lama photographs	*gonda, Dalai Lama par mindoo*	དགོངས་དག། ཏཱ་ལེའི་བླ་མའི་པར་མི་འདུག

Getting Around

Where is the hotel	*drön-khang kaba doo?*	མགྲོན་ཁང་ག་པར་འདུག
Can I stay here?	*deer day choggi rebay?*	འདིར་སྡད་ཆོག་གི་རེད་པས
How much is a bed?	*nyel-tri ray la gormo ka-dzö ray?*	ཉལ་ཁྲི་རེ་ལ་སྒོར་མོ་ག་ཚོད་རེད་
That's too expensive	*day gong chay-traggi doo*	དེ་གོང་ཆེ་དྲགས་གི་འདུག
Where are you going?	*kaba drogi yin?*	ག་པར་འགྲོ་གི་ཡིན་
I'm going to Lhasa	*nga Lhasa la drogi yin*	ང་ལྷ་ས་ལ་འགྲོ་གི་ཡིན་
Where is the bus station?	*mimang chi-chö lang-kor trising kaba doo?*	མི་དམངས་སྤྱི་སྤྱོད་རླངས་འཁོར་འབབ་ཚུགས་ག་པར་འདུག

When does the bus leave? *mimang chi-chö lang- kor kadoo drogi ray?*

 མི་དམངས་ཀྱི་སྤྱོད་སྣང་འཁོར་ག་དུས་འགྲོ་གི་རེད

Can I rent a vehicle? *lang-kor la tupgi rebay?*

སྣང་འཁོར་ལ་ཐུབ་གི་རེད་པས

How much is it per day? *nyima ray la gormo ka-dzö ray?*

ཉི་མ་རེ་ལ་སྒོར་མོ་ག་ཚོད་རེད

How much is it per kilo-metre? *gong-li ray la gormo ka-dzö ray?*

གང་ལི་ག་ཆིག་ལ་སྒོར་མོ་ག་ཚོད་རེད

I want a Japanese vehicle (i.e. a Toyota Landcruiser) *reebing lang-kor go gi doo*

རེ་པིན་སྣང་འཁོར་དགོས་ཀྱི་འདུག

Are there any dogs here? *kyee doo gay?*

ཁྱི་འདུག་གས

Do the dogs bite? *kyee so gyap gi doo gay?*

ཁྱི་གིས་སོ་རྒྱབ་གི་འདུག་གས

GLOSSARY

Acala (Tib. *Miyowa*) 'The Immovable One', a wrathful protector.

Akshobhya (Tib. *Mikyöba*) 'The Unshakable One', one of the Five Dhyani Buddhas; sometimes a name given to statues of Shakyamuni.

Amban The representative of the Chinese imperial government appointed to oversee the Dalai Lama's government in Lhasa. The post was created in 1727 and abolished by the Thirteenth Dalai Lama in 1913.

Amdo The north-eastern region of Tibet bordering on China. It has now been incorporated into Qinghai and Gansu provinces.

Amitabha (Tib. *Öpagme*) 'The One of Infinite Light', one of the Five Dhyani Buddhas; the Buddha who reigns in the Pure Land of Sukhavati. See the **Iconographical Guide.**

Amitayus (Tib. *Tsepagme*) 'The One of Infinite Life', the bodhisattva who personifies the power of longevity. See the **Iconographical Guide.**

Asanga (Tib. *Togme*) The fourth century Indian Buddhist philosopher who founded the *Cittamatra* (Mind Only) system of thought.

Atisha (Tib. *Jowoje*) (982-1055) An Indian Buddhist master who came to Tibet in 1042 to help in the revival of Buddhism. His main disciple was Drom Tönpa. He died in Netang Drölma Lhakhang. See the **Iconographical Guide.**

Avalokiteshvara (Tib. *Chenrezi*) The bodhisattva who personifies compassion. See the **Iconographical Guide.**

Bodhisattva (Tib. *jangchub sempa*) A person intent upon realising enlightenment for the welfare of others. One who is on the way to becoming a Buddha. A personification of a particular quality of enlightenment.

Bön The pre-Buddhist animist religion of Tibet.

Butön (1912-1364) A great Tibetan Buddhist scholar who organised the Tibetan Buddhist canon into its present form. He was based at Zhalu Monastery near Shigatse.

Chakpori 'The Iron Mountain', one of the four holy mountains in Central Tibet; it is situated opposite the Potala Palace in Lhasa. Formerly the site of the Tibetan Medical College, which was destroyed in 1959. Presently crowned with a radio mast.

Chakrasamvara See *Samvara*.

Charya Tantra The second of the four divisions of the Buddhist tantras.

Chenrezi See *Avalokiteshvara.*

Ch'ien-lung (1735-1796) Emperor of the Chinese Manchu dynasty who drove the invading Gurkhas out of Tibet in 1792.

Chökyi Gyeltsen (1570-1662) A teacher of the Fifth Dalai Lama who was made the fourth Panchen Lama. The writer of the textbooks of Sera Monastery.

Chuwori One of the four holy mountains of Central Tibet. It is on the southern bank of the Brahmaputra at Chaksam, the point where the Kyichu joins the river.

Dakini (Tib. *kandroma*) A female deity who personifies the wisdom of enlightenment.

Dalai Lama A series of incarnate lamas, the first of whom was Gendun Drup, the nephew and disciple of Tsongkhapa. The Dalai Lamas ruled Tibet from the time of Losang Gyatso, the Fifth Dalai Lama. The present Dalai Lama is the fourteenth in the succession. Recognised as manifestations of Avalokiteshvara. See the **Iconographical Guide** and the table on p. 40.

Deity (Tib. *lha*, Skt. *deva*) This term is mainly used to refer to the tantric personifications of enlightenment with whom the yogin identifies in meditation.

Desi Sanggye Gyatso (1652-1705) The regent of the Fifth Dalai Lama and renowned physician and scholar.

Dharmaraja (Tib. *Chögyel*) A wrathful, bull-headed protector particularly worshipped in the Geluk order. Not to be confused with Yamantaka. Can be distinguished by his standing on a bull and a human corpse.

Dhyani Buddhas (Tib. *Gyelwa rig nga*) The five Buddha 'types', or 'families'. They are Vairocana, Ratnasambhava, Amitabha, Amoghasiddhi and Akshobhya.

Dipamkara (Tib. *Marmedze*) A Buddha of the past.

Dorje Drakden The protector deity who speaks through the oracle at Nechung, traditionally consulted on all important matters of state.

Drakpa Gyeltsen (1147-1216) One of the five great masters of the Sakya order. The son of Kunga Nyingpo.

Dratsang A college within a monastery.

Drom Tönpa (1005-1064) The main Tibetan disciple of Atisha. The founder of the Kadam order and Reting Monastery.

Dugkarma 'The Lady with the White Parasol', a multi-headed deity.

Dzog-chen A form of meditation practised in the Nyingma and Kagyu schools, which seeks a direct realisation of one's innermost nature.

Ekajati (Tib. *Tsechigma*) 'The Lady of the Single Point', a wrathful female deity with one eye, one tooth, etc., who personifies mental concentration. The special protectress of Dzog-chen.

Eight Great Bodhisattvas Avalokiteshvara, Manjushri, Vajrapani, Maitreya, Samantabhadra, Akashagarbha, Kshitigarbha, Sarvanivaranaviskambini.

Emptiness (Skt. *shunyata*, Tib. *tongpanyi*) The absence of independent, self-existence, as taught in the *Madhyamika* philosophy of Buddhism. The ultimate truth of all things.

Extremity Subduing Temples (Tib. *Tadul lhakhang*) Four temples in different parts of Tibet, which were built during the time of Songtsen Gampo to subdue a demoness who was perceived in the form of the land by the king's Nepalese wife, Trisun. They are the Trandruk, Katsel, Dram and Buchu temples.

Gampopa (1079-1153) One of the chief disciples of Milarepa and a founding father of the Kagyu order. Also known as Dagpo Lhaje.

Gangpori One of the four holy mountains in Central Tibet. It is near Tsetang and is where Avalokiteshvara descended to Tibet in the form of a monkey to mate with a demoness and produce the first Tibetans.

Geluk 'The Virtuous Order', the order of Tibetan Buddhism founded by Tsongkhapa and his disciples in the early fifteenth century. The 'Yellow Hats'.

Gendun Drup (1391-1475) A nephew and disciple of Tsongkhapa who founded Tashilhunpo monastery and was retrospectively named the First Dalai Lama.

Gendun Gyatso (1475-1542) The Second Dalai Lama.

Gönpo Guru A principal protector of the Sakya order.

Guardian Kings (Tib. *Chok kyong*) The four kings of the four cardinal directions, who offer protection against harmful influences. They are found at the entrance of almost all temples and monasteries. They are Dhritarashta (east), Virupaksha (west), Virudhaka (south) and Vaishravana (north). See the **Iconographical Guide.**

Gushri Khan (1582-1655) The Mongolian emperor who installed the Fifth Dalai Lama as ruler of Tibet in 1642.

Guhyasamaja (Tib. *Sangdu*) A diety of the supreme yoga tantras. See the **Iconographical Guide.**

Gyeltsap Je (1364-1431) One of the principal disciples of Tsongkhapa and the second Throne Holder of Ganden.

Hayagriva (Tib. *Tamdrin*) The 'Horse Necked One', a wrathful protector and tantric deity. See the **Iconographical Guide.**

Hepori One of the four holy mountains of Central Tibet. It is located behind Samye Monastery.

Hevajra (Tib. *Kye Dorje*) A deity of the supreme yoga tantras especially worshipped in the Sakya order. See the **Iconographical Guide.**

Hinayana (Tib. *Teg men*) The 'Lesser Vehicle' of Buddhism, in which one is concerned with one's own salvation alone.

Jamchen Chöje (1352-1435) Shakya Yeshe, the disciple of Tsongkhapa who founded Sera Monastery.

Jampel Gyatso (1758-1804) The Eighth Dalai Lama.

Jamyang Chöje (1397-1449)) The disciple of Tsongkhapa who founded Drepung Monastery.

Jamyang Zhepa (1648-1721) A renowned scholar of Drepung Monastery who founded Labrang Monastery in Amdo.

Jangchub Gyeltsen (1302-1373) The leader of the Pamotrupa who overthrew the Sakya dynasty in 1354 and established himself as ruler of Tibet.

Jataka (Tib. *kye-rab*) Stories of Buddha Shakyamuni's previous lives.

Jokhang the main cathedral in Lhasa, which houses the Jowo image of Shakyamuni brought to Tibet by Wen Cheng, the Chinese wife of Songtsen Gampo, in the seventh century.

Jowo 'Precious One', a name given to highly venerated statues of Shakyamuni.

Kadam The order of Tibetan Buddhism founded by Atisha and his followers in the eleventh century. The forerunner of the Geluk order.

Kagyu The order of Tibetan Buddhism founded in the eleventh century by Marpa, Milarepa, Gampopa and their followers.

Kalachakra (Tib. *Dukor*) 'The Wheel of Time', one of the most complex of the supreme yoga tantras. It is associated with the mystical land of Shambhala. See the **Iconographical Guide.**

Kalki (Tib. *Rigden*) The 'spiritual presidents' of Shambhala. There are twenty-five of them, each of whom rules for one hundred years. We are now in the reign of the twenty-second, *Aniruddha* (Tib. *Magagpa*) (1927-2027).

Kamalashila An Indian disciple of Shantarakshita who came to Tibet in the eighth century to debate with the Chinese master Mahayana at Samye Monastery.

Kangyur 'The Translation of the Word', the part of the Tibetan Buddhist canon that contains the discourses attributed to Buddha Shakyamuni.

Karmapa The line of incarnate lamas of the Kagyu order based at Tsurpu Monastery near Lhasa. The First Karmapa, Dusum Khyenpa (1110-1193), was a disciple of Gampopa and the founder of Tsurpu. The Karmapas are the heads of the Karma Kagyu sub-order. The Sixteenth Karmapa, Rigpai Dorje, died in Chicago in 1981. See the table on p. 201.

Kashyapa (Tib. Ösung) A Buddha of the past.

Kelsang Gyatso (1708-1757) The Seventh Dalai Lama.

Kham The Eastern Province of Tibet, now partially annexed to Sichuan and Yunnan Provinces of China.

Khangtsen a 'house' of a college (*dratsang*) in a Tibetan Buddhist monastery, which serves as the residential quarters of the monks.

Khedrup Je (1385-1438) A chief disciple of Tsongkhapa who became the third Throne Holder of Ganden and was retrospectively recognised as the First Panchen Lama.

Könchok Gyelpo (1034-1102) The founder of the Sakya order and father of Kunga Nyingpo.

Kshitigarbha (Tib. Sa'i Nyingpo) 'The Essence of the Earth', one of the Eight Great Bodhisattvas.

Kunga Nyingpo (1092-1158) Also called 'Sachen', the son of Könchok Gyelpo and one of the five great masters of the Sakya order.

Lama (Skt. *guru*) A religious teacher and guide. A lama need not be a monk (*drapa*) and only a few monks are lamas.

Langdarma (803-842) Last king of the Yarlung dynasty, who persecuted Buddhism. Assassinated by a Buddhist monk, Lhalungpa Pelgyi Dorje.

Lhatotori (c. 347-467) The twenty-eighth king of the Yarlung dynasty, during whose reign Tibet had its first contact with Buddhism.

Longchenpa (1306-1363) A great scholar and mystic of the Nyingma order.

Losang Gyatso (1617-1682) The 'Great' Fifth Dalai Lama, who started the rule of the Dalai Lamas and the construction of the Potala Palace.

Mahakala (Tib. Nagpo Chenpo) A wrathful protector and tantric deity.

Mahasiddha (Tib. drup chen) A realised adept of the tantric path. There are traditionally eighty-four Indian mahasiddhas.

Mahayana (Tib. tegchen) The 'Great Vehicle' of Buddhist practice, in which one is dedicated to the attainment of enlightenment for the welfare of others.

Maitreya (Tib. Jampa) 'The Loving One', the Buddha of the future. Also one of the Eight Great Bodhisattvas. See the **Iconographical Guide.**

Mandala (Tib. kyilkor) The circular/spherical reality of an enlightened being visualised during tantric practices.

Mandarava One of the consorts of Padmasambhava.

Manjushri (Tib. Jampelyang) The bodhisattva of wisdom. See the **Iconographical Guide.**

Marpa (1012-1097) One of the founding figures of the Kagyu order. A translator who visited India and studied under the mahasiddha

Naropa. The teacher of Milarepa.

Maudgalyayana One of the two chief arhat disciples of Buddha Shakyamuni.

Medicine Buddha (Tib. *Sanggye Menlha*) The Buddha of Healing. See the **Iconographical Guide.**

Milarepa (1040-1123) The great poet-saint of Tibet. The chief disciple of Marpa and teacher of Gampopa. A founding figure of the Kagyu order. See the **Iconographical Guide.**

Mönlam Festival A prayer festival inaugurated by Tsongkhapa in 1409. It takes place at the Jokhang in Lhasa after the new year celebrations of Losar. It was discontinued by the Chinese from 1959 to 1985.

Naga (Tib. *lu*) A species of intelligent subaquatic being of snake-like features.

Nagarjuna (Tib. *Lu Drup*) The second century AD Indian Buddhist philosopher who propounded the *Madhyamika* philosophy of emptiness.

Naropa (1016-1100) The Indian scholar and mahasiddha who taught Marpa.

Ngog Legpa'i Sherab A renowned Tibetan translator who became the interpreter and close disciple of Atisha.

Nyingma The 'ancient' order of Tibetan Buddhism, which traces its teachings back to the time of Padmasambhava and includes in its canon works and translations dating from the early period of the dissemination of Buddhism in Tibet.

Nyatri Tsenpo The somewhat mythical first king of Tibet, whose origins are traced back to the Indian descendants of King Bimbisara, a contemporary of the Buddha.

Pabongka Rinpoche (1878-1941) An influential and powerful lama of the Geluk order, the teacher of the tutors of the present Dalia Lama.

Padmasambhava The eighth century Indian tantric master invited to Tibet by King Trisong Detsen to clear away the influences obstructing the establishment of Buddhism. See the **Iconographical Guide.**

Pakpa (1235-1280) One of the five great masters of the Sakya order, who was appointed spiritual and temporal ruler of Tibet by Kublai Khan in 1260.

Paksam Trishing (Skt. *Avadanakalpata*) A work by the Buddhist poet Ksemendra recounting some of the previous lives of the Buddha.

Panchen Lama The head lama of Tashilhunpo monastery. A series of incarnate lamas, the first of whom was Tsongkhapa's disciple Khedrup Je, and the fourth Chökyi Gyeltsen, a teacher of the Fifth Dalai Lama. Recognised as manifestations of Amitabha Buddha. See the table on p. 318.

Pelden Lhamo (Skt. *Shri Devi*) A wrathful protectress who is depicted riding a mule. See the **Iconographical Guide.**

Potala The winter palace of the Dalai Lamas in Lhasa built during the seventeenth century. Also the Pure Land of Avalokiteshvara.

Pamotrupa (1110-1170) A disciple of Gampopa and an important lama of the Kaygu order who founded Densatil Monastery near Tsetang. Also the family name of the dynasty founded by Jangchub Gyeltsen that succeeded the Sakya dynasty.

Prajnaparamita (Tib. *sher chin*) 'The Perfection of Wisdom'. Also the name of the female deity who personifies wisdom.

Pure Land (Tib. *dag shing*) A non-samsaric realm of existence created by the wisdom and compassion of a Buddha or advanced bodhisattva, in which one can be reborn through the force of meditation and prayer.

Ralpachen (805-836) Last of the three great religious kings of Tibet (the other two being Songtsen Gampo and Trisong Detsen). Considered to be a manifestation of Vajrapani.

Ramoche The smaller of the two cathedrals in Lhasa. Founded by Wen-Cheng, the Chinese wife of Songtsen Gampo, in the seventh century.

Rechungpa (1084-1161) An important disciple of Milarepa and leading figure of the Kagyu order.

Rendawa The Sakya lama who was the main teacher of Tsongkhapa.

Rinchen Zangpo (958-1055) An important Tibetan translator from Western Tibet who was a contemporary of Atisha.

Sakya 'Tawny Earth', the name of the place where Könchok Gyelpo founded the first monastery of the Sakya order of Tibetan Buddhism in 1073.

Sakya Pandita (1182-1251) The title of Kunga Gyeltsen, one of the five great masters of the Sakya order.

Samvara (Tib. *Demchok*) An important deity of the supreme yoga tantras. See the **Iconographical Guide.**

Samye The first monastery established in Tibet. It was founded by King Trisong Detsen, Shantarakshita and Padmasambhava on the northern bank of the Brahmaputra near Tsetang in the eighth century.

Sarasvati (Tib. *Yangchenma*) 'The Melodious Lady', the Indian goddess of music.

Shakyamuni (Tib. *Shakya Tubpa*) The historical Buddha, Gotama, who lived in India around 500 BC. See the **Iconographical Guide.**

Shambhala The mythological land associated with Kalachakra; it is thought to lie somewhere north of Tibet in Central Asia.

Shariputra (Tib. *Shari-pu*) One of the chief arhat disciples of Shakyamuni.

Six Ornaments (Tib. *gyen druk*) Six of the most important Buddhist philosophers of ancient India: Nagarjuna, Aryadeva, Asanga, Vasubhandu, Dignaga and Dharmakirti.

Sixteen Arhats (Tib. *netten chu-druk*) The sixteen principal saints who were the immediate disciples of Shakyamuni in the Hinayana tradition.

Sonam Gyatso (1543-1587) The Third Dalai Lama, the first of the line to be given the title Dalai Lama, which was bestowed on him by the Mongolian Emperor Altan Khan.

Sonam Tsemo (1142-1182) One of the five great Sakya masters, a son of Kunga Nyingpo and brother of Drakpa Gyeltsen.

Songtsen Gampo (617-649) The first of the religious kings of Tibet. He introduced Buddhism to the country, consolidated the Yarlung dynasty and built the Jokhang. He is considered to be a manifestation of Avalokiteshvara. See the **Iconographical Guide.**

Sukhavati (Tib. *Dewachen*) The Pure Land in the west, where the Buddha Amitabha resides.

Shantarakshita (Tib. *Shiwatso* and *Khenchen Bodhisattva*) A great Indian philosopher and abbot invited to Tibet in the eighth century by King Trisong Detsen. He helped found Samye and established the monastic order in Tibet.

Supreme yoga tantra (Tib. *lame naljor gyu*, Skt. *mahanuttarayogatantra*) The highest of the four classes of Buddhist tantras.

Sutra (Tib. *do*) A discourse attributed to Shakyamuni Buddha. Sometimes used to distinguish the exoteric teachings of the Buddha from the esoteric teachings of the tantras. The texts which make up the *Kangyur*.

Tangka Religious scroll painting.

Tangtong Gyelpo (1385-1509) Tibetan saint, doctor, engineer, and artist.

Tara (Tib. *Drölma*) The female deity who personifies the feminine aspect of enlightenment. Her most common forms are Green Tara and White Tara. See the **Iconographical Guide.**

Taranata (1575-1634) A Buddhist scholar of the short-lived Jonangpa school. A master of the Kalachakra tantra and a noted historian.

Tantra (Tib. *gyu*) A class of Buddhist scriptures that speak in a symbolic language and describe practices that involve mantra recitation, visualisation of deities and mandalas, and yogic practices aimed at rechanneling the energies of the body. There are four classes of tantra: kriya (action), charya (performance), yoga, and supreme yoga tantra.

Tengyur The 'Translation of the Commentaries', the part of the Tibetan Buddhist canon that contains the Indian commentarial literature to the Buddha's discourses. See *Kangyur*.

Tenzin Gyatso (1935-   ) The Fourteenth Dalai Lama. He now lives in exile in Dharamsala, North India.

Tertön A discoverer of texts hidden by Padmasambhava and others in the early years of Buddhism's dissemination in Tibet.

Thirty-five Buddhas of Confession A group of thirty-five archetypal Buddhas before whom the practice of confessing unwholesome deeds is performed. They are listed in the *Triskandha Sutra*.

Tibetan Book of the Dead (Tib. *Bardo Tödröl*) A text attributed to Padmasambhava in which the experiences and visions of the after-death state (*bardo*) are described. It is often read for the deceased during the forty-nine day period between death and rebirth.

Tönmi Sambhota A gifted minister of King Songtsen Gampo who devised the form and basic grammar of written Tibetan.

Torma A cake made from *tsampa*, butter and sugar, which is used as an offering in religious ceremonies.

Trijang Rinpoche (1899-1981) The late junior tutor of the present Dalai Lama. One of the most renowned lamas of the Geluk order of this century.

Trisong Detsen (742-797) The second great religious king of Tibet. He is considered as a manifestation of Manjushri. See the **Iconographical Guide.**

Trisun (Bhrkuti) The Nepalese wife of King Songtsen Gampo.

Tsampa Roasted barley flour. A Tibetan staple food.

Tsang The province of Tibet to the west of Lhasa. The capital is Shigatse.

Tsangyang Gyatso (1683-1706) The Sixth Dalai Lama.

Tsongkhapa (1357-1419) Also known as Losang Trakpa, the great 'reformer' of Tibetan Buddhism who founded what came to be known as the Geluk order.

Tubten Gyatso (1876-1933) The Thirteenth Dalai Lama.

Tushita (Tib. *Ganden*) The name of the pure land where the future Buddha Maitreya presently resides.

Two Supreme Ones (Tib. *Chok nyi*) Shakyaprabha and Gunaprabha, two Indian masters who wrote on the Buddhist monastic rule (*vinaya*). Usually represented together with the Six Ornaments (see above).

Vajradhara (Tib. *Dorje Chang*) The tantric form of Shakyamuni Buddha. See the **Iconographical Guide.**

Vajrapani (Tib. *Chana Dorje*) The bodhisattva who personifies the energy and power of the Buddha. See the **Iconographical Guide.**

Vajrasattva (Tib. *Dorje Sempa*) The bodhisattva who personifies the purity of enlightenment. See the **Iconographical Guide.**

Vajrayana (Tib. *dorje tegpa*) The 'Diamond Vehicle' of tantric practice. A division of Mahayana Buddhism.

Vajrayogini (Tib. *Dorje Neljorma*) A female tantric deity who represents the female energy of Buddhahood. See the **Iconographical Guide.**

Vairocana (Tib. *Nampa Nangdze*) 'The Illuminating One', one of the Five Dhyani Buddhas.

Vaishravana (Tib. *Namtöse*) The Buddhist god of wealth. The guardian king of the North. See the **Iconographical Guide.**

Vasubhandu (Tib. *Yig Nyen*) An Indian Buddhist scholar of the fourth century. A brother of Asanga.

Vijaya (Tib. *Namgyelma*) A female deity associated with longevity. See the **Iconographical Guide.**

Wen Cheng The Chinese wife of King Songtsen Gampo.

Yamantaka (or *Vajrabhairava*, Tib. *Dorje Jigje*) The wrathful, bull-headed deity who is the tantric manifestation of Manjushri. See the **Iconographical Guide.**

Yeshe Tsogyel The consort of Padmasambhava, formerly a wife of King Trisong Detsen, a renowned woman tantric practitioner.

Yidam 'tutelary deity', the name for the tantric deity with whom the practitioner has a special affinity.

Yoga tantra (Tib. *Neljor Gyu*) The third of the four classes of the Buddhist tantras.

Yutok Yönten Gönpo (729-854) A famous physician who founded the unique form of Tibetan medicine.

SUGGESTED READING LIST

Travel

Journey to Lhasa and Central Tibet. Sarat Chandra Das. New Delhi:
Manjusri Publishing House, 1970 (Reprint)
This is the journal Sarat Chandra Das wrote describing his fourteen
month visit to Tibet from 1881 to 1882. Das, a scholar and probably a
British intelligence agent, is a very transparent observer who provides
a clear and detailed picture of old Tibet, good and bad. He spent much
of his stay at Tashilhunpo and Drongtse monasteries and visited Sakya,
Gyantse, Lhasa, Samye and Tsetang. The final chapter describes the
social divisions of old Tibet, the ways in which marriages, funerals and
festivals were conducted, the legal system and medicine.

To Lhasa and Beyond. Giuseppe Tucci. London: East-West Publications,
1985 (Reprint)
This travelogue recounts the 1949 expedition of Professor Tucci, one of
this century's foremost Tibetologists, to Central Tibet. It covers
Shigatse, Gyantse, Lhasa, Yerpa, Ganden, Samye and the Yarlung and
Chonggye valleys. When visiting these sites today, Tucci's book acts as
a disturbing reminder of the extent of the destruction wrought over the
last twenty-five years. Often there is not even a trace left of what he
describes.

The Way of the White Clouds. Lama Anagarika Govinda. London:
Rider, 1966 (Reprinted in Rider Pocket Editions, 1984)
This beautifully written book describes Lama Govinda's pilgrimage to
Western Tibet in 1948. The account of the physical journey is greatly
enriched by the author's personal reflections on the meaning of the
spiritual path and, in particular, the mystical teachings of Tibetan
Buddhism.

The Sacred Mountain. John Snelling. London: East-West Publications,
1983
This book is an informative and entertaining study of the foreign travellers and pilgrims who managed to reach Mount Kailas in Western Tibet,
from the first Jesuit missionaries in 1715 to Lama Govinda in 1949. Original quoted passages and photographs help illustrate the often hazard-

ous journeys of these early travellers. The author also provides a lucid account of the significance of Kailas and the meaning of pilgrimage in general. An invaluable companion for anyone contemplating a trip to this part of Tibet.

History

In Exile from the Land of Snows. John F. Avedon. London: Wisdom Publications, 1985
This highly acclaimed study of the Tibetan situation is probably the most accurate and readable account currently available. It describes the historical and political background of the Dalai Lama's flight to India in 1959, the subsequent events that have taken place in Tibet under Chinese occupation, and the struggle the refugees have undergone to sustain their culture abroad, and has excellent chapters on the Nechung oracle and Tibetan Medicine.

Portrait of a Dalai Lama: The Life and Times of the Great Thirteenth. Charles Bell. London: Wisdom Publications, 1987
The author was the British Political Representative to Tibet during the crucial early years of this century. Fluent in Tibetan, he became closely associated with the Thirteenth Dalai Lama and the turbulent affairs of that time. This excellent book is an immensely readable and authentic personal account of the life of this great Tibetan leader and the events that helped shape modern Tibet.

Tibet and its History. Hugh E. Richardson. Boulder and London: Shambhala, 1984
Hugh Richardson served in Tibet for nine years as head of the British mission in Lhasa during the 1930's and 40's. This is the most thoroughly researched and accurate history available and provides detailed information on the events leading up to the Chinese occupation. The appendix contains the texts of all the relevant treaties and agreements pertaining to the political status of Tibet from the Sino-Tibetan treaty of 821 to the draft resolution of the Question of Tibet submitted to the UN General Assembly in 1959.

A Cultural History of Tibet. David Snellgrove and Hugh Richardson. Boston: Shambhala, 1986
This excellent though rather dense study explores all the principal features of Tibetan culture and provides a comprehensive view of the people, their religion, customs, literature and history. It is amply illus-

trated with fine black and white photographs that give one a good glimpse of old Tibet. Non-specialists will have trouble with the technical transliteration system used to spell Tibetan names.

Tibetan Buddhism

The Jewel in the Lotus. Stephen Batchelor (ed.) London: Wisdom Publications, 1987
This book is a guide to the major Buddhist traditions of Tibet. Each tradition – Nyingma, Kagyu, Kadam, Sakya and Geluk – is represented by a short text that sums up its particular approach. A lengthy introduction provides a clear overview of Tibetan Buddhism, putting the schools into their historical context and examining their principal doctrines.

The Tibetan Book of the Dead. Guru Rinpoche according to Karma Lingpa, a new translation by Francesca Freemantle and Chögyam Trungpa. Boulder and London: Shambhala, 1975
Although this is one of the best-known books of Tibetan Buddhism, made popular in the West by C. G. Jung, it may be rather baffling for a beginner who seeks a more explanatory account of the religion. It is nonetheless an evocative and inspiring text, which vividly describes the stages and visions that occur between death and rebirth. In Tibet it would be read aloud by relatives or monks to guide the departed person through the bewildering experiences of the post-death state.

The Jewel Ornament of Liberation. Gampopa, translated by H. V. Guenther. Boston: Shambhala, 1986
This classic text of Tibetan Buddhism describes the different stages on the path to enlightenment. Indian Buddhist sutras are quoted throughout to support the statement of Gampopa, the main disciple of Milarepa and one of the founding fathers of the Kagyu school. It may be somewhat technical for those with no knowledge of Buddhism.

Cutting through Spiritual Materalism. Chögyam Trungpa. Boulder and London: Shambhala, 1973
This popular introduction to Tibetan Buddhism is written in a clear and humorous style and makes the traditional teachings accessible to a contemporary audience. It deals with most of the major themes of Buddhism in a lively, down-to-earth way.

Wisdom Energy. Lama Yeshe and Zopa Rinpoche. London: Wisdom Publications, 1982
A simple yet compelling introduction to Buddhism by two Tibetan

lamas renowned for their insight and skill in conveying the meaning of the Tibetan tradition to the West. Written with warmth and directness it discusses the meaning and purpose of meditation, the causes of suffering and the means of uprooting negative mental states.

The Crystal and the Way of Light. Namkhai Norbu. London: RKP, 1986
This book combines autobiography with a clear exposition of the Dzogchen (Great Perfection) teachings of direct self-liberation. The author, an incarnate Tibetan lama and now a professor at Naples University, recounts some remarkable meetings with teachers he studied with in Eastern Tibet prior to the Chinese takeover. He skilfully relates the practice of Dzogchen to the other teachings of Tibetan Buddhism.

Kindness, Clarity and Insight. The Fourteenth Dalai Lama. Ithaca: Snow Lion Publications, 1984
In this collection of talks given by the Dalai Lama during his tours of the United States in 1979 and 1981, he discusses a wide variety of spiritual and human concerns with his characteristic warmth, wit and perception. His message of hope celebrates the indomitable human spirit and affirms the everpresent potential for individual and social transformation.

Tibetan Medicine

Health through Balance. Dr. Yeshe Donden. Ithaca: Snow Lion Publications, 1986
The fascinating Tibetan medical system has never been so clearly explained as in this outstanding collection of lectures presented to students at the University of Virginia by the former personal physician of His Holiness the Dalai Lama. As a special addition, many pages are devoted to Dr. Donden's lucid responses to students' specific questions. An excellent introduction to the subject.

Biography

The Life of Milarepa. Lobsang P. Lhalungpa (tr.) Boston: Shambhala, 1986
This autobiography of Tibet's most loved saint is a classic in its own country and thoroughly readable and moving in translation. Milarepa tells how he changed from a black magician to a realised yogin under

the guidance of his teacher Marpa and how he spent the rest of his life in remote mountain retreats practising meditation and teaching those who sought his instruction.

Born in Tibet. Chögyam Trungpa. London. Unwin, 1987
The vivid account of the life of a Tibetan incarnate lama who was born in Kham in 1939 and enthroned at a young age as abbot of Surmang Monastery. Trungpa describes his training as a monk and the eventual flight to India, in which he led a large party of refugees across Tibet to safety from the Chinese.

The Life and Teachings of Geshe Rabten. B. Alan Wallace (tr. and ed.).
London: Wisdom Publications, forthcoming 1988.
This is a fascinating account of a Tibetan lama's life and training. Geshe Rabten describes his childhood in Kham, his journey to Central Tibet, his rigorous studies at Sera Monastery, the flight to India and his life in Dharamsala. The second half of the book gives a clear presentation of the path to enlightenment as taught in Tibetan Buddhism.

My Land and My People. The Fourteenth Dalai Lama. New York: Potala Publications, 1977
The present Dalai Lama's own account of his life and the Tibetan situation. He recounts how he was discovered and enthroned as the Dalai Lama and brought up under the guidance of his tutors in the Potala Palace in Lhasa. He tells of his meeting with Mao Tsetung in China, his visit to India in 1956 and of the tragic events that forced him to flee Tibet in 1959. The sincerity and compassion of this remarkable man are strongly impressed on the reader as his story unfolds.

Daughter of Tibet. Rinchen Dolma Taring. London: Wisdom Publications, 1987
This is the only autobiography written in English by a Tibetan woman, and the author tells her story movingly, vividly and without artifice. 'Mary' Taring was born in 1910 into one of the oldest families in Tibet and grew up in the closely-knit world of Tibetan nobility. She was educated in India and was the first Tibetan girl to learn how to write and speak English. Her personal story covers the Tibetan history of the fifty years up to 1959. An additional chapter tells of her work in the refugee community in India.

Warriors of Tibet. Jamyang Norbu. London: Wisdom Publications, 1987
This is the story of a Tibetan Khampa warrior, Aten, and his people of Nyarong. Aten recalls his life as a child, the simple ways of the

Khampas, and the beauty of his homeland in eastern Tibet. He tells us of the history of his people and their fighting spirit. Like many other refugees, Aten related his experiences to the Dalai Lama and his statements were recorded. Years later, Jamyang Norbu, a Tibetan writer, wrote down his story.

Most of the books listed here and a wide selection of cards, prints and posters of Tibetan sacred art can be obtained from **Wisdom Mail Order, 23 Dering Street, London WI, England.**

INDEX

Numbers in bold type indicate a chapter or chapter-section devoted to the subject; numbers in italic type refer to illustrations.

PHOTOGRAPHIC
ACKNOWLEDGEMENTS

Charles Allen 74-75.

Martine Batchelor 12, 98.

Stephen Batchelor 4, 5, 8, 18, 23, 25, 28, 34, 43, 44, 45, 46, 47, 50, 58, 65, 70, 76, 77, 81, 82, 94, 95, 101, 103, 104, 107, 111, 113, 118, 120, 123, 129, 132, 135, 142, 144, 147, 148, 152, 154, 156, 159, 160, 165, 167, 168, 176, 181, 184, 188, 190-191, 194, 195, 199, 202, 207, 209, 212-213, 215, 218, 221, 222, 224, 226, 230, 231, 234-235, 239, 241, 243, 249, 256 (below),260, 264, 268, 272 (above), 274-275, 277, 281, 282, 286, 287, 288, 290, 291, 294-295, 301, 304, 316, 321, 324, 334, 335, 340-341, 342, 344-345.

Brian Beresford and Sean Jones 62, 108, 350, 354-355, 359, 361, 362, 364, 367, 369, 372, 373, 374, 375, 376, 377, 378.

British Museum Library 63.

Hiroki Fujita, x, 96-97.

Sean Jones 86.

S. W. Laden La, by kind permission of Mr. P. W. Laden La, 31.

Jonathan Landaw 347.

Hugh Richardson 14, 32, 33, 36, 67, 68, 73, 75 (below), 137, 180, 193, 196, 204, 208, 211, 236, 251, 256 (above), 265, 276, 312.

Stone Routes 2, 9, 10, 11, 13, 16, 17, 22, 38-39, 48, 56, 66, 80, 83, 90, 116, 134, 140, 150, 162, 186, 200, 205, 232, 238, 246, 252, 257, 272 (below), 278, 280 (above), 298, 300, 306, 309, 313, 314, 327, 331.

F. Williamson, Esq, C.I.E., I.C.S., reproduced by kind permission of Mrs. Margaret D. Williamson 30, 248, 280 (below), 328-329, 338.

Tibet outside Tibet: your Wisdom guide

The Wisdom Tibet Guide has shown you around the Land of Snows, but Wisdom can also be your guide to Tibet, Tibetan Buddhism and related activities outside the country. We are one of the world's major specialist publishers and distributors of books on Buddhism and Tibet. Write for our complete catalogue, but below are some titles and other information that might interest visitors to Tibet and others.

Wisdom Tibet Books

In addition to *The Tibet Guide* and the Wisdom Tibet Books listed in the **Suggested Reading List** (see page 445), the other books in this series are also highly recommended.

Tibet is my Country

Autobiography of Thubten Jigme Norbu, brother of the Dalai Lama, as told to Heinrich Harrer

Jigme Norbu, the Tagtser Rinpoche, brother of the present Dalai Lama and himself the recognised reincarnation of a high Buddhist dignitary, tells of his experiences from childhood to present-day exile in a moving account that recalls Tibet's remarkable recent history.

300pp, colour photographs, £8.95/$16.95

Memoirs of a Political Officer's Wife in Tibet, Sikkim and Bhutan

Margaret D. Williamson
In collaboration with John Snelling

In the 1930's Margaret D. Williamson spent several years travelling in Sikkim, Bhutan and Tibet at the side of her husband, a political officer for the British Imperial Government. These memoirs taken from her diary retell her life and journeys up until the untimely death of her husband in Lhasa.

240pp, b/w photographs, £8.95/$16.95 (approx)

Tibetan Reflections

Life in a Tibetan Refugee Community

Peter Gold

This is a fascinating, lively first-hand account of life amongst the Tibetan refugees of Dharamsala, a village in the foothills of the Indian Himalayas. Stupas and mantras; prayer flags, prayer wheels and offering scarves; buddhas and religious ceremonies; theatre, dance and music; the weatherman; monks, nuns and *ama-las*. And the Dalai Lama – the very centre of their lives and the source of their firm Buddhist faith. This vivid account of Tibetan life helps us understand how things must once have been in Tibet itself.

112pp, colour photographs, £6.95/$11.95

Tibetan Art Reproductions

Tibetan Art Calendar

Each year Wisdom publishes this famous calendar, which features twelve superb reproductions of *thangkas* (Tibetan religious painted scrolls) in full colour from museums and the private collections of connoisseurs worldwide. It measures 420 x 600mm and contains a detailed explanation of each painting. Back issues are also available. £11.95/$16.95

Tibetan Art Cards, Prints and Posters

Wisdom also has a growing range of cards, prints and posters of Tibetan religious and cultural art by early and contemporary Tibetan painters and Western exponents of the *genre*. A colour catalogue is available on request.

Wisdom Map of Tibet

An accurate map of Tibet has never been available. Many maps of Tibet have been produced but all have had faults. Drawing on what is correct in this source material and supplementing it with exhaustive original research, a new map, generated by advanced computerized methods of cartography, has been prepared by Mike Farmer for publication by Wisdom early 1988.

The map measures 800 x 1600mm (approx.) and is in full colour, showing contours (the most accurate topography of any readily available map of Tibet), place names (towns, monasteries etc. phoneticized in the original Tibetan for ease of communication with local people; most modern maps are in Sinicized Tibetan), roads, rivers and many other features of interest. A gazetteer to accompany it will be published later.

Tibetan Buddhism in the West

Since the Chinese takeover of Tibet in 1959, hundreds of centres for the study of Tibetan Buddhism have sprung up all over the world. The four main schools of Tibetan Buddhism are represented in most Western countries. Wisdom's *International Buddhist Directory* lists almost 2000 centres from all Buddhist traditions, as well as those of Tibet.

Wisdom is the publishing division of the **Foundation for the Preservation of the Mahayana Tradition (FPMT)**, an international organisation of Buddhist teaching and meditation centres established by Lama Thubten Zopa Rinpoche and the late Lama Thubten Yeshe. The Foundation is but one of several bodies around the world devoted to keeping alive the religion and culture of Tibet. Visitors to Tibet may wish to further their knowledge of the country after their return home and may do so through the FPMT centres listed here, which will also have information about other Tibetan centres, offices or activities in their respective countries.

Central Office, GPO Box 817, Kathmandu, Nepal (977) 413094

AUSTRALIA
Atisha Centre, Sandhurst Town Road RSD, Eaglehawk, Vic 3556 (61)(054)46 9033
Buddha House, PO Box 93, Eastwood, Adelaide, SA 5063 (61)(08)277 8522
Chenrezig Institute, Highlands Road, Eudlo, Qld 4554 (61)(071)45 9047
Tara Institute, 3 Mavis Avenue, East Brighton, Vic 3187 (61)(03)596 2465
Vajrayana Institute, 1 Guthrie Avenue, Cremorne, Sydney, NSW 2090
   (61)(02)909 1330
Wisdom Publications, PO Box 1326, Chatswood, Sydney, NSW 2067
   (61)(02)922 6338

ENGLAND
Manjushri Centre, 10 Finsbury Park Rd, London N4 (44)(01)359 1394
Manjushri Institute, Conishead Priory, Ulverston, Cumbria LA12 9QQ
   (44)(0229)54029
Wisdom Publications, 23 Dering Street, London W1R 9AA (44)(01)499 0925

FRANCE
Dorje Pamo Monastery, Chateau d'En Clausade, Marzens, 81500 Lavaur
   (33)(063)41 44 22

Nalanda Monastery, Labastide St Georges, 81500 Lavaur (33)(063)58 02 25
Institut Vajra Yogini, Chateau d'En Clausade, Marzens, 81500 Lavaur
   (33)(063)58 17 22

GERMANY
Aryatara Institut, Jaegerndorf 1½, 8382 Arnstorf (49)(08723)2396
Aryatara City Centre, Lucille Grahnstr 47,8000 München 80 (49)(089)47 14 15

HOLLAND
Maitreya Instituut, Raadhuisdijk 9,6627 AC Maasbommel (31)(08876)2188

HONG KONG
Dharma Group & Wisdom Publications, SFE, 1602 Cambridge House, 26-28
   Cameron Street, Tsimshatsui, Kowloon (852)(3)721 1974

INDIA
Root Institute, Bodh Gaya, Bihar
Tushita Retreat Centre, McLeod Ganj, Dharamsala, Kangra District, HP
   (91) Dh'sala 2266

ITALY
Istituto Lama Tzong Khapa, 56040 Pomaia, Pisa (39)(050)68976

NEPAL
Himalayan Yogic Institute & Wisdom Publications, GPO Box 817, Kathmandu
   (977)413094
Kopan Monastery, GPO Box 817, Kathmandu

NEW ZEALAND
Dorje Chang Institute, GPO Box 2814, Auckland (64)(09)60 0442
Mahamudra Centre, Colville RD, Coromandel (64)(08)4356851

SPAIN
CET Nagarjuna, Rosellón 298, pral 2a, Barcelona 08037 (34)(03)257 0788
CET Nagarjuna, Avda del Aster 28016, Madrid 28016 (34)(01)413 87 73
O Sel Ling Retreat Centre, Bubion, Granada (34)(958)76 30 88

UNITED STATES OF AMERICA
Milarepa Centre, Barnet Mt, Barnet, Vermont 05821 (1)(802)633 4136
Vajrapani Institute Box I, Boulder Creek, California 95006 (1)(408)338 9540
Wisdom Publications, 45 Water St., Newburyport, Massachusetts 01950
   (1) (617) 462 0100

Offices of Tibet

The Offices of Tibet are the official agencies of His Holiness the Dalai
Lama. As well as looking after the interests of the Tibetan people, the
Offices work towards creating a better understanding of Tibet and the
Tibetans. They supervise arrangements for His Holiness's visits and
strive to spread his message of peace and harmony in the world.

   The Offices of Tibet serve as a source of authentic information on the
culture of Tibet, on its religion, history and way of life, and on current

affairs regarding Tibet and the Tibetans in exile. With a view to improving the conditions of the people in Tibet, the Offices monitor the situation there and make available the latest information.

Since they coordinate work being done by organisations and individuals world-wide, the Offices of Tibet provide a forum for information and contacts of all kinds. They also attempt to help the various agencies of the Tibetan administration in India.

ENGLAND
Office of Tibet, Linburn House, 342 Kilburn High Road, London NW6 2QJ
  (44)(01)328 8422

JAPAN
Liason Office of HH the Dalai Lama, Rm 401, Gotanda Lilas Hi-Town, 15-12-2
  Nishi-Gotanda, Shinagawa-Ku, Tokyo 141 (81)(03)490 7868

NEPAL
Office of Tibet, Gadhen Ghangsar, PO Box 310, Lazimpat, Kathmandu
  (977)411660

SWITZERLAND
Office of Tibet, Rieterstr 18, CH-8002 Zürich (41)(01)201 3336

UNITED STATES OF AMERICA
Office of Tibet, 107 East 31st St (4th Floor), New York, New York 10016
  (1)(212)213 5010

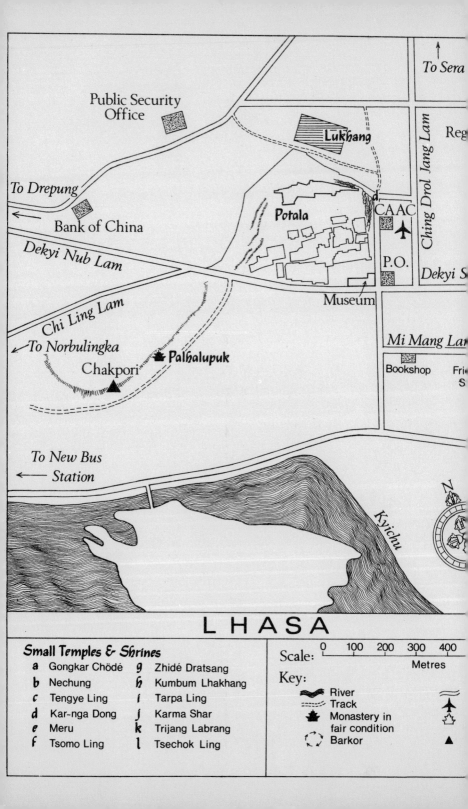

Public Security Office

To Drepung

Bank of China

Dekyi Nub Lam

Chi Ling Lam

To Norbulingka

Chakpori

To New Bus Station

Lukhang

Potala

CAAC

P.O.

Museum

Palhalupuk

To Sera

Ching Drol Jang Lam

Reg

Dekyi S

Mi Mang Lar

Bookshop

Fri
S

Kyichu

N

LHASA

Scale: 0 100 200 300 400
Metres

Key:

~~~ River
···· Track
🏯 Monastery in fair condition
↺ Barkor
✈
☆
▲

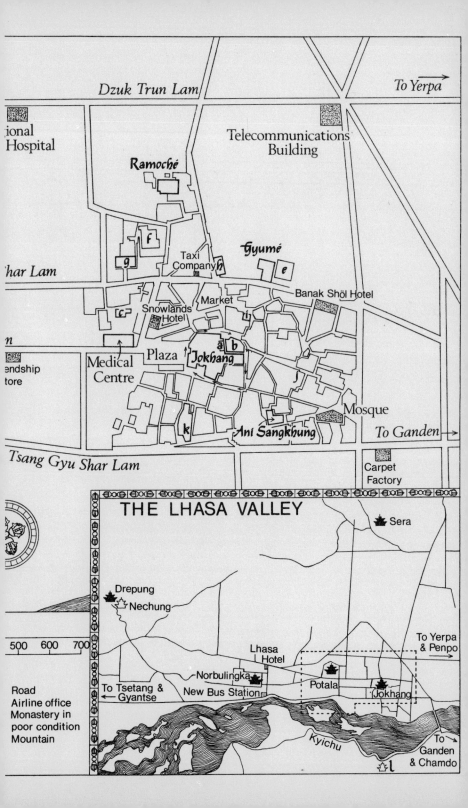

Dzuk Trun Lam

To Yerpa →

...ional
Hospital

Telecommunications
Building

Ramoché

f

...har Lam

g

Taxi
Company h

Gyumé

e

Banak Shöl Hotel

Snowlands
Hotel

Market

c

...n

Medical
Centre

Plaza

Jokhang

a b

...endship
...tore

j

Mosque

To Ganden →

k

Ani Sangkhung

Tsang Gyu Shar Lam

Carpet
Factory

THE LHASA VALLEY

Sera

500   600   700

Drepung
Nechung

To Yerpa
& Penpo

Road
Airline office
Monastery in
poor condition
Mountain

Lhasa
Hotel

Norbulingka

To Tsetang &
Gyantse

New Bus Station

Potala

Jokhang

Kyichu

To
Ganden
& Chamdo

l